PRINCIPLES OF

VOCATIONAL EDUCATION

PRINCIPLES OF

VOCATIONAL
EDUCATION

The Primacy of the Person

18429

By *FRANKLIN J. KELLER*
Principal, Metropolitan Vocational
High School, New York City

D. C. HEATH AND COMPANY · BOSTON

To

Joan and Geoffrey
Eric and Ingrid
the younger and the youngest generation
about whom this book is

Acknowledgments

NO printed word can express adequate appreciation to all the great company whose acts and convictions contribute to a book that must necessarily be a mosaic of many minds and hearts. Their thoughts and feelings, precious as they are anonymous, have become the writer's very own.

Four years ago the National Society for the Study of Education published a Yearbook on Vocational Education. As chairman of the editorial committee I wrote the first and last chapters from which, with the kind permission of the Society, I have adapted a number of passages for this volume. Communion and cooperation with thirty other contributors were invaluable discipline for the present task.

I am extremely grateful to all the members of my faculty for generous assistance. Dr. David G. Salten not only read the manuscript critically and made many valuable suggestions, but also, as Acting Principal, carried full responsibility for Metropolitan Vocational High School during my year in Germany as Head of the Vocational and Technical Section of the Education and Religious Affairs Branch of Military Government. Dr. Frank H. Paine, Mr. Nathan Luloff, and Dr. Louis Weiss have been highly competent colleagues and helpful critics. During years of arduous practical planning and administration Dr. Mary Sutton-Phelan has been the warm, glowing soul who has kept us all deeply conscious of the primacy of the person. Finally, to those important members of "the great company," all the "Metro" boys and girls but for whom this book would not have been written, I am indebted most of all. In the last analysis, they have taught me what I really know about education.

This book was written at home, on holidays and during a summer vacation. Only an interested wife can cope successfully with such a situation. So, to her I am profoundly grateful, not only for protective and stimulating ministrations during composition, but for tender and discriminating editing of the completed manuscript.

Franklin J. Keller

Table of Contents

On Work

FROM *The Prophet* BY KAHLIL GIBRAN *

Then a ploughman said, Speak to us of Work.
And he answered, saying:

You work that you may keep pace with the earth and the soul of the earth.

For to be idle is to become a stranger unto the seasons, and to step out of life's procession, that marches in majesty and proud submission towards the infinite.

When you work you are a flute through whose heart the whispering of the hours turns to music.

Which of you would be a reed, dumb and silent, when all else sings together in unison?

Always you have been told that work is a curse and labour a misfortune.

But I say to you that when you work you fulfil a part of earth's furthest dream, assigned to you when that dream was born,

And in keeping yourself with labour you are in truth loving life,

And to love life through labour is to be intimate with life's inmost secret.

But if you in your pain call birth an affliction and the support of the flesh a curse written upon your brow, then I answer that naught but the sweat of your brow shall wash away that which is written.

You have been told also that life is darkness, and in your weariness you echo what was said by the weary.

And I say that life is indeed darkness save when there is urge,

And all urge is blind save when there is knowledge,

* Reprinted by permission of Alfred A. Knopf, Inc.

And all knowledge is vain save when there is work,
And all work is empty save when there is love;
And when you work with love you bind yourself to yourself,
and to one another, and to God.

And what is it to work with love?
It is to weave the cloth with threads drawn from your heart,
even as if your beloved were to wear that cloth.
It is to build a house with affection, even as if your beloved were
to dwell in that house.
It is to sow seeds with tenderness and reap the harvest with joy,
even as if your beloved were to eat the fruit.
It is to charge all things you fashion with a breath of your own
spirit,
And to know that all the blessed dead are standing about you
and watching.

Often have I heard you say, as if speaking in sleep, "He who
works in marble, and finds the shape of his own soul in the stone, is
nobler than he who ploughs the soil.
And he who seizes the rainbow to lay it on a cloth in the like-
ness of man, is more than he who makes the sandals for our feet."
But I say, not in sleep but in the over-wakefulness of noontide,
that the wind speaks not more sweetly to the giant oaks than to the
least of all the blades of grass;
And he alone is great who turns the voice of the wind into a
song made sweeter by his own loving.
Work is love made visible.
And if you cannot work with love but only with distaste, it is
better that you should leave your work and sit at the gate of the
temple and take alms of those who work with joy.
For if you bake bread with indifference, you bake a bitter bread
that feeds but half man's hunger.
And if you grudge the crushing of the grapes, your grudge dis-
tils a poison in the wine.
And if you sing though as angels, and love not the singing, you
muffle man's ears to the voices of the day and the voices of the night.

PRINCIPLES OF

VOCATIONAL EDUCATION

Chapter 1

PROLOGUE: EDUCATION IS LIFE

DEEP down in the hearts of men and women is the desire to perpetuate themselves, both collectively and individually, through their children. Call it biological urge, fear of extinction, extension of personality, or craving for immortality, it is indubitably there. As parents and as members of the community, they want these children to know effectively and to live abundantly. This kind of learning and living is education.

When life is as simple as hunting or pasturing, the brief history of the race is recapitulated through sheer imitation. With a prod here and a warning there, boys and girls soon know as much as their parents — the folklore and the skills. Really to live is to know. As hunting and pasturing merge into a domestic economy, later to shift into commercialism and industrialism, and finally into a complexity of technology — while time piles up a backlog — the essentials of living are screened out, compacted and, too often, formalized, into what becomes "school." If it is good school, it is still good living. And education remains life.

This book is about life and education — not a segment of education, or education at any "level." It is called vocational education because vocation — what a person does to live; hunting, for instance — is conceived as a focus for many other values, as an integrating principle in a diverse life. At this point let it be an assumption, for more, much more, will develop in the sequel. This prologue is, in fact, a series of assumptions, the most stirring and the most hopeful of which are vocational. For it was Paul who said: "I, therefore, prisoner of the Lord, beseech you that ye walk worthy of the vocation wherewith ye are called, with all lowliness and meekness, with long suffering, forbearing one another in love; endeavoring to keep the unity of the Spirit in the bond of peace." If we can walk worthy, in love, and keep unity of the Spirit, in the bond of peace, education will not be mere preparation for living. It will *be life.*

4

VOCATIONAL EDUCATION MEANS A FULL, EFFICIENT, AND HAPPY LIFE.
Vocational education is not job training. It is not perfection of skills.
It is not tricks of the trade. It is not haggling in the marketplace,
wrangling in law courts, breaking of soil, or binding of wounds.
It is all of these, but it is much more. It is creative spirit in the
mechanic, service rendered by the merchant, justice won by the
prosecutor, food raised by the farmer, and life saved by the doctor.
It is attitudes, emotions, ethics, conduct, language, and beauty —
those attributes that transform jobs into vocations and men and
women into their neighbors' keepers and into citizens of the world.
It is to "walk worthy of the vocation wherewith ye are called."

Of all the things that surround a man the only ones that constitute
his real environment are those that make him change his mind or
change his words or change the direction in which he is moving.
When we say a person is "oblivious of his surroundings," we are
saying that he has no environment. So in school how often have we
been "oblivious" — of the teacher's voice, of the chalkmarks on the
blackboard, of the hieroglyphics in the mathematics book, all the
while intent upon the real environment, the adventure story under
the desk. Vocational education provides not only a genuine environment in which a person changes because he is concerned with it,
but one which is contrived and directed so as to produce positive
values. In other words, when life is interesting we pay attention.
Life *is* interesting, particularly when it means doing, aiming toward
a goal, achieving a career, being a real person.

Being *for* life, vocational education assumes the existence *of* life.
Vocational education is not something presented to or done for
young people or for men and women. It is an opportunity for
vibrant, eager, growing human beings to do something they want
to do for themselves. To use the traditional phrase, it does not have
to educe activity. It merely touches off a spark. It releases latent energy. It gives the living a chance to live.

VOCATIONAL EDUCATION ASSUMES THAT LIFE HAS A SERIOUS PURPOSE,
MANIFESTING ITSELF IN A MEANINGFUL OCCUPATION. The element of
purpose is of transcendent importance. Dawdling, loafing imply lack
of purpose. Play may arise from purpose and end in dissipation.
The liberal arts may be a titillation of the senses or an instrumentality of high endeavor. However, the word "occupation" bespeaks
purpose and, in all its radiations, comprehends the liberal arts so
often credited with "making men capable of choosing and pursuing

occupations." Occupation, activity with a purpose, gives meaning and worth to the liberal arts, to play, to leisure.

When things have meaning for us we plan to do something about them and then we do it. Consider the little boy. We say to him, "Young man, what are you going to *do* when you grow up?" Or, "What are you going to *be*?" "Do" or "be" means an occupation or a career. We are really asking our young man to state his purpose in life. He does this haphazardly and fumblingly at first, but as his environment takes hold of him, as the fullness of life taps his interests, purpose emerges and education becomes significant.

VOCATIONAL EDUCATION MAKES PROVISION FOR THE WIDE DIFFERENCES AMONG INDIVIDUALS. The capacities of individuals to pursue occupations vary from highest professional competence down to utter uselessness, even to liability. There is no assumption that high capacity or serious purpose or artistic creativeness resides in all human beings. The virtues of vocational education will not transform the world. However, recognition of the entire range of mental, emotional, and mechanical abilities, combined with awareness of the enormous range of capacities required to get the work of the world done, implies an adjustment never possible so long as the measure of intelligence is based upon ability to perform operations not directly connected with the pursuit of the jobs which the world has for people to do. Sadly enough, there are always those who can meet none of the criteria of educability, those who are not prepared to work or to learn. On the other hand, there are millions, in all brackets of the scale of "intelligence," for whom vocational education provides the purpose and the means.

In a very real sense, vocational education is concerned with enabling every individual "to make the most of himself." It is a redemption of the pledge to give everyone the opportunity to which he is entitled in a democracy.

Vocational education assumes guidance, discovery and recognition of aptitudes and capacities, and their development into socially useful activities. Not only does it assume guidance but it provides facilities the lack of which severely hampers the guidance program in most academic schools. We not only learn to do by doing but we learn not to do by doing, or rather, we learn whether or not we can do what we think we can. Training is accompanied by interpretation and appreciation which constitute education. Vocational education, tempered by guidance, escapes the evils of regimentation or excessively rigid control. It is a truism that vocational education is only as good as vocational guidance will let it be, and vocational guidance is only as good as the social facilities for adjustment. Vocational education provides the most important of these facilities.

VOCATIONAL EDUCATION ASSUMES DEMOCRACY. Not only must there be equality of opportunity. There must be free association, a common goal. People must work together. They must believe in each other's work because they feel they are serving others and others are serving them. They must be common sharers in the task of making life livable. Vocational education assumes and works upon the principle that every individual is worthy of preparation for an occupation and that every occupation is worthy of the individual who pursues it, whether it be manual, intellectual, or emotional, thus arriving at the "dignity of labor" by action rather than by preachment.

It is notable that striving toward a common end through association takes place after as well as during working hours. Eavesdrop on any discussion during a social gathering of vocal men and women and what do you hear? Talk about their work and their fellow workers, reminiscences, prognostications, and a good measure of criticism. Workers live their work at all hours. They dream about it. An occupation is the most occupying of all human activities. When it is freely shared with others, it is the most democratic.

VOCATIONAL EDUCATION IS DEEPLY CONCERNED WITH THE DEVELOPMENT OF THE LITERATE, THE EDUCATED MAN. Vocational education is interested in avoiding semantic obscurantism and in emphasizing educational reality. Reading and writing are real abilities when the symbols are closely related to acts and things that come within actual experience, experience that is pleasant because it is interesting. Nay, more, symbols that lead to the abstract are true culture — the culture of a people because they are *of* the people.

VOCATIONAL EDUCATION IS CONCERNED WITH EVERY VOCATION. Whether it is called a job, post, position, pursuit, career, mission, calling, profession, or any other name implying either dignity or odium, if it is part of the world's work, rendering service to others, and is not harmful to health or morals, it comes within the purview of vocational education. Vocational education is here concerned with well-rounded development of competent workers. It is not confined to any restricted field such as "less than college grade," manual labor, or jobs "suited to those who cannot maintain themselves in an academic school."

EDUCATION IS LIFE. Any consideration of education must be as broad as life. School education must necessarily be limited quantitatively, qualitatively, and temporally, and must therefore be restricted to only a part of life, but this part is planned cooperatively and is communally supported. Within this framework it must do everything possible to help young people to live, live as young people and later as adults. A philosophy of education is a philosophy of life, based upon personal experience, community and world experience (present and past), and upon those inner drives and impulses toward a good life, whether they be compounded of the "data and intelligent purpose" of the pragmatist, the "perfection" of the idealist, or the "inner light" or "that of God" of the deeply religious. The foregoing "assumptions" and their exposition and amplification in the following chapters constitute a tenable philosophy of education. The key words are purpose, diversity, unity, democracy, service, and work. The greatest of these is work.

Chapter 2

A CONCEPT OF WORK

I. VARIOUS CONCEPTIONS

WORK is physical or intellectual effort directed toward an end; as the *work* of a teamster, of a doctor. Effort, direction, purpose — these constitute a moral code, a plan for society. There is no more striking and fruitful exercise than running down the genealogy and history of work, for wherever you turn you find it coupled with "purpose" and with the "good." More than two pages of Webster's unabridged dictionary are devoted to "work" and its compounds. Work may degenerate into drudgery, but as "work" it is effort directed toward an end. Produced by mental labor, as a book, poem, musical composition, or picture, the end results become the work, or works, of Addison, or of Bach, or of Rembrandt. Directed toward human betterment, the outcome is "good works." Aristotle identified work with goodness: "As in the case of the flute player, the sculptor or any craftsman, their goodness or efficiency is thought to reside in their work, so it would seem to be with Man, if there is any *work* belonging to him." [1]

And yet, the curse laid on Adam expresses the popular conception of work. So "worker," "workman," used alone, connote physical labor. "Work by the sweat of their brow" — unpleasant punishment. There must be something sinister in work. The confusion is semantic in nature and it will arise again in the discussion of vocational and general education. The problem is basic.

There never has been a time when philosophers, economists, statesmen, or educators have not contended about "sound doctrine." It has been realism *vs.* nominalism, free trade *vs.* protection, national-

[1] Reprinted from *How to Read a Page*, by I. A. RICHARDS, p. 228, by permission of W. W. Norton & Company, Inc. Copyright 1942 by the publishers.

ism *vs.* internationalism, or classics *vs.* science. Amid the all-pervasive issues of fascism *vs.* communism and dictatorship *vs.* democracy, the educators still debate general *vs.* special education, progressive education *vs.* traditional education, and cultural education *vs.* vocational education.

THE SEMANTICISTS AND THE STYLISTS. The big words may serve as titles, provocative goads for the stirring up of interest, but they mean nothing until they are referred to specific, concrete, individual things or human beings, the exact size, color, and form of which (or whom) we can agree upon. They argue and they argue and they argue, but as Richards says, "A controversy is normally an exploitation of misunderstandings for warlike purposes." Even the word "individual" has tended to become an abstraction. Yet we shall have to cling to the individual, really individualize him.

The studies of the semanticists confirm the conclusions of the practicing stylists. A hundred years ago Stendhal said simply, "Style is this: To add to a thought all the circumstances fitted to produce the whole effect that the thought ought to produce." This is to say that an abstract idea has meaning only when it is supported by accurate pictures of things and accounts of events such as will conjure up in the mind of the reader the same pictures and events that were in the mind of the writer. These must be things and people that they both know. Murry comments that the writer's "sensuous perceptions are keen and precise; he has a vivid delight in the physical particularity of the persons engaged; but over and above this he has an acute sense of the psychological quality of the incident." [2]

Probably, this sense of psychological quality is the most important factor of all. It is inherent in the unforgettable school scenes of great literature, of which there are all too few. Perhaps the best remembered are the spelling-window-washing lesson in "Dotheboys Hall" and the composition contest in Thrums. "First they spells 'w-i-n-d-e-r,' and then they goes and does it." So sensitive was Dickens to the psychological quality of the incident and so powerfully did he convey it to his readers, that all England was stirred up to a reform of its social system, especially the schools. So poignantly did Barrie make his readers feel the universality of Sentimental Tommy's artistic soul in his search for the right word that the book itself is a high

[2] J. MIDDLETON MURRY, *The Problem of Style* (London: Oxford University Press, 1922), p. 105.

work of art, a compelling piece of literature. Not yet, perhaps, recognized as great literature, "The Education of Hyman Kaplan," [3] that incomparable story of the American night preparatory school for adults ("English — Americanization — civics — preparation for naturalization"), exhibits the same acute sense of the psychological quality of incident. It culminates in the final examination, in which Mr. Kaplan does badly, and in that melting "P.S." at the bottom of his paper: "I dont care if I dont pass, I *love* the class." Because Leonard Ross has given us all the circumstances and has conveyed the psychological quality of the incident, we know exactly what Hyman means.

By using concrete rather than abstract terms, by supplying concrete terms with unmistakable referents (the object or situations in the real world to which the words or label refer), by adding to a thought all the circumstances fitted to produce the whole effect that the thought ought to produce, by using active verbs that strike squarely at their objects, and by sensing the psychological quality of learning activities, it is hoped that this book will convey to its readers the meaning of vocational education.

DEFINITION OF TERMS. What is "education"? What is "American"? What is "life"? What is "academic"? What is "vocational"? What is "work"? While it is important that we know just what each of these words means, from the foregoing discussion it is obvious that no mere word cluster will make their meaning clear. In a sense, the whole book will supply the definitions. At this point it is only important to emphasize the fact that controversies, based on misunderstandings, have raged around differences of meaning. Education has been broad or narrow, cultural or utilitarian, academic or vocational, general or specialized. In sound practice there can be no such distinctions. The individual is a peculiar organism whose optimum development requires that various influences play upon him at various times, influences that are bound to be quite different in both quality and timing from those required by another organism.

The beat of the tom-tom through the forest conveys information and emotion. It says that there will be a fight and that some warriors will be happy, others sad, still others dead. The click of the telegraph key, the tap-tap of the typewriter, also tell of victory and exaltation, of defeat and despair, but with infinite variety and com-

[3] LEONARD ROSS, "The Education of Hyman Kaplan" (New York: Harcourt, Brace and Company, Inc., 1937), p. 176.

plexity. The sounds of human voices over the air, the black marks on the printed page, are only the fuses that touch off trains of thought and onslaughts of emotion. There are some major problems in describing and explaining vocational education. The writer attempts the resolution of these problems in hope and faith. He hopes that his earnestness and experience will justify the faith of those readers who come to the book seeking enlightenment, perhaps even inspiration.

WHAT IS WORK? Jacques Barzun tells the story of the student who had been given a heavy assignment of reading and had come to report. He started out, with zest, to detail the knowledge he had gained, when Barzun interrupted him with: "Never mind all that. What I want to know is, Was it fun?" If it was activity with a purpose, it was work. If it was an end in itself, it was pleasurable. If it was only a means to an end — to get a passing mark, to avoid paternal retribution, to become eligible to play on a team, then it was probably fatiguing, painful, irksome, unavoidable, and work became labor. If the "work" had no significance whatsoever, but was considered monotonous and mean, then it became drudgery. If pain and fatigue taxed both mind and body, then it became toil. Those who work without purpose so far as work itself is concerned, with only some extraneous end in view — food, shelter, clothing, recreation, avoidance of displeasure or punishment — are all in the same category. They aren't having any fun.

The best way to understand work is to consider play. An unabridged dictionary gives eleven transitive and twelve intransitive definitions of the verb. The most general is "to amuse or divert oneself." "Diversion" is the "act of turning a person from an occupation or purpose." Yet the person who *plays* an instrument or a game for a living is working! Musicians and actors are called players, though they direct their energies toward a very definite end. No one works harder, physically, than a professional dancer, while none is more fanatic in protesting the pleasure derived from his work. Two persons may go through exactly the same motion or follow the same train of thought, yet one will be working and the other playing. Obviously, the difference is not in the activity but in the purpose, the goal. If the purpose is to extract from the activity all its intrinsic values without reference to any extrinsic rewards, then it is fun. It may be work or it may be recreation, but it is pleasurable. If the purpose is to gain a completely extrinsic reward, without extracting any value from the activity itself, then the activity is drudgery. It may be work, but it is also labor, toil.

WORK AND LEISURE. We all remember how we learned our penmanship by copying out, copperplate, "Idleness is the devil's workshop." During every depression, when unemployment rises, we wrestle with the devil. During every boom period, when hours are long, we say that workers need recreation. We all want leisure time but we are afraid that the other fellow may have too much of it. We have seen that technological unemployment is very real and that the organization of compensatory industries is not a natural consequence or even a probable one. So we feel that something must be done about it. The major part of the final report of the American Youth Commission is concerned with this problem. Practical measures are suggested. However, in the last chapter Dorothy Canfield Fisher, in a beautiful piece of writing, cites the spiritual note that cannot be ignored. Assuming that our youth may again be confronted with idleness, with lack of opportunities to obtain remunerative employment, what we all need is a sense of the moral necessity of creative work.

"What we need to realize ourselves and constantly to keep before the imagination of youth is the enormous scope, range, and variety of 'skills' available to those who will make the effort to acquire them. We have a laughably absurd tendency to associate the word 'skill' with the attempt to go against the current of the times by trying to revive some manual work of the past, now performed by modern machinery. Skill means, of course, doing something — anything reasonably worth doing — *well*. This 'something' can range from such extraordinary skill as St. Theresa of Avila showed in the reorganization of convent life in her time in Spain, to the simpler skill of an American mother who tries to animate with ardor and intelligence the activities of the small local branch of the Parent-Teacher Association in the school attended by her children. Or it can range from such a mighty manifestation of the communal making of music as the annual presentation of Bach's *Mass in B Minor* by the steel workers and commercial employees of the town of Bethlehem, Pennsylvania, to the faithful work with a small church choir of a conscientious organist and leader. It may be such financial ability as is shown by the trustees of a great university in balancing its budget, or it may be the effort of a few wage earners to organize a cooperative store. In bringing this matter before the

attention of the younger generation we must untiringly remind them
of the rich diversity of the activities open to them on the sole condition that they learn, first, to protect their free time with courage and firmness from triviality and commercial exploitation, and,
second, to use it wisely and rewardingly.

"What we should do, what we must do, is to bring up into the
field of consciousness an essential truth which is already a living
part of our human experience. This truth is that the heartfelt struggle to overcome one's own limitations and to force the chaotic raw
material of human life to submit to shaping and design is not only
the most rewarding but also the most natural effort for human beings. It is not the rare prerogative, privilege, and reward of an
elite. It is an instinct innate in all human hearts, which can, if we
will wisely use the new opportunities open to mankind, grow constantly into a greater and greater element in the lives of men and
women." [4]

WHAT PURPOSES ARE HONORABLE? A frequently uttered oblique criticism of vocational education takes the form: It is not enough to
learn to earn a living, one must learn to live a life. In the light of
the foregoing analysis no such clear-cut dichotomy seems tenable.
Assuming the necessity for purposeful living, what should those
purposes be? Certainly, each individual is obligated to secure his
own personal development — subsistence, status, and ultimately,
happiness. On the other hand, as a member of a community, he is
obligated to render service to others, to live with his fellow men, to
contribute to their development along with his own. He must
"work" for others as well as for himself. Now, unless he is willing
to live a double life, become a dual personality, spend half his time
in toil, "earning a living," the other half in pleasure, "living a life,"
such a separation of activities is impossible, certainly not desirable,
and for purposes of education, quite untenable. In actual adult life
these two phases of living shade one into the other. It is only the
rare, extreme deviate who derives absolutely no pleasure from his
work and injects none of his work into his leisure.

Consider what a man does on a normal "work" day. For approximately twelve hours all his moves and all his thoughts are conditioned by his work. From the blast of the alarm clock and his slow-
growing consciousness of an outer world to the time he enters his

[4] American Youth Commission, *Youth and the Future* (Washington, D.C.: American Council on Education, 1942), p. 286.

front door for the evening meal, he is literally at work. He washes, dresses, eats breakfast, walks to the train, rides for miles, walks again, enters the factory or office, all in preparation for the work of the day. He associates with fellow workers all day, even at lunch, and in the evening reverses the morning's procedure. At home he is likely to reminisce about the day's work, cheerfully or resentfully, and then visit or entertain friends who have been acquired through work associations. There is more talk about work or workers. The physical welfare, the mental and emotional happiness of wife and children are determined by the breadwinner's work. They are likely to talk about it a great deal. Meetings of trade associations or unions, at home and in other cities, provide much of the social milieu. If the worker is a farmer, work and "life" become almost indistinguishable.

True, there are movies, theaters, concerts, newspapers, magazines, books, games, and outings, which have no direct relation to the job, and yet, to suppose that the capacity to enjoy life in these so-called cultural areas is not conditioned, or unconditioned, by work activities during the major time period of life, is to be utterly unrealistic. In any case, if the activities and human associations of the work period are congenial, the worker will live twice as much and twice as well as he will if they are not. And, of course, there immediately arises the question, toward which later chapters will be directed: For which, and for how much, of these activities, in terms of time consumed and of laudable purpose implied, is organized education necessary?

Finally, with reference to purpose, it is significant to note the tremendous role it has played in the history of mankind. The teleological aspect of philosophy has always been the most baffling. It is the essence of theology and, for many, the prime mover in religion. The scientific age staved it off for a while but more recently scientists have been on the trail of purpose. Biologists have been seeking it in the gene or chromosome. An endocrinologist looks "behind the universe" to explain glands. The Dartmouth Eye Institute suspects "purpose" in the structure of the eye. If things have purpose, certainly men have purpose. It is something they "work" for.

PURPOSE IS A FUNCTION OF POWER. In modern psychiatry persons with abnormal drive, with irresistible purpose, are known as "manics." Lytton Strachey's portrait of Florence Nightingale is an outstanding example. Whence does this energy derive? As a rule, men habitually use only a small part of the powers they actually possess and which they might use under appropriate conditions. So, William James asks, "To what do the better men owe their escape? And, in the fluctuations which all men feel in their own degree of energizing, to what are the improvements due, when they occur? Either some unusual stimulus fills them with emotional excitement, or some unusual idea of necessity induces them to make an extra effort of will. *Excitements, ideas,* and *efforts,* in a word, are what carry us over the dam." [5]

Could an occupation, a career, be such an excitement, such an idea, stimulate such an effort?

II. HISTORY OF WORK

The history of work is the history of man seeking to control his environment so that it will "work" for him. The history of vocational education is the history of ways of learning how best to exercise such control. In primitive times control was direct and manual and usually strenuous. It is a long cry from those days to the era of the push button and the lever, but continued seeking for better ways has resulted in easier, more pleasant ways. Men must always have wanted more congenial work and, no doubt, the persistent ones have found it. On the one hand, science has produced the specialist, the operative, the worker on the assembly lines; but on the other, it has produced the white collar man, the engineer, the theoretician whose heaviest tool is a pencil and whose weightiest task is to draw a line.

Purpose was first forced upon man by hunger and cold, but later it became deliberate. In the beginning, he hunted for food, but when he had enough food, he hunted for pleasure, and he is still hunting for pleasure. When the fist became a club, the club a spear, and the spear an arrow, man was beginning to make life pleasurable as well as efficient. He was making work pleasurable. He was accomplishing his purpose with less physical effort and more brain. He was gaining control over his environment and liking it. He was learning life through work.

SOME EARLY CONCEPTIONS OF WORK. Among the Hebrews the rabbis blamed the father who did not teach his son an occupation. Respect

5 WILLIAM JAMES, quoted from DOUGLAS, HITCHCOCK, and ATKINS, *The Worker in Modern Economic Society* (Chicago: University of Chicago Press, 1923), p. 25.

for manual labor was deep. On the other hand, says the Talmud, "If man does not find his food like the animals and birds, but must earn it, that is due to sin." However, the over-all history of the Jews indicates a devotion to and respect for all kinds of work.

The Greeks scorned work in every form. To them it was drudgery, a curse, and fit only for slaves. Most of the Greeks *were* slaves. Even the so-called free artisans and craftsmen were rated as hardly better than slaves. And thus the "better minds" — Plato, Aristotle, Praxiteles — were freed for the pure exercise of mind, for politics and philosophy, and for the practice of art. Work itself was for them nothing but an evil to which the bulk of mankind must bow themselves until that day, as Aristotle writes ironically, "when the shuttles fly back and forth of themselves, and the plectrum, untouched by human hands, makes the strings of the lyre resound." [6] Of course, this is no indication of what the "majority" of Greeks thought about work. There must have been proud artisans. "Greek thought" was only the thought of Greeks who wrote. How magnificently they wrote! How abjectly their countrymen must have slaved!

For the Romans, Cicero thought that two occupations were worthy of a freeman, agriculture and big business, especially if they led to honorable retirement in the rural peace of the country gentleman. All other pursuits were vulgar and dishonoring, handicraft not less than petty trade, the hiring out of one's arm not less than usury. They chained the soul to the desires of other men, to the thirst for gain. The Persians praised labor, thrift, property, and gave them ethical value. The early Christians fixed their eyes upon a future life. Work could be only a means of carrying them through this temporary existence, in preparation for the next.

Thomas Aquinas drew up a hierarchy, starting with agriculture and rising through the handicrafts to commerce. He considered work a necessity of nature, a natural right and duty, but would have had every man remain in his class and condition, carrying on from father to son. He must not use his work to pass from one class of society to another, for that would mean the ruin of the social order. St. Thomas put ecclesiastical labor above the work of the world and placed pure contemplation above labor of every sort. Luther adhered to the medieval idea of remaining in the trade of the father,

---

[6] ADRIANO TILGHER, *Work, What It Has Meant Through the Ages,* translated from the Italian by Dorothy Canfield Fisher (New York: Harcourt, Brace and Company, Inc., 1930), p. 5.

for he felt that he served God best who remained where God had put him. However, within the limits of one's own profession, whatever that might be, as long as it was legitimate, Luther held that to work was a way of serving God. All professions were needful to the common life of mankind. Hence no one was less necessary than another to piety and blessedness.

"The principle of justification by faith, denying the values of good works, permits human energies to, turn entirely to the material world. The refusal of all moral and religious authority, of all priestly authority, emancipates economic life and leaves it entirely to itself, to its own laws. It was with Luther that the German word for profession (Beruf) took on a religious color which it was never to lose and from German passed into all the analogous words of Protestant countries. Profession or vocation or calling became synonymous. Luther placed a crown upon the sweaty forehead of labor. From his hands work came forth endowed with religious dignity. The gate which gives upon modernity was from his time definitely open." [7]

ADVANCING CONTROL MEANS BROADER VISION, BETTER PLANNING. From hunter to farmer was a big step, to master craftsman a broad leap. Each of these worked for himself. He was able to do everything, his helpers simply extended the field in which his skills operated. However, the specialist worked for others. He was the hired hand. He was often a slave. Developing technology aggravated the more unsavory features of early industrialism. Naturally, in reaction, workers pooled their interests and gave birth to the early unions.

"For the relative equality in the domestic circle of the agricultural era was substituted an ever-widening inequality — an ever-widening division of classes, as *brainwork* was separated from *muscular work;* as *supervision* became distinguished from *production;* artistic *creation* from mere burdensome toil. Between the ends of the social ladder the distance increased. As the differentiation among occupations, particularly between those which allowed leisure and those which left none, became in great part realized, officials and warriors, writers and artists, the big merchants and wealthy manufacturers developed for manual labor a feeling of contempt in spite of the ever-recurring fatuous praise of toil and occasional regard for highly skilled work. Among manual workers, too, employing different tools and practices, there developed differences in social status — differences ac-

[7] TILGHER, *op. cit.,* p. 50.

centuated by the use of slave labor for the most arduous toil and of freedmen or freemen for the more skilled and more desirable forms of work.

"In a thousand years of Greek history the division of labor resulted in the creation of classes distinguished by their occupations, their tastes, their incomes, their privileges and responsibilities. Here is already the gap between *class* and *mass,* the prejudice against manual labor, the conflict of special interests between groups at various social levels which so exceedingly complicate today the task of making work easy and worthwhile for all those engaged in it." [8]

For the slave there was, of course, no freedom, no choice of work, indeed, no choice but to work. Slave economy was organized entirely in the interests of production, not of the individual. The worker received no teaching because there was no time and no inclination. In the handicraft era there was freedom, pride in work, and reasonable comfort. Then came the factory, where again production came first and man second. Finally, scientific management attempted to do with finesse what the slave driver did with the whip. The primary objective was higher production, with conservation of the worker, but the net result was the speed-up, the stretch-out, and a kind of benevolent serfdom.

Through all the ages, despite the scorn of one section of society for the work of another, it must be remembered that most men and many women were doing some kind of "work." Even the Greek intellectuals, the philosophers, the writers, had their professions. They were working very hard. Plato would have admitted that his philosophers and kings and his soldiers were "occupied with a purpose." A history of work is a history of all kinds of work, all kinds of purposeful occupation. If it is considered an evolution of non-manual control over the environment, and progress is measured in terms of diminution of manual work, no rational conclusions can be drawn for sociology or vocational education. All one can say is that as man gains control over the environment, over *processes,* he has been slow to make these improvements benefit all the workers. He has not made the improvements "work."

On the other hand, it is quite clear that no generalization can be offered for all mankind. Leaving out the effects of the Second World War, it is clear that working conditions, for all kinds of workers, vary from "ideal" to "wretched," from country to country, from

---

[8] Reprinted from *The Science of Work* by MORRIS S. VITELES, p. 13, by permission of W. W. Norton & Company, Inc. Copyright 1934, by the publishers.

city to city. But you can't leave out war, because again and again man has destroyed what he has made, and lately he has been doing this on a stupendous scale. Over the radio comes from the highest scientific authority, "in a few years it will be possible to make an atom bomb that will destroy *all* of New York City." So, even the scientist is calling for social, as well as industrial control. Thus, all workers, laborers, artisans, farmers, scientists, soldiers, editors, clergymen, lawyers, engineers, yes, philosophers and kings must improve their skills and upgrade their social understanding, but always *both,* in the interests of all. In other words, they must learn to work, to work wholeheartedly and bigheartedly at their jobs. They must help young people to grow up and prepare them to take their places. Vocational education, in its widest, fullest, richest implications, must make better history than we have ever had before.

III. WORK IN A DEMOCRACY

"Work" is a great generalizer among verbs and nouns. Like "do" it is a great replacer. Anything that anybody does can be called "work" — and often *is.* They may be sleeping at the roadside, but the sign says "Men at work." One man's work is another man's poison. All of which warns us again to consider the operation. Who is doing what? How is he doing it and where? For whom is he doing it and what becomes of the product? So, let us take the lowly shovel and then the middle-class typewriter.

HOW GLAMOROUS CAN THE SHOVEL BE? Shoveling is a simple operation. You nick a little piece out of a ball called the earth, scoop it up and throw it somewhere — just turn it over and put it back, or spread it out over the ground, or toss it into a wheelbarrow. Suppose you are a slave, chained to a rock in a dark mine. You do not see daylight for months. Day after day you pick up pieces of earth called coal. All you get for your trouble is enough food to keep you alive to shovel more coal. You don't know what happens to the coal, certainly it does not keep *you* warm. You own nothing, not even the shovel. Is this work?

Now imagine yourself the owner of a house in Suburbia. You have a garden. You insist on performing all the operations yourself. In the spring, you carve out the earth, piece by piece, turn it over and carefully replace it. Perhaps you do it in the dark of night — after a day in the office. Night after night, and on Sundays, when others are resting, you keep on spading. Then you perform many other operations that finally result in food that keeps you alive for more spading. (You already have plenty of other food, bought with money, but this is extra.) You give some to your neighbors, boasting the while about its size and succulence. Of course, you own your shovel. Is *this* work?

Consider the typewriter — and the typist. Miss A listens to each word as it comes off the cylinder and converts the sound into symbols on paper. She does this accurately and fast. She does not necessarily know the meaning of the text. In fact, efficiency precludes consideration of meaning. She is like the telegrapher who sent the message of Lincoln's death and had no recollection of ever having done so. Miss A takes pride in producing good, clean copy, and in being considered an efficient worker. She is paid a salary for her work. She will probably see the copy in print but will not be very much concerned about it. Of course, she does not own her typewriter. Is this work?

Mr. B is a poet. He writes his poems on a noisy old machine that is still called a typewriter. He has owned it for a long time. He picks out the letters with two fingers, forms them into words and lines of great beauty. He revises and revises, and finally retypes the poem and sends it to a publisher. The publisher pays him a little money but the public pays him great homage. Has the poet been working?

These combinations and permutations could be extended indefinitely, but the foregoing are enough to make clear that work can vary from dismal slavery to exultant creation. Its quality depends upon who is doing it, when, where, why, and how he performs the operation, and whose tool he is using.

ADULT BEHAVIOR OF THE INTERESTED WORKER IN A FREE SOCIETY IN A TECHNOLOGICAL AGE. Above all, the worker must be free — free to move, free to think, and free to speak. He must be free to do the same kind of work wherever and with whomever he will. Technically, this is known as horizontal mobility. In accordance with his talents and experience he must be free to move up the scale, be promoted, to reach the top. This is known as vertical mobility.

To be a free man in a free society, to be able to move horizontally or vertically, he must possess bargaining power comparable with that of his employers or competitors. If the frontier, either geographical or industrial, is closed, such bargaining power can probably be attained only through association with other workers in unions, but bargaining power he must have. With bargaining power and freedom of movement comes status.

Freedom as a worker implies freedom in all the other relationships of life. Freedom from want, freedom from fear, freedom of assemblage, freedom of worship, and always freedom of speech. These are basic considerations. For the full appreciation and enjoyment of work, something else must be added, partly by society and partly by the worker himself. Particularly vital are a sense of responsibility and a sense of creativeness. Let us see what the American scene has offered the American worker.

THE AMERICAN SCENE. The most respected — and respectable — single word in the American language is "work." From the landing of the Pilgrims to the feverish two hundred billion dollar war program the rallying cry has been work. From Governor Bradford to the latest Chief Executive, from salvation of the soul to defense of the soil, from food, clothing, and shelter to arms, ships, and airplanes, the only solution has been work, more work, and still more work. As the pioneers pressed westward through the forests, crossed the plains, and scaled the Rockies, they knew little that was not work — the hardest, the most soul-trying kind of work. Nor did those who stayed in the east — who tended the lamp of learning, who ministered to the soul — lie in the soft arms of culture or sit at the groaning table of the church. They were hard-working scholars and hard-working pastors. Using the word in its broadest connotation of "exerting physical or mental labor for the accomplishment of some object," Americans have been hard-working people. That they have respected work has been amply evident in their strong emotional reaction to such a variety of nonwork words as idler, drone, dilettante, loafer, bum. Work is the generic term for a continuous application of energy toward an end. That energy may be concentrated in the hands or the back or the vocal cords or the brain cells, but it always culminates in some product — a beet, a boat, a book, a poem, a sermon, an opera — something that not only enables the producer to live but enables consumers (who are the producers of other things) to live.

"Comfort, peace, happiness, beauty, art, culture, friendliness — all that we now consider best in life — are not characteristic of prehistoric life but of the civilization which has replaced it. In the development of this civilization no factor has been more potent than *work*. It is work, from which prehistoric and modern savages appear to be so free, which has raised man from the position of a savage and created the civilization of which we are so proud to-day. . . . The fact is that a man works only a small part of the day to escape starvation. He works the greater part to avoid living as a tramp or as a savage. 'It is his desire to live as a civilized man, with the comforts and conveniences of civilization and as many of its luxuries as he can get' that leads him to devote so large a portion of his day to work. Unless this is clearly recognized, much that occurs in the course of work in modern industry cannot be clearly understood." [9]

POSITIONS, JOBS, VOCATIONS, AND CALLINGS. Attitudes toward work range from disgust to exultation. The tramp and hobo never work except under compulsion and then only long enough to earn the next meal or the night's lodging. In a sense, Dr. Grenfell never worked, for his whole life was a manifestation of high duty to humanity. Energy and skill were absorbed and lost in the mission to which he was called. His was not a job which he "took," or a position in which he was "placed," but a vocation to which he was "called." A vocation is a calling.

Addressing college students, Elliot Dunlap Smith of Yale University has said the same thing with extreme effectiveness: "If you conceive of a vocation as something that is inevitable but not very pleasant to contemplate, something sordid, something not quite nice, then it will be just that. If a job is to you merely the means of bringing food, shelter, and clothing out of society, plus money enough to buy your pleasures, if a job is to you something apart from the important things you expect from your four years of college, then your job will be just a job. If, however, a job is to you something towards which you are striving because it will give scope to your personality, will enable you to become creative, will be a part of life itself, then your vocation will be truly what its name implies, a *calling*. More than that, what you learn in college will be truly important, it will take on new significance; it will not be mere diversion for the gentleman, or the dilettante, or the dual personality who would be cultured among his friends and hard-boiled among his business associates. Education is for life and life requires education." [10]

---

[9] VITELES, op. cit., p. 2 and p. 4.
[10] FRANKLIN J. KELLER, "The Great Dichotomy," *Occupations: The Vocational Guidance Magazine*, XIII (June, 1935), 828–29.

These concepts are of the highest practical import. They are fundamental in the selection of vocational teachers, who themselves may
be either holders of jobs or followers of vocations. They determine
the curriculum, even down to detail. The prospective businessman
may learn only to interpret sales charts and reinvest profits or, as
Adler[11] suggests, he may learn too about the Phoenicians, the
Greeks, the Venetians, about the Hanseatic League and the Steel-
Yard in London. Or, as would be said on the high-school level,
pupils should learn not only to perform manual operations skillfully but also, through social studies, to be good neighbors and good
citizens of the world. If the vocation is to give scope to personality,
then the vocational school should give attention to personality
through the so-called cultural subjects, through music, through art,
through health, even through direct teaching and exercise of good
personal habits.

ARTISTS AND SLAVES. So we come to the problem of the machine.
Even if the worker be free, how can he be responsible for and creative in his work if he is chained to the assembly line and repeats
the same operation over and over again? Art calls for skill, skill
resulting from knowledge and practice, human skill. "Fine" arts
please by perfection of execution. If you walk skillfully, then walking becomes an art—and dancing! But "art" is associated with
"responsibility," responsibility for something that pleases. You must
hold yourself accountable for what you have made, know what is to
be done with it, and be pleased with it when it finally fulfills its
function. We know ancient civilizations principally through their
art, the things they made to use and please them. We call them
"artifacts," the marks of a civilization. Where the worker feels no
responsibility, sees no outcome, he ceases to be an artist and becomes
a slave. In a remarkable essay, Eric Gill writes lyrically of the joys
of work and dolefully of the machine:

"Today our enthusiasts say that very soon, everything that is necessary will be made by machinery, then we shall all have plenty of
time to enjoy ourselves. Those who have an itch for creation will
have plenty of time to scratch it. . . . The problem of leisure is not
a moral problem. It is an intellectual problem, a problem of what
to do that is worth doing. For if all the useful things are made by
machinery, then the only things to be made in leisure time will be,

11 FELIX ADLER, *The Ideal of Culture for Businessmen* (New York: The American
Ethical Union, 1924).

will have to be, useless things. . . . The freeman does what he
wishes when he is at work, but the slave, when he is working, does
what he is compelled to do and the slave is only happy when he
is not working — but the freeman, as it says in the Book of Ecclesi-
astes, 'has joy in his work and this is his portion.'

"The word culture is derived from a word meaning to train or
cultivate. So a cultured person is one whose mind is trained in
understanding and appreciation of the true and the good and, therefore, of the beautiful. And when I say that in former times the
working life of men was their chief means to culture, I mean that
the training of their minds was chiefly attained by means of the
work which they did for their living. . . . To love a thing is not
merely to know or desire it. To love is to unite, to become one, with
what is both known and desired. . . . It is not desirable that everybody should always be talking about love; but it is absolutely necessary that, if man's work is to be a proper and normal product of
his real nature, every work of man should have the nature of a
love song. . . .

"Love, holiness, beauty. Man is a creature who loves. Ultimately
he can love only the holy. Ultimately only the holy can be pleasant to
see. The beautiful being, that which pleases when seen, must be
visible holiness. Love is the unity of the lover and the beloved. Man
can only unite with that which is connatural to him. Is the word
'holy' a stumbling block? Why be afraid or shy of the word? Primarily it means hale and hearty, whole, unsullied, perfect, and therefore of God — godly, sanctified, sacred; and therefore gay and light
and sweet and cheerful and gracious. 'Oh, taste and see how gracious
the Lord is.' But gay — above all things gay. How can the unholy
be gay? 'The morning stars sang together.' Was it a song of despair?" [12]

Every work of man should have the nature of a love song! This is
true of whatever he *does,* whether he makes something or performs
an act. He does it *for* love of someone or some idea, *to* someone, and
insofar as he is *responsible* for it and makes himself an instrument
of creation, it is art, and the doer is an artist. He is illuminated or
inspired by an idea and *designs* the act before he performs it, sees
it through, and takes the consequences. He has sung his love song.
It is beautiful and it is good.

[12] Eric Gill, *Work and Leisure* (London: Faber and Faber, 1935), pp. 42, 44, 55,
56, 116, 120, 121.

A TASK, A PLAN, AND FREEDOM. The mental hygiene approach to work and the worker leads to a strikingly similar conclusion. "The essentials, without which a person cannot be quite sound mentally and with which, apart from accident, infection, or heredity, one can have no serious mental disorder, the absolutely essential conditions are three: a task, a plan, and freedom. The task in the generic sense includes everything from the immediate and concrete goal of the moment to the objectification of the highest ideals and ends. A plan is necessary to make the work purposive activity. It must be my own task; hence freedom is necessary. It is highly necessary to dwell on the evidence that these are the essentials of mental health. Function, work, is the condition of health everywhere. Mental activity is even more essential for health, if possible, than physical activity. In all conditions of life and society, work is the condition of health and happiness. Stanley, in the heart of Africa, rousing his discouraged men every morning to face the apparently interminable forest, says that the remedy for all misery, discouragement, and despair, is work. This, which is so excellent a remedy, is still better as a preventive." [13]

THE PHILOSOPHICAL ASPECTS OF WORK. The philosophers do not help us nearly enough. While they work at their philosophy they do not say much about work. Sometimes the implications are clear, but oftener not. An often quoted reference to vocations is Plato's conception of a just man, a man in just the right place, doing his best and giving the full equivalent of what he receives. Plato would see that every man was doing the work for which he was best fitted — the perfect vocational counselor. However, unfortunately, he thought that men were destined at birth for their niche in society and that there were only three niches — that for individuals in whom appetites naturally dominated, the laboring and trading class; that for the man with a generous, outgoing, courageous disposition, the soldier; and the top place for those who could grasp the universal, those capable of the highest kind of education, the philosophers and kings. No variety and no vertical mobility. Freedom only for philosophers and kings.

Francis Bacon would "let parents choose betimes the vocations and courses they mean their children should take, for then they are

13 WILLIAM H. BURNHAM, *The Normal Mind* (New York: D. Appleton & Co., 1927), p. 207.

most flexible; and let them not too much apply themselves to the disposition of their children, as thinking they will take best to that which they have most mind to. It is true that, if the affections or aptness of the children be extraordinary, then it is good not to cross it, but generally the precept of the Pythagoreans is good — 'Choose the best; custom will make it pleasant and easy.' For 'custom is the principal magistrate of man's life.' "

"Spinoza made his living at first by teaching children in Van den Ende's school, and then by polishing lenses, as if he had an inclination for dealing with refractory material. He had learned the optical trade while living in the Jewish community; it was in accord with Hebrew canon that every student should acquire some manual art; not only because study and honest teaching can seldom make a livelihood, but, as Gamaliel had said, work keeps one virtuous, whereas 'every learned man who fails to acquire a trade will at last turn out a rogue.' " [14]

Both Tolstoy and Ruskin were famous for their extreme views on work. Tolstoy would "work as much as possible — receive as little as possible. The only work worthy of a human being is that work which is essential to life, work which meets the humble primitive needs of existence, manual work. Both Ruskin and Tolstoy considered that work is as necessary as breathing to a human being. But in work there is no titanic element of half-divine creativeness. It is for them no task of endless duration, but a necessary physiological function; not an incessant effort, but an activity as calm and uninterrupted as breathing; not a hectic rush toward an ever-receding goal, but tranquil energy which is the very act of peaceably exerting itself, bringing peace and cheerfulness and inner calm; Ruskin held that all men should work with their hands, with no help from machinery except those devices set in motion by wind and water. The product should go to the worker. It should be paid for according to justice consecrated by usage. Only in this way could the dignity of the worker be honored and the function be fulfilled with decency and decorum." [15]

THE DIGNITY OF LABOR. Obviously, the dignity of labor is not something that can be preached to the worker or that can be conferred upon him through any formal ceremony. The dignity of labor, the

[14] Reprinted from *The Story of Philosophy* by WILL DURANT, pp. 129 and 172. Copyright 1926, by Simon and Schuster, Inc.
[15] TILGHER, *op. cit.*, pp. 123–128.

virtue of a vocation, lie not in the operation itself but in the personality of the worker and all the surrounding circumstances conditioning the work. Specialization in industry may create conditions inimical to democracy, but democracy, popular over-all control over the lives of men, may eliminate these conditions or at least modify them to the point where free men can work in a free society with the essential dignity that always should adhere to work.

IV. A TENABLE CONCEPTION OF WORK

In a free society there are all kinds of jobs and all kinds of people to do them. It is the very diversity of opportunity and the variety of human beings, brought together in a given area and operating for the common good, without dictatorial direction, that make for democracy. The range of attractiveness of jobs and the range of adaptability of people who take them are both as wide as life itself. So, let us look at the picture a little more in detail.

ALL KINDS OF JOBS. Except for the unabridged English dictionary itself, probably the most fascinating expository volume in print is the *Dictionary of Occupational Titles*.[16] Spreading over 1040 pages, the Dictionary defines 17,452 separate jobs. These are also known by 12,292 alternate titles, making a total of 29,744 titles defined. The titles are coded according to major occupational groups and divisions, extending from the professional and managerial occupations through clerical and sales, service, agricultural, fishery, forest and kindred occupations, and then into what are known as skilled, semiskilled, and unskilled occupations. In the first bracket are accountants and auditors, actors and actresses, architects, artists, sculptors, teachers of art, authors, editors, reporters, chemists, clergymen, college presidents, dentists, engineers, lawyers, librarians, musicians, physicians and surgeons, social and welfare workers, statisticians, teachers, trained nurses, and veterinarians. At the other end of the scale are those laborers who require very little skill and practically no intelligence. However, the revealing information lies in the definitions, listed alphabetically, without reference to skill, intelligence, or status. Let us take a few of the A's.

Able-bodied seaman "performs all regular and emergency duties required in deck service in a ship, such as steering, lowering and

16 United States Department of Labor, *Dictionary of Occupational Titles* (Washington, D.C.: Government Printing Office, 1939).

handling lifeboat, splicing rope, making minor repairs, taking depth-soundings, and stowing cargoes. Must hold a certificate issued by U. S. Government."

Accompanist is "a musician, instrumental, who plays the accompaniment, usually on a piano, for a vocal or instrumental performance."

Accordion maker "makes complete accordions by hand: builds box section of plywood, gluing and clamping joints; cuts slots at each end for keys; makes bellows of paper covered with artificial leather; sets and tunes reeds in holding blocks, checking tuning with tuning fork; glues celluloid on box ends, keyboard, and top of keys; glues bellows on each end of case; trims material with knife; finishes accordion with lacquer or other decorative or protective covering."

Accountant, general, "devises or executes previously devised accounting systems to meet the needs of a particular concern: prepares financial statements, audits books, and does other accounting work as business requires; assumes responsibility for accuracy of the books after the audit."

Acid-tank cleaner, "a laborer, a cleaner who cleans tanks used for storing or processing acid."

Acrobat; kinker; tumbler, "entertains an audience, usually in a circus or on a vaudeville stage, with difficult and spectacular gymnastic feats, such as leaping and tumbling."

Actor, "plays an assigned part or role in a production; rehearses systematically, learning lines and cues assigned; takes comic or serious part; impersonates and portrays the character by speech and gesture. May sing or perform dancing routines."

Agricultural engineer, "a term applied to one who is versed in the technical phases of agriculture, supplemented by engineering fundamentals, but who engages in the development, design, or supervision of the engineering phases of agriculture, such as farm structures, dams, sedimentation boxes; light, heat, and power systems, and other applications of electricity to farming; farm machinery; rural roads, soil erosion, and flood control; or irrigation and drainage. Classification is made under such titles as civil engineer, electrical engineer, and mechanical engineer, according to the basic branch of engineering engaged."

Air-filler; air-tester (cooperage), "a laborer, process. Fills tight barrels with compressed air preparatory to inspection by *barrel inspector, tight;* pushes check valve into bunghole of barrel containing small quantity of water; connects air hose to bung valve, and manipulates hand valve to admit air into the barrel and to regulate the pressure of the air; removes hose from check valve and sets barrel aside."

Thus, within eight pages of over one thousand appear the most diverse occupations of the modern age. Imagine the air-filler with his thousands of barrels, each one looking like every other. He pushes the check valve into the bunghole, admits the air, removes the hose from the check valve and sets the barrel aside. Then comes the next barrel. He pushes the check valve into the bunghole. . . . Repetitive, monotonous, but a job that somebody does. Compare the air-filler with the agricultural engineer, whose activities range over the entire countryside, whose studies take him into all the sciences, whose work means idea, design, creation, human betterment, a finer civilization. Whoever could be a good air-filler could never be an agricultural engineer, nor could the agricultural engineer be a good air-filler, for more than a few valves. The expert able-bodied seaman would not be likely to respond to the artistic demands made upon the accompanist, nor would the accompanist probably steady himself for long aboard ship.

There is no need to labor the point. The curious-minded person requires no occupational dictionary, for within twenty-four hours he can observe as wide a variety of occupational skills as is possessed by those he meets in his daily life — the train conductor, the shopkeeper, the waiter, the policeman, the musician, the architect, the engineer.

ALL KINDS OF PEOPLE. Who are these people who choose, or gravitate to these jobs? Well, the able-bodied seaman is certainly able-bodied. He likes the sea and its freedom. Perhaps he loves ships and the stars and becomes an officer, a navigator, a master, responsible for a beautiful mechanism that plies the seven seas, taking food and machinery and people to foreign lands and bringing spices, coffee, sugar, what not, and always more people, to our own shores. His intelligence, physique, and temperament make him a good able-bodied seaman and a potentially good skipper, but probably an impossible accompanist.

On the other hand, watch our accompanist on the concert stage, slight of physique, of sensitive disposition, and of high musical intelligence. He has had long training in technique and interpretation and not only must know how music should be played, but must be responsive to the last degree to the interpretation of the musician he accompanies. The concert hall is no place for an able-bodied seaman, but in a raging storm, the wheelhouse would be equally uncomfortable for our musician. Neither able-bodied seaman nor accompanist would have even the prerequisites for agricultural engineer and all three would be unsuccessful in pushing that check valve into ten thousand bungholes.

Consider one other aspect of these jobs in relation to people. The agricultural engineer works with the greatest of freedom and the minimum of direction from others. The able-bodied seaman works under the closest supervision of his boatswain. If he has no ambition or capacity to rise higher, he continues under that supervision, but if he becomes the master of the vessel, he is completely master. The air-filler and the acid-tank cleaner (whom we have neglected) are under strict supervision, and probably like it. Some people prefer to direct their jobs and themselves, others are only happy when they are told what to do. With these illustrations in mind, and hundreds of others will crowd into the consciousness of the reader, let us cull the good points of good jobs for the right people.

WHAT DO WE WANT IN OUR WORK? 1. "Money is not as strong an incentive as it is usually supposed to be." [17] Undeniably, the worker wants as much money as he can get because he wants as many of life's comforts as he can buy, but when he is looking for a job, he feels, very literally, that "money isn't everything." How many people would work in the mines for any amount of money? How many people would work at sea for any amount of money? And, of course, how many could be successful in either place, no matter how hard they tried? This is important because it is a clear indication that people want to live well on their jobs, that they consider their jobs part of life and not merely a means of earning money that may be used to "live" after working hours. Incidentally, to the seaman this is exceedingly important because, except for time in port, he literally lives his job.

2. Job efficiency and job satisfaction must be considered not only

[17] VITELES, op. cit., p. 366.

in terms of the job itself but also in terms of the personality of the worker. It is these elements of personality, in reaction to job environment, that determine the life adjustment and happiness of the individual, primarily as worker, but also most significantly as member of a family, of a community, or of the world.

3. In most human beings there is some element of desire for mastery of others. This ranges from the dictator to the fifth assistant helper. It may be blatant in practice or stifled in frustration. The immature youngster, least capable of assuming responsibility, is likely to grasp for it at the first opportunity. For many, life immediately becomes sweeter when they can tell others what to do.

4. Variety must be so balanced with monotony as to suit the individual's needs. Your secretary does not *always* want to be doing *new* jobs. We are not at every moment ready to be original, inventive, creative.[18]

5. Some people want a boss all the time, others none of the time. Most people like a gentle mixture of authority for themselves and direction from others. Many college professors have voluntarily relinquished all the perquisites of administration in order to return to the calm and "irresponsibility" of teaching and scholarship.

6. The artist-worker wants to see the end-product of his endeavor. He wants to feel responsible for what he has done. Most factory workers miss this pleasure, many do not care. As Cabot points out, too many teachers, engrossed in special subjects, have little regard for the finished student, another evidence that human frailties are no respecters of the ultimate social or professional status of workers.

7. We do want status. Sometimes it is the title of the job. Often it is a uniform. It may be only a handle to our name. It may be gained through association with others, the college in which we teach, the labor union to which we belong. It is evidenced in the second degree when a woman says with pride, "My husband is the head man. . . . He handles all the big machines. . . ."

8. We like to work among pleasant people, people that we like. Nothing will drive a man from a job more quickly than uncongenial companions, still another evidence that workers live their jobs. As a matter of fact, it is largely from these very fellow workers that they draw their associates during after-hours.

9. Says Cabot: "Payment can be given a working man only for

18 RICHARD C. CABOT, *What Men Live By: Work, Play, Love, Worship* (Boston: Houghton Mifflin Company, 1914). A most human, understanding treatment of incentives for work.

what some other man might have done. The man himself you cannot pay. Yet anyone who does his work well, or gets satisfaction out of it, puts something of himself into it. There is spiritual value in being paid in hard cash. It gives precious assurance of *some* value. The value of gratitude begins just where the value of pay ends. It is personal. Workers are hungry for *reality* — doing something that counts. The sense of somebody's need is the most powerful in the world. Every one of the goods we buy with our work is itself a means to something else, a coin with which to purchase something more." [19]

What is the ultimate value? Happiness? Perfection? Love?

BEING A REAL PERSON. "Along with love and friendship, one of the most durable satisfactions in life is to lose oneself in *creative work*. Every wise man seeks a task to dignify his days. No man can be himself until he gets out of himself into work with which he identifies himself. Even beavers build their dams, bees their honeycombs, and birds their nests. Rooted in a long past, there is in man an impulse to construct, an urge to create, a deep need to invest himself in work that becomes an extension of himself. This is why more people become neurotic from aimless leisure and laziness than from overwork, and this is why unemployment is one of the worst of tragedies, its psychological result quite as lamentable as its economic ills. As Michelangelo said, 'It is only well with me when I have a chisel in my hand.'" [20]

"I cannot conceive of life without a vocation, an inner summons. The vocation arises from the vital spring, and from the vocation is born the project of life which, at every moment, constitutes 'my life.' The vocation of an individual may coincide with one of those forms of life which have been dubbed with the names of professions. There are individuals who genuinely are painters, politicians, businessmen, clergymen. There are many more, however, who execute these professions without genuinely being them." [21]

"Work gives every man an audience and a message. . . . To find one's work is to find one's place in the world. Work pulls people out of the misery of a self-centered existence. Idleness is corrosive. Human energies, like human stomachs, turn inward perversely and

[19] CABOT, *op. cit.,* pp. 73–85.
[20] HARRY EMERSON FOSDICK, *On Being a Real Person* (New York: Harper & Brothers, 1943), p. 92.
[21] Reprinted from *Toward a Philosophy of History* by JOSÉ ORTEGA Y GASSET, p. 260, by permission of W. W. Norton & Company. Copyright 1941 by the publishers.

self-destructively if they do not have material to work on. *Thought plans action; action executes thought.* Good thinking feels its way by action — good manual work is full of thought. Loyalty is a force that holds a man to a job even in the moments when he hates it and sees no great significance in it. No man who loves his work sees it without its halo.

"When we try to serve the world (or understand it), we touch what is divine. We get our dignity, our courage, our joy in work because of the greatness of the far-off end always in sight, always attainable, never at any moment attained. Service is one of the ways by which a tiny insect like one of us can get a purchase on the whole universe. If we can find the job where we can be of use, we are hitched to the star of the world, and move with it." [22]

Pleasure or displeasure in work is inseparable from an inner drive (interest) and conditions of work (especially status). Desire to work, and certainly *creativeness,* may be entirely lacking. The only satisfaction in work may be status, bathing in the (supposed) admiring glances of others, in lording it over one's "superiors," "betters" — shouting, insulting, belittling. In other words, as has already been shown, it is futile to discuss work in abstract terms or in terms of any general human qualities or social conditions.

Work in a democracy is joyous; one works for himself, and for others. In a totalitarian state, it is drudgery, work is all for others, except for mere subsistence.

People who are not occupied are at loose ends, footless, waiting for something to strike, killing time. They ask that their senses be titillated — eyes, ears, flesh, taste.

What more important aspect of citizenship is there than the production of *goods* and the rendering of *services* to others? Education for leisure cannot be confined to mere tickling of the senses and, if it is, why education? Leisure activities might well be production — photographs or paintings (for others to enjoy), playing musical instruments (for others to listen to), games (well played with, and against, others), acting (with and for others), and so on. Does mere observation — spectatorship, auditioning — require training or education?

Most people, even educators and philosophers, would agree on how a mature adult should act in a scientific age, but they disagree upon the knowledge that should be put into his head and how it should be put there, in other words, about subject matter and meth-

[22] CABOT, *op. cit.,* pp. 12, 13, 16, 42, 44, 67, 72, 85.

ods in education. For centuries we took work as we found it. By learning what kind of work we like, pursuing and advancing in it intelligently we may even beat the technological age. Obviously, the "good life" is neither drudgery nor play, but a combination of both, so, preparation for the good life — education — must comprehend both. Since vocation is so vital a part of living, vocational education can very well be the integrating principle. And the integrating principle of vocation, as has been abundantly shown, must necessarily be *purpose, goal, end*. Every boy or girl should be a young man or a young woman going somewhere.

Chapter 3

AN INTERPRETATIVE HISTORY OF VOCATIONAL EDUCATION

I. VOCATIONAL EDUCATION AS RELATED TO WORK

PATENTLY, work is much more than "work," and knowing *how* to work is much more than knowing how to perform an operation. In all its radiations work is vocation, life with a purpose. So, vocational education is much more than knowing how to work, it is education with a purpose, for a purpose. Vocational education is learning how to work, but it is learning how to work in a milieu, among people, with people, for people. It is learning how to live with other workers, at home, at play, and in the community. It is learning to live efficiently and morally. It is *everybody* learning to work, first of all, *you,* your butcher, your baker, your electric light maker, your professor, your barber, your doctor, your favorite movie actor, your clergyman, the architect who planned your house, the maid who keeps it tidy, and the plumber who made America sanitary. Then all the others, some of whom you have never seen and therefore do not know so well — the aitch-bone breaker, alley boy, ballyhoo man, animated-cartoon artist, and the delayed-bill-analysis-clerk, final touch-up man, pigs' feet boner, anthropologist, ash man, pants maker, strip-tease artist, and sweeper.

In its manual and technical phases, vocational education is teaching others how to work. In the rise from savagery to civilization, people have learned to work in many different ways. At first they must have learned by accident, the Lamb-roast-pig method. Down through the ages, the most popular method has been trial and error, mostly error — the auto-mechanic-learning-on-your-car. Slaves learned under the whiplash, duller folk often learn best when they are "yelled at." Average people learn by being told how and by being shown. Bright boys and girls need only watch the expert and then imitate. They learn by observation and doing.

It is obvious that, through these casual, fortuitous methods, all adult persons who earn a living must have received some kind of vocational education. Planned, organized vocational education comes late in the history of work. Apprenticeship is one of the early forms, the public vocational school one of the latest.

Vocational education has generally been identified with the manual and technical phases, and very naturally so. For vocational education, as a means of human development, has usually been a protest against neglect, and in its earlier, organized phases, was almost solely a teaching of manipulative ability. The history of what has been known as vocational education is largely the story of men and women who have recognized the importance of teaching people how to perform manual operations well. The history of what has been called professional education has included better performance but has emphasized theory, the scientific basis, the knowing *why* as well as *how*. Modern vocational education for all vocations — industrial, agricultural, commercial, professional — comprises not only performance and theory but the whole life of the worker. The history of vocational education is revealing even in as brief a treatment as the following must be. In truth, it is more a history of opinion than accomplishment, but it clears the way for understanding.[1, 2]

II. OPINIONS AND ACCOMPLISHMENTS IN VOCATIONAL EDUCATION

Throughout the ages the father has taught his son a trade. Even in a time of widespread industrialism this is probably the most prevalent type of occupational teaching. It may be casual, indirect, and inexpert, but it has the merit of being conducted by a teacher interested in his pupil, and both teacher and pupil probably have respect for the trade itself. An extension of the paternal situation is the father's placement of the son with another craftsman who not only takes over the instructional duties but treats the boy as his own son. This is apprenticeship in its simplest form. In a simple society, it is obviously a convenient arrangement for any kind of work existing at the time, whether manual or intellectual. As already noted, the emphasis of the Jews upon the desirability of learning a trade placed

[1] Charles Alpheus Bennett, *History of Manual and Industrial Education Up to 1870* and *History of Manual and Industrial Education, 1870–1917* (Peoria, Illinois: The Manual Arts Press, 1926 and 1937).
[2] Paul Monroe, *A Textbook in the History of Education* (New York: The Macmillan Company, 1905).

the responsibility upon the father to teach that trade and in no way set up any formal program of vocational education. Indeed, "school" was for instruction in religion, "trade" was for the home or shop, for "he who applies himself in study alone is like him who has no God."

Monasticism offers one of the most fascinating examples of vocational education. Cloistered as they were, monks led their own life, a life to which they had somehow to be adjusted. In a very real sense, all of monasticism was their profession. They entered the monastery to live a religious life. To live the religious life they must read the Scriptures and therefore must be taught to read. They must have books and therefore must be taught to copy manuscripts. They must maintain themselves and must therefore perform manual labor which, in itself, was most salutary in keeping them out of temptation. Without being so proclaimed or recognized, here, in a very real sense, education was life. Life was the profession, a most effective kind of professional education. Fortunately, after a time, the surrounding communities benefited.

"It is true that until the organization of the teaching orders in the sixteenth and seventeenth centuries, the monastic orders did not make education the controlling aim. On the other hand, it is also true that from the seventh to the opening of the thirteenth centuries, there was practically no other education but that offered by the monks, and that the Church and the monastic institutions were responsible for the fact that no other conception of education existed and that no other educational institutions were tolerated. . . .

"Thus it happened that the monasteries were the sole schools for teaching; they offered the only professional training; they were the only universities of research; they alone served as publishing houses for the multiplication of books; they were the only libraries for the preservation of learning; they produced the only scholars; they were the sole educational institutions of this period." [3]

Later, when life broadened, escaping from the narrowness of the monasteries, the medieval university became predominantly vocational, its purpose being the education of doctors of law, theology, and medicine. Their texts were Latin and Greek but the subject matter became the technical equipment of the graduates. Paralleling this education for the professions was the ancient master-helper relationship, more fully developed through the supervision of trade

[3] From PAUL MONROE, *A Textbook in the History of Education,* pp. 253 and 255. By permission of The Macmillan Company, publishers.

guilds and formal indenture. The apprentice had to serve his master faithfully, work diligently and make himself useful as a member of the family. The master obligated himself to teach the apprentice all phases of the trade, and to give him all the care owing to his own son — shelter, food, clothing, and most importantly, moral and religious instruction. Foreshadowing the more formalized vocational education of today, apprenticeship was expected to provide not merely a good craftsman but a good citizen. And, traditionally, the apprentice was expected to, and very often did, marry the master's beautiful daughter. Again, the worker lived his education and, for seven years, education was his life.

It is interesting to note that, while Luther railed against the teachings of the monastic schools, he too believed in several hours of academic education in school and in spending the rest of the day at home learning a trade, all of which was a forerunner to the modern continuation school.

In philosophy, in religion, in science, in education there has always been, and must always inevitably be, a search for the ultimate, the real. Whether it be the "Ding an sich," or God, or electron, or — well, what is it in education? "Though not usually included within the Renaissance period, realism represents but a later and higher stage of that movement. As the Renaissance in the fifteenth century revealed itself primarily in ideas of individual attainment and effort after personal culture, and hence became chiefly literary and esthetic; so the same movement in the sixteenth century became primarily moral, reformatory, and hence chiefly religious and political or social. In the seventeenth century, through a yet further development of the same spirit and of the same forces, the Renaissance became impersonal, nonsocial, and directed toward a new determination of reality. Hence it became philosophical and scientific. Modern science, which received its first formulation in the seventeenth century and began to modify educational ideas and practices in these tendencies collectively called realism, is the full product of the Renaissance revolution in thought." [4]

The realistic movement was, of course, *the* real thing. In modern parlance, this was *it!* The humanistic-realists used the classical languages and literatures to reveal all that was fundamental in human nature, in societal organization, in the surrounding physical world. As with the modern scholastics, they went to the great books for the

[4] MONROE, *op. cit.,* p. 442.

realities of life. Milton was a humanistic-realist and gave us the well-known definition, conspicuously occupational in intent: "I call therefore a complete and generous education that which fits a man to perform justly, skillfully and magnanimously all the offices both private and public of peace and war."

The social-realists, of whom Montaigne is the outstanding exponent, went even further in their advocacy of education for occupational life. "Education should shape the judgment and the disposition so as to secure for the youth a successful and pleasurable career in life. This view regarded education, in the frankest and most utilitarian manner, as the direct preparation for the life of the 'man of the world.' Holding a view as far as possible from a high idealism, or a rigid asceticism, or a fervid emotionalism, these educators looked with unconcealed skepticism upon the ordinary routine of the school and the accepted deification of the humanists' studies. To them, education should be a frank preparation for a practical, serviceable, successful, happy career of a man of affairs in a civilization formal enough in its pretenses, but not over rigid in its standard of conduct. To them education was to culminate, if it was not chiefly to consist in, an extensive period of travel for the sake of acquiring experience and familiarity with men and customs. Through travel one would acquire practical knowledge and the culture which comes from actual contact with places and people made familiar through literary study. With the social-realists, however, this view usurped practically the entire scope of education." [5]

The first intimations of the modern scientific and mechanical age came from the sense-realists, of whom Bacon and Comenius are the outstanding exponents. Here was something very "real," something that man must touch or see or hear or taste or smell to know that it really existed. Of course, it is the stuff of the training phases of vocational and scientific education and it gives rise to the theory that makes it possible to handle it intelligently. Bacon had very little to say about education itself, but his whole theory of knowledge implied a method of acquiring it. Then too, he saw how the acquisition of "truth" would set to rout his well-known "idols." He classified them as "idols of the tribe, those that 'have their foundation in human nature as such, and in the tribe and race of men'; idols of the den, or the personal bias of the individual; idols of the market-place, or those which arise from the manners, customs, and usages of men in

[5] MONROE, *op. cit.*, p. 452.

their social intercourse; and idols of the theater, those which depend upon doctrines, dogmas, and traditions." [6]

Comenius, a remarkable educational philosopher and a practical schoolman, was the great sense-realist. While, for him, religion was the ultimate aim of education, the knowledge of the universe came through the senses, whatever was to be taught must lend itself to practical application and be useful in life.

Rousseau, of course, first preached the political and social gospel of the common man and gave him an education as a right by birth. Emile learned a trade "less for the sake of knowing the trade than for overcoming the prejudices which despise it. Emile is industrious, temperate, patient, firm, and full of courage. . . . He has little knowledge, but what he has is really his own; he knows nothing by halves. . . . Do you think that a child who has thus reached his fifteenth year has lost the years preceding?" [7] This seems to be Rousseau's prescription for the dignity of labor.

This brief mention of the educational philosophers closes appropriately with Pestalozzi, whose whole plan of education was based upon the developing mind of the child. It was he who emphasized the importance of the object lesson. Children were to learn through things, not words. "Here is the principle upon which I acted: Seek first to open the heart of the children, and, by satisfying their daily needs, mingle love and benevolence with all their impressions, experience, and activity, so as to develop these sentiments in their hearts; then to accustom them to knowledge in order that they may know how to employ their benevolence usefully and surely in the circle around them. . . . Thus faith must be cultivated by our own act of believing, not by reasoning about faith; love, by our own act of loving, not by fine words about love; thought, by our own act of thinking, not by merely appropriating the thoughts of other men; and knowledge, by our own investigation, not by endless talk about the results of art and science." [8]

PRACTICAL APPLICATIONS. Out of all the theory and tentative approaches to vocational education very little organized vocational school education evolved until the latter part of the nineteenth century. The one outstanding institution was Fellenberg's School at

[6] MONROE, *op. cit.* p. 476.
[7] Quoted by PAUL MONROE, *op. cit.,* p. 563.
[8] Quoted by PAUL MONROE, *op. cit.,* pp. 606, 612.

Hofwyl in Switzerland operated during the years 1806 to 1844. For its time it was a remarkable school. Technically, socially, and pedagogically, it broke new ground and exerted a tremendous influence. First, Fellenberg wanted to bring together young people of different social strata and thus get them to know and understand each other better. Second, he wanted to give them the type of education that, considering their probable later employment, would be useful to them in taking their places in the world. Third, he wanted to present this instruction in a way that would capture their interest and stimulate their effort. So he trained the youth of the peasant class in agricultural and technical pursuits, giving them a modicum of academic education. At the same time and in the same area, he gave youth of the upper class the ordinary classical education. Both groups worked in school gardens and on the farms. He also established a school for girls and a normal school for teachers. Even today such a venture would be exciting.

Toward the end of the nineteenth and the beginning of the twentieth century the father-son relationship and apprenticeship gave way to the more formalized continuation school which the young worker attended for one half or a whole day a week, spending the rest of the week on the job, presumably learning how to work. Continuation schools varied from those that gave purely academic instruction to those that gave direct training in shops. Between those two extremes were the schools that gave theory related to the pupil's job and also presented material of a general civic nature. The large factory, often managed by foresighted and civic-minded industrialists, frequently took the continuation school into the factory itself, transforming the program into what has become known as modern apprenticeship.

In the meanwhile, the value of manual activity for culture as well as training had become recognized and the sloyd and manual training movements were launched. The next development was the spread of trade and technical education in the United States, France, England, and Germany. Parallel with these later movements came the mechanics institutes, where organized classes in drawing, mathematics, science, and other subjects useful to the mechanic, were presented in evening classes to men engaged in their trades during the day. In 1917, in this country, the National Association for the Promotion of Industrial Education brought about the passage of the Smith-Hughes Law, with its federal aid provision, thus giving stimulus to a widespread program of vocational education on the less-than-college-grade level. In the meanwhile, on the college and university levels, professional education had grown by leaps and bounds. It is difficult to realize that within a hundred years the surgeon, the nurse, and the lawyer have risen from the point where no education whatsoever was required beyond that which individuals cared to pick up for themselves, to the point where they may not engage in these occupations at all without first having met high general and professional education requirements and having attained, after severe testing, a state license.

III. SOME INTERPRETATIONS OF HISTORY

Undoubtedly, what is most striking in the history of work is the persistent strength of its innate characteristics. Through all the changes in social economy, activity with a purpose has played the same dominant part in the life of man. However, man has shown no easy comprehension of the potentiality of work for the full development of body, mind, and soul. So, while men have always, willy-nilly, learned to work, the history of consciously organized vocational education is brief and desultory. Curiously enough, the social evils of industrialism and technology emphasize the indispensability of creative work by responsible workers, so, while the first isolated trials in vocational education were made two to three hundred years ago, organized programs appeared first in the nineteenth century and became effective only in the twentieth. Out of this story emerged persistent trends of extreme importance in any consideration of education in general or vocational education in particular.

1. Occupations have been learned, and are still being learned predominantly on the job. Learning has been a by-product of ordinary living. Somehow or other the work of the world has been done without the conscious intervention of the educator.

2. Even in early Jewish and monastic education, where the importance of learning a trade was emphasized, job-learning was incidental to daily life. Teaching was casual, unpremeditated. The primary motive was not job efficiency but moral prophylaxis.

3. Among the crafts teaching became conscious with the fostering of apprenticeship by the medieval guilds. For the professions it became conscious in the medieval universities.

4. Except for the guilds and the universities, the first plans for group training in manual occupations were directed toward deviates:

a. In the early days of this century it was a tragic quip that, if a boy wanted to learn a trade, he had to commit a crime. Trades were taught regularly to delinquents before normal boys and girls ever had a chance. Trade training was reformatory.

b. The "ragged-schools" of England are typical of trade training for the poor. At first the tattered children of the destitute were gathered in the shop of a craftsman to learn a trade. Later the program became more formal, but the youngsters had to be ragged.

c. For a long time trade training has been given to mental subnormals as a last resort in attempting to educate them.

d. Trade training has been used similarly for all kinds of mental and physical deviates. As manual activity it has taken an important place as "occupational therapy."

All these programs have unquestionably been exceedingly valuable to the unfortunate persons in them. However, one of the difficulties encountered in organizing programs for normal children has been the assumption by the public and by most teachers in academic schools, that anybody who does poorly in language and arithmetic is sure to be good in "mechanical work." The assumption is utterly false, but it has given rise to some unsavory practices and horrible words, such as "dumping them into the trade schools."

5. While trade training was for the unfortunates, manual training came to be recognized as an essential element in a cultural program. The phrase has been, "training hand and eye." For a while sloyd was the trademark of a good school. It should be noted that, of course, manual training was not intended to prepare boys or girls for trades but rather to give them good general education by teaching them to make various articles for use in the home, to make them entirely by hand, and without reference to trade practices.

6. Despite a considerable literature describing the experiments and expounding the theories of ardent individual educational reformers, it is clear that these efforts were not followed by any general practice of their principles. However, it is probable that, in totality, these men had considerable influence over later developments.

7. Strangely enough, despite the stress of the reformer upon the importance of work in the educational program, it is clear that up until a very late date occupational practice constituted the core of the educational program only in certain professions such as law and theology. Generally speaking, educators have been chary of admit-

ting that sound education in an occupation can be sound education for complete living.

8. It is only recently that vocational education, in all its radiations and ramifications, has been conceived as a means of education for all and for life. There are still comparatively few who accept the thesis wholeheartedly.

9. It is again only recently, probably since 1870, that methods of teaching in a vocational education program have been subjected to close analysis and have not been merely an imitation of the methods used in apprenticeship training. In other words, vocational education has subjected itself to the same discipline as general education.

A PLAN OF DISCUSSION. Out of all these considerations arises a conviction that vocational education cannot be discussed adequately without a close examination of basic assumptions and an analysis of its relation to the fundamentals of general education. Therefore, a major portion of this book is given over to these crucial issues:

1. The primacy of the person, the development of all individuals through a wholesome concept of work, is paramount. The inclusion of everybody means that the scope of the problem is enlarged and must be defined and described. It means that vocational education does not accept the rampant current forces, but places the individual first and expects him, through education, to come nearer not only to his own heart's desire but to the demands of the finest spiritual forces that can be evoked.

2. The development of any one individual can be complete only in relation to the development of all other individuals. His contribution of life and spirit and work to others determines his own development. He lives and acts in a democracy, and he seeks the good life among other people who, he hopes, will also live in the democratic spirit. So, democracy and internationalism become vital problems in education.

3. It is a truism that no one ever learns anything unless he is interested, interested either in the thing learned or in something that will result from learning it or from not learning it. We pay attention only to things that interest us. Vocational education is based upon primary interest and holds that interest can be transferred to so many other "interests" in life that it becomes a major force in education. Interest means good teaching and good teaching means good method. Interest and method become outstanding themes for discussion.

4. The quest for reality is universal and everlasting. Many seek it, but few find it. Often, those who find it do not know they have it. In any case, vocational education has an interpretation for reality and believes that it can evaluate the outcome. Evaluation and reality will be treated in detail.

5. From the Spartan "emphasis on physical education" to the monastic "mortification of the flesh" the human body has run the gamut. Democratic education accepts the body as part of the complete personality and works for its maximum improvement. Vocational education is vitally concerned with the mechanism that enables the individual to work and live efficiently and happily. Good physique is a vital element in its program.

6. Vocational education adopts no philosophic theory of epistemology. It does not preclude "ideals intuitively cognized," but it does test them. It believes that most knowledge comes through doing, through experience, and it does preclude the exaltation of the abstract, obtained through words alone. It believes that intelligence is not "intellectual" but is an instrument for solving the problems of life in whatever form they present themselves. Vocational education has effective ways of stimulating intelligence.

7. Ultimately, we judge a person by his or her behavior, as Conant puts it, "adult behavior in a democracy in a scientific age." Conduct, ethics, is the test of a good life.

IV. THREE CURRENT INTERPRETATIONS

Disputation regarding reality, personality, and discipline eventuates today in the argument regarding specialism or vocationalism versus generalism. This will be discussed in the chapter on Reality, but at this point it is desirable to launch into the specifics of vocational education by first listening to two writers in opposite camps and to a third who synthesizes both views. John Dewey, in *Democracy and Education,* emphasizes the centrality of occupation:

"A vocation means nothing but such a direction of life activities as renders them perceptively significant to a person, because of the consequences they accomplish, and also useful to his associates. The opposite of a career is neither leisure nor culture, but aimlessness, capriciousness, the absence of cumulative achievement in experience, on the personal side, and idle display, parasitic dependence upon the others, on the social side. Occupation is a concrete term for continuity. It includes the development of artistic capacity of any kind, of

special scientific ability, of effective citizenship, as well as professional and business occupations, to say nothing of mechanical labor
or engagement in gainful pursuits.

"An occupation is the only thing which balances the distinctive
capacity of an individual with his social service. . . . An occupation
is a continuous activity having a purpose. . . . A calling is also of
necessity an organizing principle for information and ideas; for
knowledge and intellectual growth. It provides an axis which runs
through an immense diversity of detail; it causes different experiences, facts, items of information to fall into order with one another.
. . . The only adequate training *for* occupations is training *through*
occupation.

"In the past, education has been much more vocational in fact
than in name. The education of the masses was distinctly utilitarian.
It was called apprenticeship rather than education, or else just learning from experience. . . . To a considerable extent, the education
of the dominant classes was essentially vocational—it only happened that their pursuits of ruling and of enjoying were not called
professions. . . . By a peculiar superstition, education which has to
do chiefly with preparation for the pursuit of conspicuous idleness,
for teaching, and for literary callings, and for leadership, has been
regarded as nonvocational and even as peculiarly cultural." [9]

While Mark Van Doren, in his book *Liberal Education,* speaks
eloquently for generalism, he recognizes the essential role of skill:
"Education is of the hand as well as of the head and heart. Some
of our gray matter seems to be in the fingers, which had better be
familiar with their hidden wisdom. Mere readers and talkers are
never subtle enough. 'The second-handedness of the learned world,'
says Whitehead, 'is the secret of its mediocrity.' There is in men a
'deep natural instinct to translate thought into manual skill, and
manual activity into thought.' " [10]

"Newman says the medicine for a student is 'the habit of method,
of starting from fixed points, of making his ground good as he goes,
of distinguishing what he knows from what he does not know.'
Such treatment is heroic because it is hard, but it is necessary if the
student's practice is to be intelligent and if his theory is to be self-
understood. The medicine is best administered in laboratories where

9 From John Dewey, *Democracy and Education,* pp. 358–65. By permission of The
Macmillan Company, publishers (1916).
10 From *Liberal Education* by Mark Van Doren, p. 96, by permission of the publishers, Henry Holt and Company, Inc. Copyright, 1943, by Mark Van Doren.

thinking can be done through the refractory medium of things; and not only scientific laboratories, but laboratories in the arts, in history, in philosophy, and in mathematics. If no such laboratories are available, they must be conceived. Knowledge is not knowledge until it operates." [11]

In his article on "Education" in *Encyclopaedia Britannica,* T. Percy Nunn reconciles the specialist and generalist points of view: "A well-based theory of the curriculum should find a place for all that is sound in the conflicting ideas involved in these antitheses. Such a theory must undoubtedly start from the long view. In other words its leading principle will be that the school society must include among its formative influences all those modes of intellectual, esthetic and practical activity which have played a major part in the evolution of the human spirit and have shaped the mind of the present age. Letters and art, music and handicraft, mathematics and science, geography and history are thus indicated as necessary constituents of the complete curriculum; but not only may they enter into it in a variety of ways, they must do so if the principle is to be elastic enough to fit the varying needs of different types of scholars. For instance, training for a specific vocation conforms with the principle if it aims not merely at imparting skill in the use of tools or empirical technical knowledge, but at putting the learner to school in the ethical and scientific or esthetic traditions of some essential occupation or profession which has played and continues to play an important part in our civilization. Thus conducted, a vocational training may be, for large sections of the population, the appropriate way of completing and rounding off a truly liberal education. On the other hand a training based mainly on the study of the ancient classics is not entitled to be called liberal unless given in such a way as to make the student a freeman of the modern world, sensitive to its ideas and awake to the significance of its intellectual and social movements." [12]

[11] VAN DOREN, *op. cit.,* p. 118.
[12] T. PERCY NUNN, Article on "Education" in *Encyclopaedia Britannica,* Vol. VII, p. 965.

Chapter 4

SIZE AND QUALITY OF THE PROBLEM

I. QUESTIONS TO BE ANSWERED

THE deep-seated purpose that eventuates in work, its expression of energy, its universality, gives direction to life. Yet, in the long course of history, educationally, work has been an indirect force, powerful but unorganized. However, recently, science, industrialism, technology have forced work into the field of direct education. The factors that make a vocation effective for education — interest, personality, reality, democracy, method, physique, ethics — can operate only in a framework of practicality, raising the problems of milieu, of social and professional prejudice, of number and quality of persons affected, of number and characteristics of occupations available, of present educational program, and of attainable ideals. The history of vocational education abounds in efforts to foster the integrity of the individual in a changing and insistent environment. Vocational education tries to fit the inner man to the outer world.

Education happens to people, particular people, you and me. It happens in some place, at some time, often with the help of somebody else. *Vocational* education happens when a particular person (student) is learning a specific occupational act or fact (trade, course of study), with all its ramifying theory and human associations (science, mathematics, drawing, labor relations, etc.) and with the civic and cultural accompaniments of good citizenry; in a selected work and social environment (school, factory, office, farm, home); under the guidance of a skilled worker (teacher); at a definite, appropriate time (grade or unit); and in a prescribed manner (method). This book tells, among other things, who these people are, or should be, what they should learn or teach, and when, where, and how they should do it. All of which means that answers must be given to the inevitable questions: Why? Who? What? Where? When? How?

II. WHY?

Above and beyond the fundamental nature of "work" and its historical implications, are the social needs, the needs of the individual to find a place in society, and the need of society for competent, purposeful, good individuals. On the one hand, hundreds of thousands of young people join the labor force each year. Their intelligence, temperament, and physique, in the aggregate and in the long run, make up the very society that welcomes them one by one as individuals. On the other hand, the peculiar gyrations of the same society, bringing about technological changes and social revolutions, create very definite demands for these individuals who come to make up the necessary labor force. The people as a whole determine the need for people as individuals, while the individuals are remaking the society that creates the need. What do youth need?

1. Youth need to know themselves. Obviously, self-revelation is the product of various and divers influences, many of them casual and unorganized. But "know thyself" is still a serious injunction to the young person who would gain access to other people and who craves understanding by them.

2. Youth need to know other people. There are so many other people and they are found in so many places — the home, the church, the school, the workshop, the office, the street, and the theater. They should know about people of the past as well as of the present. Therefore, they should know history, geography, and literature.

3. Youth need to know their environment, immediate and remote. Their outlook should be global, in peace as well as in war. They must reach out to the ends of the earth to make all other people part of themselves.

4. Youth need to develop an attitude toward life, a philosophy. Morals, character, religion, are essential for good conduct.

5. Youth need to know about occupations. They must know *about* a great many occupations. They must know enough to choose the right occupation in terms of what they have learned about themselves. When the knowledge *about* occupations begins to grow full and rich, then youth can essay a series of tentative choices, usually culminating in the adoption of a definite vocation.

6. Youth need to learn how to work. Vocational education provides for such learning. However, it concerns the entire human being in relation to all of society, thus recalling the thesis that "work," in all its radiations, is an effective focusing point for education.

PROVIDING FOR THE GENERAL WELFARE. What the human being needs as an individual must be provided by all other individuals in what is known as society. People come singly but are greeted by the whole world. The good of the world at large is the general welfare. What are its foundations?

1. Full employment is a sine qua non. To the extent that he is physically and mentally capable, every individual must carry his own economic weight and a little more. Children, very old people, the physically and mentally handicapped, incarcerated delinquents, must be supported by society at large. Normally, most people are willing and anxious to work and want nothing more than the opportunity to do so. So, full employment is an utterly necessary basis for a sound economy.

2. To be useful to society, full and continuous employment must be accompanied by high production. During the Second World War, under pressure of the enemy, production rose to unprecedented, almost undreamed of, heights. Motivations of desired victory, eagerness to save lives of sons and brothers and husbands, drives of patriotism and, yes, love of money rewards, made more people work harder than ever before. Scientists stepped up research, engineers devised new techniques, administrators streamlined their business procedures, and personnel managers and vocational teachers taught newer and better methods. Thus far, the blessings of peace have never been as soul-stirring as the horrors of war, so, postwar production has always sagged. While society, collectively, believes in high production and prosperity, recurrent depressions make it obvious that society, both collectively and individually, either does not care or does not know how to maintain it.

Certainly, one way to maintain it is to see that the skills and the theories and the mores of the fathers and mothers are transmitted to the sons and daughters, that *all* the sons and daughters shall have opportunity to learn all these skills and theories and customs according to their aptitudes and potentialities, and that they shall then have opportunity to use them in the interest of society at large. Technology has become too complicated, competition too keen, skill too specialized, and theory too important to make it possible to carry on the world's work through "pick-up," "by-education," or other fortuitous methods. A manual and pedestrian world has given way to the machine and to speed. Casual, itinerant, and rule of thumb services have become professions. Society demands that its workers be educated men and women.

For better, for worse, we live in an age of discovery and invention. Atomic energy, with its first, sinister application to the destruction of man, has become available through intensively and extensively planned concentration of technical, vocational skill. Once upon a time the discoverer, the inventor, was a lone visionary who somehow, single-handed, brought his vision down to earth. Today, discovery and invention go on simultaneously among thousands of men industrially, scientifically, and corporately organized. They work with a body of knowledge and a complement of equipment that, as individuals, they could never have mobilized.

So, more and more, discoverers and inventors are highly trained, highly educated, highly literate men and women. That flash of vision, that spark of intuitive imagination, must be there, but without the knowledge and skill that characterize modern productive life, it would, except in rare instances, waste itself in barrenness. Out of vocational education and its fruits are coming and must continue to come the discoverers and inventors.

Thus, in effect, vocational education becomes an indispensable means of transmitting a most important segment of our social inheritance. Whether it be radar or plastics or rockets or steel or oil or cotton or wheat or penicillin, vocational education, which teaches individuals to use these forces and products skillfully in the interests of mankind, is the medium through which this social inheritance is passed along from one generation to another. All the books and lectures in the world can never make these modern developments either as comprehensible or as useful to the men and women of tomorrow as can vocational education. The culture of a people is what they do and what they do is what vocational education teaches them.

3. Implied in high production is a plenitude of services. The services are what make available to people the fruits of production and, during the past few decades, the number of people engaged in services has shown an enormous proportionate increase over other occupations. All the mechanical gadgets, radio, automobile, refrigerator, must be "serviced." Milady's hair and nails must be serviced. John Doe's income tax statement must be serviced. The building in

which he lives must be serviced. For comfortable living in the twentieth century services must be both varied and abundant.

4. Full and continuous employment, high production, and a plenitude of services mean a high standard of living. And yet, these material benefits may degrade rather than uplift mankind unless there is an appreciation of values. The welfare of society requires that consumption shall be discriminating as well as adequate. The consumer must have a sense of values, restraint even amid abundance. The evils of conspicuous consumption, in the Veblen sense, are only one degree removed from those of famine. Spiritually, a case could be made out for death of the body along with preservation of the soul, as against the fatty degeneration of both body and soul. Vocational education includes a generous inculcation of consumer values.

5. The general welfare requires that the right workers work in the right places. "Right" means that the worker shall be happy because he is well adapted to the kind of work he is doing, that he earn enough to maintain a high standard of living, and that he produce to capacity for the benefit of all other workers. Vocational education will have enabled him to arrive at this point only if good vocational guidance has oriented him into that kind of job. Often enough, guidance fails in its endeavors because society has not made it possible to carry out the best conceived guidance program. The potentially famous surgeon can never become one in actuality if neither his parents nor society provide the wherewithal to maintain him in school until he is twenty-six to twenty-eight years of age. Wasted lives make for a wasteful economy. A soundly conceived guidance program is basic to a sound economy.

6. By promoting the foregoing objectives, society provides, in a very real sense, for the safety of the state. A high standard of living means a healthy, happy citizenry, presumably with pride in country and strength for defense. Of course, the political unit (for us, the United States) should share with other units the benefits of a sound economy and educational program, thus extending itself so as to produce a unified, cooperative development which, in the last analysis, is the best defense. If such a development is attained through the United Nations, no specific defense will be needed. That is to say, there will be no war. If these relationships break down and there is war, high productivity will have built up a strong nation for defense. Before the United States was drawn into the Second World War vocational schools throughout the country were called upon to train

civilian workers in the crucial industries. This is only a special instance of the place of vocational education in a world economy.

Intensification of productive powers to the point of exploitation is a threat to the internal safety of states. Child labor is an instance. No amount of goods produced for society or of wages paid as a contribution to family support can justify the physical and moral injury to children put to work before their time. For society is entitled to the full productive capacity of every adult and this cannot be attained if some children are not allowed to receive education up to that time and are physically handicapped throughout their lives. Good guidance and sound child labor laws effectively curb this tendency. Vocational education, at every point, keeps the prospective worker aware of social dangers and occupational hazards so that, while exercising free choice as to occupation, he can avoid the more dangerous occupations. This applies not only to mines and factories but to every conceivable type of occupation. The weakling cannot stand the rigors of the family doctor's life any more than he can stand those of the coal mine. The safety of the individual and of the state demands that every worker should be in the right place.

Besides setting legal standards for the protection of individual workers, the state is obligated to protect consumers from the incompetence of the same workers. These standards obtain especially in the field of public health. Doctors, dentists, plumbers must pass rigid examinations before they can be licensed to serve the public. Ships' officers are licensed to protect travelers and merchandise. Lawyers and engineers are licensed to assure the public of their competence. And finally, teachers are licensed or, at least, minimum educational qualifications are set, to protect the children. Moreover, the professional schools have operated as quasi-licensing institutions by setting standards for graduates that mark them ever afterwards as competent in their professions. The names of the best medical schools, law schools, engineering schools have become hallmarks truly as significant as the word "sterling" on the table silverware. Vocational education has thereby contributed to the safety of the state.

7. The welfare of society requires that all workers, at all times, and in all places, constitute an intelligent and well-behaved citizenry. Vocational education is not mere job training, but includes all the "common learnings" — history, literature, art, and so on, as integral parts of the program. What society needs is men and women capable of producing a good life for all and capable themselves of living in

it effectively. Stupendous as the task may be, vocational education must perform this miracle.

III. WHO?

THE CLASSES AND THE MASSES. The answer to the question "Who?" is, in a democracy, exceedingly simple. It is "everybody." Yet the conflicting opinions of well-intentioned persons are baffling. "Everybody should have vocational education." "Vocational education is for dumbbells." "Everyone should learn to use his hands." "Vocational education neglects culture." Obviously, these loose generalizations are nonsense. Vocational education is not a wassail bowl from which each member of the multitude ladles out his fill. Nor is vocational education a therapeutic for a sick mind. Nor is it a training in gymnastics. Vocational education is learning how to work — for all those who can work and who need to be taught to work. And, be it remembered, work is directed activity with a purpose. In this sense, it is for the masses *and* for the classes. In this sense, it is for everybody, but for *each* body to the extent, in the place, under the auspices, and during the time that he can benefit from it.

Vocational education cannot lay claim to any unique recognition of the importance of the individual, but it can point out that its program is based upon such recognition. The interests, aptitudes, and capacities of every child are to be developed to their fullest extent to the end that all people who can work may learn to work effectively. This implies the widest possible spread of opportunity for vocational education and for a thoroughgoing system of vocational guidance. Physically and mentally handicapped children must receive vocational education because their personalities are respected by all other, better endowed personalities. Vocational education covers the entire sweep of occupations from those requiring a minimum of skill to those demanding the highest possible professional qualifications. And for those who have become enmeshed in the legal net, vocational education is indicated to the end that they may redeem their personalities and take their places in normal society. Vocational education is for all who can learn to work.

THE MAGNITUDE OF THE PROBLEM. Obviously, the number of persons to be trained for work is the total population of the country minus the number of those who, because of mental or physical handicaps, cannot be expected to work. However, no such simple calculation will present a clear picture. Many factors are involved. For instance, the population, fourteen years and over, in 1940, was 101,103,000, but the "labor force" was only 53,299,000, or 52.7 per cent. This figure excludes, of course, such persons as housewives whose failure to receive money compensation takes them out of the "labor force." It is estimated that 1,750,000 additional youth enter our national labor market every year. Presumably their education has fitted them for work. But *has* it? In 1942 high school graduates totaled 1,242,375 and college graduates, 185,346. The high school graduates constituted 51.2 per cent of the total number of persons seventeen years of age. The increase in high school enrollment in the fifty years after 1890 has been enormous. The 1942 enrollment was 1835 per cent of that in 1890, and the number enrolled per 100 of population, fourteen to seventeen years of age, rose during that period from seven to seventy-two.

All this indicates that the number of potential candidates for vocational education is enormous, that the number who have been trying to prepare themselves for life through high school education has been growing by leaps and bounds. Whether or not this education has been effective is questionable, but the numbers and the problem are there. The fact that they are not all benefiting from continuous education up to the level of their capacities is indicated by the fact that 1,273,141 who were graduated from high school in 1942 were the residue from 4,040,558 who were in the first grade in 1930.

That the educational system itself is a sorting and selecting agency operating under principles not related to occupational efficiency is all too patent.

"The educational system may be thought of as an enormous, complicated machine for sorting and ticketing and routing children through life. Young children are fed in at one end to a moving belt which conveys them past all sorts of inspecting stations. One large group is almost immediately brushed off into a bin labeled 'nonreaders,' 'first-grade repeaters,' or 'opportunity class' where they stay for eight or ten years and are then released through a chute to the outside world to become 'hewers of wood and drawers of water.' The great body of children move ahead on the main belt, losing a few here and there who are 'kept back' for repeated inspection.

"At a station labeled 'high school' there are several types of inspection and the main belt divides into smaller belts which diverge slightly from each other. From some of the belts the children, now become youths, are unceremoniously dumped down chutes into the

56

outside world, while the other belts, labeled 'college preparatory,' 'commercial,' 'vocational,' roll steadily on. The young people are inspected not only for brains and learning ability, but also for skin color, pronunciation, cut of clothes, table manners, parental bank account. Strangely enough they are not inspected for moral integrity, honesty, or other qualities which go under the name of 'character.'

"At the end of the high school division several of the belts project their human freight into the outside labor market, and the sorting machine is now much smaller, housing a few narrow conveyors labeled 'college,' 'professional school,' and 'trade school.' The inspectors quickly shunt aside the majority of this small band of young men and women into the labor market, leaving a few indeed who reach the next station, labeled 'bachelor's degree,' which is the end of the machine really, though there is a small extension called 'graduate school.' "[1]

Obviously, the only criterion for sending an individual out from school into the labor force is his ability to cope with life, especially in its occupational phases. All those who are not yet ready to make this departure constitute the answer to the question, "Who shall be educated?"

IV. WHAT?

The content of vocational education is determined by the interests and capacities of the potential learners and by the demands of society for competent workers and good citizens. The demands of society are determined by the kind of world we live in and the kind of world we would like it to be. We have become fond of calling our living place a "changing world." How much has it really changed? What is old and what is *really* new? Has human nature changed or can't you change human nature? How different are the new jobs from the old jobs? How different are people's daily lives, at home, at play, at worship, at work?

THE POTENTIALITIES OF THE INDIVIDUAL. To reveal these potentialities is one of the tasks of elementary and early secondary education. It is the specific task of vocational guidance. Patently, if every indi-

[1] WARNER, HAVIGHURST, and LOEB, *Who Shall Be Educated?* (New York: Harper & Brothers, 1944), p. 49.

vidual were set to learn the vocation in which he was most interested, society would be plagued with a plethora of, for instance,
unwanted movie actors. Interests must be tempered by necessity and
opportunity. The vocational guidance program must reveal not only
a single dominant interest but many interests. It must even create interests. The desires of the individual must be gaited to desires of all
other individuals.

THE WORLD'S WORK. Another task assumed by the vocational guidance program is to paint for the individual a large-scale picture of
the world's work so that, on the one hand, he may choose what he
likes and, on the other hand, reconcile himself, if necessary, to the
doing of something that he does not like so well. The task of the
vocational education administrator is to build a vocational curriculum that will include those vocations that need to be taught to provide the world with the services it demands.

TYPES OF VOCATIONAL EDUCATION. Traditionally, on the secondary level,
vocational education has been industrial, agricultural, commercial,
and homemaking. On the university level, it has been legal, medical,
engineering, theological. These have been convenient classifications
but they have been misleading and, as technologies change, will ultimately become untenable. Such areas as mining, maritime, and forestry occupations have been ignored. The injection of machinery into
farming has produced an industrial-agricultural occupation. Whatever the names of the occupations, the actual operations and the latest
technical knowledge must be taught. This information is made available through continuous surveys and analyses conducted jointly by
boards of education or university boards of trustees, and advisory
boards of employers, professional men, and employees.

COMMON LEARNINGS, CULTURE, GENERAL EDUCATION. With work as a
focus, vocational education presents to the student a picture of the
world's affairs in all their ramifications. Art, literature, mathematics, science, human relations, all find their place in the curriculum,
coordinated, integrated, made significant with relation to the directed, purposeful activity of the pupil. It is tempered to the capacity
of the individual and prepares him for total living with all other individuals.

TECHNOLOGICAL CHANGES. Whatever other doubts we may have as to the capacity of our world for change, we are certain that those changes we call technological are very real indeed. We are also certain that they make definite changes in the subject matter we present to students. They deserve careful consideration.

The invention of machines and their use in industry gave rise to social revolt and to a classical debate. This was the sequence of thought: More machines, less labor; less labor, more unemployment; more unemployment, greater poverty. Again, more machines, less manual skill; less manual skill, smaller wages. Once more, more machines, less skill; less skill, less education. For one hundred and fifty years people have argued about machines, some saying that they create unemployment and are therefore a great danger, others contending that every new machine creates new jobs and that the balance is maintained. The classical debate drew in such famous names as those of David Ricardo, Karl Marx, and John Stuart Mill. It has been carried down through the years on a more or less subjective and philosophical basis, culminating in objective studies, the most recent being that of the Temporary National Economic Committee.

Instances of labor-saving devices, with accompanying skill saving, can be readily and dramatically cited. The continuous strip mill employs 126 men instead of 4512, a reduction of 97 per cent. In Boston four thousand telephone operators are employed as against twelve thousand on the 1925 basis. In one large automobile plant 43 per cent of the men are on jobs that require one day to learn; 36 per cent, up to eight days; 6 per cent, up to two weeks; 14 per cent, one month to one year; and 1 per cent, more than one year. In 1931 in the metal-working industry 4 per cent of the workers required training of less than one-half month; in 1936, 20 per cent were in this category.

The Temporary National Economic Committee considered all new industries and noted four with possibilities: (1) Prefabricated housing encounters various obstacles and there is generally only 10 per cent saving. (2) Air conditioning has gone far but will advance greatly only when cheap enough for mass buyers. (3) Television encounters technical difficulties and will in large degree substitute for other industries. (4) Diesel engines present many possibilities.

The committee comes to the general conclusion:

"It seems apparent that technology will continue to increase labor productivity, to displace skilled occupations, and to reduce unit labor costs. In the absence of effective offsetting forces economic and social distress may be expected to accumulate.

"While technology on one hand creates tremendous economic problems through the displacement of labor, on the other it induces concentration, thereby impeding the operation of the compensatory force of price reduction." [2]

Even a casual study of the problem leaves us with an impression that we can come to no definite conclusion as to the effect of technological changes upon the need for vocational education. We have only a collection of pictures of many kinds of vocations. We know that in some of them the number of jobs requiring little or no training is increasing. There we see less need for skill and therefore less need for vocational education. On the other hand, there are some vocations which have risen from classification as unskilled services to that of professions. This is true of most of the health services — doctors, dentists, and nurses. Even teaching, now considered a profession, was not so long ago only a job that any literate person could undertake.

V. WHERE?

THE CONCEPT "SCHOOL." People should learn to work wherever they can do so most economically in terms of time, energy, and money and where the environmental influences will be such as to make them desirable social beings as well as skillful workers. Such places of work-learning should be accessible and available to everyone. They should be called schools.

A person who went to school a generation ago is astounded at the machinery, the activity, and the adult freedom of a vocational school. These new attributes require reorientation, a new concept of school, not entirely new, but drastically modified.

WORKER-TEACHER FOR PROSPECTIVE WORKERS. A job can be learned by trial and error, very badly, very slowly, very uneconomically. It can be learned effectively and quickly under the constant supervision of a master worker. This is old-fashioned apprenticeship. The old worker teaches the young worker. He must teach with the tools and materials that create a work environment. That is why trades must be taught in trade schools. That is why agricultural education is organized around farm enterprises, why every boy or man centers his

[2] Temporary National Economic Committee, *Technology in Our Economy*, Monograph No. 22 in the Investigation of Concentration of Economic Power (Washington, D.C.: Government Printing Office, 1941).

study upon a farm project. That is why doctors learn in a hospital. That is why homemaking is frequently taught in a cottage. That is why each girl plans for experiences in her own home with home equipment and supplies. All of which leads to a consideration of the comprehensive high school.

THE COMPREHENSIVE HIGH SCHOOL. We have assumed that vocational education means a full, efficient, and happy life; that life has a serious purpose, manifesting itself in a meaningful occupation; that vocational education makes provision for wide differences among individuals; that vocational education is deeply concerned with the development of the literate, educated man. If these assumptions are valid, we can also assume that the good secondary school, college, or university offers within its four walls or within the boundaries of its campus, sound practical, theoretical, civic, and cultural education to all comers. In other words, on the secondary level, the comprehensive high school is an effective institution. Its offerings embrace both of those types of education that have come to be known as "vocational" and "general." This is the ideal situation. It is the theme developed in the succeeding chapters. However, some hard facts must be faced. The criteria set up in the preceding paragraph are such that the attempt to give both vocational and general education in the same building has rarely succeeded.

The fundamental reason seems to be that the older, experienced worker in a trade is so different a person from the older, experienced worker in words that the two find it exceedingly difficult to understand each other and to cooperate in the education of young people. This is doubly true of administrators. A trade school often subordinates general education to the point where it almost disappears, and an academic school dilutes trade education to the point where it becomes mere dabbling in manual artistries.

The outcomes are not inherent in the situation. They have simply been "usual." But that usualness is highly significant. It indicates that the so-called comprehensive high school, if it is to fulfill its function of giving an appropriate kind of education to every individual, must be a strictly controlled institution in terms of the criteria for both trade and general education:

(1) The trade teachers must be experienced and practical.
(2) The academic teachers must be experienced and scholarly.

(3) The two kinds of teachers must be personally acquainted with, understand, and appreciate each other.

(4) A strong guidance department must assure each pupil a program appropriate to his interest and capacity.

(5) The principal and other administrators must be those rare combinations of worker and scholar that can keep the various phases of the entire program in balance.

SOCIAL SYMBIOSIS. The school can and should set out to provide the young person with vocational competency. Unto vocational competency should be added all the academic, cultural, social essentials and graces that can be effectively acquired. Vocation must contribute to culture and culture to vocation. The principal must see that they do so contribute. Such is social symbiosis.

There *can* be a comprehensive high school. In smaller communities there is no other way. But it is a fact that there have been few successful ones and are likely to be few until a new generation of administrators arises who have had rigid training in both the vocational and general fields and are zealous and stubborn enough to administer a school in the interest of both. It is always a soul-stirring but often a soul-trying task.

COOPERATIVE, CONTINUATION, APPRENTICE EDUCATION. It is a truism that people learn to work best on the job. Such was the apprentice and master worker relationship. However, it is recognized that, while manual operations are thus learned most effectively, the related technical knowledge is often neglected. Continuous, organized group instruction supplies the need. A combination of work experience and classroom teaching proved desirable. Thus arose cooperative education (half time on the job, half time in school), continuation school (five days at work, one half or a full day in school), and modern apprenticeship (five days in the shop, a half or full day in the public trade school or in the factory school).

Where is the worker "learning"? In the shop, the store, the farm, the home, the office, or in the "school"? Obviously, he is learning wherever he is acquiring skills and knowledges economically and effectively. School is where the learner is.

BUILDINGS AND EQUIPMENT. Work environment means buildings and equipment designed for work. The ordinary classroom is designed for work with paper and pencil. Double the size and install office machines and it may take on the atmosphere of a business office.

A building designed for the teaching of academic subjects may be used for some kinds of vocational education. But the limitations are severe. Sturdy construction for the support of heavy machines, power lines, special lighting, blower and exhaust systems, freight elevators, runways, high-ceilinged rooms, and small cubicles are all features that distinguish a vocational- from an academic-school building. The place for vocational education is in a work environment.

THE TRADITIONAL CATEGORIES. Practical considerations have led to the establishment of vocational schools in separate buildings, either as general vocational schools including many trades, or as special schools devoted to a particular type of occupation. Thus we have had industrial, agricultural, and commercial schools. Girls' vocational schools have usually combined industrial, commercial, and distributive education. In some cities specialized, central schools have been set up for building trades or printing trades or needle trades or automotive trades or maritime trades. Technical institutes have usually taught many different trades although there has been some specialization. On the college and university level specialization has been definite, as in medical, law, theological, engineering, education, and business schools. On the high school level vocational education has usually been public but beyond high school the private and quasi-private schools have predominated.

VI. WHEN?

More than a generation ago, when the movement for vocational education was gaining strength, the argument was that many boys and girls could not profit from academic education, that they became restless, unruly, delinquent, and went either to work or to jail. Now that we have, in many communities, vocational education beginning at the ninth or tenth school year, we note many educators advocating a program of general education exclusively during the high school period and the postponement of vocational education until the thirteenth or fourteenth school year.

This trend toward a postponement of vocational education to the later school years is one of the most curious and inexplicable occurrences in the history of education. It does not make sense pedagogically, economically, socially, or historically. It runs counter to the psychology of learning and any sound, democratic philosophy of education. It ignores all experience derived from the operation of vocational guidance programs.

GENERAL EDUCATION, VOCATIONAL EDUCATION, AND FAMILIES OF OCCUPATIONS. The attempt to get away from vocational education, but not too far away, is evidenced by the substitution of "family of occupations" for "trade." The line of reasoning is represented by the following passage:

"These factors raise the question of the relation between vocational education and general education at the high school, junior college, and college levels. The program of vocational education we have had in the high school is not an adequate answer to our present problem. It has already been pointed out that job opportunities are not available to many high school graduates. Recent studies also indicate that among the unemployed as many young people may be found who have had vocational education as have not had it. Also, the trends in enrollment in the technical schools in our large cities indicate that many of those enrolling in the technical schools are already high school graduates. It should be noted further that most of those who drop out of school before completing the high school go into the unskilled trades. Technical training of a specific sort, therefore, is inappropriate to these youth, save for a generalized vocational training for a 'family' of occupations. Considerable research done by the United States Employment Service indicates unrealized possibilities of generalized vocational training for such 'families' of jobs.

"These facts indicate that we are now approaching the time when the high school can be relieved of the responsibility for vocational education of a specific sort and thus devote itself almost exclusively to a program of general education.

"Thus we have arrived at the conclusion that the high school in the future is to be primarily a place for general education — a form of education so much more important than any of the electives or the vocational courses that no school should omit it." [3]

This would seem to be one of the most unrealistic passages in recent educational writing.

WORK EXPERIENCE. To call the foregoing statement unrealistic is in no way to belittle the importance of general education or to make

[3] HOMER P. RAINEY, "Social Factors Affecting General Education," in *General Education in the American College*, Thirty-Eighth Yearbook, Part II, National Society for the Study of Education (Bloomington, Illinois: Public School Publishing Co., 1939), p. 21. Quoted by permission of the Society.

extravagant claims for vocational education. Moreover, the proposal to postpone vocational education may not mean to the vocational educator what it means to the general educator. Perhaps some sort of synthesis may be reached through a new conception of work and a consideration of what the general educator has, in recent years, lauded as "work experience."

1. Obviously, if work is not hard labor or drudgery but is directed activity with a purpose, joyfully pursued, it is something that the child is eager to embrace and that makes his school work pleasurable. Of course, in the child's early years, it does not take the form of a job for which money can be earned, that is to say, a payroll job. But it is nevertheless work, effective work, with valuable educational by-products. It is never too early to begin this kind of activity. When the spark of interest is visible, then the time for education has come.

2. If "vocational education is learning how to work," and work is the basis of economic status, this learning must begin on an honest workmanlike basis as early as the child develops an interest in such work. This workmanlike basis cannot be supplanted by amateur, hobby projects, no matter how valuable these may be in themselves.

3. The whole trend of and justification for vocational education has been its potency as a motivating catalyst. Yet, when vocational education has demonstrated its effectiveness in this respect there are those who would denature it and revert to the educational dark ages from which we have presumably emerged. In reaching out for reality Fellenberg built a living school on the concept of sense-realism. Shall we turn the educational clock back one hundred years? Perhaps Fellenberg's institution was a comprehensive high school. In any case, it is clear enough that the emphasis has been laid again and again on vocational education and should certainly not now be lost in general education.

4. General educators have been generous in acclaiming the value of work experience — after high school and sometimes in parallel with college. The benefits of N.Y.A. and C.C.C. have been recognized. However, there has been less understanding and, hence, less recognition of traditional types of work experience that might be even more effective if financed as generously as N.Y.A. and C.C.C. Apprenticeship and continuation schools are good examples. The diversified occupations program is a more recent variation. Work experiences in vocational schools often utilize the going farms and factories for instruction or provide farms or factories closely parallel-

ing private establishments. If there is general agreement, as there seems to be, as to the value of work experiences, and general agreement, as there certainly is, as to the importance of recognizing the continuity of the individual's experiences, there should be hearty agreement upon the desirability of making those experiences available as early as boys and girls can take advantage of them in one form or another. For the vast majority of children the time to start is early in the high school period.

5. If we agree with Dorothy Canfield Fisher on the moral aspects of work (*vid.* p. 12) then certainly children should be introduced to the realities of work as early as possible, even though they do not become paid workers until well into the adolescent stage.

Finally, to argue for vocational education early in the life of the child is not to make a case for vocational education or against general education. We are here concerned with the whole education of the whole child — and of the whole adult. General, cultural, academic education is an indispensable element. But it is part of a greater whole and of an integrated child.

VII. HOW?

The distinguishing characteristic of a worker at work is his activity. He is making a product or rendering a service. He is doing something. To become efficient he must learn to do it well. The way in which he learns to do it, especially if he is helped by another person, constitutes probably the most important phase of learning. The content, the place, and the time must be appropriate. The method must be right. It must be pleasant, quick, economical, otherwise the learning process may well remain the by-education that it has usually been, for the essence of good school education is what actually happens to a person in a shop or classroom at any particular time.

The laws of learning a vocation are not necessarily very different from the laws of learning anything else, but the emphases are different.

OCCUPATIONAL MOTIVATION. It is a rare human being who does not want to stand on his own economic feet, who does not want to earn his own living, who does not want to work. So the work motive is usually present and provides the first and most important step in the learning process. It has been suggested that the schools capitalize upon this motive as early as possible in the student's career. Not only is the motive potent in enabling the school to teach the student how to work, but it carries over into the field of general education.[4]

ANALYSIS OF THE OCCUPATION. As has been frequently reiterated, ever since the beginning of human life people have learned to work. Inevitably, some people have learned quickly to work well. Methods of learning and of teaching have developed. Obviously, good school methods can result only from a preliminary analysis of the methods of by-education. Vocational educators have been fully aware of this necessity and have made many occupational analyses and job analyses, thus revealing both content and method. In the field of general education, educators have made similar analyses of social, political, and economic phases of life, that is to say, of consumer rather than producer values. Vocational education is therefore committed to continuous occupational analyses to keep prospective workers abreast of the times as to both content and method.

TEACHING JOB BY JOB. The occupation or "job" usually consists of a series or complex of acts also known as "jobs." "I have this job to do today and that job to do tomorrow." Sometimes such a job, often today's job, has no relation to tomorrow's. The auto repairman fixes a flat for a customer today and repairs a spring for another customer tomorrow. On the other hand, he may spend a week overhauling an engine for a third customer, thus doing a number of small jobs, the series constituting the big job.

The content of vocational education has been subjected to most careful analysis, resulting in series of jobs of greater and greater difficulty. Assuming that the analysis of the occupation has been accurate and comprehensive, it is then safe to assume that ability to perform all the jobs revealed by such analysis is a fair measure of occupational efficiency, of vocational competence.

TEACHING RELATED KNOWLEDGE. In vocational schools knowledge is an inevitable accompaniment of skill. It is the "why" that explains the "how." A bit of science, a mathematical operation, a working drawing, may all be essential factors in enabling skill to do its work. So, motivation works in series. A student is interested in learning an occupation, is therefore interested in learning a skill, and is, in turn,

[4] MARK ELLINGSON, GEORGE W. HOKE, and L. L. JARVIE, "Occupational Motivation in General Education," in *General Education in the American College, op. cit.,* p. 277.

interested in learning about science, mathematics, and drawing. He wants to get along with other workers, to be liked by customers, to live happily with his neighbors, to buy food and clothing economically, to be a good citizen; so, as a prospective worker, he is or can be interested in general as well as vocational education.

APPROPRIATING THE METHODS OF GENERAL EDUCATION. While the special conditions of work do indicate special methods of learning to work, good vocational education has appropriated the best methods of general education. The best techniques of group instruction are just as useful in one field as in the other. And even though the effectiveness of the job instruction sheet may not be quite equaled in the general education field, the techniques of individual instruction developed in the general field are certainly useful and effective anywhere. The good vocational educator is an eclectic.

Chapter 5

PRIMACY OF THE PERSON

THE inescapable fact about people is their diversity. The depressing truth about curricula is their uniformity. A curriculum is a course to be run — by the fleet-footed, the lame, the well, the sick, the bright, the dull, the intellectual, the athletic — and the well-educated are those who finish on time.

Schoolmen believe in the individual, they exalt him, but — he must run his course. If he takes too long or quits the race, he is a poor student or a "drop-out." Teachers, counselors, administrators give him good advice. They help him along. They may even change his course. But, speaking generally — of general education — he must finish to win.

Now, recognition of the individual, respect for personality, carries with it the obligation of educating that human being in terms of his own nature as well as of the composite nature of two billion other human beings. Therefore, fundamental and precedent to the educational process itself is a determination of what that education should be. This is not a single act, but a series of evaluations or re-evaluations. It is a guidance program. Such a program is not merely a diagnosis of the individual, it is, in the final analysis, an evaluation of education itself.

I. THE SIGNIFICANCE OF PERSONALITY

THEORIES OF PERSONALITY. Of utmost significance is the unanimity with which educational theorists regard the importance of personality. Viewing education from diverse philosophical standpoints, they see the individual as the key to sound education. For instance, in a study embracing the opinions of strong proponents of the experimentalist, realist, idealist, Aristotelian, and Catholic educational philosophies, the editor concludes:

"On one ground or another each holds that the individual is the primary end of education and that the claims of society or the state are to be subordinated to him. This is perhaps the most striking instance of unanimity of viewpoint among the diverse philosophers of education presented in this volume. Even though the experimentalist and the realist stress the acquisition of the group culture as an aim of education, this is in order that the individual may achieve adequate selfhood or personality. Indeed, the realist makes respect for the demands of the individual equal with those of society; and the experimentalist lists first among his half dozen most fundamental philosophic principles that 'each person is to be treated always as end and never merely as means.' The idealist too subscribes to this Kantian dictum. Because he can think of nothing higher or more valuable than personality, the effect on personality, as already noted, is the ultimate test of any social system. Moreover, it is the core of the idealistic teacher's method. Sustaining this unanimity of viewpoint, the Catholic places the individual ahead of the state in educational importance because his end is supernatural while that of the state is purely natural. But he would hold to this priority of worth even if he considered nothing more than the natural order alone." [1]

Agreement as to the importance of individuality does not carry with it agreement as to the origin or precise nature of the personality that constitutes the individual. Through the ages there have been propounded two opposite theories. In one, all man's behavior is determined by his inner nature. In the other, it is conditioned by external influences. According to the first theory, education can only give play to whatever already exists in the individual. According to the other, education can make out of the individual almost anything it likes. We recognize the time-worn controversy between nature and nurture. However, even the nature theory allows for considerable modification by environment, indeed calls for the most studious arrangement of that environment so that the "best" in nature may be revealed and the "worst" be suppressed. The inner drives are made more meaningful. And personality becomes the entire mental and physical organization of the individual. It embraces every phase of human character: intellect, temperament, skill, morality, and every attitude that has been built up in the course of his life.

Interestingly enough, the word personality derives from "persona,"

---

[1] *Philosophies of Education*, Forty-First Yearbook, Part I, of the National Society for the Study of Education (Bloomington, Illinois: Public School Publishing Company, 1942), p. 315. Quoted by permission of the Society.

the mask worn by the actor. The theory based upon nurture is often called the "mask" theory and is offered most frequently by the behaviorists as the sum of activities that can be discovered by actual observation over a long enough time to give reliable information. In other words, personality is but the end-product of our habit systems.

THE COMPLEXITY OF INDIVIDUALITY. Most significant to the individual is his own individuality. The very idea of individuality is opposed to classification, yet both scientific and popular thinking have been engaged for centuries in classifying people. Out of all the complexity of personality, we tend to select the dominant, perhaps the most annoying trait, and forever label friend or foe — we classify him. Freud held that man wanted most of all to be loved, Jung that he wanted to be secure, Adler that he wanted to be significant. Yet where love is dominant, security and significance may be of little importance, or where security is most desired, significance and love may become wholly subordinate. A still later classification, resembling the old idea of temperament, but buttressed by more scientific evidence, is based upon physique — the endomorphs (soft and comfortably rounded), mesomorphs (hard and muscular), and ectomorphs (slender bones, stringy unemphatic muscles, and short, thin-walled gut), all with corresponding temperamental traits. The endomorph has the viscerotonic pattern (relaxation in posture and movement, slow reaction, profound sleep, love of physical comfort, love of food, love of company, and desire for the affection and approval of other people). The mesomorph is the somatotonic type (assertive, loves physical adventure, enjoys risk, lusts for power). The ectomorph has the cerebrotonic temperament (overalert, oversensitive introvert, lives in his own thoughts, and has a passion for privacy).[2]

Of course, the well-balanced person possesses all three traits in moderation. All others possess them in varying degrees. So, since the possible permutations are practically innumerable, the number of different kinds of people is as great as the number of people themselves. Somewhat recently such variety has been expressed in so-called "profiles" in which the amount of each of many traits is represented by a line of corresponding length. These personality profiles are as different as facial profiles and are equally useful in recognizing the individual.

[2] ALDOUS HUXLEY, "Who Are You?" *Harper's Magazine*, November, 1944.

DIGNITY OF PERSONALITY. "Dignity of personality" is no mere catch-phrase. The sheer variety of personalities in this world makes respect for each individual a sacred obligation. "First in any list of values strategic to democracy and to spirituality is respect for persons, a sense of their dignity and worth which requires that they be treated as ends, not means merely, individuals with feelings and preferences and desires, with potentialities to be developed. . . . Along with the right of the individual to respect and consideration so long as he does not affect others adversely goes the responsibility of the individual to see that each other also receives this respect and consideration." [3]

PERSONALITY AND CURRICULUM. As trite as it sounds, never too often can it be repeated that the attainment of a well-balanced personality is the end-all of education. Vocation, both as cause and effect, is totally bound up in personality. The history of the world is a history of personality. "The process of the organization of the totality of one's acts into a pattern is what we mean by the development of a personality. . . . The problem of developing a unified personality in a culture which is full of conflicting patterns is one of the significant problems of education." [4]

As a measure for mental hygiene, and thus for fine personality, a sound educational program is indispensable. "Provision of an enriched and flexible school curriculum, to be determined in each case by the needs and interests of individual human beings and the group, and giving major attention to the arts and other creative activities, rather than to traditional subject matter," is cited as one of the essential next steps in education. [5]

"The gradual building up of personality and its extension in theory to every member of the community was the great contribution of the prophets and redeemers: a process that reached a new plateau in Christianity. Lloyd Morgan's doctrine of emergent evolution has sociological as well as metaphysical significance. . . . Even historians forget too easily that the largest part of every culture is transmitted,

[3] *The Public Schools and Spiritual Values,* Seventh Yearbook of the John Dewey Society (New York: Harper & Brothers, 1944), p. 125.
[4] RALPH B. SPENCE, "Personality," in *Readings in the Foundations of Education,* Vol. II (New York: Bureau of Publications, Teachers College, Columbia University. 1941), p. 384.
[5] W. CARSON RYAN, *Mental Health Through Education* (New York: The Commonwealth Fund, 1938), p. 285.

72

not through a few institutions and a handful of texts, but by a million daily acts and observances and imitations." [6]

II. EDUCATION AND PERSONALITY

"All men are created equal" has now become "All men are different." "All men are equal before God and the law and, if sane, are equally responsible for their acts, but they differ biologically and, even under the best conditions, would presumably strive for different ends." [7]

If, because of these differences, respect for each individual becomes a sacred obligation, then the educational program devised for the development of his personality automatically becomes a sacred obligation. In both spirit and technique it must enable the individual to develop his own peculiar powers, always, of course, with regard for the interest of his fellow individuals.

THE NATURE OF INDIVIDUAL DIFFERENCES. The elements that make up human personality are bewilderingly multifarious and elusive. And yet, within recent years they have yielded to a certain degree of classification and evaluation. As we have already seen, even temper and temperament lend themselves to a kind of measurement that makes them objectively understandable.

1. The range in *intelligence* is enormous, from idiocy to genius. Intelligence tests are legion. For better, for worse, the I.Q. is the most widely accepted datum in educational diagnosis. Whatever contentions there may be as to the nature of intelligence or as to different kinds of intelligence, the significance of the intelligence quotient is enhanced by common observation. Our references to bright and dull people, "intelligent" and ignorant people, all point to the fact that there is something we can call general intelligence.

2. In *aptitude* we detect latent capacity for certain fields of *activity*, ability to *do* things. These abilities we recognize as exceedingly important indices of the person's individuality. Discovery of aptitude, which may later develop into ability, is essential to the individual's satisfactory adjustment to his environment.

3. Akin to, but not necessarily identical with aptitude, is *interest*.

[6] LEWIS MUMFORD, *The Condition of Man* (New York: Harcourt, Brace and Company, Inc., 1944), p. 61 ff.
[7] PAUL H. BUCK and others, *General Education in a Free Society*, report of the Harvard Committee (Cambridge, Massachusetts: Harvard University Press, 1945), p. 82.

Interest is basic. Without interest, no attention. Without attention, no learning. No learning, no education, no vocation, no avocation, no life. Interest is a major factor in the viability of vocational education.

4. Fully functioning intelligence, aptitude, and interest are essential to a whole and wholesome personality. A falling off in effectiveness in these areas means a decline in *mental health*. And such is human frailty that, mentally, individuals vary from those with sound, superior minds to those with extreme defects even to the point of idiocy or raging insanity.

5. Reason does not always triumph, even over itself, much less over the emotions. A fine mind may wallow in uncontrolled emotions. *Emotional stability* is a crucial measure of the person. It is closely related to will power and is antecedent to fidelity of purpose.

6. Commanding greater general recognition perhaps than any of the foregoing elements of difference is that of *physical well-being*. A healthy man works fast and well. A sick man works ineffectively or not at all. Of course, there are notable exceptions — Keats, Spinoza, Carlyle. The chemistry and mechanics of the body are as varied as differences in billions of component cells can make them.

THE OUTER SPHERE OF OPPORTUNITY. Directing a scornful glance at other countries, we have often been pleased to think of our country as the land of opportunity. For the pioneer no doubt it was, but the frontier has moved on and out and we are not certain that the same opportunity is now open to all persons, even to those of similar gifts. There are differences not of the individual, but of the environment into which the individual is thrown by birth or circumstance.

1. No matter how remarkable his gifts for medicine and surgery, a boy cannot become a doctor unless he can afford to go to school for twenty years. *Financial ability* determines his career. His parents' resources, his own ability to earn money while going to school, the availability of scholarships, determine the education, the career, and the social life of the individual. And among all individuals the differences are very, very great.

2. The *type of community* in which the individual lives not only determines, in part, the availability of educational facilities but the likelihood that they will be used even if they are available. Respect for education itself, traditions as to desirable types of schooling, accessibility of information regarding opportunities outside the com-

74

munity, all these are strong, though often subtle, influences upon the pupil.

3. Within any community lie all the differences in *social and economic status*. These pervade not only home and social life but life on the job. Subconscious drives toward the "gentility" of professional life are often more powerful than reasonable dictates of recognized aptitudes. Superficial aspects of "dignity" are more apparent than true worth of conscientious service. Desire for status manifests itself in surprising, even weird, forms.

4. Determining to a considerable degree the type of community in which the child lives and the social and economic status under which he has been born are the *parents' attitudes and cultural backgrounds*. These are passed along to the younger generation and are markedly changed only through new and powerful social or educational influences. Individual differences are not confined to the younger generation. They derive from fathers and mothers, and are passed along to the children's sons and daughters. In a closed and static society, without schools, life goes on without change. This is the story in primitive society, where individual differences are not significant.

Obviously, the outer sphere of opportunity begins in the family, widens out into the community, and spreads to state and nation. Within that area the diversity is enormous, seemingly infinite. To Americans, "education" has been very largely schools in the United States. This concept is no longer tenable, for politically, financially, militarily we have moved out over the whole world and the whole world has moved into us. So, however complex and innumerable these differences may be in our own domain, they become astounding in a world that includes the Chinese, the Germans, the East Indians, the Russians, the Argentines, the inhabitants of Morotai — us.[8, 9]

SELECTIVE FUNCTION OF EDUCATION. Fundamental to a sound economy and a happy society is "intelligent election of vocation-mode." [10] Vocation-mode is a happy term connoting all those situations — among family and friends and fellow workers — that do not arise from particular skills but rather from the total way of life. It is with this total way of life that vocational education is concerned and it is for this way of life that it must devise its techniques. Since it is

[8] Education Policies Commission, *Education for ALL American Youth* (Washington, D.C.: National Education Association, 1944), p. 15.

[9] BUCK and others, *op. cit.*, Ch. III.

[10] Reprinted by permission from *Education and Vocations* by T. H. EATON, p. 128, published by John Wiley & Sons, Inc., 1926.

dealing with *different individuals,* the techniques must be governed by these differences. Methods of teaching must be various to suit the wide range of capacities. Subject matter must be drawn from the whole field of human accomplishments and sifted out for all kinds of students. It must be a subject matter of reality, reality for those to whom it is taught. Teachers must be understanding, understanding of humanity in all its varied and curious aspects. Children must be taught to act like adults and adults like citizens of the world. Education must be for ethics as well as for knowledge and performance. It must be normative as well as descriptive.

Above all, there must be a broadly conceived, carefully implemented program that will assure full play of the best educational forces on all these individual differences and of all sociological forces on the conditions that determine the development of the individual. This is the *guidance program.* It is the educator's way of respecting personality.

III. THE GUIDANCE PROGRAM

Over a period of several decades during which the word "guidance" has grown from a word in the dictionary to a hallmark, there has been profound discussion as to the difference between educational guidance and vocational guidance and the difference between these two and just plain guidance. Moreover, there have been marked differences of opinion as to who should perform the acts that constitute guidance. Some have said that only highly trained and officially certified counselors can guide, while others have contended that all good teachers are counselors, that guidance exists everywhere in the well-conducted school. Precise definition must be subordinate to a true understanding of the educative process itself. What appears in this chapter constitutes a conscious projection of educational influences upon the personal development of the individual, and this projection is called guidance. If it turns out that good method of teaching or careful choice of subject matter also projects itself toward the individual and helps him develop himself as an individual, that too may be called guidance. However, experience clearly indicates that classroom procedure, the procedure necessary for the teaching of *groups* of children, is never concerned *primarily* with the individual, and that to assure attention to the individual and to his development as a person, certain special attitudes and devices, usually designated as "guidance," are necessary.

Guidance in a vocational school becomes primarily vocational guidance because selection of and preparation for a career are foci for so many of life's other activities. With a view to formulating procedures that would serve the whole man, the following definition has evolved: "Vocational guidance is the process of assisting the individual to choose an occupation, prepare for it, enter upon it, and progress in it. It is concerned primarily with helping individuals make decisions and choices involved in planning a future and building a career — decisions and choices necessary in effecting satisfactory vocational adjustment." [11]

OCCUPATION AS DIRECTED ACTIVITY WITH A PURPOSE. Any conception of occupation as directed activity with a purpose subsumes a number of criteria for a guidance program:

1. Insofar as an individual lives among other people and must adapt himself to them, guidance must be a lifetime, or at least an early lifetime service. It is continuous, beginning with the young child and moving through various age levels up to college and university, even beyond. Since children engage in no formal work that can be called vocational, the main concern of "child guidance" is the child's behavior. However, as he moves on, many of the so-called manual or artistic activities introduce him to phases of vocations. Special subjects — art, music, woodworking, metal working, sewing, and cooking — while cultural in intent, are exploratory and vocational in actuality. In junior high schools they are known as "exploratory" and "orientation" courses and they become specifically associated with the vocational guidance program. And so, through high school and college and university, as play with material things and with elementary science and geography and so on, develops an interest in their practical application, the individual needs counsel as to how to use them wisely. Guidance is a continuing, almost a lifetime process.

2. Guidance deals with the intimacies of life, the hopes, fears, the tribulations of growing, developing human beings. It is a highly personal and critical process.

3. The making of decisions and choices involves whole families, groups of friends, street companions, the fringe around the home

[11] "The Principles and Practices of Vocational Guidance." Report of the Committee of the National Vocational Guidance Association, *Occupations: The Vocational Guidance Magazine*, XV (May, 1937), 772–80.

known as the neighborhood, the larger community, sports and leisure, and finally the job.

4. The essence of guidance is the same in any school at any age
level, but it becomes tense and explicit in those schools where vocation is held to be a vital, most important phase of teaching. Thus,
the vocational school provides a peculiarly fertile ground for growth
of individuals through good guidance.

5. At every point guidance must mean adjustment, action. Mere
counsel, important as it may be, too often wears itself out in words.
Guidance should ultimately result in firm decisions and in forth-
right action.

THE GUIDANCE PROGRAM. The techniques of guidance are diverse and
various. They range from devices for teaching elementary facts in
occupational information to interpretation of tests in personality.
Very subtly and cleverly contrived procedures may yield a minimum
result, whereas a casual word dropped by a highly respected teacher
to an emotionally involved pupil may change the course of a whole
life. However, the wholly desirable delicacy in dealing with human
beings, the spiritual touch that so successfully eludes analysis and
classification, does not preclude the use of scientific procedures.
Workers in the field of guidance have been diligent and earnest in
search of effective ways of enabling young people to set themselves
on a true course leading to an appropriate occupational goal. The
texts are numerous and excellent and should be carefully studied by
those who wish to make guidance the indispensable feature of vocational education that it certainly should be.[12]

12 RICHARD D. ALLEN, Organization and Supervision of Guidance in Public Educa-
tion (New York: Inor Publishing Co., 1933).
JOHN M. BREWER, Education As Guidance (New York: The Macmillan Company,
1932).
ARTHUR J. JONES, Principles of Guidance (New York: McGraw-Hill Book Co., 1945,
revised edition).
FRANKLIN J. KELLER and MORRIS S. VITELES, Vocational Guidance Throughout the
World (New York: W. W. Norton & Company, 1937).
GEORGE E. MEYERS, The Principles and Techniques of Vocational Guidance (New
York: McGraw-Hill Book Co., 1941).
National Society for the Study of Education, Guidance in Educational Institutions,
Thirty-Seventh Yearbook, Part I (Bloomington, Illinois: Public School Publishing Co.,
1938).
HAMRIN and ERICKSON, Guidance in the Secondary School (New York: D. Appleton-
Century Co., 1939).
KOOS and KEFAUVER, Guidance in Secondary Schools (New York: The Macmillan
Company, 1932).

Writers on vocational education have usually laid considerable
stress on guidance.[13]

GUIDANCE IN THE CLASSROOM. Insofar as the teacher of any subject,
whether it be mathematics, woodworking, Latin, or art, can get close
to the mind and heart of the individual, he can exercise a beneficent
guidance influence. If he is really concerned with his students as individuals, he can consciously and systematically provide effective
guidance. The books of Cox and Duff and of Dunsmoor and Miller
point the way.

In colleges and universities the tutorial system is an attempt to
rescue the individual from the mass, to recognize practically and
honestly the dignity of the person. It makes education something
more than reception of knowledge or making of grades. It gives
dignity to education itself. When college and university add to this
useful device a student personnel department, soundly conceived
and well administered, then education seems to attain a fusion of
the best in science with the best in humanism, making science serve
rather than dominate man. Where this type of service is provided in
a professional school, it recognizes an exceedingly important fact —
that choice of vocation is not final because the student has chosen a
vocational school nor is progress in preparation for a vocation smooth

RUTH STRANG, *Pupil Personnel and Guidance* (New York: The Macmillan Company,
1940).

DUNSMOOR and MILLER, *Guidance Methods for Teachers* (Scranton, Pennsylvania:
International Textbook Co., 1942).

Cox and DUFF, *Guidance by the Classroom Teacher* (New York: Prentice-Hall, 1938).

E. G. WILLIAMSON, *How to Counsel Students* (New York: McGraw-Hill Book Co.,
1939).

WILLIAMSON and DARLEY, *Student Personnel Work* (New York: McGraw-Hill Book
Co., 1937).

PATERSON, SCHNEIDLER, and WILLIAMSON, *Student Guidance Techniques* (New York:
McGraw-Hill Book Co., 1938).

HOPPOCK and LULOFF, "Vocational Guidance," in *Vocational Education,* Forty-Second
Yearbook, National Society for the Study of Education (Chicago: University of
Chicago Press, 1943). A concise treatment of vocational guidance in a vocational
school.

GERTRUDE FORRESTER, *Methods of Vocational Guidance* (Boston: D. C. Heath and
Company, 1944).

A. E. TRAXLER, *Techniques of Guidance* (New York: Harper & Brothers, 1945).

[13] EDWIN A. LEE, *Objectives and Problems of Vocational Education* (New York:
McGraw-Hill Book Co., 1938). Chapter on "Trends in Vocational Guidance," by
HARRY D. KITSON.

CHARLES A. PROSSER and CHARLES R. ALLEN, *Vocational Education in a Democracy*
(New York: The Century Co., 1925).

DAVID SNEDDEN, *Vocational Education* (New York: The Macmillan Company, 1920).

because he happens to be enrolled. New problems of guidance continue to appear throughout life. Very frequently old ones recur.

IV. SELECTIVE FACTORS

Despite all controversy as to the time when vocational education should begin and the place where it should be given, obviously such a time eventually must arise and a decision must be made not only as to where the education shall be given but as to the vocation for which it shall prepare. In a small town it may very well be given in a comprehensive high school where the student, at the beginning of the ninth or tenth or eleventh school year requests a new program, to include a "shop" or part-time employment in a cooperative program where specific training is given. In a city large enough to maintain specialized high schools, the student may choose, at the end of the eighth or ninth year, the high school that prepares for his trade or profession or, if he has not yet fixed upon a specialty, he may choose a general or neighborhood school either for further tryout in the trade or for continued academic instruction. At this point the school system must intensify its efforts to help the students decide wisely and, in the specialized high schools, must carefully select those students who are likely to succeed in that particular specialty. What are the valid factors in selection?

SELECTIVE FACTORS. No item in a school program reveals the educational standards of a teaching staff so plainly as those of admission. Moreover, it is clear that these standards are not always based on educational considerations but frequently stem from a desire for prestige or for preservation as an administrative unit. When students clamor for admission to a school with limited accommodations, the standards of admission are "raised." When registers fall and teaching positions are jeopardized, a spirit of "liberalism" creeps in. Some vocational high schools scoop off the upper layers of intelligence quotients, leaving the lower layers to settle where they may. Other vocational high schools take anybody who will come, regardless of intelligence. Again, some elementary and junior high schools send *their* top layers to the academic high schools, sometimes under protest from students themselves, directing all others to vocational high schools on the theory that a low intelligence quotient connotes "mechanical-mindedness" and — "Where else are they to go?" These practices are human and must be recognized, if not respected. The relation of intelligence to aptitude will be discussed in the next section, but at this point it is useful to note that:

1. A high I.Q. does not necessarily incapacitate an individual for manual work although it does suggest a range of vocations in which that level of intelligence would be most useful. No elementary or junior high school can legitimately refuse to send a high I.Q. to a vocational school. At the same time, a high I.Q. does not justify a vocational high school in accepting its possessor solely on that ground. There are a dozen other major factors that may either cancel out or reinforce the factor of intelligence.

2. A low I.Q. does not guarantee a good manual worker. As a matter of fact, generally speaking, records of vocational high school students indicate that poor manual work is usually accompanied by poor work in academic subjects. At the same time, students with low I.Q.'s often do excellent manual work. It is not the low I.Q. in itself that is the determining factor, but rather a constellation of traits that determines success.

3. If the student is not word-minded there is likely to be little value in the usual academic education though it is imperative that he be given opportunity to make the best of his physical equipment. In other words, preparation for jobs must be provided for young people of this type, but such provision should not be allowed to validate the belief that vocational education for trades is for dullards only.

General, neighborhood, vocational high schools should admit all who wish to come. Providing a variety of vocational experiences, the school should allow the student almost literally to play around in it, to taste of the different offerings until he finds his métier. Such "tryout" should reveal both aptitude and ability and, in a sense, no further test should be necessary to determine admission to a course preparing for a specific trade. However, certain other factors do require consideration. They are the same factors that operate in admitting students from elementary and junior high school to vocational high school.

1. The over-all consideration is the student's previous performance. This should be recorded on the cumulative record card and provide a comprehensive picture of the personality. Insofar as it approaches this ideal, it is a sound instrument of selection. Of course, it requires expert interpretation. First of all, it should give evidence of *interest* in the chosen trade or profession. Without interest, no attention. Without attention, no learning. Every effort should be

made to check upon the genuineness of this interest. In every case of doubt the student should receive the benefit. Better to give opportunity to prove that interest is not genuine than to choke off the aspirations of a really sincere student.

2. Effectiveness in the manual arts — drawing, woodworking, metal work, electricity, printing — is important for the manual trades. Good performance in English, penmanship, typewriting, mathematics, suggests adaptability to commercial occupations. High ratings in science and mathematics provide prerequisites for the engineer.

3. The interpretation of general behavior must be approached with extreme caution. The child may be troublesome in elementary school just because he has not had those opportunities that are peculiar to the vocational high school. On the other hand, misbehavior in the lower grades is not, as is sometimes held by the teachers of those grades, prima facie evidence of successful candidacy for the vocational high school. Again, the student must receive the benefit of the doubt. The aggressive personality, so abhorrent to the traditional classroom teacher, may be the makings of an excellent salesman and worthy citizen. The extrovert with sensitive perceptions may find complete satisfaction in dramatics and not only cease to annoy his teachers and neighbors but actually contrive to entertain them.

4. Physical equipment for an occupation is, of course, just as important as mental or emotional. While, more and more, employers and schools are appreciating the adaptability of physically handicapped persons to many kinds of work that have heretofore been denied them, the watch repairer must still have acute vision, the salesgirl good feet, the trial lawyer a good voice, the coffee taster a sensitive palate, the tool maker a delicate touch, the photographer's model good looks, and the stevedore a strong back. Any illness or weakness that raises the threshold of the senses or takes the tone out of the muscles is a hindrance to success. If, upon application for admission to a specialized vocational course, a boy lacks the requisite physical equipment, he must either remove the disability within a reasonable time or give up hope of entering that occupation.

5. There are many extraneous, but very real, conditions of entrance to occupations that should not act as a bar to admission to a specialized course but which should be carefully explained to the applicant so that he may decide whether to challenge the condition or submit to it. Where race and religion are traditional handicaps he should know about them. If the occupation is controlled by unions

which limit their membership to relatives and close friends of current members, the applicant must be prepared, sooner or later, to hurdle this obstacle.

6. In the interest of the general welfare society has a right to determine, at least roughly, the number of workers in each occupation, especially if the public pays the bill for their preparation. If, practically, the preparation of too many doctors militates against the preparation of enough miners to keep us warm, thus making more work for doctors, the public, through the trade and professional schools, must attempt to keep a sociological balance. Moreover, the public is interested in preventing the production of poor doctors, bad lawyers, and unreliable airplane pilots. Therefore, applicants who are technically qualified but who are poor risks, may well be excluded from the trade or profession of their choice, and be encouraged to make a second choice within the range of their abilities and for the greater welfare of their fellow beings. In other words, as with all other phases of vocational education, the purpose is to develop to the full a unique personality in a social organism of other unique personalities.

TRYOUT. The traditional and common sense method of learning whether we like something is to try it or to try it out. The way we come to like people is by trying them out, by working with them, by playing with them, by visiting them in their homes. And tryout is experience, far superior to reading about or being told about. The ideal way to learn of our liking for a job, as well as to learn to do the job, is to work at it, to try it out. Actually, this is what many people do, sometimes deliberately but usually casually. If one could find out whether one liked to be a doctor by being a doctor or about being a machinist by being a machinist or about being a minister by being a minister, that is to say, if life were long enough and other people patient enough, both choice of and proficiency in all occupations would be a simple matter. Only to a very small extent is such procedure practicable. Yet, the principle is so important that, in recent years, the trend in curriculum building has been to inject as many experimental elements as possible. As already noted, "activities" with vocational implications, spread over the elementary school years, have provided indices of vocational aptitude. Drawing, wood and metal work, singing, instrumental music, hobby clubs, have all played an important part.

The industrial arts movement has been a special, consciously devised means of providing tryout experiences. It has been much more than this, a notable contribution to general education, and under that heading, we shall deal with it again. As tryout it provides data that constitute a most important selective factor in the introduction of students to the specialized vocational high school. In the junior high school industrial arts assumes a very special tryout function. Whether it be taught in "general shops" or in several different shops, each one devoted to a particular medium, such as wood, metal, leather, and the like, it is devised to draw out the aptitudes and interests of the students. It is intended to enable them to choose the type of work for which they would like to prepare. Its purpose is laudable and sound. Combined with other equally important guidance procedures, it has produced good results.

On the other hand, the tryout program has some serious defects, principally of omission. For one thing, no school, no community can give experience in the seventeen thousand, four hundred and fifty-two separate jobs listed in the Occupational Dictionary, nor even a taste of the one hundred and thirty industries in which these jobs are found. Viewed objectively, the fifteen or twenty different kinds of shops found in the largest and best schools are a travesty on the diversification of industry. Machine shop practice, electrical work, printing, woodworking, plumbing, bricklaying, sheet metal work, foundry work, watch repairing, do not comprehend the industries of the United States. Even if we add a few commercial courses and homemaking and agriculture (a rare addition except in rural communities), we are still a long way from painting an adequate picture.

Again, a school shop is an artificial and unrepresentative attempt to bring the occupational world to the child. Specific skills may be faithfully taught, but the hundred conditions that make a job a real job are missing. Pressure for production, struggle for better wages, atmosphere created by adult workers earning a living, long hours of application, are a few among many factors that make the real job so different from the school job.

Once more, to assume that the future of any group of children from a cosmopolitan neighborhood will confine their future occupations to those selected for teaching in a tryout program, is futile. Except in highly specialized communities, their gifts and inclinations will lead them all over the geographical and occupational map.

However, despite all these objections to a junior high school tryout program, the principle is sound and may be made to work out toward practical success. This can be brought about first, by making the shops as representative as possible of broad occupational areas and second, by associating with the activities in the shop all the facts and activities, all the school subjects, all the ideas and emotions, that play around these representative shop subjects. Choice of vocation is emotional and volitional as well as mental. In many cases, we must realize, it is purely accidental.

In the vocational high school, where shops are used primarily for the teaching of skill, tryout is accomplished through flexibility of program. This is essential in a general vocational high school. In a specialized vocational high school, careful admission procedures reduce the need for tryout to a minimum, but it should never be abandoned. Changing social attitudes, changing physique, changing understandings, lead to changes in occupational desire, and at any point, in high school, or college or university, the program must be flexible enough to aid the young man or young woman who, even after years of training in a specific field, desires to change over to another.

All this simmers down to the problem of acquainting young people in a restricted area and in a small institution with what is going on in a large, highly complex world. The close and familiar world of domestic economy has moved away from them. It has to be brought back through representative activity, through picture, through word. When possible, young people must be taken out into the world, on excursions, into cooperative work. Good general education makes the vocational phases significant, and good vocational education makes general education meaningful. More will be said about this in the section on occupational information.

V. REVEALING PERSONALITY

The student comes to a vocational high school with a considerable record of achievement or failure behind him. The data continue to pile up so that at whatever point he starts preparing for a specific vocation, much is known about his personality. Some of this has been recorded on the basis of teachers' observations, some through ratings on examinations, and some from tests of physique, mentality, personality, and so on. However plentiful the data, it usually seems advisable to learn still more about the student. It is always best to get these items through experiences in real situations. And it is never necessary to get them all at once. However, it is highly desirable that they be obtained economically. Therefore, despite the large number of test data that are likely to be found on present-day cumulative record cards, it proves advantageous to give further tests to provide missing data and to check on those data that seem inconsistent with other known facts. Tests of general intelligence, achievement, special aptitudes, personality traits, interest, and physique should be available in the personnel department of any institution basing its educational procedures on vocation as a goal. Their number is now legion. Standardization has made them exceedingly useful, and manuals for their administration and interpretation are plentiful.[14]

GENERAL INTELLIGENCE. Every school, whether academic or vocational, boasts or would like to boast about the high general intelligence of its students. Academic ratings correlate very closely with results of general intelligence tests. General intelligence is related to success in given occupations and failure in these occupations can be predicted when an individual score falls below the floor for that occupation. Successful engineers with I.Q.'s below 100 are rarities, as are successful laborers with I.Q.'s above 100. So, up and down the scale, there are maxima and minima for success and any individual score can be fitted into the range of occupations suitable for the person by whom the score was made. Occupations in the professional brackets require preparation in mathematics, science, and language that make up a large part of the tests in general intelligence. Therefore, it is in these areas that the high I.Q.'s are found. Vocational schools are justified in requiring high I.Q.'s for professions that also require them, but they are not justified in requiring these I.Q.'s when the training is for low I.Q. jobs. Vocational education must be as realistic as academic education often is not.[15]

SPECIAL APTITUDES. An aptitude is a latent ability. It may be so well revealed as to mark the man to all observers, or it may be so well concealed that the possessor himself does not suspect it. Aptitudes rise to the surface during activity, when problems are to be solved, and somebody with aptitude attempts to solve them. A pseudo-activity in the form of an aptitude test may reveal aptitude. Aptitude testing has made great strides in recent years and, although there is not yet sufficient validation for many of the tests, especially for me-

14 OSCAR K. BUROS (ed.), *The Mental Measurement Yearbook* (Highland Park, New Jersey: Mental Measurement Yearbook, 1941).
WALTER V. BINGHAM, *Aptitudes and Aptitude Testing* (New York: Harper & Brothers, 1937), pp. 35–59.
15 BINGHAM, *op. cit.,* p. 44 ff.

chanical ability, the tests are useful. They require validation and confirmation. They certainly do not reveal aptitude in highly specific occupations, but they do seem to mark out large areas of occupations and give the subject some first clues as to favorable occupations. Where tryout is varied and effective, aptitude tests may have no place at all. In a vocational school that makes intensive and conscientious use of data on the cumulative record card and that has an otherwise extensive guidance program, aptitude tests are useful only where other phases of the program have seemed to fail. Where men or women have never come into contact with such a guidance service or, indeed, with any vocational education program, aptitude tests often come up with unsuspected talents and enable the counselor to turn the subject in a direction he has never before traveled.[16]

PERSONALITY. In such phrases as "primacy of the person" or "dignity of the person" or "revealing personality," "person" and "personality" are meant to designate all those things that make up the whole man. Tests of personality are usually confined to a few emotional and volitional reactions. In any case, they exclude other types of traits mentioned in this chapter, especially intelligence, aptitude, achievement, interest, and physique. They purport to measure such traits as introversion and extroversion, behavior under specific influences, and what is generally known as temperament. Temperament in relation to the occupation is of paramount importance. It is quite probable that as many people choose jobs because they think they can get along with other people on the same kind of job, people who will be congenial to them, as those who choose jobs for the skill required or the salary paid. Personality in this narrow sense is an exceedingly important influence upon success or failure.

INTEREST. Interest plays such a significant role in vocational education that a whole chapter is devoted to it. However revealed or stimulated, it is basic to learning.[17]

ACHIEVEMENT. Strictly speaking, achievement is not an element of personality, but outstanding achievement or marked failure in any field of current activity, especially if interest is present, leaves a mark on personality. Success begets confidence, failure undermines security. It is sense of achievement in a field never before explored that

[16] BINGHAM, *op. cit.* The entire book is an indispensable tool for the counselor.
[17] BINGHAM, *op. cit.,* Ch. VI and VII.

gives direction and reality to the lives of many vocational high school and college young people who have previously wallowed in deep frustration. Therefore, it is incumbent upon the vocational school to check up unrelentingly to the end that self-recognition of achievement may fortify the personality of the succeeding student and that the frustration of the failing student be short-lived. One of the most heartening features of vocational education is the satisfaction and confidence that exude from young men and women who have "achieved" in their trades or professions. A job completed satisfactorily is in the best sense of the word an "achievement." It is for the world to see and admire. The school must foster such self-realization and at the same time provide incentive for still greater achievement. In a school system organized for vocational education it is possible for a vastly greater percentage of young people to achieve success than it is in a system that ignores vocational education.

PHYSIQUE. The recent emphasis upon psychosomatic medicine recognizes more clearly than ever the intimate and sensitive interrelationship of mind and body and soul. The ancient ideal of a sound mind in a sound body becomes even more significant. Again, the topic is so important for vocational education that an entire chapter will be devoted to it. Here, suffice it to say that every known resource should be brought to bear upon painstaking physical examination of every child in the lower schools and upon continued checking throughout his entire school career. Only through an intimate knowledge of the individual's strength and weakness of body can he be understood as an individual or can he be optimally adjusted to the demands of an occupation.

PERSONAL INTERVIEWS. Whatever has been revealed about personality through all the data appearing on cumulative record cards and through additional testing, must be continuously supplemented and interpreted through personal interviews which must be recorded, in turn, on the cumulative record card. Interviews must be held not only with the student himself but with others who are close to him. Who these are will be indicated in the nature of the case — father, mother, older brothers and sisters, doctor, clergyman, representatives of welfare agencies, employers (future or part-time) and so on. The more informal, the more intimate, the more friendly these conferences are, the more likely are they to reveal fully the personality of the student. It is a truism that completely revelatory information comes not through systematized inquiry, although this is indispensable, but through casual remarks made in unguarded moments. The soul is bared when one's mental guard is down.

VI. THE CUMULATIVE RECORD CARD

In name, the most impersonal of all instruments in the guidance program, the cumulative record card can become as exciting as a documentary film. In fact, if it be considered as history in the making, the history of pulsing, living human beings, that is exactly what it is. It is not the form, nor even the substance that makes it vital, but the use to which it is put. It is not a mere listing of subject ratings or a device for bookkeeping. In significance, any one item, character, for instance, may outweigh everything else in the record. It enables teacher, counselor, principal, doctor, nurse to pick up a student's life, from birth to the crucial present moment, and hopefully to project it into the future. Here is a person who came into the secondary school as a child, has been growing the while, and, in a few moments, will be leaving as a young man or woman. Any judgment passed upon such a person is bound to be quite different from that accorded a mere name in a particular class on a certain date who wants to change his shop because he cannot get along with his teacher, or who wants to be accelerated because he has done the whole term's work in half the usual time.

THE SUBSTANCE OF THE RECORD. Of course, there are certain basic data — name, address, birthplace, names of parents and their places of birth and occupations, names of brothers and sisters and their ages. Then there is the rating for each subject, along with the teacher's name. The results of all tests are given — intelligence, achievement, aptitude, personality, interest, or other standardized tests. There appears a complete health record — results of examinations, diagnoses and prescriptions. All co-curricular, extra-curricular, and out-of-school activities, school service, honors and awards find their place in the record, also any after-school or cooperative employment.

Even with all these data the record is still a record, potentially useful but still not alive. It begins to be meaningful when character traits are entered — interest, industry, initiative, courtesy, cooperation, self-control, appearance, dependability, health habits — and when work traits appear — care of tools and equipment, ability to follow instructions, ability to plan, neatness, speed, attitude, use of English, safety, workmanship. Then, most vital of all, successive characterizations of the student which often become an anecdotal record. There is a large open space where anybody concerned with the student may write anything that seems important.

The record card, usually 8½" × 11", is kept in an envelope sturdy enough to hold notes, letters, records from previous schools — any pertinent documents.

Such a record card opens up the opportunity for a dramatic history but in no sense does it in itself induce teachers, counselors, and administrators to write such a history.[18]

THE SPIRIT OF THE RECORD. The innocuousness of the cumulative record is its inactivity, its place in a file. It is usually guarded sacredly so that the student will never see it. It is too far away from those who know the student for them to use it conveniently. It has no conspicuous utility except at term-end, for promotion purposes. There are no inducements to make it live. The remedy is simple. A few fundamental practices, well publicized to the students and the staff, bring the cumulative record into the foreground of their attention along with the student whose story it tells.

1. Take the cumulative record out of the central file and give it to the advisor who is primarily and continuously, throughout his school life, responsible for the student. The advisor is responsible for the entry of all ratings and other data. He is responsible for the upkeep of the card. He is thoroughly familiar with it, for it remains in his possession usually for four years. It can become his pride as well as his responsibility.

2. Let the student see his record. Let him too feel that he is making history. Let him take it to the counselor, to his teachers, to the principal, whenever he has a request for adjustment or has an honor bestowed upon him, or has been delinquent. Let him know that his card is his passport. If he loses it, destroys it, or lets it be destroyed, he will be like a person in a foreign country without his credentials.

The only answer to any objections to this procedure is that it has worked. Over a period of eight years, with probably eight thousand cards involved, we know of one that was destroyed and another that was lost. In both instances the cards were reconstructed from original data. The extreme of solicitude occurred when a boy in the maritime school, while leaving the training ship, accidentally dropped his card

[18] U. S. Office of Education, *Handbook of Cumulative Records* (Washington, D.C.: Government Printing Office, 1945).

into the East River, and promptly dived in after it. He retrieved a very soggy card but he still had his passport.

Schoolmen question the desirability of letting students see the results of general intelligence and other tests. So far as we can discover, only good effects result from friendly, cooperative consideration of a student's whole personality in terms of its full development for a useful life, especially in its vocational phases.

3. The principal, head counselor, and other administrators demand the card, along with the student, whenever making any decision regarding the welfare of the student. The principal will not see a boy without his card. The principal makes his entries in red ink, reading them aloud as he writes. He takes every opportunity to dignify the record in the eyes of the young person. If any pertinent data are missing, he sends the record back to the advisor for completion. He writes notes of commendation to those advisors who keep especially good records. He nearly always has a few cards on his desk, pending decision, and regards them as respectfully as if they were the boys and girls themselves.

KNOWING THE WHOLE CHILD. Parents try to be wise about their children with the thought that they have known them ever since birth. They remember the illnesses, the delinquencies, the lovely experiences. They see their youngsters in terms of development and, in accordance with their own wisdom, or lack of it, deal with living personalities. The judge of the Children's Court decides no cases without a long documentary history from the probation officer. The school, in solicitude for its charges, can hardly do less. The cumulative record must make the personal history of the child live.

VII. ADJUSTMENT TO LIFE

The negation of individuality is mass education in a large school — the lost child without a teacher who is responsible for him as a personality. Interest unsatisfied, desires frustrated, programs denied, because nobody meets a freshman and says, "You're my boy for the next four years and at the end of that time I'll be on the platform to hand you your diploma." We speak of the "whole child," the "integrated personality," but too often we dissect him into hundreds of pieces, each one treated by a different person, each term with a different result. At the end of the course we try to fit all the pieces together into a pleasant picture. Only in exceptional cases of strong, intelligent self-direction does it work. For the remainder, chance and good luck are the only salvation.

Whatever ideals, whatever techniques a guidance program may offer, the heart of the matter is continuous, vigilant, painstaking adjustment of the student to school and social life by one who cares and who accepts the responsibility. The familiar grade advisor, when he follows a class through all four years, is an approach to the problem, but when his family reaches one hundred fifty, two hundred, three hundred, as it often does, the opportunity for understanding and intimacy just disappears. Daily immediacy is a primary condition of human adjustment.

THE ADVISORY SYSTEM. In the advisory system the entering student meets his advisor in home room period every morning of his stay in school. The advisor is his parent-teacher-friend who listens to his woes, rejoices in his good fortune, punishes his transgressions, fights his battles, and only incidentally marks his attendance. The advisory group is heterogeneous as to intelligence, grade, age, achievements. Its components are as unlike as the members of a family, and as unified. The older members are big brothers and sisters. The young ones are taken in with solicitude and kindness. The group aims to be the "best section in the school." The advisor backs his charges against all comers, and assures their effectiveness by helping each individual to surpass himself.

The advisor's duties are heavy and responsible. Of course, he marks attendance in the roll book. The cumulative records of his students are all in his possession and he keeps them up to date. He receives reports on studies and deportment from all the other teachers. He counsels with individuals during at least one assigned period a week. He conducts the home room activities. He sees that all the services of the school — curricular, extra-curricular, and personal — play upon each individual in his section. He is a very busy, but usually happy counselor and friend. Incidentally, his effectiveness as a counselor is not conditioned by the subject he teaches during the remainder of the day. He may be a teacher of English or mathematics or music or automobile mechanics, or she may be a teacher of art or homemaking, but in relation to the members of a home section, the advisor is primarily a friendly and concerned man or woman.

THE HOME ROOM PERIOD. The essence of the home room period lies in the spirit and activity of the advisor. Home room lessons are lessons in personal adjustment, group-considered. They may take any form that the group elects and to the extent that they are student-managed they are good lessons. One period a week is devoted to discussions of a report on student activities by the section president, who is a delegate to the Student Council. The section, as an "election district" or "county," contributes to the spirit and unity of the entire school. Under inspired leadership the home room becomes really a home, where the problems of adolescence are threshed out with candor and satisfaction.

TEACHERS AS COUNSELORS. Now and again is heard the statement, "No special vocational guidance program is necessary in a good school, for every teacher is a counselor." Like every other specious statement, in it lies a modicum of truth. Every teacher can be and often is a counselor, but usually in an unplanned and ineffective way. On the other hand, unless the subject teachers cooperate wholeheartedly with the counselors and administrators, and especially with other teachers in the capacity of advisors, the guidance program can be only partly effective. One of the advantages of the advisory system is that nearly every subject teacher is also an advisor, appreciates the problems of the advisor, and can therefore be expected to cooperate with all other advisors.

The competent instructor, no matter what the subject, makes every effort to reach students as individuals, and even in large classes succeeds to a considerable extent in doing so. Individual instruction and solicitude for the young person at all times make of the subject teacher a most important adjunct of the guidance program.

Then again, the teacher who adopts classroom procedures that provoke discussion, call for judgment, and elicit information, especially about occupations, is performing one of the functions of a good counselor. The planning and teaching of occupational information is of itself one of the principal functions of guidance, often performed by a trained counselor. However, there is every reason why this type of information should also be disseminated by instructors in all subjects, for it is a poor subject that does not have some occupational implication.

Finally, the teacher's personality is always, for better or for worse, a guidance factor. The friendly, glowing, interested man or woman inspires worshipers who want to be "just like him," or "just like her." His or her words are carefully weighed by the students and are often translated into action. Students crowd around that kind of person before and after sessions for a chance to ask questions and to be beamed upon. The value of such guidance cannot be measured, but anyone who has the good fortune to sit at the feet of a real mentor has a very keen sense of being "guided."

SPECIAL COUNSELORS. In the very small school it is likely that all special counseling services are rendered by the principal. As the school grows larger these duties fall upon an assistant, then upon a part-time counselor, and finally upon a full-time counselor, a person fully trained in all the techniques of guidance. In a very large school the head counselor has assistance from a testing counselor, placement counselor, health counselor, social welfare counselor, and perhaps others. These again are trained in their specialties and render expert service in adjusting students to school and outside life. It is to these special counselors that advisors and teachers appeal for authentic data and competent assistance in taking care of students in their sections. The advisors and teachers, in their guidance capacity, are primarily interested friends. The counselors, in their guidance capacity, are trained technicians.

In a system of schools there is a director of guidance to coordinate the guidance activities in all schools (junior high, academic high, vocational high) and to disseminate among all counselors information regarding the educational opportunities in all schools and the occupational opportunities in the community.

PERSONALITY ADJUSTMENT AND TRAINING. Admittedly the strongest and most persuasive influences upon personality arise from fortuitous and casual contacts with other people. However, no institution of vocational education can justify its existence without making a direct attack upon the personality problem. Relationships between teachers and students, counselors and students, advisors and students, and between student and student, when consciously conducted on the highest level of cooperation and amity, cannot fail to influence the personalities of young people. If these relationships are supplemented by direct teaching of personality techniques in classes organized for the purposes and staffed by persons of outstanding personality, then definite results are bound to ensue. Home room, assembly, and club activities can be readily directed toward the same end.

While differences of personality in social relationships can be good enough to hold together large families, even communities, and can be bad enough to result in abandonment, divorce, and even mayhem and murder, polite and friendly relationships in industry and business not only make for good human fellowship but actually become marketable skills. Thus personality development becomes an integral part of sound vocational education.

SOCIAL WELFARE. Schools are not primarily organized to provide home relief, medical services, or advice on marital affairs. Yet in some instances personalities of young people are profoundly changed, sometimes wrecked by unbearable home circumstances. A failure in mathematics may very well be traced to lack of space or time or quiet surroundings for requisite study. No advisor, no counselor can operate successfully for any length of time without encountering these problems. The social welfare counselor must mobilize all the social welfare services in the community in the interest of the students of the school. And it is a clear-cut function of the school to follow through with each young person to see that he has availed himself of those facilities.

THE INDIVIDUAL STUDENT'S PROGRAM AND THE FLEXIBLE SCHOOL PROGRAM. Ideally, every student's program for an ensuing term is made out strictly with reference to his or her needs and without regard to the possible program offerings of the school. These programs are then collated to determine what subjects should be taught and in which terms. Wherever there is a sufficient number of students to maintain a class, that class is established. If individual programs have been painstakingly constructed in the sole interest of each individual, the resulting school program is more than likely to become an impossibility, in some cases an absurdity, in the light of teachers, space, and time available. Yet every effort must be made to accomplish even an absurdity if education for all young people is to be provided. The school program must be flexible, adaptable, and student-created. Individuality and flexibility are the attributes of a school organization dedicated to human personality.

PERSONAL ADJUSTMENT IN THE SMALL "INDEPENDENT" SCHOOL. The "special counselor," the "home room period," the "advisory system," are organizational devices to counteract and minimize the mass education defects of the large public school. They can do so effectively. However, for many years the best of the small, privately financed,

independent schools have operated under conditions highly conducive to the personal intimacy and individual diagnosis so essential
to sound orientation. Vocational guidance, in the usual sense, is
rarely attempted; but in recent years numerous private schools have
built up strong departments of "guidance," or "tests and guidance,"
interested especially in determining scholastic aptitude, in planning
the student's course, and in aiding personality development. Though
most private schools are essentially "college preparatory," some put
greater emphasis on "doing your own best" than on covering a prescribed course. A "controlled environment" is generally considered
one of their most distinctive features. "Dignity of personality" — regardless of creed, sex, ability, or color — has been a living ideal in
Friends' schools for three centuries. Small classes are the rule; they
have been maintained and strengthened by the conference method,
even in such large schools as Andover, Exeter, and Lawrenceville.
The smaller boarding schools can even approximate the closer, continuous relationships of family life. At George School they justly
claim that every teacher and every phase of the program are part of
the personal guidance process. In a word, it is generally recognized
that efficient independent schools — within whatever limitations their
selective form of organization may place upon them — enjoy several
definite advantages in giving personal, individual guidance to their
students, advantages which educators wish to see shared as rapidly
as possible by the public schools.[19]

VIII. OCCUPATIONAL INFORMATION

If decisions were always to be made in the clear light of reason,
the only data needed for valid choice of occupation would be those
provided by analysis of the individual personality and by analysis of
all occupations for which that individual might be a likely candidate.
While, as is well known, choices are based upon many other factors,
accurate information still plays an important role. For this reason
the teaching of occupational information is usually considered a vocational guidance function. It is sometimes thought that it ought to
be taught only by a trained counselor in a special period set aside for
the purpose. In this way, effectiveness is assured. However, in consideration of the scope of subject matter provided by general education and of the importance of extracting from the so-called general

19 ERNEST B. CHAMBERLAIN, *Our Independent Schools* (New York: American Book
Co., 1944), pp. 42, 65-68, 128, 191-92, 195, 224.

subjects every item of value for vocational orientation, the teaching of occupational information will be considered in the chapter on Reality.

It should be noted that the vocational guidance movement in this country has laid great stress upon the dissemination of occupational information. Occupational information makes the initial impact upon the school curriculum. We shall always be reminded that Benjamin Franklin's father took him around town to observe men at work in various vocations so that he might make a wise choice. Benjamin Franklin's father was the original American vocational counselor.

IX. PERIODIC STUDENT EVALUATION

One of the more frequent arguments for late choice of occupation and for postponement of the training period until after high school graduation is that the child does not understand himself or the occupation well enough to make a valid choice. Moreover, his own developing powers and the rapid changes in industrial, business, and professional life may alter the desirability of a particular occupation. These arguments are sound enough except that they ignore the element of interest upon which all learning is based and they do not take into account the possibility and desirability of frequent, periodic evaluation of the student's attainments in terms of his occupational purpose. Of testing and tryout and continuous counseling we have already spoken. Of interest more will appear in the next chapter. At this point we may note a simple administrative device.

CLEAR-CUT GOALS. The usual high school diploma attests to the completion of a course and to good character. A college diploma confers "rights, privileges and immunities" deriving from the feudal Middle Ages. The university diploma, professional in nature, carries with it the right to practice a profession or to take state examinations conferring that right. The rigidity and inevitability of these professional tests provide a strong stimulus to study and personal preparation. In college and high school, where occupational aim is hazily conceived and often entirely absent, these specific goals do not usually appear. However, in the vocational high school they are definite in character although not always clear and detailed. For this reason, it is important that students entering upon an occupational course have impressed upon them the qualifications for success in that occupation and that, from time to time, the student's accomplishments be evaluated in terms of those qualifications.

The ratings on the comprehensive cumulative record should be considered from term to term and steps taken to bolster up the weaknesses of the student for, if these weaknesses indicate probable failure to attain the goal of graduation in that particular occupation, the pupil should be reoriented. In those occupations requiring a specific talent, such as music, pupils should be auditioned early in their course by a recognized member of the profession, and, even though found satisfactory at that time, should be auditioned again shortly before graduation. Successful members of industry, business, or the professions will, as a matter of course, be organized into advisory boards that consider it part of their duty, whenever called upon, to evaluate the vocational assets and liabilities of young men and women preparing for their vocations.

CRITERIA OF VOCATIONAL COMPETENCE. Obviously, graduation should not be determined merely by excellence in performing the skills of the occupation. At every stage in the student's progress there should be emphasized, and evaluation should make explicit, the fact that the good worker is "good" in a many-sided situation. He has a well-rounded general education. He has developed favorable personal traits. He has the attributes of a good physique — sound health, good appearance, and strength and dexterity to whatever extent may be required by his occupation. His general intelligence is on a level essential to that occupation.

He knows about the world he is to live in and knows how to live in it so that he may be respected by his fellowmen. He is not content to be merely a successful individual but wants to take part in the activities of the community. He has high ethical standards and applies them in both his professional relations and civic and family activities.

We have suggested that the student share in building up the cumulative record, that he look upon it as his passport. If he is thoroughly aware of the goal to be reached and is confident that teacher, counselor, advisor, and principal are working with him to put their visa on that passport so that the world of occupations may be opened to him, he responds with enthusiasm, competence, and appreciation.

X. PLACEMENT

Through an advisory board or commission, the vocational school, whether conducted on the high school, college, or university level, maintains close contact with the industry, business, or profession. The audition, examination, or inspection of students, mentioned in the previous section, acquaints employers and other workers, as individuals and as associations, with the workers of tomorrow. Commission members who have assisted in formulating courses of study and practice leading to placement in their own vocations, feel a proprietary interest in the product — the young men and women who, upon graduation, seek employment. So, the early stages of placement occur long before the final act of accepting a job, in some cases, upon admission to the school. It has long been the practice of large corporations to comb the engineering schools for talent, for colleges and universities to look to their own and other institutions for new instructors, for major league baseball clubs to maintain "farms" (minor league clubs for the training of young players) so that they may employ the product. Similarly, advisory boards on vocational education, with their attendant specialized commissions, look to the vocational schools for young blood for their working forces.

TEACHERS AS PLACEMENT OFFICERS. Competent teachers of vocations, whether printers, architects, garment designers, artists, physicians, or welders, maintain their old occupational associations and acquire new ones in order that they may assist in opening up opportunities to their graduates. It is only when teachers keep in close contact with the realities of life that their teaching is vivid and their products are useful.

STUDENTS AS THEIR OWN PLACEMENT OFFICERS. An effective vocational guidance program, through individual counseling, through lessons in occupational information, and through continued emphasis upon the importance of individuality, stimulates students to make their plans for employment long before graduation and urges them to use their own initiative and not to depend upon others for help to any greater extent than the circumstances warrant. This is the normal, salutary procedure which should not be weakened by unnecessary help and direction. It is only when the young person is on his own and faces up to the realities of life, with its disappoint-

ments and bitternesses, that he appreciates the successes that come
his way.

THE PLACEMENT OFFICE. All of this in no way belittles the importance of the organized placement office, whether conducted by an
individual school, a school system, a municipality, a state, or the
federal government. Organized, systematic solicitation of job opportunities; carefully planned, scientific analysis of individual ability; and finally, the conjunction of opportunity and man or woman,
can be effectively carried out only by those who devote themselves
assiduously to this specialized task. They perform an indispensable
function. For effective functioning a placement office should meet
certain criteria:

1. The placement office should cover as wide a geographic area
and as great a range of occupations as is likely to be tapped by applicants to the bureau. It should bring richness of opportunity to the
individual. A university placement office may very well be national
in scope while a municipal employment office will necessarily confine itself to openings in the city.

2. The placement office should be generous in its dissemination
of information to all types of vocational schools. Data regarding job
qualifications, trends in employment, and technological changes are
indispensable to continual revision of the curriculum and of the
guidance program itself. The placement office is not merely a job-
getting device, but is rather an integral part of the school program.
When it is conducted by the educational institution itself, this obligation weighs heavily upon it.

3. The placement office should itself offer guidance to all who
register with it, for it is an educational agency. The placement officer
should be among the most effective of counselors.

XI. FOLLOW UP

Follow up constitutes a kind of continuous placement or replacement, with all its attendant problems. Adjustment to occupation is
not accomplished by entrance upon the first job for which a graduate qualifies. Even the doctor who theoretically is competent to
treat all human ills, must start humbly and simply with his first
case. If wise, he has frequent recourse to the institution in which he
was trained, and if that institution is sensitive to its obligations, it
follows up the experience of the young physician and offers its as-

sistance during the period of difficult adjustment. All this is equally true of the young man who begins as an apprentice in a skilled trade. He has many steps to take before he reaches the level of the full-fledged skilled craftsman. For some the road of advancement is smooth, for others exceedingly rough. Some employers establish sound personnel policies, others have none at all. For the employees of the latter, who get caught up in a maze of conflicting policies and unsympathetic supervisors, the counsel of the school can be of great value.

THE IDEAL FOLLOW UP. In an ideal plan of post-school follow up, the school requests and receives periodic reports from all its graduates, who have been so strongly imbued with the importance of sending in this information that, after graduation, they rarely forget to do so. A staff of coordinators visits their employers to acquire general information useful not only in counseling the young people but also in enriching the fund of knowledge and wisdom of the counselors. A coordinator makes, for each individual, such adjustments as he can, and adds the data to the store of information already existing in the school. The school sets up in its guidance program a consultation office for graduates, conducted in the evening, where former students can be counseled in ways of securing advancement, of finding other and better jobs, on subjects and places of further study, and on relationships with fellow workers. In other words, with exceedingly valuable data at hand, the school helps its graduates solve the problem of genuinely facing up to reality.

XII. RESEARCH

Just as the total problem of the school is to bring about continuous and progressive development of the individual, so is it the task of the guidance staff to bring about continuous and progressive development of the program itself. Almost any question that may be asked about the adjustment of the individual to the school program and to his future occupation, can become a research problem. It is only through such research that the potentialities of the individual can be revealed and made useful to himself and to society.

SOME RESEARCH PROBLEMS. What is the correlation between ratings in academic subjects and ratings in shop subjects? Also the correlation between intelligence quotients and ratings in shop work?

What is the minimum I.Q. necessary to succeed in any particular kind of manual work? Or for successful study in a profession?

Can pupils who have been successful in shop work in a vocational high school sustain themselves in college? What is the minimum I.Q. of a vocational high school pupil that warrants his admission to college?

What are the minimum I.Q.'s for various types of occupations for which preparation is given in vocational high schools?

What are the characteristics of entering pupils and how do they differ from those exhibited upon graduation?

How can the school's testing program be made more effective?

What motivates pupils to choose the vocational high school? What are the incentives to study and work?

In one vocational high school, without too great burden upon the administrative or teaching staff, it has been possible within recent years, to make profitable studies of (a) comparisons of reasons why boys and girls enter the school, with their evaluation of the school shortly before graduation, (b) relation of scores on the Armed Forces Institute General Education Development Tests to intelligence quotient, school grades, and qualification for admission to college, (c) feasibility of combining standard shopwork and traditional academic high school practices within the usual high school day, (d) a number of other problems suggested by the questions in the foregoing paragraph.

All the above studies can be made by a well-trained counseling staff. However, it may be useful to draw into the research program professors from community institutions, especially if there are colleges or universities in the immediate area. If the term "research" sounds too formidable, and it often does, it is no great task to start a research program with common-sense procedures and a minimum amount of expertness in dealing with figures. Most important of all is a desire to improve. The ways and means are usually not too far away from the source of instruction to make it possible to get help. In any case, the guidance program should be continually re-evaluating itself.

XIII. PRIMACY OF THE PERSON

Guidance may be either a philosophy or a catchword. It may express a deep-lying conception of the processes of human development or a missionary zeal for regimentation. It may be a means of implementing the "evil works of fastidiously bigoted school teachers" (phrase from Frank Swinnerton) or it may be a way of life for educators. It may soar in the stratosphere of character and culture or wallow in crass utilitarianism. Some say it is individualized education, others that it is education itself. Still others maintain that it is rightful heir to a long line of shibboleths, stemming from Froebel and culminating in Dewey. It is a word that attracts to itself important adjectives like moral, social, physical, mental, educational, ánd, most commonly of all, vocational.

In point of fact, guidance historically earned its right to a place in educational thinking through its association with vocations. It connoted choice of a life work, orientation in the field of occupations, decision in an economic situation. It provided a chart, a guide book for exploration in a confusing environment. It aided the individual in a complex society. It was the first groping for release from the thraldom of competition in a surplus economy. In its vocational sense guidance takes on a maximum of meaning, at least for the child. Health and morals are vague, even undesirable goals in the eyes of many children; but they all understand the necessity for a job that will sustain life, and, incidentally, health and morals. During adolescence it is a powerful motive which is utilitarian only in the sense that it is useful. So, vocational guidance becomes a powerful aid to educational guidance.[20]

SOME IMPORTANT PERSONS. The only fitting conclusion to a chapter entitled "The Primacy of the Person" is the story of persons, persons who have had the benefit of all the scientific techniques, educational procedures, and human influences that comprise vocational guidance. These are persons in whom vocation has been a powerful motive, persons whom the present writer has known intimately and of whom all other personalities may well be proud. They are products of a program but, much more than that, they have helped to make and to justify that program. Their cumulative record cards are dramatic biographies, their advisors have been in every sense counselors, friends, and school-parents, and their adjustments have been adjustments for life.

All his young life Joseph Cannon looked forward to a career at sea. Well before his graduation from junior high school, at thirteen years and nine months of age, he cast about for a school that would serve this abiding interest and, through his vocational counselor,

20 FRANKLIN J. KELLER, Editorial, *Child Study*, Vol. XII, 1935.

learned of Metropolitan. Skeptical of any workable combination of practical seamanship and secondary education, he spent three days visiting the courses and finally convinced himself that this was *his* educational institution. Graduating three months short of his seventeenth birthday, he was still too young to get his seaman's papers, but ultimately he did sail and was on one of the first vessels torpedoed after Pearl Harbor. Nine days in a lifeboat gave him his first taste of the hazards of the sea. The experience only confirmed Joe in his early choice of a vocation. He has served responsibly and continuously since then. He now holds a Master's license for steam and motor vessels and is Master of the Liberty Ship "Thomas W. Kerns" of the North Atlantic and Gulf Steamship Company at a salary of $610 a month plus maintenance — an extraordinary accomplishment for a young man twenty-three years old. Joe is married and has three children.

At sixteen years of age Edward Fitzgerald found himself in an academic high school, passing in most of his subjects, but unhappy and restless. He too had the sea as his goal, so he transferred to Metropolitan. Originally planning to sail on deck, he moved down into the engine room because a physical examination indicated that he probably would not meet the eyesight standard required for work on deck. He made an excellent record in his shop, and by dint of extra work performed on the S.S. "Brooklyn" (a war-time training ship annexed to the school) after regular school hours, was able to ship out two months before regular graduation time. After his first ten days in the engine room, while the ship was still in port, and during which he stood watch for the second engineer, he remarked: "Gee, it's great to stand in the engine room and look at all those gadgets and know just what to do with them, just because you went to school." Eddie went out to sea and made an excellent record as third assistant engineer on T-2 tankers running oil from South America to Okinawa during the dangerous war period. Then something happened. During prolonged heavy weather he developed a compulsive fear that the ship would capsize. There was nothing to do but come ashore to take psychiatric treatment. He fully recovered but the danger of a revival of his fears was too great for him to return to sea, so he sought a shore job. Like all those young men who have been subject to the advisory system, he returned to school for counsel. Through the principal's reference to a fellow member in the New York Rotary Club, Eddie was placed in a Consolidated Edison power plant where he found himself at home and happy. Edward is now attending a junior college in New Jersey.

Theodore Sandlin is one of those boys whose cumulative record card is embellished with such enthusiastic adjectives as "cooperative," "studious," "willing," courteous." His shop marks were always "E," an exceptional rating; in character and work traits he was not rated less than 5, the top mark. From the outset of his high school career, he wanted to be a radio operator. His accomplishments were so outstanding that he was not only accelerated to the point of graduating at seventeen and a half years of age, but he completed all regents' requirements for admission to college. He obtained the second class radio telegraph operator's license and the second class radio telephone operator's license, and sailed as radio operator on a merchant vessel a few days after graduation. During the war he was an ensign in the Maritime Service, and at present he is chief radio officer on a Lykes Brothers ship. Keen, dynamic, cooperative, Teddy was not only carving out a career which was intensely to his liking, but, during his entire school career, was helping to establish the validity of radio instruction and rendering invaluable assistance in building and equipping new shops in the department. "Sparks" has been the hero in many rescues at sea. Traditionally, he and the skipper are the last to leave the sinking ship. At all times his skill, ingenuity, and unswerving sense of duty are major factors in assuring the safety of passengers and crew. Teddy will play this role perfectly if the occasion ever arises. He plans to attend college in the near future and will specialize in electrical engineering.

Where there is a genuine urge for the sea, it is difficult to resist. If there are any physical handicaps, the true salt finds ways of overcoming them. There is the classic story of Matthew Fontaine Maury who, as a young man, had his leg so badly injured in a stage coach accident that he was never able to sail again in any working capacity. However, he compensated for his handicap by intensive study of weather and water to the end that he became the founder of the United States Hydrographic Office. This office is now responsible for all the charts and reports that enable navigators to find their way in any kind of wind or weather. So it was with Alexander Waigandt who came to Metropolitan bent upon being a deck officer, hoping to become a skipper some day. In his second term his advisor wrote the following characterization: "Romantic type. Good address. Uncertainty has crept into his plan for the future since he learned that he is color blind. He wanted to become a navigator. He is reorienting himself. Wishes to become a marine radio man." His final orientation was brought about when he was placed aboard ship as a purser. However, the day came when everything in Alec's makeup found opportunity for self-expression and for service to his country. In May of 1943 the "Daniel Huger" was docked at Bone, Algeria, loaded with 6000 tons of high octane gasoline. Seventeen German planes began a high level bombing attack, which took the lives of a Navy gunner and the third mate, and started a fire between decks. Terrific explosions resulted and flaming gasoline was sprayed over the two holds of the ship. With flames rising 300 feet above the vessel, the order was given to throw all live ammunition overboard, to flood the magazine, and to abandon ship.

For his part in the subsequent events, Alec received the Merchant Marine Distinguished Service Medal. "Upon arrival of the shore fire brigade it was decided to save the ship with foamite," reads the citation, signed by Rear Admiral Emory S. Land, Chairman of the Commission. "It was necessary to have a few men return to the ship, enter the adjacent hold and play a hose on the heated bulkhead to prevent the raging fire from spreading. Purser Waigandt was one of the four who volunteered to risk their lives in an attempt to save part of the cargo, which was so necessary to the continuance of war operations. That the fire was eventually brought under control and most of the cargo saved was due in no small measure to his outstanding bravery. His willingness to risk his life to save his ship and his heroic conduct during the fire are in keeping with the finest traditions of the sea."

Camille Lupinacci's father was a tumbler, an acrobat. Camille inherited the aptitude and aspired to become a dancer. Of average scholastic ability, she had no interest in academic work and would probably not have finished the four years of high school had it not been possible to work out a program in terms of her vocational interests. She realized the uncertainties of dancing as a career and felt that it would be wise to prepare for office work at the same time. On the face of it, the resulting program looked like a crazy quilt, but in actuality it served a most useful purpose. Music, dramatics, sewing, and extra periods of physical training contributed to the preparation for dancing, while stenography, typewriting, and special English prepared her for office work. The combination helped to develop an excellent personality with the result that dancing became a pleasant and slightly profitable avocation while the office training gained her a position in the Corn Exchange Bank at Chatham Square.

From the outset Jerome Aronberg wanted to be and probably will be a theatrical manager. Well-above-average intelligence and an ingratiating personality made him most successful in acting and directing while in school. In his spare time he was a radio announcer at WNEW and WNYC. Later, he attained third place in a countrywide audition and became announcer at WWCO in Waterbury, Connecticut. Excellent grades in academic work gained him admission to college. When drafted, the Navy sent him to Harvard and upon discharge he went back to Harvard to finish the course. A dominant interest in the theater has enabled him to acquire technical skills and cultural assets that constitute for him a well-rounded education.

Salvatore Ficalora came to high school with the handicap of three terms of retardation. His elementary school career had not been a happy one. Somehow or other, "education" had not clicked. His father was a photographer and Sal wanted to be one too. From his very first day in the photography course he made a name for himself in excellence of both shop and academic work. He was first elected president of his section, then president of the Students' General Organization, and finally president of the Honor Society. He was accelerated to the point where he was graduated at the normal age of eighteen, and has since then been highly successful as photographer in the Army Signal Corps. Together with his brother, Anthony, Salvatore is now proprietor of a photographic studio on Second Avenue. From a youngster of great reticence he has blossomed out into a normal, extremely personable young man. This could never have happened in an academic school without career motivation and facilities.

Carolyn Clarke is one of those finely superior persons who would have been outstanding in any type of school. With high intelligence, excellent home environment, and a delightful personality, everything has been in her favor. However, she chose Metropolitan for its opportunities in vocational music and around this core of interest built up an outstanding record in performing skill and in the book subjects. Exhibiting great skill on the French horn, she majored in music in college, graduated with honors, and has been playing with the National Symphony Orchestra.

Frank Hoag was one of those fine, normal, wholesome boys who made a good average record and was well liked by everybody. His desire for the life of the sea brought him to Metropolitan where he soon became president of the Students' General Organization. Catherine Sandow was a sweet, pleasant personality, full of life and ambition, and very active in school social affairs. The stage was her goal and while still in school she obtained professional engagements in dancing. The Maritime Deck Department was called upon to assist the Vocational Dramatics Department in setting up its scenery. Once he had set his eyes on Catherine, Frank became an indefatigable worker in dramatics. But his regular school work slumped badly, and only shortly before graduation, when romance was apparently on the rocks, it became evident that Frank would not, apparently could not, meet the requirements for his diploma. The most sympathetic and persuasive counseling was of no avail. He was "through," and was joining the Navy. Here he made an excellent record for himself. In the meanwhile Catherine, who was graduating, again cast favorable eyes on Frank and insisted that there be two diplomas between them. So Frank completed his graduation requirements at sea. He re-enlisted in the Navy as a quartermaster, married Catherine. She has been doing professional modeling and illustration for "True Romance Magazine." They are two very happy people who visit the school frequently for renewal of pleasant associations. The time and thought and energy devoted by teachers, counselors, and principal to assistance in adjusting these two fine personalities would be difficult to total, but no figure would be too high to justify its worthwhileness.

THE BALANCED PERSONALITY. The foregoing personality sketches are indicative of a kind of personal balance described by Lewis Mumford. "The ideal personality for the opening age is a balanced personality: not the specialist, but the whole man. Such a personality must be in dynamic interaction with every part of his environment and every part of his heritage. He must be capable of treating economic experiences and esthetic experiences, parental experiences and vocational experiences, as the related parts of a single whole, namely, life itself. His education, his discipline, his daily routine must tend toward this wholeness. To achieve this, he must be ready to spurn the easy successes, in a dying culture, through self mutilation.

"Such a dynamic balance is not easily achieved: its consummations are precious and its stability is precarious: it demands a vigilance and an athletic readiness for new shifts and stresses that more specialized vocations do not habitually achieve. For balance is not a

108

matter of allotting definite amounts of time and energy to each segment of life that requires attention: even our mechanical partition of functions does that. It means that the whole personality must be constantly at play, at least at ready call, at every moment of its existence and that no one part of life should be segregated from another part, incapable of influencing it or being influenced by it.

"But qualitative balance is as important as quantitative balance: many kinds of experience have the role in life that vitamins have in the diet: quantitatively minute elements may be as important for spiritual health as the vitamins and minerals are for bodily health. Most of man's higher activities are in the latter category. No healthy person can look at pictures all day any more than he can make love all day. But for even the humblest person, a day spent without the sight or sound of beauty, the contemplation of mystery, or the search for truth and perfection is a poverty-stricken day; and a succession of such days is fatal to human life. That is why even the most superstitious forms of religion, which have at least kept alive some wraith of beauty or perfection, still contain for the mass of mankind something valuable that a bare scientific positivism has allowed to be lost both in thought and practice." [21]

It is this kind of balanced personality that vocational education, especially through its guidance functions, can attain.

[21] LEWIS MUMFORD, *The Condition of Man* (New York: Harcourt, Brace and Company, Inc., 1944), pp. 419–20.

Chapter 6

MOTIVATION, INTEREST, AND LEARNING

THE never-ceasing wonder of children is their activity — always moving — forever going somewhere. After the first vague gropings of babyhood we see them moving in some direction — following a ball, chasing a playmate, sailing a boat. True, these are short excursions, with frequent changes of goal. As the years go on and adolescence succeeds childhood, the body becomes quieter, the movements less impulsive, and the goals more distant. Immediate satisfaction gives way to sustained purpose. The more or less common goals of children give way to the highly varied, sometimes fantastic purposes of adults. Among the most baffling of human problems are the purposes of men. Why do they do what they do? Only the sick, the imbecile, and the dead have no purpose, no interests, no goals. What determines men's purposes?

I. MOTIVATION AND LEARNING

It is through constant *doing,* with a purpose, that we learn — to do — to *live.* We learn what we do. Without those drives that begin immediately after birth and continue throughout life to make impact upon the environment, we should never learn even enough to remain alive, for learning is a condition of survival. Nothing is learned through mere stimulation of the senses. The learner must actually take part in the experience, for the attitude of the participant is quite different from that of the onlooker. He identifies himself with what he sees or hears and then is interested enough to do himself. Interest is fundamental to learning.

PERSONALITY AND PURPOSE. A personality is a person going somewhere — he has a *purpose.* The dull clod, the idiot, has no considered purpose and therefore has no personality. A person is an individuality, a personality by virtue of his interests, his traits, and his attitudes. The significance of interest lies in its *drive,* from suckling at the mother's breast to the formulation of a cosmic philosophy. Interest is dynamic, directive, purposive.

MOTIVATION. Motivation is that something that explains why we do what we do. We cannot observe motivation, we can observe only the resulting behavior. We know there must be causes. Behavior cannot be completely spontaneous. Causes lie in the condition of the organism in relation to changes taking place in the external environment. When we say that the individual is motivated, we are explaining nothing. We are simply saying that something makes him act the way he acts. The word "motivation" is derived from the Latin *movere* — to move, stir, excite to action, arouse feeling, purpose, take action. The practical problem in education is indicated in the dictionary definition of "motivate" — to stimulate active interest (in some study) through appeal to associated interests or by special devices. So, while we cannot observe motivation we can observe the behavior of individuals and then try to relate it to such conditions of the organism as can be observed.

What is the nature of the factors related to the release and direction of activity? Psychologists list many of them,[1] the most important being: wants, needs, traits, attitudes, interests, habits, skills, purposes, and emotional conditions. Both wants and needs are requirements of the organism. They are not learned, they are there. Traits are both natural and acquired patterns of response which predispose the individual to more or less common reactions in a wide range of situations. Attitudes are learned patterns of response which predispose the individual to rather specific behavior in given situations. An interest may be classified either as a trait or as an attitude, depending, largely, on whether it is broad or narrow in its reference. Interests are *learned* responses which predispose the organism to certain lines of activity and which definitely facilitate *attention.* Habits and skills serve as motives to the extent that new learning which is in line with existing response patterns will be more easily acquired. Furthermore, achievement breeds interest; the interest value of new learning is enhanced by its relationship

[1] DAVID G. RYANS, "Motivation in Learning," in *The Psychology of Learning,* Forty-First Yearbook, Part II, National Society for the Study of Education (Bloomington, Illinois: Public School Publishing Co., 1942), p. 309.

with earlier learning. Purpose is a need of which one is aware and which one carries out by striving to attain the goal toward which it is directed. Feelings and emotional states are obviously important contributors to the preparatory set for an activity. What one likes one learns easily.[2]

As can be readily seen, the fundamental factor in learning is the state of the organism, the extent to which it is prepared to make a response. This is known as *set*. When we say we are "all set," we are prepared to act. So with the organism. It is motivated.

The goal we want to reach, the object we want to attain, that something that stirs the organism to a response, is the *incentive*. When we have attained the object of our desire, the effect is known as *reinforcement*. The relationship of the drive to incentive is strengthened but the drive itself may be decreased.

INTEREST. Out of all these factors related to motivation emerges the most important for educational purposes. *Interest* is that excitement of feeling which gives rise to *attention*. This mental excitement may be intellectual or sympathetic and emotional, or merely personal, as an interest in philosophical research, in human suffering, in money getting.

For practical school education, for effective learning, then, interest must be present, however derived. And in subsequent pages we shall speak most of interest and of those finally imagined goals toward which the individual directs his energies — *purposes*. And most of all we shall speak of directed activity with a purpose.

II. INTEREST AND EFFORT

The controversy between proponents of "interest" and of "effort" was seemingly resolved at the turn of the century.[3] Yet, the blitheness with which many educators ignore the one factor that can guarantee learning makes it necessary to revive and restate the problem. We have already noted that, in the strictest psychological sense, there are other factors related to motivation, to that something that

[2] Adapted from RYANS, *op. cit.*
[3] JOHN DEWEY, *Interest and Effort in Education* (Boston: Houghton Mifflin Company, 1913).
WILHELM OSTERMANN, *Interest in its Relation to Pedagogy* (New York: A. S. Barnes, 1899).
CHARLES DEGARMO, *Interest and Education* (New York: The Macmillan Company, 1902).

moves people in the direction of learning. However, wants, needs, traits, and emotional conditions, all combine to make people *like* to do something. And that is *interest*.

INTEREST AND FEELING. Interest has its origin in *feeling* which, for all practical purposes is, psychologically, an ultimate. To go beyond feeling is to enter the realm of mysticism. Interest is feeling in the two-fold sense that either it is itself feeling or it has developed from feeling by means of other psychological processes. The object of interest may be sensuous or ideal. Bright colors and graceful forms please the eye. Sweet tones and soft spoken words please the ear. They are sensuous objects of interest. Ideal interest may be intellectual, esthetic, sympathetic, ethical, religious, patriotic. "Interest" means that we attach "value" to these objects — we are "conscious" of worth. By being pleased we identify ourselves with those objects. We make them a means of our own self-expression. Interest demands that we be able to understand the objects, to know their meaning. Otherwise the original feeling subsides and interest wanes. In other words, they must be meaningful, they must have something to do with us, and we must have something to do with them. They must be part of our lives.

All this is a kind of "pleasure theory," and for the advocates of "effort" in education, represents a weakening of the will, a softening of the backbone, and calamity for the nation.

INTEREST AND WILL. Of course, no such thing is true. Otherwise, where would our ever-active child be? He does not sit around waiting for something to affect him pleasantly. He is already moving in some direction. He is seeking pleasure, if you like. And it is in this dynamic seeking that he discovers the things or movements that help him to attain his ends. He is already exercising his will. Interest gives it direction.

If pleasure arises from primary action, we call the process *play*. Whether child or adult, the individual who thoroughly enjoys what he is doing at the moment, is at play. If adult, he calls himself an amateur. If, perchance, he makes money from play, he calls it work. If, on the other hand, the individual engages in immediate activity only to gain a more remote end — food, clothing, and shelter, for instance — and he has an interest only in the end, not at all in the means, then he is at work and his interest in that work is only indirect. He may call it "hard" work because he has to put effort into it. And he will put effort into it if the end result is interesting enough. He will be disciplining himself.

Happy is the man, the artist, to whom his work is so significant and to whom the processes are so pleasurable, that work is play. If all work were effortless, the millennium would have come. It probably never will. As a matter of fact, all artists have their stretches of effort-making, and that effort-making requires an exercise of will. But again, if the goal is of transcendent interest, such effort never becomes drudgery.

INTEREST AND GROWTH. So, interest is normal, indeed, indispensable. It is an accompaniment of those movements that lead to experience, the experience that is education, and the education that is growth. The soft, wishy-washy interest that is merely a tickling of the senses has no place in education. However, interest that springs from the life processes, that moves the individual out into the world, interest that is the springboard for self-realizing performance, interest that gives fire to a worthy purpose, is of the essence of education.

It is in this very process of growth, of development, that vocational education fits into the psychological picture. What is a career but an imagined goal? What is striving for a career but an expression of purpose? What are the successive steps in such striving but the process of growth? And what greater and more sustained effort does man put forth than to achieve the status guaranteed by a career? Even love and passion are contained within it for, regardless of pleasure in the job itself, the protection and security guaranteed by that job are sought more fervently for loved ones than for oneself.

III. OCCUPATION: PLAY AND WORK

The kindergarten has more in common with the vocational school than has any other part of the educational system. The insight of Froebel was uncanny. He cluttered up his pedagogy with a good deal of futile symbolism, but fundamentally he was sound. Not only let the children play, but help them to play well. Release their energy, but canalize it. Above all, give them an opportunity to create. And so, in the kindergartens of today, not only do we have games and singing, but construction, building, making things. When the children "play" house, they make the house, they furnish it, and they operate it. It is a child's world, but it is patterned after an adult model. And much effort is expended. The children put a great deal of "work" into it.

Then see how active they are. They keep on until they are ex-
hausted. What they do is all clearly within their powers. They are
happy. The teacher does not have to interest them. There are a few
whose organisms do not respond, forerunners of adults who cannot
or will not work, but by and large the children react with enthusiasm. We ask then, why, at any time, must we teach what the organism cannot learn, cannot identify with itself? Why must play become
drudgery rather than wholesome, happy work? What immediate
interests can be tapped? What abiding interests can be conjured up?
What purposes can be developed?

The answer lies in the engagement of children in activities to
their liking, with gradual but insistent development of these activities
into occupations that reproduce on the child's level the occupations
of adults. These "occupations" will not all be money-producing, in
fact, many of them will be humane and contributory. However, they
will all represent life at its best. As is so true later, when the vocational phases of an occupation become explicit, it is exceedingly
important that the occupation be conceived as service to others rather
than as mere bread-getting for the worker. It is exceedingly important that this early training in "industry" be on so high a plane
that it sets the standard of value for the remainder of the child's life.

OCCUPATION — INTEREST TO PURPOSE. The "occupation" of the child
carries with it faint adumbrations of "What I want to be" — "What
I want to do." The academicians always express great horror at the
early choice of an occupation, when "the child knows nothing about
the world and very little about himself." Regardless of its usefulness,
children do, sooner or later, express preferences. Sooner or later —
with varying degrees of earnestness, with backgrounds that vary
from zero to considerable. As with the doctrine of interest, emphasis upon the individual has been strong in educational writings.
At the same time, fear of too early a choice of occupation has been
generalized into frequent recommendations that vocational education begin only after the high school period. As if interest, purpose,
drive, imagination, all lay dormant in the child until he had absorbed
this thing known as general education. Some children know what
they want to do as soon as they can talk. True, they change their
minds again and again, but the mere expression of desire is a signal
for seizing the opportunity to "educate." Wisdom, intensity, vary
with the child, and in any one child, vary with age. Other children go on to the time when they must work without ever thinking

or caring about what they will do for a living. Between these extremes lie all the variations of individual difference. Moreover, economic and social conditions change as the child grows older. We remember periods when all boys wanted to be locomotive engineers, then chauffeurs, then airplane pilots, then radio mechanics. Whatever the particular drive may be, it is incumbent upon the school to make it move along the lines of both individual and social development.

SOME CHARACTERISTICS OF VOCATIONAL INTEREST. As with many other phases of vocational education, research in vocational interests, despite some noteworthy attempts, has been all too meager. However, in 1931 Fryer brought together the results of studies made up to that time. His conclusions still have considerable significance: "The vocational interests of early adolescence during elementary school, are exceedingly impractical, far removed from reality and subject to enormous fluctuations. . . . The vocational interests of early and of later adolescence are both impractical when interests and opportunities are compared. There would appear to be less than fifty per cent who do achieve their vocational interest when the time comes to take a position and to adjust to the occupational world. . . . The reasons given for these vocational interests do not lead to the conclusion that there is a very close correlation in the mind of the individual between interest and fitness or opportunity. . . . A measure of fluctuation of vocational interest from early adolescence to adulthood shows a median of six different major interests for one hundred and forty-five subjects. . . . There seems to be practical value in these fluctuations of interests in a try-out of opportunities. . . . For the boy or girl interested in a particular occupation, there is usually a trend of occupational development over a fairly long period. . . . The vocational interest estimate is of little significance for prediction. It is only important when linked with other significant criteria of selection and guidance. . . . *It is the total picture of interest that is valuable in the adjustment of the individual — their practicality, the presence of various interest trends, their synthetic relationship as indicating development, their relation to fitness, abilities, and achievement, their fluctuations in a functional field of the occupations, and so on, that constitutes the clinical evidence useful in furthering a vocational adjustment.*"[4]

[4] DOUGLAS FRYER, *The Measurement of Interests* (New York: Henry Holt and Company, 1931), pp. 176–7.

Practically all studies of validity and permanence of a vocational choice have been made upon children who have not had the benefit of either vocational guidance or vocational education. It is these very agencies that not only take into account "the total picture of interest" but that actually seize upon it as an invaluable factor in the educational process itself. To ignore any expression of a child's preference, whether it be of vocation, of person, of religion, of politics, however naive, is to ignore the child himself. Not to seize upon these expressions is to let slip through one's fingers the very stuff upon which learning depends. No interest, no learning. No learning, no school. No school, no teachers. No teachers, no education. What are we, who pretend to be teachers, doing if we do not capitalize upon preference for vocation, vocation that constitutes the life work of any individual?

IV. FITNESS OF VOCATION FOR MOTIVATION

Activity, or self-activity, has long been a fundamental principle in learning. Dewey emphasizes four types of activity as providing educative interest: physical activity (including mental), intellectual activity, social activity, and the use of tools — work. He makes the point that "it is the *discovery and use of extra-organic tools which has made possible, both in the history of the race and of the individual, complicated activities of a long duration* — that is, with results that are long postponed. And, as we have already seen, it is this prolongation and postponement which requires an increasing use of intelligence. The use of tools and appliances (in the broad sense) also demands a greater degree of technical skill than does mastery of the use of the natural organs — or rather, it involves the problem of a progressively more complicated use of the latter — and hence stimulates a new line of development." After distinguishing between work and play, Dewey then goes on: "A child engaged in making something with tools, say, a boat, may be just as immediately interested in what he is doing as if he were sailing the boat. He is not doing what he does for the mere sake of an external result — the boat — nor for the mere sake of sailing it later. The thought of the finished product and of the use to which it is to be put may come to his mind, but so as to enhance his immediate activity of construction. In this case, his interest is free. He has a play motive; his activity is essentially artistic in principle. What differentiates it from spontaneous play is an *intellectual* quality; a remoter end in time serves to suggest and regulate a series of acts. Not to introduce an element of work *in this sense* when the child is ready for it is simply arbitrarily to arrest his development and to force his activities to a level of sense-excitation after he is prepared to act upon the basis of an idea. A mode of activity that was quite normal in its own period becomes disintegrating when persisted in after a person is ripe for an activity involving more thought. We must also remember that the change from an activity with an end nearby to one with an end farther off does not come all at once, not at the same time with respect to all things. A child may be ready for occupation with tools like scissors, paint and brush, for setting a table, cooking, etc., while with respect to other activities he is still unable to plan and arrange ahead. Thus there is no ground for the assumption that children of kindergarten age are capable only of make-believe play, while children of the primary grades should be held to all work and no play. Only the false idea about symbolism leads to the former conclusion; that only a false identification of interest and play with trivial amusement leads to the latter conclusion. It has been said that man is man only as he plays; to say this involves some change from the meaning in which play has just been used. But in the broader sense of wholehearted identification with what one is doing — in the sense of completeness of interest, it is so true that it should be a truism. Work in the sense in which it has been defined covers all activities involving the use of intervening materials, appliances, and forms of skill consciously used in achieving results. It covers all forms of expression and construction with tools and materials, all forms of artistic and manual activity so far as they involve the conscious or thoughtful endeavor to achieve an end." [5]

And to arrest his development is to commit an educational crime.

MOTIVATION IN THE CLASSROOM. Motivation in the classroom too often consists in contriving devices that will "make interesting" the subject matter that the teacher decides to present. These devices are useful in themselves but, divorced from intrinsic motivation of subject matter, they are pernicious in their deception and futile as to intention. Selecting one of the best of these listings, it will be useful to note the fitness of vocations for such motivation:

1. "Emphasis on 'meanings' and relationships contributes to the individual's set for learning. Materials lacking in meaning are relatively more difficult to learn than those the meaning of which is

[5] JOHN DEWEY, *op. cit.,* p. 65 ff.

understood." Certainly a sincerely conceived preference for a vocation is full of meaning.

2. "Interests, attitudes, and purposes must sometimes be developed,
or needs created, as a first step in learning. . . . Needs may be
created through introduction of projects which tap a major interest
of the individual but, at the same time, demand that he learn a
variety of previously unencountered facts or skills in order to bring
the task to completion." Projects of a vocational nature are especially useful for this purpose.

3. "Goals and standards to be met function successfully as incentives only when adapted to pupil abilities. Individual differences in
potentiality for achievement at any given time are widely distributed
in a classroom." All that has been said about individual differences
and vocational interests indicates the possibility and desirability of
setting up valid goals and standards.

4. "Definite objectives are necessary if motivation is to be effective. . . . Distant goals, where attainment is more desired than anticipated, are not generally considered to be so useful as incentives
as are more immediate goals." True, a vocation is a distant goal, but
in the minds of the children it is very definite.

5. "Pupil interests are important sources of motivation." The cas-
ualness of this remark takes one aback. Pupil interest *is* motivation.
Without it there is no learning. Vocation is a vital pupil interest.

6. "Specific directions and suggestions for learning," "reward and
praise," "punishment," and "the teacher," are factors that affect
motivation in any type of education. The teacher who really knows
the trade or profession that he is teaching can, through the authen-
ticity of his knowledge and the appropriateness of his personality,
become a very strong factor in stimulating the interests of the pupil.[6]

END AND MEANS. "Many educators have felt that the only worthwhile motivation is so-called 'intrinsic' motivation and that emphasis
upon the end (an incentive) rather than on the means (the learning) of attaining the end is undesirable. Statements regarding the
desirability of extrinsic versus intrinsic motivation are, of course,
largely matters of opinion. It may be true that intrinsic motivation is
more generally and permanently effective than is learning for some
material reward. However, it is the behavior that is being acquired,
the learning that is taking place, that is most important. So long as
the desired learning does take place and becomes available for ap-

[6] RYANS, *op. cit.*, p. 324.

plication in the individual's life activities, the incentive which was used to learning is, perhaps, of relatively little significance. That is, so far as the learning itself is concerned, it may matter little that the incentive was a material reward, praise, or simply satisfaction in doing the job well; the incentive itself drops out of the immediate picture, and the pattern of behavior which was learned becomes the important feature of the individual's experience." [7]

It may be "a matter of opinion," but how important the opinion! The end does not justify the means, socially, morally, or pedagogically. The very intensity of the means, necessary to "teach" uninteresting subject matter, is, by mere association, bound to leave its mark on the "learner." The means become part of the end, so the means had better be good means. If learning is stimulated by reference to a worthy career and the means are related to that career, the end result will be incomparably superior.

Says Dewey: "The school cannot immediately escape from the ideals set by prior social conditions. But it should contribute through the type of intellectual and emotional disposition which it forms to the improvement of those conditions. And just here the true conceptions of interest and discipline are full of significance. Persons whose interests have been enlarged and intelligence trained by dealing with things and facts in active occupations having a purpose (whether in play or work) will be those most likely to escape the alternatives of an academic and aloof knowledge in the hard, narrow, and merely 'practical' practice. To organize education so that natural active tendencies shall be fully enlisted in doing something, while seeing to it that the doing requires observation, the acquisition of information, and the use of constructive imagination, is what most needs to be done to improve social conditions." [8]

ADULT MOTIVES. It is interesting to note the relationship of children's motives to adult motives and the part that craftsmanship or workmanship plays in the motivation of the adult: "It seems to be neither the perfected talent nor the automatic habit that has driving power, but the imperfect talent and the habit-in-the-making. The child who is *just learning* to speak, to walk, or to dress, is, in fact, likely to engage in these activities for their own sake, precisely as does the adult who has an *unfinished* task in hand. . . . The active motive sub-

[7] RYANS, *op. cit.,* p. 322.
[8] From JOHN DEWEY, *Democracy and Education,* p. 160. By permission of The Macmillan Company, publishers (1916).

sides when its goal is reached, or, in the case of a motor skill, when it has become at last automatic. . . . Now, in the case of the permanent interests of personality, the situation is the same. A man whose motive is to acquire learning, or to perfect his craft, can never be satisfied that he has reached the end of his quest, for his problems are never completely solved, his skill is never perfect. Lasting interests are recurring sources of discontent, and from their incompleteness they derive their forward impetus." [9]

MOTIVATING DEVICES. The outstanding advantages of vocational education as to motivation lie principally in the depth and breadth of purpose and in the concreteness of the subject matter. Most other incentives are usually mere devices and may be used in any kind of education. Some of these incentives lend themselves particularly well to vocational education procedures: posters and charts, models and samples, visual and sensory aids. Assignments can be made very definite. Common interests make the socialized recitation a natural procedure. Discussions of social-economic forces and material culture become more relevant to the entire school program. Avocational interests grow out of vocational interests. In the shop the blackboard is more useful and demonstrations are more practical. Field trips are more purposeful. The shop teacher is more likely to be competent in making teaching aids. Traveling museums and collections are feasible.[10]

V. VOCATIONAL EDUCATION *IS* EDUCATION

Sometimes a mother or father will blaze into a vocational school to which, somehow or other, an enterprising son has gained admission without parental consent, exclaiming wildly, "I want my boy to go to an academic school where he will get an *education.*" And "education" means books, not tools. Happily, these instances are rare, most parents expressing gratitude that their children have found themselves. Unfortunately, a good many teachers in all types of academic schools harbor the idea that education is what *they* got in school and the real thing must be academic. Latterly this academic education has been called general education and the demand has been for

[9] From *Personality: A Psychological Interpretation* by GORDON W. ALLPORT, p. 204. Copyright, 1937, by Henry Holt and Company, Inc.
[10] F. THEODORE STRUCK, *Creative Teaching, Industrial Arts and Vocational Education* (New York: John Wiley & Sons, 1938), Ch. VI on "Motivating Learning."

"good general education, followed, if necessary, by vocational education." The foregoing discussion has emphasized the fact that vocational education *is* education. It is not a little something extra piled up on top of the real thing. Vocational education is education itself, begun when the first interest in activity presents itself to the individual, terminated only when the last interest in work has died.

INTEREST PERMEATES ALL PHASES OF VOCATIONAL EDUCATION. In a previous chapter on Primacy of the Person it was shown that interest is a major concern of guidance. Later it will be shown that profitable subject matter is not only a product of the environment but is a function of individual interest. It will be pointed out that good method grows out of valid interest. In Chapter 4 we have referred to the proposal that the high school confine itself entirely to general education and that all vocational education "of a specific sort" be postponed to the post-high school period. This conception of secondary education finds its champions here and there from time to time and will be dealt with more fully in the chapter on Reality. If for no other reason but that of the transcendent importance of interest, the conception must be considered wholly unsound. Note the Harvard Report: [11]

The question of the nation and age, say the authors, is: How can general education be so adapted to different ages and, above all, differing abilities and outlooks, that it can appeal deeply to each, yet remain in goal and essential teaching the same for all? Their answer is, in totality, satisfactory, but it is hesitant and never emphasizes the one key word, *interest*. Take the following phrases and sentences. Do they not add up to interest, and again, interest, and once again, interest? "For better guidance and testing are clearly a first necessity. . . . Again, the relationship of special to general education needs far more thought. . . . They must make increasing use of what appeal directly to the senses and clothe ideas with warmth — movies, singing, plays — yet never to the neglect of reading and discussion. . . . Again, since the whole rise of vocational and manual courses has come about not primarily to train young people for jobs but as a means of reaching them through what they respect and think real, the carrying over of general education into these subjects has special importance. Students whom ideas will hardly touch will yet feel them in more specific forms — mathe-

[11] PAUL H. BUCK and others, *General Education in a Free Society,* report of the Harvard Committee (Cambridge, Massachusetts: Harvard University Press, 1945).

matics when it turns up in some mechanical task, history when it touches some trade, design when it is part of making, and speech and clearness of mind running through all. Hence follows the need already expressed for devoted and broadly educated teachers of these subjects, who will teach them with these higher ends in view. . . . It has been said that one of the challenges of our age is so to rouse in students the sense of connection between ideas and day-to-day action that their wills will be enlisted for what their minds accept, and for none has this point more importance than for those who see life primarily as action. There exists no one body of knowledge, no single system of instruction equally valid for every part of it." "General education should strive to enrich society by freeing the full scope of people's native gifts."

The foregoing quotations are acceptable criteria for sound education, for sound general education. However, the Report does not carry them to a logical conclusion. It compares general education with the trunk of a tree from which branches, representing specialism, go off at different heights, at high school or junior college or college or graduate school. This is an inverted view of interest which is inherent in the child during his earliest school days and which should be nurtured at every age so that general education will adhere to it. The school may have available and the teachers have in mind a broad field of ideas that comprise general education, but the pupil will take into his mind only those ideas in which he is interested. The Report quotes Alfred North Whitehead as saying that a student should not be taught more than he can think about. Certainly he does not think about anything in which he is not interested.

The Report adopts a better figure when it speaks of general education at high school level as being like the palm of a hand, the five fingers of which are so many kinds of special interests — mathematics and science, literature and language, society and social studies, the arts, the vocations. These fingers would stretch for all beyond the common core, and all would follow one or more than one. At some point "actual work comes to take its place, for some, as a part of high school, that would be, illogically, yet a sixth finger. All then, whatever their future intentions, would have the binding experience of the common core; all would follow some field of special interest." This is putting the cart before the horse. It assumes that all are interested in the common core and therefore will work hard at it. This is exactly what does not happen. However, give each one a chance to work at his special interest and, as these special interests either clash or coalesce, the common core will emerge. This is what vocational education does. This is "enriching society by freeing the full scope of people's native gifts." [12]

THE SO-CALLED THREAT OF SPECIALIZATION. Those who decry vocational education are also those who decry specialization, repetitive work, the assembly line. Certainly the creative impulse cannot exercise itself if it is repressed, if it is allowed to languish in academic barrenness. The scholar of the future, whose interest is primarily in language and ideas, will always fare well in the academic atmosphere. And so he should because, for him, it is undoubtedly a good vocational school. One way to combat the assembly line (not the only and probably not the controlling method) is to stimulate growth of the creative impulse to the point where it will burst through the barriers of specialization. At worst, it will provide an avocation for those who have become automata in the factories.

The lament regarding the machine age is probably unrealistic both as regards the jobs and the workers. What were electrical engineers, doctors, dentists, chemists, architects, airplane pilots, auto mechanics, locomotive engineers, and nurses doing two thousand years ago? Were they not doing some repetitive, backbreaking work? Give *interest* a chance in all fields — mechanical, artistic, commercial, professional. Let interest and ability compete for the richest opportunity. Both individual and society will benefit. Never yet has it appeared that there were too few men and women to man the assembly line without violence to their creative impulses. The assembly line may dull the interests of a few, but on the other hand, it may provide jobs for the many who are not up to anything more original. We do not know much about the individual artistry and sensitivity of the factory worker. We need to know. In the meanwhile let those who fear for the outcome take cognizance of the importance of interest and of vocations in the schools so that they too do not become assembly lines turning out book-crammed students fit only for the factory.

INTEREST NOT AN AIM IN ITSELF. "Some means must be found to overcome the separation of mind and subject matter; problems of method in teaching are reduced to various ways of overcoming a gap which exists only because a radically *wrong method* had already

[12] FRANKLIN J. KELLER, "A Democratic Philosophy of American Education — The Harvard Report," *High Points,* December, 1945.

been entered upon. The doctrine of interest is not a short cut to 'methods' of this sort. On the contrary, it is a warning to furnish conditions such that the natural impulses and acquired habits, as far as they are desirable, *shall obtain subject matter and modes of skill* in order to develop to their natural ends of achievement and efficiency. Interest, the identification of mind with the material and methods of a developing activity, is the inevitable result of the presence of such situations.

"Hence it follows that little can be accomplished by setting up 'interest' as an end or a method by itself. Interest is obtained not by thinking about it and consciously aiming at it, *but by considering and aiming at the conditions* that lie back of it and compel it. If we can discover a child's urgent needs and powers, and if we can supply an environment of materials, appliances, and resources — physical, social, and intellectual — to direct their adequate operation, we shall not have to think about interest. It will take care of itself. For mind will have met with what it needs in order to *be* mind. The problem of educators, teachers, parents, the state, is to provide the environment that induces educative or developing activities, and where these are found the one thing needful in education is secured." [13]

What can do this better than vocational education as described in these pages?

[13] John Dewey, *Interest and Effort in Education, op. cit.,* p. 95.

ADDITIONAL REFERENCES

Leonard T. Troland, *The Fundamentals of Human Motivation* (New York: D. Van Nostrand, 1928).
Edward L. Thorndike, *The Psychology of Wants, Interests and Attitudes* (New York: D. Appleton-Century, 1935).

Chapter 7

REALITY: THE APPROACH TO VALID SUBJECT MATTER

SCHOOL is a succession of momentary situations in a pupil-teacher environment. These moments may be static, inert elements in haphazard and unrelated patterns that dissolve one into another like the colored pieces of glass in a kaleidoscope, or, they may be minor crises in a developing life directed by purpose. To change the figure slightly, life may be lived piecemeal and then put together as in a jigsaw puzzle, and the curriculum, supposedly reflecting life, may be put together in the same way. Or, the curriculum may be a series of way-stations on a road leading to a clearly envisioned goal. At each of these stations is enacted one dramatic situation out of which emerge fragments of knowledge, elements of skill, phases of attitude, surges of feeling, and, it is hoped, flashes of desire to push on toward the next new situation.

The "logical" curriculum is the piecemeal affair. It adds up the "subjects" until they meet the "requirements." It fits the pieces into a picture of "what should be known." The "functional" curriculum is the way of life. It is experiential in content and psychological in method. Learning is natural and vivid. It runs the danger of leaving out elements that may be encountered in some other situation, but it possesses the over-all merit of guaranteeing learning. What is learned, is really *learned*.

The vocational education curriculum is functional. It is experience, powered by interest and guided by purpose. It is true that, for practical administration, certain bodies of subject matter must, at times, be injected into the curriculum because they are "necessary" to make some other subject matter intelligible, but when this *is* necessary, it can always be motivated in terms of real, not imaginary necessity. Over reasonable stretches of time people will learn what they "ought to know," but only when frequent reference is made to a fully sensed reality.

The first sentence in this book is: "Deep down in the hearts of men and women is the desire to perpetuate themselves, both collectively and individually, in their children." What these children, adolescents, young men and women, should *know* and be able *to do* — and how they should *feel* about it — is the subject matter of vocational education.

I. WHAT DO PEOPLE WANT THE SCHOOL TO TEACH THEIR CHILDREN?

Educational aims are an expression of what people want their children to be. That is, in a democracy, they are the aims of a majority of people, or at least of people who make themselves felt in the electorate. In a totalitarian country, it is the few who dominate and determine what the schools shall teach. Then everyone must conform. In a democracy the schools teach what the majority want taught, but those who want some other kind of learning are free to give it to their children. Hence, the independent schools, both secular and sectarian.

The independent schools are excellent illustrations of the thesis that educational policies are ultimately based on conceptions of what is "good" — they are embodiments of ethical ideas. Parents who send their children to expensive private schools do so because they believe it is "good" for their children to associate with "people of their own kind," or to live away from home during the adolescent years, or to be under the influence of a noted headmaster, or to be under military discipline, or to receive daily religious instruction, or what not. These are various kinds of "good" which they do not find in the public school.

"Every statement of educational purposes, including this one, depends upon the judgment of some person or group as to what is good and what is bad, what is true and what is false, what is ugly and what is beautiful, what is valuable and what is worthless, in the conduct of human affairs. Objectives are, essentially, a statement of preferences, choices, values. These preferences are exercised, these choices made, these values arranged in a variety of ways." [1]

"Schools are expected to promote a desirable present and future family life for the children in their care. But why is this purpose given prominence? Clearly, it is emphasized because people gen-

[1] Educational Policies Commission, *The Purposes of Education in American Democracy* (Washington, D.C.: National Education Association, 1938), p. 1.

erally believe that the home and the family are wholesome institutions, capable of contributing to a good and significant life. If we thought that the home was an unimportant and worthless institution, we would not include education for home life among our educational purposes.

"This purpose of the school is frequently summarized in the phrase 'worthy home membership.' Again, what is *worthy* home membership? The objectives of the school in this area acquire concrete meaning only when that word 'worthy' is defined. The definition must be made, ultimately, upon an ethical basis. We have all known families ruled by a stern, personal, yet not unkindly autocracy. Many look with favor on this type of home membership. Others believe in a more democratic family regime. Whichever party is right, it is clear that the two types of home membership are quite different and that each would require a different education. Which of them is the worthy one? Or are they both unworthy? The answers to these questions involve a choice of values, essentially ethical or moral in nature. And that ethical choice determines the real purpose of the school in this regard." [2]

WORK AND GOODNESS. The ethical concept applies to all other phases of education. Who is the *good* citizen? Who has *good* character? What is a *good* job? Who uses his leisure time *worthily*? The anxious parent sums it up in saying, "I want my boy to have a good job and a nice family," thus passing judgment on both vocation and home membership. What does she mean? Does she want her boy to express himself through his job, to be wholly absorbed by it, to be, in essence, an artist? Or does she want him to use all his powers in serving others, to be "called" to the ministry, to medicine, to education? Or would she like him to work for the State, for the State exalted to Godhood, for the State as supreme ruler over all individuals, the Nazi ideal? Or, as is more likely, does she want him to make lots of money, do only a moderate amount of work, and be generally free to live a comfortable life outside working hours? Whatever she wants, she is evaluating the job in relation to all other life activities and, whether or not she knows it, she is evaluating vocational education.

What do people want of their jobs? The extremes are obvious. There are those whose very existence is in their work, and there are those for whom work is only a necessary and unfortunate accompaniment of life. These attitudes are expressions of individual ethics.

[2] Educational Policies Commission, *op. cit.*, p. 5.

Attitudes toward life, ethical judgments, play queer tricks with subject matter in both secondary school and college. A half century ago Veblen [3] wrote a scathing chapter on "The Higher Learning," pointing out that colleges, even high schools, can be leisure class establishments or, at least, some people can think them so. Surviving belief in the occult, reverence for form, subservience to precedent, admiration of rank, and enjoyment of ritual, all play a part in determining the subject matter in the curriculum. A knowledge of the classics, prowess in sports, and precision of speech are obvious evidences of participation in college life and therefore tend to make the college curriculum an inflexible medium of social satisfaction. True, since Veblen's day many of the colleges have become responsive to the more "worthy" aims of education and their subject matter has changed, or at least the student has a wider choice. Nevertheless, there are always reactions, notably, in recent years, the Aristotelian, "great books" curriculum of Hutchins and St. John's College, and still more recently, the tremendous drive of the G.I.'s on the colleges, under the spur of veteran support. During the war the only subjects that were "good" were those that prepared directly for action. They prepared soldiers for their jobs. After the war many veterans held to the same goal, that is, preparation for jobs — this time, of peace. However, in vast numbers, they streamed into the colleges for whatever "good" the colleges could provide.

GOODNESS AND SELF-REALIZATION. We recall, in Chapter 2, on Work: "Effort, direction, purpose — these constitute a moral code, a plan for society." Now we see that educational policies are also based upon ethical considerations. Each person, for himself, wants the kind of education that will satisfy his particular urge. The urge determines, and is reciprocally determined by, the individual's scale of values. Veblen wrote about the higher learning before Freud and Jung and Adler wrote about self-realization. Then we recall Gill's artist with his weighty sense of responsibility and Cabot's workers with their diverse ideas of what constitutes job satisfaction.

What knowledges, what skills, what attitudes will enable the individual to realize himself and at the same time serve society? What must the state provide through its educational system? What should the individual provide for himself, either through his own efforts or through independent, private schools?

[3] THORSTEIN VEBLEN, *The Theory of the Leisure Class* (New York: The Macmillan Company, 1899).

II. WHAT DO THE EDUCATORS PURPORT TO TEACH YOUNG PEOPLE?

In order to live efficiently, effectively, and happily, what should one *know,* what should one be able *to do,* how should one *feel* about these knowledges and abilities? Feelings, attitudes, are usually mentioned in any discussion of the curriculum, but feeling is such an elusive element that very little can be said about ways of instilling it. It is suggested that feeling is what makes for the alleged difference between vocational and general education. If we examined the two types from this point of view, or perhaps one should say, with a generous feeling toward both, some supposed differences may tend to disappear.

What is general, what is vocational? One proposed distinction is that everything that prepares for a specific vocation is vocational education, and everything that prepares for consumer efficiency is general education. Of course, if the two types of education are separated physically and scholastically and neither is expected to supplement the other, this may be a useful distinction. However, it is quite obvious that much general education is basic for vocational efficiency but that considerations of prestige and scholastic respectability impel people to call it general education. They deny that it is vocational but assert that no one can be successful vocationally without it. The distinction is so tenuous that, upon examination, it disappears. For instance, teachers of history and literature have been prepared for their trades by other teachers of history and literature, and these later teachers are preparing more young people for the trade of teaching history or literature, or at least for trades requiring the same skills. They claim that "common learnings" are a necessary foundation for vocations as well as for "living." Then how do they justify the delay in giving what they call vocational education? Much depends upon how you feel about history and literature. If they contribute to prestige, if they are the mark of the "educated man," that is one thing. If they are life itself, as lived by everyday men and women, then they are part of common learnings, and that is another thing.

THE ORIGIN OF SUBJECT MATTER. Subject by subject, the matter taught in public schools has been lifted out of the home. Parents hired people to teach these subjects to their children when they no longer had time or facilities or abilities to do the job themselves.

Reading, writing, and arithmetic at first constituted the entire curriculum. When printing spread knowledge of the world about them, then people not only had to read but they had to know something about the world in which they were living. People might discuss world affairs in their homes, but any real knowledge had to come from the schools. Somewhat later science became important in the lives of people, and children had to know about that too.

In the meanwhile, in a domestic economy, children learned their future occupations in and about the home or, as in apprenticeship, in somebody else's little shop and home. When the industrial revolution was well on its way, it became apparent that another function of the home was being usurped. Children would have to learn their trades on a job that was far from home or in a trade school.

So the story of subject matter in the school is not different for vocational subjects from what it is for general subjects.

At this point it should be noted and emphasized that, regardless of the extent to which these types of instruction have been taken out of the home, many homes still wield an important influence in areas where the school is supposed to dominate. For instance, "good speech" often fights a losing struggle against the poor speech which has been taught much more effectively in the home. "Worthy home membership" is, in a way, an implied condemnation of unworthy homes. However, in these days, no such unfair competition exists in the teaching of occupations, because, except for agriculture, the home just does not have it to teach. Industrialism and democracy drove vocational education out of the home into the school. What are the educators doing about all this?

EXPRESSED AIMS IN EDUCATION. These expressed aims constitute largely the history of education and of philosophy. The rest of it is subject matter, the stuff of the school, and the ways of using it (method). While this is not the place for a history of education, it is the place for noting recent formulations of objectives along with either implied or expressed opinions as to the subject matter necessary to attain those objectives.

The "Cardinal Principles of Secondary Education," issued by the Commission on the Reorganization of Secondary Education, appointed by the National Education Association in 1918, still constitute a kind of norm against which all later proposals are measured. Not that the norm itself is not riddled in the process. Ten years later the Department of Superintendence of the N.E.A. issued its yearbook on "The Development of the High School Curriculum" in which the general objectives of all education are stated as follows:

"1. To promote the development of an understanding and an adequate evaluation of the self

"2. To promote the development of an understanding and an appreciation of the world of nature

"3. To promote the development of an understanding and an appreciation of organized society

"4. To promote the development of an appreciation of the force of law and of love that is operating universally" [4]

Out of these large objectives the Yearbook culls somewhat more definite subject matter. "What can the secondary school do to help the youth to know himself? By respecting him, it may teach him to respect himself; by setting an example of righteous living, it may teach him to lead the good life; by revealing to him the great achievements of the human mind in all ages, it may help him to discover the latent powers within himself; by having sympathy with his questioning, it may cultivate in him the true spirit of inquiry; by providing opportunities for wholesome and vigorous living, it may add to his experience and make his selfhood evident through the activity."

The Yearbook goes on to stress the importance of developing health, both mental and physical; of teaching science, history, and government. Under the objective, "To promote the development of an appreciation of the force of law and of love that is operating universally," the Yearbook states: "No greater task rests upon the secondary school than to help its pupils to find their God. How this is to be done is the greatest of problems. Of one thing only are we sure: We cannot solve this problem by ignoring it. There is no single way to apprehend Infinity. Each in his own way may draw near." Two principles are stressed: to afford an opportunity for adventure and to afford an opportunity to create, and a little later on, "One fundamental principle needs to be emphasized. The activities of pupils constitute their curriculum."

Another and very different approach to the curriculum was made by Bobbitt. Instead of deducing the curriculum from general principles, he built it up from an analysis of human activity, which he then classified into: (1) language (social intercommunication),

---

[4] *The Development of the High School Curriculum*, Sixth Yearbook of the Department of Superintendence, National Education Association (Washington, D.C.: Department of Superintendence, 1928), p. 51.

132

(2) health (physical fitness), (3) citizenship, (4) general social activities (meeting and mingling), (5) spare-time activities (amusements and recreations), (6) mental fitness, (7) religion, (8) parental, (9) unspecialized or nonvocational practical activities, and (10) vocational activities.[5]

In 1938 the New York State Regents' Inquiry produced *High School and Life* by Francis T. Spaulding, who later became State Commissioner. The Educational Policies Commission of the National Education Association published *Education for ALL American Youth* in 1944, and in 1945 the New York State Education Department published a Report of a Consultative Committee entitled *Basic Issues in Secondary Education.* Comparable statements in the field of higher education brought forth Mark Van Doren's *Liberal Education,* sponsored by the Association of American Colleges in 1943. *General Education in a Free Society,* Report of the Harvard Committee, appeared in 1945 and Sidney Hook's *Education for Modern Man* appeared in 1946.[6] While, in a few paragraphs, it is impossible to make altogether valid comparisons of objectives, it is enlightening at least to note those objectives that are mentioned at all and to take into account the differences in emphasis.

COMPARATIVE STUDY OF PROPOSED SUBJECT MATTER. 1. Three of the reports on secondary education make specific provision for vocational instruction. *Basic Issues:* "The Committee is firmly convinced that the general pattern of vocational education under the federal act providing for 50% vocational training, 25% related work, and 25% general academic work is too inflexible a plan for the education of youth. The trend in many states is illustrated by California which provides that 'vocational subjects should be scheduled largely in the eleventh and twelfth grades.' With the developments that are taking place in all fields, scientific, technological, cultural, and social, as well as vocational, a rephrasing of this formula may be desirable." The Committee is clearly opposed to vocational education on the secondary level. The positive recommendations of the Report call

[5] JOHN FRANKLIN BOBBITT, *How to Make a Curriculum* (Boston: Houghton Mifflin Company, 1924), p. 7.
[6] *Regents' Inquiry* (New York: McGraw-Hill Book Co., 1938).
Education for ALL American Youth (Washington, D.C.: National Education Association, 1944).
Basic Issues in Secondary Education (Albany, New York: The University of the State of New York Press, 1945).
SIDNEY HOOK, *Education for Modern Man* (New York: Dial Press, Inc., 1946).
MARK VAN DOREN, *Liberal Education* (New York: Henry Holt and Company, 1943).

for the mandating of academic subjects to the point where it would be impossible to give adequate vocational education. *The Cardinal Principles* provides for vocational education but does not indicate how it would be made part of the regular program. *The Regents' Inquiry* states: "For every pupil who is to complete his formal education at school, each secondary school ought to provide the necessary minimum of definite preparation for a vocation." *Education for ALL American Youth* gives time to vocational education, increasing from one sixth in the tenth year to one third in the twelfth year, and provides for much intercorrelation. On the college level both the Harvard Report and *Liberal Education* discuss "specialism" and "vocationalism," but only to point out that the liberal arts can, under certain circumstances, become vocational. Neither report deals with the problem of practical vocational education on the college level. However, Hook insists that "schools and colleges must revolutionize their entire attitude toward the vocational future of their students. They must recognize the vocational future of the students as in large part the present responsibility of the educator." He emphasizes the importance of relating this vocational education to liberal education in such a way that the first will not become narrow and the second will not become futile.

2. All four of the secondary school reports agree on the seven cardinal principles, on the need for exploration and guidance and for flexibility of organization and administration. In addition, the three later reports stress the importance of science and also of the teaching of methods of analysis, "learning independently," "thinking rationally," and "independent and critical thinking." The unanimity makes all the more surprising the failure of *Basic Issues* to sense the importance of vocation.

3. It is difficult to compare the college reports, but it is fair to say that except for attitude toward vocation, they pretty well agree on aims. However, after his magnificent thesis on the task of the college, Van Doren closes his book with a eulogy on the trivium and quadrivium which is a startling *non sequitur*.

4. All the aims of predominantly academic institutions are the aims of vocational education and one naturally asks, What is the difference and why the controversy? The answer lies in spirit and method of approach and, of course, in the time and attention given to the various subjects. It also lies in nomenclature. Some high schools call any manual work "vocational," even though it is diverse and exploratory in nature and purely cultural in intent. As the Har-

vard Report says, "A general education is distinguished from special education, not by subject matter, but in terms of method and outlook, no matter what the field."

5. On the basis of this analysis, it would seem that reconciliation of so-called general and vocational education on the secondary level should be a very simple matter. Yet, practically all high schools throughout the country, except those specifically designated as vocational, do not teach vocations. Why then this sharp divergence between protestation and practice? Many answers are available but they simmer down to a few that are basic. First, traditional respect for academic subjects. This persists and will die hard, if ever. Second, and closely related, is scarcity of teachers with occupational experience. The vast majority cling to the academic subjects, the only things they know. Only as vocational teachers climb into the supervisory and administrative saddle will they be able to affect the hidebound academic curriculum. Third, lack of research results and effective public opinion to show that vocational schools have produced a high caliber of young person who is of exceedingly great use to society. Fourth, failure of the general public to understand that vocational education is not merely "training," but is a combination of practice, knowledge, and social attitudes.

6. If it can be shown that the best vocational high schools do all that is really requested by the parents and that they comply with the suggestions of the writers of these reports, then, with their parents' blessing, the students will flock to the schools where they can satisfy their craving for both a remunerative occupation and preparation for college. Vocational secondary schools, setting the highest standards, do prepare students for both occupation and entrance to college. True, the student cannot accept both of these opportunities at the same time (except where evening college courses are available), but the doors are wide open to him on both scores. He can go to college immediately and defer his wage-earning experience until after he graduates, or he can go to work and postpone the college experience until he has earned enough money to support it. In some rare instances he may be able to merge both of these desires. On the college level the objectives of both general and vocational education are being admirably met in some institutions, such as Antioch College and Bennington College.[7]

[7] ALGO D. HENDERSON, "Vocational Education in Liberal Arts Colleges"; ALVIN C. EURICH and JAMES A. McCAIN, "Programs of Vocational Colleges and Vocational Education in Universities"; in *Vocational Education,* Forty-Second Yearbook, Part I,

III. WHAT DO THE YOUNGSTERS WANT OF SCHOOL?

The youngsters want life, activity, interest. Education *is* life. We learn what we *do*. We do what *interests* us. The inescapable fact about people is their *diversity*. The depressing fact about curricula is their *uniformity*. These are the theses of preceding chapters.

When children become old enough, they do not go to school, they are sent. When they are placed in class, they do not choose what they want to do, they are usually told. If they are fortunate enough to find themselves in a good kindergarten, they play. Their interests are short-lived, fifteen minutes being a generous attention span. But differences quickly manifest themselves. One child likes this activity better than that and wants to stay at it longer than the others, and the clever teacher observes these differences and capitalizes upon them. These major interests often become absorbing. Watch this little girl playing house, almost literally for hours at a time. Look at that little boy constructing a mechanical toy, creating for the time being a world of his own. Such activities take on some of the aspects of "work." At a little later stage some children pore over books with all the tenacity of real scholars. Here and there a child "loves arithmetic." At home some "play school." Boys collect stamps, construct radios, fly pigeons, sail boats.

These are the things that youngsters want to do. Different youngsters want to do different things. They do not care where they do them. School would be a nice place if it provided the facilities and there were sympathetic grownups to help them on their way. As a matter of fact, children like people who suggest new activities, open up interests never before realized, propose long-range purposes for the time "when I am grown up." So, the school that capitalizes upon what the youngsters want in order to teach them what the world needs of them, that is to say, the job of living and working in a complex environment, is on the way to selecting useful subject matter and providing sound education. Of course, "what the world needs" is of utmost importance. So, let us look at the social scene.

IV. THE SOCIAL SCENE

What parents want, what educators want, and what youngsters themselves want, when added up, may still not constitute sound edu-

National Society for the Study of Education (Chicago: University of Chicago Press, 1943).

cation, for educational policies are ultimately based on conceptions of what is "good." There may be a still higher "good." It is difficult to say whose judgment it should be, for no matter how "high," it has to be expressed by a human being. However all this may be, the ethical judgments of parents, educators, and students must be sharply tempered by a realization of the kind of world in which they live. "This changing world" has been a favorite phrase. The world has always been changing. Perhaps the change is now relatively more rapid, even startling. It is recognized by all as being technological.

THE TECHNOLOGICAL AGE AND THE "BUTTON-PUSHER." Response to the incursions of technology is, again, ethical. One person says, "Technology is doing marvels for civilization. It brings more and better goods to more and poorer people. Education should train people for participation in this accelerated production. Let us train engineers, technicians, and operatives to provide us with a better life. There is no limit to consumption and whatever time is left over for play will be used wisely by well-fed, well-clothed, well-housed people. Technology is good."

The next person comes along and exclaims, "Aha, you would plunge the world into an orgy of making *things*. People will be corrupted by their possessions. Technology will take care of itself. People will learn on the job. Teach people how to *live,* to use their leisure time wisely. Stress the humanities. The humanities are good."

Incidentally, those who fear the effects of too great stress upon vocational education, always speak of "narrow vocational training" or "narrow specialization." As a matter of fact, "narrow vocational training" is of the rarest occurrence among adolescents in a full-time school. Such training is almost always reserved for those who have received all the general education that they will take, and are usually adults. Again, while "narrow specialization" is used as a criticism of vocational education, "broad generalization" might very well be used much more effectively and justly of such general education as is pointless, purposeless, and unsusceptible of evaluation.

As has already been shown, skill and theory are only two of a long series of "learnings" that, over the centuries, have moved from the home into the school. After moving in, certain constellations of skills have been backed up with so much theory and dignified with so much prestige that they have become professions. The most striking example is the nurse who, in the time of Florence Nightingale ranked with the charwoman, but is now on the level with the college graduate. Homemaking itself has become specialized and — dignified. Agriculture has become scientific. Most of the deck and engineer officers operating merchant vessels today learned to do so on the job. They came up "through the hawse hole." They took successive government examinations leading ultimately to a license as master or chief engineer, but they learned on their own. However, a few skippers and engineers received their first training in a State Maritime Academy, and now, in the United States Maritime Academy at Kings Point, New York, and the New York State Maritime Academy at Fort Schuyler, young men are learning to operate ships in four-year college courses leading to the degree of bachelor of marine science. Those skills and knowledges that, a few years ago, they would have "picked up," "learned the hard way," they now acquire as a profession. This may constitute a trend. In any case, skills and knowledges that, at one time, existed only in the muscles and the heads of nurses and ships' officers are now written down as subject matter in college courses.

It is a great temptation to adopt extreme views on the effects of technological changes, either to assume that the world will become a maze of push buttons and nobody will need to know anything any more except which button to push, or, that the world will be so full of complicated machinery and abstruse science that everybody will have to know everything. Both positions are manifestly absurd yet they are not far removed from those held by some otherwise responsible men. We are here concerned with the skills and knowledges that young people will have to acquire in order to live, the subject matter they will have to learn. The whole problem bristles with difficulties and no adequate research has yet been attempted. The best we can do is to examine the data on trends, to draw from the most authentic reports and opinions, and then to lay a reasonable course for a curriculum. Corresponding to the two extreme opinions are two educational proposals: (1) If, for the most part, jobs are drab and uninteresting, then teach the liberal arts to brighten and humanize the lives of the workers. (2) If these jobs are really not drab at all, then teach the worker to realize how much humanity there is in every job and, of course, teach him the job itself.

THE TRENDS. Always remembering that there are all kinds of people in the world and that their reactions to work and leisure and politics and poetry and science and religion differ as night from day, we can, with a great deal of profit note the available evidence in business and industry and agriculture and home as to the changes of skills and knowledges that determine modern living.

1. Most striking are the changes in the major occupational fields. Between 1870 and 1930 the number of workers employed in agriculture declined from 53 to 21.4%. Forestry and fishing, extraction of minerals, and domestic and personal service remained almost static, but manufacturing and mechanical industries increased from 20.5 to 28.9%, transportation and communication from 4.2 to 7.9%, trade from 6.8 to 12.5%, public service from .7 to 1.8%, professional service from 2.6 to 6.7% and clerical occupations from .6 to 8.2%. In other words, all the striking increases were at the expense of agriculture.[8]

2. From 1910 to 1940 the number of professional workers increased from 4.4 to 6.5%, clerks and kindred workers from 10.2 to 17.2%, and semiskilled workers from 14.7 to 21%. The percentage of skilled workers remained exactly the same, 11.7%, while proprietors, managers, and officials decreased from 23 to 17.8%, and unskilled workers from 36 to 25.9%.[9] Notable among these figures is the fact that the percentage of skilled workers and foremen did not decrease and that the number of semiskilled workers increased apparently at the expense of unskilled workers. Or, putting it another way, nearly one quarter of the unskilled workers moved up into the group of semiskilled workers. The Census report notes that "the 'unskilled workers' form a particularly significant social-economic group. Although the group has been changing in size more rapidly than any other group, and fortunately, has been decreasing, it nevertheless was considerably the largest of the social-economic groups in 1940, when it included more than one in four of all workers. . . . The professional class will grow in relative importance. . . . Farmers will decrease and other proprietors will increase in relative importance. . . . Clerks and kindred workers may continue to increase in relative importance. . . . Skilled workers probably will decrease in relative importance after the war. What is a skilled occupation today may become, with the introduction of a new invention or a new process, a semiskilled occupation tomorrow. . . . Semiskilled workers will become the largest group. These statistics suggest that with the probable further mechanization of industry a larger and larger proportion of manual workers will become machine operators — that the semiskilled group will draw somewhat from the

[8] United States Bureau of the Census, *Population: Comparative Occupation Statistics* (Washington, D.C.: Government Printing Office, 1943), p. 101.
[9] United States Bureau of the Census, *op. cit.,* p. 187.

skilled group above and largely from the unskilled group below. The manual workers of the future probably will be concentrated more and more in a great middle class of semiskilled workers. Indeed, the semiskilled group probably will rapidly become the largest group in the nation's labor force. . . . Unskilled workers will continue to decrease in relative importance." [10]

3. It must be remembered that technological changes are not solely a twentieth century phenomenon. Particularly at the turn of the nineteenth century economic distress began to stir up the English nation, especially in the textile industry. Arguments pro and con at that time closely parallel those of more recent date.[11] It is therefore significant that, in the early part of the twentieth century, when technology was stepping up its pace, the problem was examined anew. Particularly enlightening are the studies of an economist and two educators. Stuart Chase, a prominent writer in the field of economics, states:

"From the mass of evidence, often conflicting, often incompletely documented, certain conclusions nevertheless emerge.

"First. The initial effect of the machine age was to hurt the worker physically and mentally. It killed him, maimed him, infected, poisoned, and above all, bored him, as perhaps no other culture has ever done. This effect still obtains in altogether too many areas, particularly in countries which are just developing the factory system, and in backward regions of highly mechanized nations — say sections of the industrial South, in the United States.

"Second. By and large during the past generation, the health of the industrial worker has been improving. He is living longer, suffering less from sickness, working shorter hours, sharing more in the comforts of civilized life. Since 1920, in the United States, the accident rate has risen, but the phenomenon is perhaps temporary.

"Third. The percentage of those engaged in monotonous competitive machine work relative to the total population is small, and judging by factory employment figures in the United States, steadily growing smaller. At the present time not more than five per cent of all persons are so engaged. Greece in her great days had 5,000,000 freemen standing on the backs of 12,000,000 slaves. I dare you to conclude that a population 70% slave is a more wholesome combination than one possibly 5% slave to the machine.

10 United States Bureau of the Census, *op. cit.,* p. 180 ff.
11 DOUGLAS, HITCHCOCK, and ATKINS, *The Worker in Modern Economic Society* (Chicago: University of Chicago Press, 1923), p. 108 ff.

"Fourth. Of the five million or so persons in this group an unknown total, possibly the majority, do not object to the character of their work, however strenuous may be their objection to rates of pay. Physiologically it does not appear to harm them, and psychologically they are glad to be relieved from all sense of responsibility. The question remains, however, whether industry is not guilty of deliberately conditioning them to a status lower than that which they are capable of achieving. Might they not be saved from their own stolidity and made into free, thinking — and suffering — citizens?

"Fifth. The remainder of the group who do not readily adjust to the repetitive regime constitute a major industrial tragedy. Unwilling robots, they are crucified in a ghastly and relentless process. No stone should be left unturned in setting up proper psychological tests to prevent them from ever entering the treadmill.

"Sixth. Meanwhile two agencies are at work to lift the burden from both processes. Automatic machinery displaces the robot and replaces him with a skilled man. The 'philosophy of fatigue' is beginning the long-awaited task of adjusting the job to the physiological imperatives of the worker. Both have far to go.

"Seventh. Finally we should remember that unskilled labor and premachine civilization was frequently dull, hard, debasing work. Consider the Pyramid builders, the galley slaves, the hewers of wood and drawers of water. The machine comes to save us much of this grinding toil. Insofar as it is successful — and it has made an impressive beginning — it lifts the load of monotony from that group, and reduces the necessity for gorillas or robots in the whole social structure." [12]

Prosser and Allen are even more optimistic:

"First. The work performed by each individual has become more and more important and in sufficient performance correspondingly so.

"Second. The shift is away from mediocre performance of most jobs to the highest possible efficiency in every job.

"Third. The modern demand upon every worker in every occupation is for specific efficiency in a specific occupation.

"Fourth. The shift in this demand for specific efficiency in the performance of all work is, in general, away from purely mechanical to technical demand.

[12] From STUART CHASE, *Men and Machines,* p. 166 ff. By permission of The Macmillan Company, publishers (1929).

"Fifth. The shift is away from manual dexterity and skill toward the exercise of specific job intelligence in the specific occupation.

"Sixth. The shift is away from a training content for a few jobs to a specific training content for every job.

"Seventh. This specific training content, whether it be small or large for different occupations, is vital to the specific efficiency of any modern worker in any specific occupation.

"Eighth. The specific training content may be given in various ways, but whatever scheme is employed constitutes vocational education." [13]

4. In 1940 the Temporary National Economic Committee of the Seventy-sixth Congress conducted an "investigation of concentration of economic power" and explored the likelihood of the development of new industries to take up the slack caused by technological and economic changes.[14] The fields of investigation were photosynthesis, atomic power, long-range weather forecasting, synthetic materials, chemical cures of disease, genetics, human relations, and mobilization of scientific knowledge. The Committee concluded that further developments in these fields would undoubtedly greatly benefit mankind but that it was unlikely that a great employment-creating industry would emerge from any one of them in the near future. Neither did it feel that much additional employment would be created by the development of any of the four promising specific new industries — pre-fabricated housing, air conditioning, television, or diesel engines. However, what the Committee did not find out was that these are all industries requiring the highest excellence of engineering and scientific ability and that while they might not create additional employment, they might tend to stimulate that movement of workers out of the unskilled group into the semiskilled and possibly into the skilled and professional. In 1927 the National Resources Committee painted a fascinating picture of the effect of technological changes upon the social economy, without, however, specifically indicating the effect upon the subject matter of education. The implications are nevertheless clear. Whatever the number of persons employed in the industries affected or whatever the character of their jobs, the total amount of scientific knowledge and corresponding

[13] CHARLES A. PROSSER and CHARLES R. ALLEN, *Vocational Education in a Democracy* (New York: The Century Co., 1925), p. 80.
[14] Temporary National Economic Committee, *Technology in Our Economy*, Monograph No. 22 (Washington, D.C.: Government Printing Office, 1941), p. 185.

skill necessary to carry on these industries will be tremendous. They can only be reflected in the subject matter of the schools.[15]

5. In World War II training for all the army services became a major operation. Never before had so many men been prepared for specific jobs, most of them not of a strictly combat nature. Transportation and communication were exceedingly important and the techniques were very little different from those of peace. In the emergency training had to be intensive and quick, and it was, of course, essentially *training*. In addition, both soldiers and sailors were given the opportunity to take specific theory courses or general education courses through correspondence with the Armed Forces Institute. Men at war, a highly technical war, needed both training and education.

6. The increasing importance of technology must, of course, be considered along with the rise in demand for professional services and the increase in number of those engaged in such services. Among the sciences is that of human relations, to which increasing attention must necessarily be given wherever there is personal contact between professional man and client, seller and buyer, employer and employee.

7. Even on the trade level there is demand for more and more science and scientific understanding. The radio repair man is finding himself in greater and greater difficulties insofar as he operates by rule of thumb and not by a knowledge of electronics. Television will make occupational life hard for him unless he is willing to become a student. The introduction of automatic controls is often cited as an instance of lessening demand for skill on the part of those who operate machines. However, this point of view often turns out to be quite fallacious. For instance, these automatic controls are being used more and more on steamships, easing the daily burden of the engineer. On the other hand, these very automatic controls, usually based upon electronic and thermodynamic principles, make it necessary for the engineer to know ever so much more than he did before, because an automatic control is only automatic so long as it works. If it breaks down (and all machinery suffers from fatigue and abuse), then the engineer must know how to repair it, or get along without it. In all fields served by machinery this same problem arises. Less manual labor perhaps but more and more understanding, alertness, and flexibility. All this is subject matter to be learned.

[15] National Resources Committee, *Technological Trends and National Policies* (Washington, D.C.: Government Printing Office, 1937).

8. There is little evidence to indicate to what extent persons doing repetitive work are unhappy — or happy. If they do not complain about monotony, it is fair to assume, and to a considerable extent we know it to be true, that they would not be capable of more highly skilled work and certainly would not be happy while doing it. In many cases it is quite likely that, if they were not employed on repetitive, unskilled, or semiskilled jobs, they would not be employed at all. Of course, if such an assumption is correct, then no "subject matter" of job skills and knowledges can exist. However, human relations, safety precautions, care of physique, and a certain amount of paternalism may very well become functioning subject matter.

9. Whatever else may be said about specialization, it certainly does make necessary many highly skilled workers to design, build, and maintain the machines of specialization. The skills and knowledges necessary for these purposes constitute a vast body of techniques and information to be passed along to workers.

EDUCATIONAL IMPLICATIONS OF SOCIAL CHANGE. 1. All the evidence points to one inescapable conclusion: We know very little about the specific effects of technological change and we can predict less. The most we can say is that it causes some dislocation. Many individuals must change their jobs, must learn new skills, must acquire new knowledge, but, in totality, how many are seriously and permanently disadvantaged, we do not know. Here is a field for extensive and continuing research.

2. In any case, the drive toward technological improvement goes on. If man is curious enough to split the atom, then he will split it even though it culminates in an atomic bomb. It is safe to say that this everlasting curiosity will not abate. The only remedy is still more curiosity about the effects of technology upon man and, of course, a driving desire to dedicate all discovery to man and his own improvement.

3. Preparation for this kind of world is a major operation. It cannot be a product solely of the schools. It must draw its substance from economic life and it can only be successful with the support and cooperation of those who are responsible for the work of the world. Subject matter must derive from the source that will later be replenished by the product of the schools.

4. A consideration of the work to be done in this world precludes any acceptance of the idea that secondary schools or colleges should

devote most of their time to preparing young people for worthy use of leisure, teaching them how to play, just play. In the best sense of the word "play" — work with a purpose — yes. Teach them primarily to work, and wholesome play will follow. Teach the skills and knowledges required by vocation — the things one has to do to live comfortably and in relation to his fellow men. That is something that arises out of a sense of reality.

5. Whatever jobs there are to be done, it is fitting that they should be done by those best able to do them. At the same time, all those who are willing and able to work for their own support and, wherever possible, to work because they have a vocation, must be permitted and encouraged to work. And they must be trained for work. It is not conceivable that any American boys or girls should be allowed to drift into economic life without being prepared to bear their own weight. This applies to those of high and low intelligence, excellent and poor physique, and of any economic standing whatsoever. Moreover, when they are prepared, society must offer them jobs. This is democracy, and of democracy and vocational education we shall speak in the next chapter.

V. THE TIME FETISH

If, as has been pointed out, school is a succession of momentary situations in a pupil-teacher environment, those moments add up to time, and time, for human beings, is finite. Limitations of energy, attention span, family and social obligations, and the basic twenty-four hour limit to the day, all make time a factor in presenting subject matter. So many subjects to be taught, so many hours to teach them, and it becomes necessary to make allotments, five periods of this, three periods of that, for so many years. Despite all the differences in individuals, in teachers, in the subjects themselves, five periods a week for a year count as one point for everybody.

Despite the convenience, the practicality, and perhaps the inevitability of a system of accreditation based on time, there seems no reason for failing to modify or at least to supplement it with a more rational type of evaluation. In fact, this has often been done. The Pennsylvania Study [16] not only proved that some college freshmen may know as much about a particular subject as some seniors, but

[16] Learned and Wood, *The Student and His Knowledge* (New York: The Carnegie Foundation for the Advancement of Teaching, 1938).

also indicated how to take such differences into account and thus to make education more meaningful to the student. At this point we can only point out the importance of the time factor for subject matter that belongs primarily in a vocational curriculum. It should also be noted that the educational development tests of the Armed Forces Institute have made it clearly evident that young people may grow intellectually while they are out of school and may have learned just as much from normal contacts with life as they would have learned in school, or even in spite of school. Assuming the validity of the tests, the fact that so many boys, with only one or two years of high school education, returned from the war to score as well on these tests as the vast majority of high school graduates scored, is something to give us pause.

What is the purpose of time prescription for secondary and college subjects? Why are so many subjects and so many units mandated? The obvious answer is that such and such a subject is necessary to make a competent citizen, or that no educated person can afford to be graduated without having studied a particular subject, or that, to become a competent worker, a pupil must have so many hours at a particular machine. It is all in the interest of the pupil. However, there is clearly another factor. Time prescriptions are set up as bulwarks against incursions of the enemy. If the consultative committee of the State Education Department insists on nine credits in academic subjects, then the vocational people will not be able to jeopardize the lives of young boys and girls by giving them too much shop work. On the other hand, if the Smith-Hughes Law mandates 50% of shop work, then the academic people cannot spoil a good workman by giving him too much English or social studies or what not. There is no doubt that these bulwarks have been necessary, assuming a correct moral judgment on the part of those who decide that one subject is more desirable than another. So this is all done in good faith and in good conscience, but where does it leave the pupil?

Knowledge has been gained when it can be reproduced or appropriate action can be taken on the basis of that knowledge. A skill has been learned when it can be performed. Measures of the acquisition of knowledge or of skill in performance have long been available, and certainly objective tests should be used periodically in determining the future program of a student. Learning subject matter is not solely a matter of time exposure.

There is another aspect. In recent years much stress has been laid

upon the importance of adding or lengthening general subjects in
vocational schools. As will be made amply clear, these subjects are
all important. However, there is grave question as to the length of
time an educational institution should take to teach a subject. If
the high school teacher complains that his admissions from lower
schools do not know anything about arithmetic and "I must stop
my regular work and teach them to add and subtract and multiply
and divide," he is saying that after eight or nine years the schools
have not been able to teach simple numerical operations and that
the only way to correct the situation is to start all over again. The
same applies to English and history and geography. The child does
not know arithmetic because either he is mentally incapable of grasping the subject at all, or he has not been interested. If the former,
the school ought to quit. If the latter, then it is about time to
interest him in arithmetic, preferably by presenting vocational problems that require its use. Time is a condition of growth, both mental
and physical, growth of interest and purpose as well as of mind and
body. However, some individuals learn everything, or so it seems,
in no time at all, while others learn nothing in all the time there is.
So time should be used for *growth,* and then only as a kind of norm
against which to plot the individual differences of pupils. Time
sinks into insignificance in a student-planned curriculum, where
traditions and proprietary interests do not operate. Moreover, in
that kind of institution, subjects are mandated not in terms of time,
but in terms of objective accomplishment. Each student's program
is built around individual needs, and the school program is built
around the individual programs.

SPECIFIC LEARNINGS. How long does it take to learn
- (a) to be healthy?
- (b) to talk, read, write, figure?
- (c) to be a worthy home member?
- (d) to use leisure worthily?
- (e) to acquire an ethical character?
- (f) history and geography?
- (g) science?
- (h) to think?

Certainly, no one can answer these questions in terms of minutes,
hours, and days. Translating the aims implied in these questions
into classroom, laboratory, workshop, or seminar procedures, that
is to say to make a curriculum, is the most delicate of tasks and no

school with a normally constituted faculty can be entirely free from pedantry, not even a vocational school.

We know that subject matter — *pieces of knowledge* — put down on paper, gets over to any one individual according to:

    (a) the individual (interest)
    (b) other individuals in the group
    (c) the teacher

Skills get over to an individual according to:
    (a) the individual (interest and muscular coordination)
    (b) tools and equipment

These factors provide innumerable permutations which cannot be served by a rigid curriculum. One answer is to set up objective standards in all subject matter, general and vocational, and to "promote" when these have been met. Vocational subject matter lends itself much more readily to this treatment than does academic, and a sound vocational program makes full use of it. It works.

It works on any level. In criticism of the Hutchins-Adler-Barr school of educational thought, Hook says: "Let us borrow a metaphor from Plato and Aristotle to make this clear. They often compare goodness of the soul, which the educator aims to develop, with the health of the body, which the physician aims to help us to achieve. Now the elements of health are the same for everybody. We can indicate the conditions which must be satisfied before any individual can be declared healthy. That is to say, the formal criterion or definition of health is the same for everybody — namely, certain optimum levels of physical and mental activity. But would a scientific physician prescribe the *same* regimen, the *same* diet, the *same* medication for *all* individuals independently of their history, their constitution, and their specific deficiencies? Such procedure is an unfailing sign of a quack. Similarly, it is a kind of educational quackery to demand that, because the elements of a good education in a democracy should be the same for everyone, everyone should get it in the *same* way, by the *same* courses, in the *same* time and order, independently of differences in aptitude, interests, and past educational experience. One would imagine, in view of these differences in personality and background, that identical methods and curriculums are hardly likely to lead to identical results, and that the more uniform we wish the educational achievement of students to be, the more varied and flexible our methods and curriculums must be without denying the likelihood that they will exhibit certain constant features." [17]

VI. ELEMENTS OF A SOUND VOCATIONAL PROGRAM — FOR ANYBODY

Somehow or other most people learn to earn and to live. Too many of them have just jobs, not vocations. In light of the foregoing discussion, devising a curriculum that would prepare for a livelihood and at the same time make all of life worth living should not be too difficult a task. Only a few schools in either category, academic or vocational, match up with the criteria. What are these criteria? What should the curriculum provide?

1. Elementary skills in communication. Speaking, reading, writing — skills that are necessary for any kind of living with people, at home, in company, at work.

2. Health. The promotion of good health should be largely a family matter and, on the upper economic levels, is. However, so long as society cannot guarantee economic support for privately purchased health service, it must do so through public agencies, preferably through the school in cooperation with the local Board of Health.

3. Interests. This may mean much or little, depending on the school. The traditional school "makes" the traditional subjects "interesting." The newer school provides for all kinds of interests, interests that may be passing or abiding, hobbies or vocations. To the extent that both kinds of interests are served, both types of education are furthered. However, it is all-important that these interests be genuine, realistic, and humanistic.

4. Training in specific vocational skills. This training provides for all skills that are useful in pursuing an occupation — machine shop practice for the machinist, art for the artist, music for the professional musician, radio for the radio repairman, sports for the professional player or coach, sewing for the dressmaker, typing for the typist, architecture for the architect, law for the lawyer, medicine for the doctor, theology for the minister, and so on. And, of course, whatever manual skill or occupational theory is not used for the purpose of earning a living, may be turned to account for better consumption or more enjoyable play.

[17] SIDNEY HOOK, *Education for Modern Man* (New York: Dial Press, Inc., 1946), p. 141.

5. *Training in study, execution, analysis, and the like.* Any attempted general training for application to all situations is of doubtful validity but insofar as such training is specific it can be useful, whether for vocation or hobby.

6. *Vocational guidance.* This is a feature of all good education, whether general or vocational.

7. *Social relationships.* Such relationships are as important at work as they are at play or in the home. For work they must be taught realistically and under work conditions.

8. *Work experience.* Under any auspices work experience must be real experience. When it is made available in school, it must be on real jobs, whether they are classified as auto repair in a trade school or orthodontia in a dental school. It must be strongly motivated. It must be activity with a purpose.

9. Wherever education takes place, *interest must be present* and activity must eventuate, not only in skill but in knowledge and understanding. If preparation for a vocation is the aim, it must still be human.

10. *Wisdom and sincerity must be in the teacher.* The vocational teacher must know a great deal about human relationships, and the academic teacher must know something about occupational techniques.

VII. THE VOCATIONAL CURRICULUM

We have traveled a long and seemingly circuitous route to arrive at a determination of the substance of each of these momentary situations, in a pupil-teacher environment, that we call school. We have looked at work and life and have traced the developing thought of educational philosophers who have also looked at work and life from our point of view. We have considered each potential student as a personality with motivating interests and a susceptibility for learning. We have glanced at the parents' desires, the educators' aims, and the youngsters' demands. Now, after a brief comparative study of curricula usually designated as academic or as vocational, we come to our conception of a vocational education program, whether it be designated as academic, liberal arts, vocational, technical, or what not, so long as it gives full consideration to the vocational career of the student, in all its ramifications, as well as to his other relationships with people. What should be the content of such a curriculum?

PROVISION OF VARIED FIELDS OF INTEREST FOR CONTINUED TRYOUT. Under diverse names and with differently expressed explanations, this element has appeared in many curricula. Core curriculum, activity program, industrial arts, occupational information, fields of interests, work experience, and many others, have all had, as one of their reasons for being, the presentation of life situations in which the pupil may explore his interests. Exploration, discovery, finding oneself, these have been the key purposes.

Practical arts is a generic term which includes what is better known as industrial arts. It also covers a large part of the field of vocations, but does so for general cultural and for exploratory purposes. For instance, school gardening and garden club activities in a junior high school give the pupil some idea — very elementary, of course — of agriculture. An elementary business course, a general home economics course, or diversified manual activity in a shop, does the same for business, the home, or industry. There has always been question as to the validity of interest based upon such imperfect replicas of actual occupational conditions, but in principle, and perhaps often in practice, there is educational soundness in the plan. At least, it goes further, much further, than traditional academic education that ignores the basic interests of the child.[18]

In teachers' colleges, general colleges, and universities there are practical arts courses that play a similar role, with emphasis, perhaps, on culture rather than on exploration. The making of fine furniture and of art metal work are examples. In junior high schools exploratory and tryout courses are common practice. They often fall far short of their aim, but they must, even at their poorest, excite some curiosity as to what lies in the occupational world beyond. In vocational high schools practice varies. Perhaps most schools expect their new pupils to have made valid choices. However, many general vocational high schools and some special schools have a ninth or tenth year tryout for further orientation.

On both the secondary school and the college level the work experience program has been in growing favor, especially when it is conducted on the cooperative basis. Again, necessarily restricted because of lack of opportunity for *all* kinds of experience, the program has nevertheless provided opportunity for sparks of interest to burst into flame and for young people to find themselves amid a

[18] F. THEODORE STRUCK, *Vocational Education for a Changing World* (New York: John Wiley & Sons, 1945), Ch. II.

baffling variety of callings. The best known examples are Antioch
College and Bennington College.[19]

In Fieldston School, the high school of the Ethical Culture Society,
students are given opportunity to study in special fields of interest,
to explore occupational possibilities, and to visit institutions where
these occupations are carried on. Since the group is of generally
high intelligence and of college caliber, interests are usually directed
toward the professions. For instance, science is one of the fields and
the occupations range from physician to laboratory technician.

For effectiveness of learning we know that activity, real participation, ranks highest. Then comes observation, and lowest in the
scale — books. So, work experience, even when limited, is the best
means of orientation. Visits to industry or business are of lesser
value, but still effective. The acquisition of occupational information
through classroom teaching is least valuable, but, because of the almost infinite variety of occupations in the world, and the restricted
area in which any individual can move for experience and observation, the teaching of occupational information remains an exceedingly important phase of the orientation procedure, especially when
enlivened by all the arts of the good teacher. On every level occupational information courses find an important place. In the junior
high school they are called just that. In the academic and vocational
high school the information may be taught in similar classes, but
much of it also comes through related instruction classes, home room
classes, and classes in social studies. In the colleges classes in economics and sociology provide orientation.[20]

Finally, the young person is helped to discover his interests through
opportunity to try himself out in a wide variety of courses offered
by an institution or even in different institutions. True, such "shop-
ping" finds disfavor among most administrators and, when aimless,
undoubtedly deserves such opinion. However, when unwarranted
freedom becomes "guidance" and free electives become "flexibility
of curriculum," then untold benefits may be conferred upon the
student. In other words, no curriculum worthy of educational respect is unaccompanied by an orientation program for the individual.

Education is life and the educational institution that fails to bring
life to the young person who is preparing for it, fails of its mission.
Tryout, orientation, exploration, all the terms used in the last few

paragraphs, are attempts to express this idea of life-knowing. For vocational education it is basic.

THE GUIDANCE PROGRAM. For the most part, guidance is an operational procedure rather than a part of the curriculum. Except for group teaching in occupational information and industrial arts, it is essentially individual counseling. It has been described in detail in the chapter on Primacy of the Person. However, it is listed here under the curriculum because the curriculum is meaningless without it.

LEARNING SKILLS. When a foreman hires a machinist, when a patient consults a physician, when an editor engages a writer, when a producer casts an actor, when a young man asks a girl to take charge of his home, he wants to know not what the prospective worker *knows,* but primarily what he or she can *do.* Knowing is important, and we shall speak of it presently, but inability to translate knowing into action is futility insofar as relations with other people are concerned. However acquired or however accompanied by wisdom, there must be skill.

Vocational education bases its program on the teaching of skills, skills for earning a living, skills for enjoying living, skills for serving other people so that they may enjoy living. These skills are as varied as is human capacity for learning them — plowing, cutting, decorating, operating, designing, serving, arguing, writing, singing, playing musical instruments, digging, and composing. Learning a skill is coordinating eye, ear, senses, muscles. Skills are learned by doing, by doing with material, under conditions as nearly like those of actual life as possible. In fact, skills are best learned on the job under close supervision. However, for obvious reasons, such conditions cannot often be created. Therefore skills must usually be learned in a school shop or laboratory or on a demonstration project or in a seminar or clinic. When a person is graduated from a vocational education program, he is able to exercise skills the products of which other people are anxious to buy. Whatever other differences there may be between what is usually known as academic education and as vocational education, this one is basic.

THEORY, KNOWLEDGE, WISDOM. A simple skill may be learned by observation and repetition, driving home a nail, let us say. As long as the conditions remain exactly the same, size and composition of material in nail, size and kind of hammer, size and character of wood into which the nail is driven, the worker can keep on driving nails perfectly forever, without *knowing* anything. However, change one element, the hardness of the wood, say, and, unless he *knows* what effect hardness of material has upon type of nail or kind of hammer or force that must be used, he is lost. In other words, the teaching of skills must be accompanied by explanations, reasons, knowledge, that will enable the worker to change his mode of operation whenever conditions change, however slightly. He must know the "why" of the "how." This is related science, or just science. It is theory, knowledge. As subject matter it may have many names — mathematics, biology, chemistry, physics, anatomy, theology, law, sociology, history. For a justice of the Supreme Court related theory constitutes the wisdom of the world. Whatever it is called, it is the stuff of thinking. Each fact is the tool of mind rather than of hand. It may be necessary for measuring a two-inch piece of steel or for calculating the distance of a star. It may assist in recognizing a kind of lumber or in determining the structure of the atom. It may be essential to trouble-shooting on an automobile or to diagnosis of a rare disease.

HUMANITY AND THE HUMANITIES. Parents want their children to be "good" boys and "good" girls. They want these children to act decently toward other people. However they phrase it, they want their offspring to establish good human relations. The employer wants his employees to be congenial with each other. He knows that personal friction reduces production, increases the number of separations, and gives rise to labor trouble. The patient looks to his physician for kindliness, understanding, and sympathy, as well as for medicine. In fact, any doctor knows that a word of assurance is often worth much more than a pill. Good human relations are nothing new in the world but their recognition as an essential phase of sound education, in all its aspects, is comparatively recent. As a specific goal, they relate themselves neatly to the teaching of skills and their application to real occupational situations. A sound program of education not only stresses these relations as they arise in connection with the teaching of skills and theory, but makes them explicit in lessons on personality set up either as a separate course or as units in the home room program.

Deriving its name from the same source, "the humanities" have come to mean something quite different from essential "humanity."

"The humanities are the branches of polite learning regarded as primarily conducive to culture, especially the ancient classics and belles-lettres." These are the stories of human beings in other days. They may be, and often have been, of deep human contemporary concern. Insofar as they represent human thinking and feeling in recurrent and timeless situations, they are effective education. As with any other products of the human mind, they deserve study. However, their real worth for any single individual depends upon his own personality, his interests, his intelligence, his environment, and the teacher who presents the material. All these factors have been or will be discussed. Vocational education embraces humanity and the humanities as ardently as traditional academic education, but it insists that humanity and the humanities must be genuinely human, very real, and warmly intimate.

Sound vocational education sets up no rigid mandates as to the relation of every item of knowledge to a vocational skill. Science and the humanities may be taught piece by piece in such relationship or as separate subjects named "physics" or "history," or in "integrated" courses, according to the exigencies of the school program. However, it does insist that this knowledge be meaningful and that "meaning" is a function of interest, background, and *doing*. However and wherever this relationship is firmly established, sound education is taking place.

General skills are frequently vocational skills. The elementary skills of communication — speaking, reading, writing — are fundamental to success in many vocational fields. In fact, efficiency in communication often decides the occupational level of the worker. Effective guidance helps the individual to find this level. When choice of vocation and training for that vocation become an issue, proficiency in these arts of communication is well established. Where further development seems possible, it is motivated by the prospect of a desirable career and is upgraded by special work in remedial English and speech. Vocational education is deeply concerned with "good English."

ESTHETICS. This is a streamlined age. True, there is plenty of ugliness in the world, but the impulse is to make it beautiful. Automobiles, trains, ships, houses, furniture, books, and, of course, all kinds of apparel, are being treated for line and color. The radio is demanding beauty in speech. Art is applied, seemingly, to everything. Vocational education must necessarily be concerned with art and young workers must be taught not only to appreciate, but to apply it. Beauty enriches life.

HEALTH AND PHYSIQUE. If a sound mind in a sound body is necessary for general living, it is certainly essential for occupational efficiency. Vocational education is deeply concerned with the physical welfare of every future worker. A whole chapter will be devoted to this topic.

"TEACH HIM TO THINK." How often this injunction has been laid upon the schools! It is often considered the special province of the academic school. Thinkers and doers have been placed in separate categories. However, we hold that occupational education provides a superior motivation and implementation for real thinking, as will be shown in the chapter on Intelligence.

TEACHERS AND METHODS. We return again to our picture of school as a succession of momentary situations in a pupil-teacher environment. Subject matter is just the stuff that is tossed around. It can be meaningful and useful only if there is pupil-interest, teacher-effectiveness, and expert methodology. A chapter will be devoted to each.

Chapter 8

DEMOCRACY IN EDUCATION

PROBABLY the most familiar recent phenomenon in American education is the mushroom growth of secondary school enrollment during the twentieth century. As already noted in the chapter on Size and Quality of the Problem, in 1890 only seven out of every one hundred boys and girls, fourteen to seventeen years of age inclusive, attended public high school. In 1942 seventy-two out of every one hundred attended. As far back as 1870 there were only eighty thousand students in these schools, but taking 1890 as a more accurate base, we find the enrollment to be approximately 360,000, and in 1942, approximately 7,000,000, an increase of 1835%. During the same period the numbers in private preparatory schools increased from 94,931 to 457,768. While there was some falling off during World War II, the return of peace will undoubtedly find the trend to be toward a norm of secondary education for everybody. The total educational facilities are the result of a great variety of independently supported, or nontax supported, schools and colleges as well as of public schools and colleges. "Everybody" includes the bright and the dull, the word-minded and the hand-minded, the well-integrated and the neurotic, the magnificent physique and the weakling. That is the whole range of "demos," and "democracy" means education for all.

Let us look at the colleges. During the same period, from 1890 to 1942, while the total civilian population increased from approximately 63,000,000 to 131,000,000 (108.1%), and the eighteen to twenty-one inclusive population from approximately 5,000,000 to 9,000,000 (73.4%), enrollment in institutions of higher learning increased 792.4%. In 1890 .25% of the total population and 3.04% of the eighteen to twenty-one inclusive population went to college, while in 1942 1.07% of the total population and 15.66% of the eighteen to twenty-one population attended.[1] The impetus of veteran attendance has swollen this figure enormously. Certainly a considerable number will not find the traditional college curriculum congenial. More and more, there will be education for everybody. Opportunity will have opened wide the doors of the school. Will democracy in education have, at long last, been attained?

I. THE NATURE OF DEMOCRACY

Democracy is that attitude and those devices that strike a delicate balance between my desires and your desires. It predicates the full and harmonious development of personality, along with a sense of restraint and love that leads to just as full and just as harmonious development of all other personalities, known collectively as "society." This is life and education is life. If democracy is life (the good life), education must *be* democracy. This is the education we have been describing.

As Dewey points out: "A democracy is more than a form of government; it is primarily a mode of associated living, of conjoint communicated experience. The extension in space of the number of individuals who participate in an interest so that each has to refer his own action to that of others, and to consider the action of others to give point and direction to his own, is equivalent to the breaking down of those barriers of class, race, and national territory which kept men from receiving the full import of their activity. These more numerous and more varied points of contact denote a greater diversity of stimuli to which an individual has to respond; they consequently put a premium on variation in his action. They secure a liberation of powers which remain suppressed as long as the incitations to action are partial, as they must be in a group which in its exclusiveness shuts out many interests." [2]

Full and harmonious development, opportunity for self-development, freedom for activity, are not enough. Activity must have a purpose, not merely the purpose of self-development but also the purpose of serving others so that they too may develop themselves. There must be neither unrestrained individualism nor totalitarian

[1] U. S. Office of Education, *Statistical Summary of Education,* 1941–42 (Washington, D.C.: Government Printing Office, 1944).
[2] From JOHN DEWEY, *Democracy and Education,* p. 101. By permission of The Macmillan Company, publishers (1916).

control. Rousseau's misguided naturalism and Hegel's institutional idealism have both run their course. Rather, we accept for democracy a liberalism that calls for continued readjustment in the light of reason and in the warmth of love, love of all mankind.

II. HOW DEMOCRATIC IS AMERICAN EDUCATION?

Here we have the democratic ideal of education for all and a rapidly growing secondary and college program seemingly on the way to accommodating all. What actually happens to these young people?

THE NATURAL SELECTIVITY OF EDUCATIONAL INSTITUTIONS. Some of the following observations lend themselves to statistical proof, others emerge from intimate experience, still others are matters of general knowledge:

1. Children in the upper social and economic brackets do not choose to attend a vocational school early in life. Their course lies through public academic high school or independent preparatory school, liberal arts college, and then through a vocational school preparing for one of the professions or for business.

2. Children on the top economic levels, and even those on somewhat lower levels, do not go to public school at all. They get both elementary and high school education in private schools. For the parents there are various inducements: small classes, 24-hour boarding facilities, country environment, religious training, individual attention, and social economic homogeneity.

3. On the middle and lower levels there is still a marked preference for academic high schools, schools that prepare for college and, in the minds of some parents and young people, provide "real education."

4. It is a general practice of elementary and junior high school principals and teachers to advise pupils of higher intelligence to attend academic high schools and those of lower intelligence vocational schools. Many an intelligent pupil whose interest in a vocation has indicated the wisdom of attending a vocational school, has had to struggle with his elementary or junior high school teachers for the privilege.

5. Principals of academic high schools estimate that from 25% to 50% of their students "are not fit to take the standard courses studied."

6. Only 20% to 40% of students entering academic high schools are graduated. Neither the graduates nor the drop-outs have acquired any specific vocational competence. True, some of them fit themselves into jobs for which the elementary skills of communication have prepared them, and many of the graduates go on to college and professional school.

7. The vast majority of students who leave school are ill-adapted to life.

8. The courses in most high schools are selective and have not necessarily been established because of their interest to students.

9. Democracy is working in the school, as is indicated by a certain amount of vertical and horizontal mobility. However, prestige and status play very important parts.

10. Students come to vocational school for two reasons. Those in the first group deliberately choose a vocation and want to learn to become competent in it. The ones in the second group come because they have been unsuccessful in academic work and are therefore ready to turn to something mechanical. Strong purpose usually carries the first group through to success. Many of the second group find themselves, and probably all would do so if the school and community facilities were varied enough and the sanctions were powerful enough.

11. Strong purpose does the same for those who are adapted to academic high school work. However, between the purposeful ones in academic high school and the purposeful ones in vocational high school there is a large group to whom the opportunity for development of purpose has been denied.

12. On the professional school level most of the phenomena just cited also occur, with modifications. Greater maturity and a somewhat broader view of the world's work tend to make for better adjustment wherever the bedeviling factor of prestige has not become dominant.

PREPARED FOR LIFE? The criticisms of "narrow vocational training" are usually based upon the assumption that "general education" prepares young people for "life." Even a proponent of "sound vocational education" says, "Vocational education conceived as job training represents the greatest threat to democratic education in our times." One might readily counter with, "General education, conceived only as citizenship training, is the greatest threat to the life of our nation at any time." And there would be some support for that point of view. One study of the Regents' Inquiry resulted in some startling findings:

"1. The former pupils, especially those in larger communities, had few contacts with adults.

"2. The young people just out of school had little home life.

"3. Lines of educational and recreational activity started in school were usually discontinued immediately after the pupils left school.

"4. After the pupils left school, they had very little contact with it. Most schools made little or no attempt to find out about the activities of their graduates and withdrawals. Few attempted to act as agencies for advice and help for out-of-school youth. Few provided any activities for the former pupils.

"5. The guidance program for pupils in the schools was decidedly inadequate.

"6. High school diplomas were not at all descriptive of the individuals who received them, although they may roughly indicate differences among the large groups of pupils enrolled in different curricula.

"7. Pupils left school with certain attitudes which made it difficult for them to adjust themselves to the out-of-school situations."

Each of the foregoing statements is based upon considerable validated evidence, and is expanded into some detail. However, if only the last statement were validated, it would be a severe indictment of the schools. On this point the authors write:

"a. No matter what type of community these young people lived in, or what occupations their parents engaged in, former pupils wanted white collar jobs, and were discontented and unhappy if they found it necessary to take some other kind of job.

"b. Pupils left school under the impression that it was wrong and weak to seek advice.

"c. Pupils were not at all realistic about their plans for the future. Many looked forward to entrance into the professions, even though there was little chance that these hopes might be realized." [3]

Another study considers the question, "Who shall be educated?" in the light of certain "hard facts":

"1. Children are not born equal.

"2. Only a limited number of people can be accommodated in the upper social and economic levels of our society.

"3. Economic mobility is probably decreasing.

---

[3] By permission from *When Youth Leaves School* by ECKERT and MARSHALL, p. 310 ff. Copyrighted, 1938, by McGraw-Hill Book Company, Inc.

"4. Such economic mobility as now exists is largely resultant from the low birth rate of people in the upper socio-economic group.

"5. Economic improvement is widely identified with moral improvement.

"6. Failure to rise in the social scale and consequent frustration are inevitable for many."

The identification of economic improvement with moral improvement is explained as follows:

"Economic increase is identified with moral improvement by a large middle section of our society. The professional man or small business man wants to build up a small fortune, hoping to establish his sons and daughters more comfortably in life than he has lived. The clerical worker, the farmer, and the mechanic slave to give their children a college education which means an 'easier time' in life. The unskilled laborer often denies himself comforts and even necessities in order to send his boys and girls through high school so that they may start higher on the ladder than he will ever reach. All these people face their fellow citizens with feelings of pride and assurance of approval at thus pushing their children upward. This is a large part of their morality. Often the labor union member, proud as he is of his union card, does all he can to prepare his children for a position with management or to promote them into a profession. It seems as if there is something immoral about earning one's bread by the sweat of one's brow for two successive generations. The children catch the notion quickly and often come to feel guilty if they do not justify their parents' hope and sacrifices by rising in the economic scale. The young man or young woman who will deliberately cast in his lot with the laboring class, in spite of superior education, is a rare person, looked at with some suspicion and interest by his fellow workers as well as by his friends and relatives." [4]

WHAT IS THE REMEDY? If secondary education were adapted to all pupils we would not have the continuous flow out of the schools, beginning at the minimum compulsory age. Of course, the ideal school need not be conceived as one that will hold all students up to a certain age, whether it be eighteen or twenty or twenty-two. Allowance must be made for educational saturation and for the possibilities of learning, especially certain types of jobs, outside the school. Nevertheless, the present maladjustment is obvious, and there is no argu-

[4] WARNER, HAVIGHURST, and LOEB, *Who Shall Be Educated?* (New York: Harper & Brothers, 1944), pp. 149–156.

ment as to the tremendous need for the adaptation of the schools to the education of all these youths. Watering down of the existing academic curriculum, lowering of standards, will not do it. A new and varied education with personality, interest, and purpose at the core, must be evolved.

The Harvard Report [5] makes the point: "It has been estimated that algebra, for instance, is successfully taught to fourteen-year-olds of slightly superior gifts but that, as now taught at least, it is more or less meaningless to fully half of the age group. What does such a fact mean? The answer if it could be fully known would certainly be most complex, and no claim is made here to knowing it. But this much seems clear: that, however firmly rooted in native endowment (the mere physical and nervous makeup of the brain), intelligence depends also on habit and outlook which in turn go back to earliest opportunity. . . . Assuming that a young person's abilities to some extent reflect his surroundings and both together color his hopes of life and expectations of himself, a truly democratic education must perforce try to equalize opportunity by counteracting impediments. But it cannot do so simply by offering the conventional academic subjects to all students indiscriminately. These again, as now taught at least, are too alien to the backgrounds of most students to be anything like generally effective in breaking down the barriers of circumstance. Something closer to their experience is needed which, by meeting them half way, will lead them out and beyond themselves. That is not the case, to be sure, with the very gifted. Their vivid minds, like powerful currents, overleap all breaks between life and study, supplying by imagination what they have missed in experience. Much has been written, and rightly so, about the need of seeing to it that such students, whatever their means, find their paths clear to the topmost reaches of education. . . . Certainly few subjects touch more closely the spirit of democratic education. But democracy is not only opportunity for the able. It is equally betterment for the average, both the immediate betterment which can be gained in a single generation and the slower ground swell of betterment which works through generations. Hence the task of the high school is not merely to speed the bright boy to the top. It is at least as much (so far as numbers are concerned, far more) to widen the horizons of ordinary students that they and, still more, their

[5] PAUL H. BUCK and others, *General Education in a Free Society,* report of the Harvard Committee (Cambridge, Massachusetts: Harvard University Press, 1945), p. 10.

children will encounter fewer of the obstacles that cramp achievement."

Finally, going back to the Dewey of 1916: "School facilities must be secured of such amplitude and efficiency as will in fact and not simply in name discount the effects of economic inequalities, and secure to all wards of the nation equality of equipment for their future careers. Accomplishment of this end demands not only the adequate administrative provision of school facilities, and such supplementation of primary resources as will enable youth to take advantage of them, but also such modification of traditional ideals of culture, traditional subjects of study and traditional methods of teaching and discipline as will retain all the youth under educational influences until they are equipped to be masters of their own economic and social careers. The ideal may seem remote of execution, but the democratic ideal of education is a farcical yet tragic delusion except as the ideal more and more dominates our public system of education." [6]

Today this ideal does not seem so remote. Some children have always liked school, the traditional, academic school. They have liked to read and write, to work with books, to bask in sunshine radiated by the teacher. They have arrived at school early in the morning to greet the teacher at the front door and have had to be almost literally ejected at the end of the day. These students have reacted naturally. For them, this has been the happy life, and the school has been the ideal school. Then there have been many others who have found school tolerable but for whom the happy life has lain in other fields. The fortunate among these have found some other center of interest, often in a vocational school where *they* have been found waiting at the front door for the opportunity to get into a shop from which it has been necessary to drag them away at night that they might go back to the uninteresting demands of play and the home. Most teachers and many parents know this kind of child and know that school can be fascinatingly attractive to the few. It can be just as attractive to the many.

III. A DEMOCRATIC HIGH SCHOOL

With whatever assurance we speak of a democratic high school as a reality, it is tempered with humility and pride, for the features here described, as well as the curriculum and guidance program and

[6] DEWEY, *op. cit.,* p. 114.

other elements of a "sound vocational education program," are the life of Metropolitan Vocational High School, of which the writer is principal. Falling far short of the ideal, but always struggling toward it, this school is typical, we are sure, of others, and offers its own practices only that they may be matched and surpassed. We do not think that America has to wait too long to be educationally democratic.

GENERALIZED AND SPECIALIZED EDUCATION. Metropolitan has passed through four stages. It began as a full-time elementary school with a small part-time continuation department. The rapid growth of the continuation department finally forced the elementary school out of existence and the organization became the East Side Continuation School with, at one time, 14,000 part-time students. With the raising of the compulsory school age from fourteen to sixteen the part-time school dwindled but was rapidly replaced by a full-time general vocational high school which, since 1936, has gradually evolved into a specialized vocational high school with the maritime trades (deck, engine, radio, steward, and boatbuilding), commercial photography, and vocational music and vocational dramatics as its major features. During all these transformations, caused by shifting social and economic conditions, the school has operated on the principles set forth in this book. As will be shown in more detail in the chapter on Administration, these principles would have been applied if the organization had been the one vocational high school in a moderate sized town or had been a department in a comprehensive high school in a still smaller town. While size, large or small, must necessarily be a determiner of organization, it need not change the spirit or the ideals if the members of the faculty and the school system's administrative officers persist in holding to them. The school, like all of education, should be for democracy and life.

PREPARATION FOR A VOCATION AND COMMON LEARNING. The school prepares for vocation and for "life." It operates on the Smith-Hughes formula, 50% for practical shop work and 50% for all other subjects. For many reasons this seems to be a workable formula, but the important point is that it is only a formula. To the extent that the teachers of the "other subjects" take advantage of the motivation offered by the shop subjects, and at the same time, infuse these shop subjects with the rich content of theory and of human relationships, education becomes a unitary process. The vocation is not "narrow" and the academic subjects are not "academic." "Work" becomes something that youngsters like to do because through it they realize their own personalities. There is nobody more fanatic than the young man who wants to go to sea and some day become the captain of a vessel. He is closely matched by the talented musician or actor whose "shop" is the concert hall or the theatre. And budding photographers are not only omnipresent but are clearly omnipotent when they are set upon taking a particular picture. When all of these prospective workers mingle in the students' general organization or in the honor society or in special assembly programs or in school festivities, they are learning to live democratically.

INTEREST AND APTITUDE ARE THE BASES OF ADMISSION. With some exceptions, students are admitted to these courses with reference solely to interest and aptitude in, and physical fitness for, the vocation for which they wish training. If the interest is genuine, it seems to stimulate aptitude. In any case, a boy who wants to go to sea ought to have his fling at it. With radio it is different. It is possible to test for aptitude in code work and it is also possible to set a lower limit of intelligence for the learning of electronic theory. It is to the definite disadvantage of a boy to struggle for several years to become a marine radio operator when a few tests will determine readily whether he has the prerequisite qualifications. If his interest in radio is genuine, good counseling will guide him into some other phase, perhaps the radio mechanics of the repair man.

Prospective musicians can be auditioned for performance and tested for aptitude. Experience indicates that the results are valid. So, intense interest and passable aptitude, regardless of school ratings, previous conduct, or any other conditions, guarantee the individual a chance to become a professional musician. Obviously, differences in scholarship call for differences in programing, and later, probably for reprograming. Individual student programs and easy changes of program, under guidance, are conditions for the adequate adjustment of the student.

GENERAL EDUCATION FOR EVERYBODY. Such an admission policy means I.Q.'s ranging from 60 to 160. It means students from classes for the mentally retarded in elementary school, elementary school graduates, and junior high school graduates. It means that classes in theory and in academic subjects must be graded so as to provide an approach to homogeneity. It means that some students stay for two or three years without even earning an elementary school diploma while others, within the same period, become eligible for admission to college. It means that, regardless of one's vocational goal, eligibility for college education is open to all with power to pass in the required subjects. As has already been pointed out, college graduation for the mariner seemed, only a few years ago, a fantastic goal. Now, through the United States and the State Maritime Academies, it is a definite possibility, and the vocational high school is equipped to prepare him for it. For those who argue the narrowness of the Smith-Hughes formula, it should be noted that the combined vocational and college preparatory work is carried on within the terms of that formula. A high school ranging in population from subnormals to those in the top ranks of intelligence, basing its program on interest and self-development in services useful to mankind, would seem to be democratic.

MEETING THE TIME FACTOR. Obviously, the highly talented musician attains a high degree of efficiency much more quickly than his less talented brother. All students must take private, individual lessons on their instruments. Some have better teachers than others and progress more rapidly. So, some may graduate sooner or, if they prefer, may take more intensive or varied work in music. Or, they may concentrate upon the academic studies. If a boy has become an ardent amateur photographer, has his own camera and dark room, and spends hours at home each day at picture-taking and -making, he will naturally accelerate himself in the photography course at school. Such acceleration is based on very definite standards of accomplishment, but the time factor is entirely within the student's control. Similar adjustments are made in the academic work although, where college entrance is the goal, state regulations and the rules of the colleges themselves make this more difficult. However, learning is measured in terms of accomplishment and not of time spent.

GUIDANCE. As has been emphasized again and again throughout these chapters, the individual, the personality, is always the heart of the program. He, or she, *is* the program, and all the principles and practices of a good guidance program are what make education work. Since it works only if the full and harmonious development of the individual is accomplished, and guidance is what guarantees this accomplishment, a school with that kind of program is democratic.

PLACEMENT AND FOLLOW-UP. As noted in the Eckert and Marshall Study, few students have contact with their schools, or acknowledge much help in making adjustments, after leaving. Well-oriented vocational education has a definite purpose that comprehends the individual purpose of each student. Upon graduation, adjustment means placement and no graduate leaves without a place in which to use the skills and knowledge he has acquired in school. It is a definite task of the school to effect such placement, to follow up the young worker in his employment, and to insist on replacement whenever it becomes necessary. One test of a functioning school is the return of former students for help. When, for three or four years they have been guided through school by an advisor with whom they have had daily contact, such return to school becomes customary, almost standard practice. Democratic education cannot discharge itself of responsibility with the presentation of a diploma, or with the casual approval of a drop-out. It is responsible for its clients until their feet are firmly planted on the road to success.

WORK EXPERIENCE. In recent years much recognition has been given to the educational value of "work experience." Of course, for centuries that is just the kind of education that most people have had and the present emphasis is, in a curious kind of way, a "return to nature." However, it is salutary. Even in a vocational school, where half the time is spent on practical work, experience on paying jobs is exceedingly useful. The job gives the boy an insight to commercial demands. He brings this back to school with the result that instruction becomes much more meaningful. Then, of course, he takes instruction back to the commercial job and makes it much more effective. For instance, on the cooperative plan, boys who are old enough (at least sixteen and a half years) go to sea for two or three months as ordinary seamen or wipers or messmen, and are given credit in school. The more talented musicians are already playing in dance bands or orchestras long before graduation. The photographers are working part time in high class studios. Sometimes arrangements for such work experience are made formally by the school. Just as often they are arranged by the young workers themselves, always with school approval, of course. This interplay between the school and commercial life is an exceedingly important factor in the education of the young person. The freedom with which it occurs, the associations it develops, and the public approval that it wins, are all vital elements in democratic education.

HORIZONTAL MOBILITY. One of the frequent criticisms of vocational education on the secondary school level is that the boy is too young to make a choice and that training for one kind of job is dangerous for two reasons. After spending several years in preparation, he may find that ultimately he does not like that kind of work and would much rather do something else, or, after devoting himself whole-heartedly to it, and liking it better and better, he ultimately finds that the trade itself is on the decline and he cannot obtain a job. Of course, if the problem could be stated so simply, the results might be tragic. In the first place, as against straight academic education, it is obvious that the boy is no worse off than the academic high school graduate and is certainly better off in being proficient in at least one trade. However, "one trade," if well taught, carries with it proficiency in a number of ancillary trades. For instance, the marine engineer makes an excellent stationary engineer, has a good start as machinist, and knows the elements of plumbing, sheet metal work, electrical maintenance, and gas engine maintenance. He is really a very versatile fellow. The photographer has received instruction in art and has learned a good deal about advertising. Moreover, photography takes on many different forms in various kinds of business. The boat-builder is, of course, an excellent carpenter and can operate in wood for hundreds of different purposes. The very essence of the argument for the democratic school is that it is not narrow, that it is expansive, that it extends itself into many places and numerous persons. Of course, the necessity for transferring to other trades is unusual at the end of four years of high school. In the first place, the student has had plenty of time to know his own mind and ample opportunity to change his trade if he wished to. In the second place, the school and the school system are alert to trade fluctuations and are guided by them. One of the important functions of advisory commissions, to be discussed presently, is to keep the curricula of the school in tune with the demands of business and industry.

VERTICAL MOBILITY. The imaginative, ambitious, purposeful student wants to "go to the top." And so he should. Whether or not he can do so is a matter of birth, locality, money, to mention only three factors. There has been considerable vertical mobility in American life. Given present conditions, we do not really know whether it will become greater or less. However, we do know that neither the country nor the educational system will be thoroughly democratic unless such vertical mobility is an actual fact. The vocational school can contribute to it by giving the kind of thorough, basic training in skills and instruction in theory that will enable the young worker to make his way up through the ranks of his trade, even to attain a professional status. That is a contribution, but it is not enough. Lack of money, lack of time, family obligations, must be compensated for by some kind of subsidy based upon occupational success, worthiness of character, and prognosis as to advancement. Democracy cannot afford to allow fine talent to languish for lack of sustenance.

DIVERSITY IN TRADE, COMMERCE, AGRICULTURE, HOMEMAKING. The foregoing discussion has deliberately drawn its examples from the specialties in Metropolitan. Moreover, it has referred only to boys. However, the principles apply to both boys and girls, to countless different trades, commercial occupations, homemaking pursuits, and agricultural vocations. It is this myriad of applications in a country of wide occupational variety that makes vocational education democratic.

"LOWERING STANDARDS, CHEAPENING THE SCHOOL." The organization and maintenance of a democratic secondary school is, as would appear from the small number of instances in which it has been accomplished, no easy task. It is immensely rewarding, but it has its drawbacks and its disappointments. Perhaps the most vexing of these is the strong tendency of schoolmen to consider the school a "dumping ground." True, in answer to the protestation that the vocational school has positive standards for admission rather than the purely negative one of unavailability for any other type of school, the elementary school principal or teacher says, "But, what else can I do with him?" Under usual conditions there is *nothing* else that he can do with him. And so, the vocational school takes him. Only, instead of being considered a haven, a sanctuary, a holy place for the redemption of a lost soul, it becomes, in the mind of the bemused principal or teacher, a — dumping ground. Of course, vocational education, as set forth in these pages, should be able to, and does, take care of the "problem cases." Otherwise it would not be democratic. However, in a small community, with one comprehensive high school, that school should be equipped to give education to every boy and girl who wants it, and also to those who do not want it, but should. Part of each youngster's program should be vocational, but the program must be based upon all the facilities of the entire community and should not be considered a desperate nostrum for the rejects of traditional schoolmen. Moreover, the vocational interests and potentialities of the brightest students, the non-problem children, must be recognized and provided for. No schoolman is justified in saying, "But, what shall I do with him?" if he cannot also say, "What will you do vocationally for my brightest student?" A vocational program is for all boys and girls and not solely for problem cases. It is democratic for the "nice" ones as well as for the "bad" ones.

A shop class in a comprehensive high school, a vocational department in an academic high school, or one vocational school among ten others in a large city can acquire a reputation for "low standards" or for "taking all the bums" (more despicable words are frequently used, even by schoolmen), if that school is the only one in the group that recognizes its responsibility for democratic education. The explanation is simple. To use another figure of speech, "Bad money drives out good." Gresham's Law operates in education as well as in economics. When the number of troublesome students of low intelligence reaches a point where their presence begins to affect the tone of the school then, not only do the other students note the effect, but word passes on to other schools, and the number of "good" admissions tends to fall off. This is the way in which slum areas grow in a city and, as with such areas, there is only one answer. No one school, no one area, should bear the burden of the difficult child or the substandard dweller. The whole school system, or the whole city, should take its share so that the substandard, whether child or adult, will feel the influence of the best people and will be upgraded. This is democracy at its best.

Vocational education can do this job in the secondary field if, in the first place, it is understood for what it really is. It is based on work, the work of all men, the laborer, the mechanic, the commercial artist, the grocer, the civil service worker. It grows out of interest, purpose, and is the great respecter of personality. So conceived, it is education in its highest and best sense. And it is democratic.

IV. DEMOCRACY IN THE COLLEGES

The essence of democracy, as already stated, lies in the freedom of the individual to develop himself to the utmost, not only that he may live happily through self-realization, but that he may serve others, and be served by others in the development of their personalities.

SOME COROLLARIES TO THE DEMOCRATIC CONCEPTION OF EDUCATION. To this conception there are several important, but sometimes forgotten, corollaries:

1. The individual should be free "to take" or to engage in any kind of education he wants, or his parents want, short of instruction in crime. The state may well mandate that he should learn the fundamental arts of communication and should become familiar with the customs, institutions, and government, as well as the history of the country. This means not only that independent, private schools should be permitted to operate but that, in a democracy, they are a good thing.

2. Free competition among educational ideas is salutary. The sharper the issue, the more salutary it is. So, if a church or a political party or a group of private citizens sets up an educational program and proclaims it the "best," even the "ideal," and pays for it, and if it is not anti-democratic, that is good for democracy.

3. While it is fair to insist that each individual shall become economically independent, that he shall earn his living in an honorable occupation, there can be no compulsion as to the way in which he learns this vocation. He may learn it in school in two weeks or ten years, or he may learn it on the job.

CERTAIN PRACTICAL CONSIDERATIONS. While freedom of thought, and therefore freedom of education, is a major tenet of democracy, the size and complexity and ever-changing character of the country demand that this freedom from restriction be accompanied by certain positive measures in the public interest:

1. The genius, perhaps the glory, of American *public* education, education planned, established, and maintained by the majority of the people, tax-supported education, is that it shall be free and accessible to all — to *all*, without exception.

2. If accessible to all, public education must be suitable to all, effective for all. It must do what we have just said the democratic high school must do. It cannot set up an "ideal" curriculum and say, "Here, boys and girls, is education. If you can take it, you will be educated men and women. If not, you are forever doomed to move among the proletariat." Since free, public secondary education has become general and standard in the United States, it must be truly public.

3. But now we come to the post-high-school period, a field in which free, public education is neither general nor standard. Even

the land-grant colleges and the state universities do not provide subsistence for students or for parents in need of their support. The old-line standard colleges, with their high tuition fees and social screening, are even more inaccessible to the poor. After the Second World War veterans were the freest individuals, educationally speaking, but the limitations of space and other facilities made admission to college a scramble for them, and complete prohibition for many civilians who would otherwise have been admitted.

4. Another consideration: When does the process of education, unaccompanied by earning, stop? Psychologically and morally, when should young people begin to produce and serve, to say nothing of specifically and earnestly preparing for production and service? What considerations warrant extension of the learning period? To the age of twenty, twenty-two, twenty-four, thirty? No one questions this extension of youth if the end result is a physician equipped to serve humanity, a public servant who could not have acquired that equipment in any other way. Moreover, does any one object if twenty-odd years of education produce a salesman who could have been just as competent at the end of eight years of education? That is, is the individual "worth" that much education and is a liberal arts (in any case a nonvocational) program "worth" the outcome?

5. Democracy connotes not only freedom, but *responsibility*. Such responsibility demands not only that vague entity known as "good citizen," but "good worker," yes, to use an old-fashioned term, "good provider."

WHEN AND WHERE SHALL OCCUPATIONS BE LEARNED? Everybody agrees that all mentally and physically competent persons should work, but disagrees as to when and where they should learn how to work. One position is that, except for the professions, all work should be learned on the job, that all schooling should be "general." The opposite position is that the individual should begin to make a tentative choice of occupation when his first interest appears and that he should begin to prepare for that occupation when the interest becomes strong enough to provide a focus of activity. In its stress upon interest and purpose and responsibility and work our own position has been made clear. In principle, it extends through the period of higher education. In practice, it would be modified in the light of the considerations in the foregoing paragraphs. There remains only the necessity of considering what has actually been happening in American colleges.

THE AIMS OF HIGHER EDUCATION. American colleges began as vocational institutions for the professions, primarily the ministry and teaching. The A.B. degree was a certificate of competency, a license to perform the job. The curriculum was the trivium: grammar, rhetoric, and logic; and the quadrivium: arithmetic, music, geometry, and astronomy. Or, in the Harvard version: "Logick, Ethicks, Politicks, Arithmetick, and Geometry, Astronomy; to syntax, prosodia, and dialects, grammar, Hebrew and the Easterne tongues, the Old and New Testament, and declamations." The "liberal arts" constituted a thoroughly satisfactory education for those professions. They were also highly satisfactory for the training of "gentlemen." As time went on and more gentlemen than ministers graduated from the colleges and, of course, pursued other occupations, the liberal arts were justified for their disciplinary and presumably for their gentleman-producing qualities. The Civil War brought the Morrill Act and the land-grant colleges which, along with the state universities that developed toward the end of the nineteenth century, were specifically vocational in their aim. They set out to prepare young men and women for their life's work. Since then the trend has been to introduce vocational aims and courses into the curricula of many of the colleges, to use the vocations to give meaning to the liberal arts, and to use the liberal arts as enrichment for the vocations.[7]

The curriculum of St. John's College at Annapolis, Maryland, is a reaffirmation of the virtues of the trivium and the quadrivium. This throwback to Aristotelianism, sponsored by Chancellor Hutchins and Professor Adler of the University of Chicago and directed by Stringfellow Barr, has received an enormous amount of attention as a "significant experiment in American education." The curriculum consists of "one hundred great books," constituting, supposedly, the grand classical tradition in Western thought. The books are discussed in small seminars twice a week, daily tutorials are held in languages and mathematics, and the students use instruments and make experiments on the basis of the scientific classics in the book list. Greek, Latin, French, and German are each studied for a few months. And that is the starkly naked curriculum of St. John's. Its merits or shortcomings as a liberal arts curriculum are not pertinent here. They have been competently discussed elsewhere.[8] However,

---

[7] BENJAMIN FINE, *Democratic Education* (New York: Thomas Y. Crowell, 1945).
[8] SIDNEY HOOK, *Education for Modern Man* (New York: Dial Press, Inc., 1946), pp. 197–229. Also FINE, *op. cit.,* Ch. VIII.

in the light of the thesis of this book the St. John's program is found
wanting on every score. Being as old as college education itself, it is
hardly an "experiment." Moreover, even if the idea were new, it is
not set up with any elements of "control" or "evaluation." Yet, as
has been said, as a private, independent educational venture, it is
helpful for a democracy. It should be watched with kindly understanding and should be appraised with scientific care. Then we shall
probably be able to determine the validity of Mr. Barr's conviction
that "St. John's may serve as a model for the reorganization of liberal
education in the United States," or Mr. Van Doren's statement that,
"It will take time to get the proposal accepted. Until it is accepted
everywhere in America, we shall lack the right to say that liberal
education exists among us," or Mr. Adler's opinion that, "St. John's
is the only college in the country which is making a proportionate
effort to adopt means that may succeed in achieving the ends of a
liberal education," or Mr. Hutchins' insistence, "that no matter how
environments differ human nature is, always has been, and always
will be the same everywhere," and that therefore, education should
everywhere be the same, and finally Mr. Hutchins' dictum that "the
thing to do with vocational education is to forget it. As the War
Training Programs in industry have shown, industry can train its
hands if it has to, and can do it at lightning speed."

VOCATIONAL EDUCATION IN LIBERAL ARTS COLLEGES. We have stressed
the importance of a vocational field of interest for the secondary
school and have indicated how general education can be made meaningful through such interests. A few high schools have carried on
such programs with success. On the college level the outstanding exponents of that idea are Antioch and Bennington. What they are
attempting to do is best explained in the words of those who are
carrying on the programs.

"'What are you going to be? What vocation in life are you preparing yourself for?' These are perhaps the most insistent, the most
recurrent questions which boys and girls face. From cradle to college, this cultural pressure forces them to think about vocations. . . .
That students should be vocationally-minded is not undesirable.
A student with a vocational goal acquires more meaning from
his educational experiences. Perhaps inarticulately, he correlates
his educational program with his expressed or unexpressed goals,
thus making the educational process a more integral part of his life.
Both from general cultural courses and from technical courses he

excerpts the material that relates to his conception of his vocational goals. . . .

". . . Educational and occupational orientation, to be effective, must both operate from the same sets of facts about the students. Succinctly stated, they must both be organized upon the foundation of a thorough clinical analysis of the student's abilities, motivations, and other pertinent facts about his qualifications and limitations. The objectives of educational orientation are not unitary; neither do they conflict with the objectives of occupational orientation. Educational orientation aims at assisting the student to make the most of his educational opportunities. In the liberal arts college, this means educating him toward becoming a broadly cultivated individual, *at the same time* preparing for participation in a life activity which will be socially useful and personally satisfying. Occupational orientation is concerned with one aspect of this general objective, namely, assisting the student to choose and enter a vocation for which he is qualified. Those objectives are not in conflict. Rather they are overlapping and supplementary. Moreover, neither can be attained except in terms of the individual student's personal configuration of abilities, goals, interests, and motivations. To make a man cultivated, the arts college must cultivate him in terms of his personal assets and liabilities. Occupational adjustment stems from the same source — individual diagnosis. From an analysis of the pertinent facts about a student, the college can determine what kind of orientation, educational, occupational, or both, the student requires." [9]

The application of this philosophy at Bennington College is indicated in the following:

"(1) That education is a process continuing through life, persisting most effectively in the years after college when the habit of educating oneself has been acquired; . . .

"(3) That such educational self-dependence can be developed most effectively if the student works at tasks which have meaning and interest for her; . . .

"(4) That continuing education, self-initiated, is most likely to take place where the student has attained expertness, or a sense of mastery in a few fields of enduring interest or use, rather than smatterings in a great many fields; . . .

"(6) That direct experiences — planning, organizing, manipu-

[9] W. H. COWLEY, ROBERT HOPPOCK, and E. G. WILLIAMSON, *Occupational Orientation of College Students,* Study Series VI, Student Personnel Work, Vol. III, No. 2 (Washington, D.C.: American Council on Education, April, 1939).

lating, constructing, and investigating, in conjunction with reading and the acquisition of knowledge — are valuable means for developing permanent interests pursued voluntarily;

"(7) That tools of learning such as statistics and the use of English, to have meaning as well as to be most economically mastered, should be connected immediately, or in the process of learning, with the ends for which they are instruments rather than acquired as separate disciplines related vaguely to possible distant use; . . .

"(9) That intellectual development cannot and should not be isolated from the development of the whole personality, and that general arrangements, and especially individual guidance, should give proper weight not only to intellectual factors in personal growth but also to physical, emotional, moral, and esthetic factors as well. . . .

"In the case of those vocations which are entered directly from college, Bennington College includes training in the necessary techniques and skills they require. There is no hesitation in relating senior division requirements to vocations growing out of work in the field. The type of intellectual asceticism which fears that contact with practice or reality will destroy the field for culture is not encouraged. The winter period is frequently used to test vocational aptitude and to acquire practical training. A valuable part of the student's education is the assessment, early in her undergraduate career, of her real capacity for the actual work toward which she is aiming. On the other hand, vocational training is never permitted to interfere with the fundamental purpose of the senior division. Breadth and thoroughness of work requiring sustained intellectual or artistic effort, whether directed toward the vocation or as a preparation for leisure, is the test of success. The college seeks to avoid the false sense of security connected with too specific vocational preparation, and to provide breadth and flexibility of training suited to the special uncertainties of woman's life as well as to the general uncertainties of supply and demand which affect all occupations." [10]

These quotations are taken from an article by President Algo D. Henderson of Antioch College where, for a number of years the vocational motive has been successfully used in making a liberal arts college a reflection of American culture.[11] After describing activities at Antioch similar in spirit and execution to those at Bennington,

[10] *Bennington College Bulletin,* Vol. X., No. 1, 1941–42.
[11] ALGO D. HENDERSON, "Vocational Education in Liberal Arts Colleges," in *Vocational Education,* Forty-Second Yearbook, National Society for the Study of Education (Chicago: University of Chicago Press, 1943).

President Henderson goes on to describe the cooperative plan that has been one of Antioch's significant contributions in the field of college education:

"The cooperative plan of work and study at the college is the principal medium through which vocational orientation and education are secured. Each student, before graduation, must have had a minimum of six quarters' work experience. Ordinarily, this is provided by regular jobs in industry, institutions, and professional and governmental services, on a plan under which the student alternates twelve weeks of work experience with twelve weeks of study at the college. These jobs are scattered over about twenty states and include nearly every kind of experience appropriate to the student's age and capacity for responsibility. The job experiences provide many educational values, of which those of personal maturity and development, supplementation of the college curriculum, vocational orientation and training, and direct observation of the experience in contemporary society are the principal ones.

"By actually trying an experience in a supposed vocational interest, the student secures an occupational orientation which is not possible otherwise. In this way, vocational-interests tests and other counseling devices are supplemented by the trial-and-error process. That this is important is indicated by the fact that more than half of the Antioch students, before they have graduated, have shifted to interests other than those they announced as first choices in their freshman year. As they work along, too, the students get considerable vocational training. For example, a major in the field of chemistry ordinarily will work several hundred hours in industrial or institutional laboratories. Finally, having had experience with one or more companies or institutions, his placement at graduation is greatly facilitated. Even if he does not choose permanent placement with the particular company with which he has worked, he graduates as an experienced and vocationally self-reliant person."

Mr. Henderson concludes: "For if liberal education has a function today, that function must be much broader than it has tended to be in the past. Liberal education must serve some larger purpose than that assumed by Fowler in his *Dictionary of Modern English Usage:* 'It is the education designed for a gentleman (Latin *liber,* a free man), and is opposed on the one hand to technical or professional or any special training, and on the other to education that stops short before manhood is reached.' The true function of liberal education would seem to be to prepare students for active leadership in a dynamic society and to furnish some guidance for finding the basic values to be used in solving the essential problems in society today. Liberal education may be defined as the education which tends to produce the liberal individual — the person who, because of his perspective of history, his critical observation of contemporary society, and his understanding of social dynamics, helps to facilitate needed changes in the world. In this setting, the past becomes a source of light upon ways and means of advancing contemporary culture.

"Probably in at least ninety cases out of one hundred, the life work of the individual becomes the primary medium through which he finds his greatest personal happiness and makes his greatest contribution to society. Especially if he has leadership capacity, it is important that his life work be enriched by the perspective of knowledge and breadth of judgment which should come as a result of a liberal education. The vocational education of the student then takes its natural place as a part of the total educational objective."

It is contended that this type of education, carried on in the colleges, is of the essence of democracy.

VOCATIONAL EDUCATION IN THE UNIVERSITIES. As post-college institutions, with students normally twenty-two years of age or older, it should be expected that the universities would, at long last, provide young people with vocational preparation. Sixteen years of "common learning" or "general education" should be enough to satisfy even the most ardent advocate of the liberal arts. And this has been the case. Even graduate students in the liberal arts are graduate students because in one way or another they intend to use the liberal arts vocationally — usually as teachers or writers. So, at Harvard, for instance, we find professional preparation in journalism, engineering, theology, law, dentistry, public health, business administration, design, education, and public administration. At the University of Chicago there are professional schools of divinity, law, business, medicine, social service administration, and library administration. The catalogues of all American universities would give similar lists.[12]

THE DEMOCRATIC COLLEGE. The General College of the University of Minnesota accepts for admission every high school graduate who wishes to enter college regardless of his grades in the academic sub-

---

[12] EURICH and McCAIN, "Vocational Education in Universities," in *Vocational Education, op. cit.*

jects. They must have been graduated from an accredited high school, but without any prescribed subject credit. According to the University:

"A numerically large and educationally important group of high school graduates enter college with no very clear understanding of their assets and liabilities or their hopes and aspirations, and with no very well defined plans for the future. The General College program aims to help them find themselves both personally and vocationally. It helps them to know themselves as individuals, to develop realistic goals in keeping with their interests and abilities, and starts them making progress in achieving such goals."

The General College program is an attempt to deal with human beings and their aspirations in friendly, helpful, common-sense fashion; to take them as they are, to discover their interests, to capitalize upon their strength, to bolster up their weaknesses; in other words, to deal with these young people on the college level much as the vocational education program does on the secondary level. It is designed to give each individual an opportunity for self-realization. As Fine puts it: "If at the end of the first year a student has failed in chemistry, English, and algebra, the average college will drop him. He will be labeled poor college material and be told to shift for himself. The student, despite his poor academic record, may wish to continue in college. To throw him out will not solve any problem, except perhaps to rid the college of an unwelcome burden. But what of society? Can the student be expected to become a better citizen or more intelligent voter? Today a freshman who fails to pass his term examinations is virtually told that college is no place for him and that his 'education is finished.'

"However, the college of the future must in all honesty say to the young man: 'Evidently you are not able to continue in the field of medicine or law. That type of program is a bit too much for you. But don't get discouraged. Just because you failed in your first try is no reason to assume that you should drop all learning. If you wish you can stay on at college. You may need more remedial work in arithmetic and English. Perhaps you might find smoother going in animal husbandry, or forestry, or in business administration. Stay as long as you wish. We feel that the longer you remain at college, the better citizen you will be when you finish. Education, you see, is unending and you are not to be penalized for failing in one phase, even if it is the liberal arts. There is far more to education than that. If, after another try, you feel you might do better by going to work, suit yourself. We shall give you all the help and encouragement that you need if you wish to remain with us.' " [13]

To this should be added, as the author would undoubtedly agree, the caution that such an institution must maintain a strong guidance program calculated to hold the student at all points to full responsibility for what he does, and to make it impossible to become either a scholastic or vocational hobo. "Stay as long as you wish, yes, but not one day longer than your conscience tells you and our observation proves to you that you are putting forth every effort to realize that full and harmonious development which good education is supposed to provide."

V. DEMOCRATIC CONTROL OF THE PUBLIC SCHOOLS

Invariably, throughout the United States, public schools are controlled by local boards of education the members of which are elected by the people or appointed by an elected official. Especially in smaller communities, the schools are most responsive to popular demand, sometimes, unfortunately, to their detriment. Of course, there is always the State Department of Education with its usual standard-setting powers and its right to intervene where gross inefficiency or political maneuvering interferes with sound educational practice. This has not always operated to keep the curriculum in step with economic and social changes or with advances in pedagogic or administrative practice. Tradition and inertia still play their part. However, when the vocational education program, of less than college grade, was first given financial and moral support on a national basis through the Smith-Hughes Law in 1917, it was fortified by the mandate for advisory boards on vocational education, the membership of which was to represent employers, employees, and the public.

THE ADVISORY BOARD. Usually a state advisory board on vocational education requires that a local advisory board be appointed wherever a vocational education program is set up. These boards are what their title implies — advisory. They have no administrative powers. Boards of education do not have to accept their advice. They can therefore be as powerful as their constituent personalities make them, or as weak as their lack of interest and inactivity allow them. In fact, they range from powerful to impotent. At best, they are most valuable adjuncts to the school system. Occupationally, they are close

[13] FINE, *op. cit.,* p. 225.

to life. Any member is not only a farmer, say, but a parent, a member of the Rotary Club, a member of the Grange, and is bound to be vitally concerned with the effectiveness of vocational education in his community, especially as it relates to agriculture. Put together a group of men and women representing permanent vocations, either as employers or employees, place upon them the responsibility for keeping the community board of education alive to its responsibility for vocational education, and the result is likely to be startlingly good. Moreover, this is democratic control, control through advice, intimate knowledge, practical experience, and, if necessary, public pressure.

OCCUPATIONAL SURVEYS. Frequently pointed out by skeptics is the impossibility of bringing all of industry, commerce, agriculture, and homemaking into the school, for either guidance or training purposes. Certainly the field is enormous, altogether inexhaustible, but because of the impossibility of doing everything, there is no warrant for doing nothing. Moreover, there are "typical" trades, and in any community there are predominant trades. In any area, large or small, there are some occupations which engage a great many workers and others hardly any. Again, some trades have rich educational content, others little. It is the purpose of the occupational survey to uncover these facts and make them known to the community, especially through the Board of Education.

"For a long time the terms 'curriculum construction' and 'curriculum revision' have been current in the field of general education. 'Occupational survey' and 'job analysis' are, roughly, comparable terms in the field of vocational education. Careful consideration of the functions of an advisory board indicates that, if these functions are exercised on a high plane of efficiency and in close cooperation with the board of education, they constitute a kind of continuous occupational survey and repeated revision of job analyses. They keep education close to life and make a specific preparation for life.

"Experience with vocational surveys has been varied. Sometimes they have produced good results, at other times negative results. No one can predict the reaction of school system or public. It can always be predicted if one general principle is kept in mind: purposes, methods, and personnel of the survey must, at every stage, be freely and frankly discussed with the administrators and teachers who are expected to carry out the recommendations of the survey — indeed, these administrators should be put to work on the survey itself.

182

Needless to say, comparable discussion must take place with the public, as represented by the board of education and other civic bodies." [14]

Indeed, this is the essence of democracy.

On the basis of such a survey the advisory board must bring to the board of education a full and accurate picture of occupational community life so that a sound vocational education program may be organized and maintained. This program cannot be rigidly limited to occupations in the community but must have due regard to the potentialities of the children in the community for employment in occupations in other communities. The choice may often become a delicate one, obscured by local pride and social prestige, but it is one that must be made. It is the duty of the advisory board to make it.

THE CURRICULUM. The occupational survey turns up rich detail to be translated into instructional material. The vocations are taught in an atmosphere of reality and this reality comes out of the shop, the store, the office, and the farm. While professional school teachers accept the task of translating it into daily lessons, the advisory board, assisted by the same teachers, is responsible for providing authentic occupational information.

THE TEACHING AND ADMINISTRATIVE STAFF. Standards for selection of teachers of subjects in the general curriculum are of long standing. Examinations are readily given and, normally, the number of available teachers is adequate. Moreover, the tradition has been for a great number of young women and a smaller number of young men to choose teaching as a career and to begin preparation for it during their college days. In vocational education the situation is quite otherwise. The most important prerequisite for teaching a trade is adequate experience in that trade, variously calculated as being from five to ten years as a journeyman. Obviously, it is a rare person who starts out on a five or ten year stretch with the aim of becoming both expert in the trade and proficient in teaching it. Actually, opportunity for teaching comes fortuitously to the trade man or woman, and training in the new trade of teaching is a kind of post-graduate and unexpected affair. For this reason it becomes most important for members of an advisory board to be alert for prospective voca-

14 STEPHEN F. VOORHEES, "Community Relations in Vocational Education," in *Vocational Education, op. cit.*

tional teachers, literally to entice them out of industry and then to certify to the board of education their competence as workers. Sometimes they may even have to go to the extent of subsidizing such workers until the community can see fit to pay them wages equal to or better than they received in industry.

STUDENT PERSONNEL. Just as they assist the board of education in selecting teachers, advisory board members serve in selecting students. With the same wisdom that characterizes personnel programs in their own establishments, they choose prospective workers for training in the trades. This does not necessarily mean actual personal choice, but it does mean cooperation with the school in setting standards.

PLACEMENT. If members have done well in the selection of teachers and students, at the end of the training period they have young workers whom they are proud to place in their own establishments or those of fellow-employers or fellow-employees. Moreover, periodically the members, or representatives whom they select from trades with which they are less familiar, examine the students in the trade courses to see whether they are coming up to expectations. Finally, before graduation, they pass upon the students' competence, either through special projects (masterpieces, if you will), or through an examination of their regular work in course.

BUILDING, EQUIPMENT, AND SUPPLIES. Building, equipment, and supplies should all conform to trade practice, subject, of course, to pedagogical considerations. The advisory board is especially competent to advise the board of education on these matters.

ADVISORY BOARD MEMBERS AS INDIVIDUALS. As is always the case, much better understanding can be established between two individuals than between two corporate bodies. So, individual members of the advisory board function most effectively when they visit schools as individuals, confer with principal and teachers personally or over the telephone, invite teachers and students to observe industry at work, in fact, consider themselves as very special personal consultants to the vocational program. Friendly relationships established in this way promote sound practice and effective coordination more readily than the longest and most solemn formal group meeting.

PUBLIC RELATIONS. These friendly contacts *are*, of course, good public relations. It is incumbent upon the advisory board to pass along to parents, community officials, clergymen, newspaper editors, Rotary and other service clubs, chamber of commerce, union officials, in fact, to the entire community a knowledge of what is being done in vocational education and, even more important, what should be done.

COOPERATION WITH LABOR. "The average schoolman, only superficially acquainted with occupational problems, is always skeptical, even cynical, about the possibilities of cooperating with organized labor. Too often, to him, 'unions' are synonymous with 'strikes' and other 'labor troubles.' The fact is that, throughout the United States, the cooperation of organized labor in promoting vocational education has provided notable evidence of the possibility of establishing live curriculums in live schools; in other words, this cooperation is making the schools prepare for life, as they have always been supposed to do. True, unions are not uniformly understanding and cooperative, but neither are employers' associations. Nevertheless, the average is high. It is a matter of common experience that, when organized employers' and employees' groups are brought together in conference, they frequently indulge in sharp discussions regarding wage-and-hour conditions, but when they focus upon problems of their children, the children of the community, and attempt to formulate educational plans, the interests of both groups begin to merge to the end that they combine their forces and give support to sound vocational education.

"The official attitude of the American Federation of Labor is reflected in a resolution passed at its 1937 Convention calling for more active interest of affiliates in vocational education and insisting upon high standards in performance. While no such similar declaration of policy is available from the Congress of Industrial Organization, the practical cooperation of the C.I.O. unions in New York City is evidence of understanding and appreciation similar to that of the A.F. of L. For instance, the National Maritime Union, a C.I.O. affiliate, is not only represented on the Maritime Educational Commission (a subcommittee of the Advisory Board on Vocational Education), but all graduates of the maritime course in the Metropolitan Vocational High School are automatically accepted as members of the union and are placed aboard ships." [15]

Union cooperation, like all human cooperation, depends, first of

15 VOORHEES, *op. cit.*, p. 73.

all, upon complete knowledge of the objectives of the cooperators. Frankness, sincerity, free give-and-take of information, and frequent meetings for friendly discussion are the principal factors in good school relations with unions. After all, the school is training workers and most of these workers are going to be union members. The union is just as much interested in getting good workers and good people as is the community at large. On this common ground the unions are bound to cooperate. The answer is that in most cases they already have cooperated.

VI. JEFFERSONIANISM VERSUS JACKSONIANISM

The classes or the masses? Traditional academic education has certainly been for the classes, and early vocational education in the professional schools was also for the classes. Vocational education, in terms of individual differences, is for everybody, both classes and masses. In a democracy differentiation is tolerable only in terms of capacity and personal worth, not in terms of birth or wealth. The Harvard Report concerned primarily with general education, the common learnings rather than special training, states the case for democracy, and for vocational education, with telling effect:

"Are Jeffersonianism and Jacksonianism in fact complementary or do they struggle against each other? Much of our future will be written in the answer to this question. The terms are of course vague and relative. Thus we have criticized the school system as too Jeffersonian, because it gives quite different honor to academic and technical subjects from which students go on to relatively assured futures, from any that it gives to subjects pursued by humbler students. The standard of our education is a strongly middle-class standard, which must disappoint and may embitter those (perhaps half of all the students in the high school) who find themselves cast for another role. Their good is still almost wholly to be discovered. On the other hand, it can equally be said that the high school is Jacksonian, in that it largely fails to find and force the able young person. And the same, as has been noted, applies to outer influences, radio and moving picture, which aim, often calculatingly, at the mass. It has been gloomily said that no man and no society can do two things well at the same time. Certainly the human tendency is so to see one goal as to forget the other, and writers on education have not uncommonly erred with this fault, setting either a standard of culture which cruelly neglects the great mass or indulging in a flat and colorless egalitarianism. But the belief that one good is purchasable always and only at the expense of another ultimately goes back to a belief in the natural right of the stronger; it runs counter both to religious faith and to the best experience of civilization. The hope of the American school system, indeed of our society, is precisely that it can pursue two goals simultaneously: give scope to ability and raise the average. Nor are these two goals so far apart, if human beings are capable of common sympathies." [16]

[16] Buck and others, *op. cit.*, p. 35.

Chapter 9

METHODS OF TEACHING

THE curriculum is a series of way stations on a road leading to a clearly envisioned goal. At each of these stations is enacted one dramatic situation out of which emerge fragments of knowledge, elements of skill, phases of attitude, surges of feeling, and, it is hoped, flashes of desire to push on toward the next new situation. Thus we have already written about subject matter. The teachers and students move from one situation to another. The way they move, the way they make each situation dramatic, is method. So closely are subject matter and method related that it is often impossible to distinguish one from the other. Good method grows out of, and often determines the selection of good subject matter. Method is the difference between good teaching and bad teaching. It depends on all that has gone before — attitude toward work, regard for personality, solicitude for interests, choice of subject matter, and so on. It is the determiner of what actually happens in school, of what goes on in education. It is not a coldly calculated procedure (although planning is essential) but rather a warm, human experience. The plan, like the written drama, may, when it is acted out on the stage of the classroom or shop, turn out a failure or a notable success, depending upon all the circumstances, especially the actors.

An outstanding characteristic of vocational education is its engrossment in activity, in *doing,* the prerequisite for all learning. Affairs are always moving, and it is no fortuitous circumstance that, when the action touches off emotions, a drama is said to be "moving." That is the method of the dramatist. It should be the method of the teacher. Good teaching is always dramatic.

I. HOW PEOPLE LEARN

In the rise from savagery to civilization, people have learned to work in many different ways. At first they learned by the accident, the Lamb-roast-pig method. The most popular method has been trial and error, mostly error — the auto-mechanic-learning-on-your-car. If a job is to be done, and we want to do it, or, at least, we want to enjoy the products, and we are on our own, that is the natural way of learning. Trial and error is a costly method — in time, energy, and material. Observation and imitation of a good, experienced workman is better, but still wasteful. If a good worker demonstrates, shows how he does it, and explains each step, the bystander may be taking a desirable first step in learning. But the best way is to combine the natural method — plunging in and doing the job — with careful, step-by-step supervision by one who knows how it should be done — the teacher. This applies to the learning of anything — individually or in a group.

Before the advent of organized vocational education the most common way of learning a job was by the "pick-up" method. Pretend to be an experienced machinist, get a job, bungle it for a day, and be discharged but — learn something. Try again, hold the new job for two days — and learn some more. A persistent man could step up the periods of employment to one week, a month, and finally hold on as a really experienced worker. This was systematized natural learning. Our economy can now no longer support it.[1]

WHAT IS METHOD? Method is a "general or established way or order of doing anything or the means or manner by which it is presented or taught." The dictionary definition is a clue to the disrepute into which method often falls. The "general or established way" easily becomes an outmoded and inefficient way. So, there are good methods and bad methods. We speak of a good way or a best way of doing things. Practically, it is the way that accomplishes its purpose in the shortest time, at the lowest cost, with the least expenditure of energy, and, most importantly, with a maximum of pleasure. If we are talking about a method of teaching, "maximum of pleasure" means that the learners and the teacher are eager and interested. No method is wholly bad because it does not fully meet all these criteria, nor is it wholly good because it does. Method is a function of time, place, materials, and people. What is good method in a large urban school may be poor method in a small rural school, and vice versa. But, in

---

[1] CHARLES A. PROSSER and CHARLES R. ALLEN, *Vocational Education in a Democracy* (New York: The Century Co., 1925), p. 152.
CHARLES A. PROSSER and CHARLES R. ALLEN, *Have We Kept the Faith?* (New York: The Century Co., 1929), Ch. XVI.

any case, it should be the "best" way, under the circumstances, of learning something.

Obviously, *arrangement of subject matter* in an orderly manner is the first step in good method. Such arrangement begins with simple facts, interesting because they are familiar and because they apparently lead to a goal in which students are interested. From here on the plan moves along to the next related fact, and the next, and so on. The teacher carves out units of subject matter to fit a school period or a day. He plans each topic so that it will arouse a desire to *do* something about it, to *learn*. All this is method that functions before the teacher gets into a shop or classroom, or even sees a student. It is a way of employing subject matter to accomplish a purpose. It is virtually indistinguishable from the subject matter itself.

METHOD IS PERSONAL. "Methods remain the personal concern, approach, and attack of an individual, and no catalogue can ever exhaust their diversity of form and tint." [2] It is the differences in individuals, differences in knowledge, temperament, muscular coordination, in whatever makes a person an individual, or an individual a personality, that makes method something more than an arrangement of subject matter. If the primary intent of a lesson is to transmit knowledge, that knowledge assumes a different "form and tint" in each individual. It means something different to each person. If skills are being taught, they are not learned uniformly, no matter how mechanical they may seem. Each worker holds a tool in *his* way, according to the conformation of his hand and the responsiveness of his muscles. True, there is a "best" way and a "right" result, but the worker who is an artist varies the method, even if ever so slightly. Painters, for instance, are known by their style and they sign their work. So, *every* worker might very well sign *his* work, for, to the practiced eye, it already bears the earmarks, or better, the hallmark of the maker.

The active nature of vocational education, the dynamism of its subject matter, and therefore of its methods, grows out of the nature of the learner. Insofar as these methods require physical activity, allow for full expression of one's impulses, are creative and moving, they are more likely to develop personality than are those methods that depend upon passive learning (if passive learning is ever possible) and even go so far as to frustrate the pupil.

[2] From JOHN DEWEY, *Democracy and Education*, p. 204. By permission of The Macmillan Company, publishers (1916).

METHOD OF TEACHING IS THE METHOD OF AN ART. Teachers in a program of vocational education are teaching students how to work, and like the work of the students, the teacher's work should have the nature of a love song. His work is an art and its method should have the nature of an art. It is activity directed by a purpose, the purpose of enabling the men and women of the next generation to direct *their* activities with a purpose.

GOOD METHOD IS GOOD THINKING. In the next chapter we shall discuss intelligence and thinking in relation to vocational education. At this point it should be noted that good method follows the procedure of good thinking. First, there is the problem set by the goal. Then there is the collection of data bearing upon the problem, after which, through study, discussion, the data are analyzed for their significance. Next come experiment, application, and testing to determine how the data affect the problem. Finally, judgment is passed and a conclusion is reached. Whether this conclusion be an abstract formula, or a repaired automobile engine, or a skill learned by a class, the essential procedure is the same, and sound thinking has been promoted.

All this is accomplished smoothly and effectively when subject matter and method are so merged in their orientation toward a goal that they become fused into a unitary act. Consider the boy bent upon becoming a professional photographer or the master of a seagoing vessel. Everything in the photographer's equipment, from unexposed film to finished, mounted enlargement, is, in his hands, an instrument of art. Or, rather, it is an extension of himself, an element in a unitary, photographic world. The future skipper, learning to pull an oar in a lifeboat, identifies himself so completely with the oar and the boat and the purpose, that subject matter and method never become entities in his consciousness. Nor should they in the consciousness of the teacher, the master mariner, who is teaching the lesson. "Experience, in short, is not a combination of mind and world, subject and object, method and subject matter, but is a single continuous interaction of a great diversity (literally countless in number) of energies." [3]

METHOD AS BEST PRACTICE. In the attempt to identify subject matter and method it may seem that method has dissolved into a mere abstract attribute of subject matter, and that respect for individuality

[3] DEWEY, *op. cit.*, p. 196.

has negated the value of the teacher's experience and wisdom. However, that is far from being the case. The experienced photographer, for instance, ready at hand to suggest, advise, warn, is available to the eager young photographer to convey to him, as occasion demands (and the occasions are ever so frequent and imperative) the "best practice" that has developed through the experience and the experimentation of thousands of photographers, including the teacher himself. The student experiments and blunders, but his very desire for a perfect picture leads him to call upon the master worker (who may in turn refer his student to a book) for the accumulated experience of the profession. To return to our definition, if the "general or established way" produces good results, the student is satisfied. If not, then his individuality should, and often does, drive him on to seek a better way which, if he is clever and lucky, may become the "general and established way."

II. THE PROBLEM — MOTIVATION

Interest and motivation have engaged us for a whole chapter but, in relation to method, several points need to be made. First, the setting of a problem, or rather, the discovery of a problem that is besetting a student, is of the essence of method. The person without a problem to be solved has had all his problems solved for him by death. It is to solve problems that one has to put forth energy, to think, to work, to earn. The desire to solve problems is motivation. We have stated the thesis that "work" may, to a very large extent, be self-motivating, may be activity with a purpose. However, we have also pointed out that the range of susceptibility to work impulses is very great and at the lower end may be entirely lacking. There may be just no "creative" impulse in the individual.

So, in the school lesson, or in work of the world itself, it may be necessary to resort to extraneous impulses, and this necessity should not be minimized. Speaking of "schools of basic vocational education" (what today would be called "narrow vocational training"), Snedden is "strongly of the opinion that we must yet utilize the motive of gain."

"But we are still very much in the dark as to how far these instinctive tendencies alone supply motive force for modern conditions. Often they seem to rise scarcely above the level of primitive social life. They seem excessively dependent upon the play spirit. Only under strong extraneous motives, often, can men and women be depended upon to 'work hard,' to subject themselves to painful routine, to postpone pleasurable 'excursions.' Everyone who has tried to assist the poor and irresponsible, to hold adolescents to systematic effort, or to organize for productive purposes the dwellers in warm climates or the primitive humans of any part of the world, knows how imperfectly functional for the conditions created by crowded population, large utilization of natural forces, and rising standards of living, are the motives dependent directly upon instincts of workmanship.

"But social life abounds with examples of successful use of extraneous motives. Strong men early learned to drive their fellows to work by fear. The desire for 'gain' — that is, for much-wanted consumable or capital goods — can be extensively utilized. Desire for approval (or to escape disapproval) plays a very large part in holding modern man to toil. Finally, habituation, rendering that which was unpleasant, pleasant in time, and drying up the fountains of competing incentives, makes toil welcome and even necessary. Thus civilized society makes the worker, the man of routine, the provident investor, the inventor, the power harnesser." [4]

We are certain that a considerable number of boys and girls drop out of school without having developed a strong desire to pursue a particular vocation or even to work at all except for money reward. However, unless a concept of work such as we have developed can take hold of adults and can be passed along to their children, we shall be driven back upon such motives as Snedden mentions — desire for gain, craving for approval, and just plain fear. As a nation, as a world of nations, we cannot afford to retrogress into any such state of mind or spirit. We just must line ourselves up on the side of those who work in the service of mankind.

TOTAL ABSORPTION. A method of teaching that grows out of activity, that respects personality, that follows a line of abiding interests, and is therefore strongly motivated, is one that is bound to capitalize upon developed worthy attitudes. In that atmosphere learners have complete confidence in the possibilities of education. They see life growing before their eyes and want to take it in more abundantly. Their minds are receptive to new ideas, even to the danger point. They exhibit the touching faith of children. They are carried on by a unity of purpose that is as refreshing as it is sometimes inexpli-

[4] From DAVID SNEDDEN, *Vocational Education*, p. 141. By permission of The Macmillan Company, publishers (1920).

cable. Finally, they are like our worker-artist who loves his craft because it is his own. It is something for which he is responsible.[5]

III. "GOOD PRACTICE" — SPECIFIC METHODS

Just as a good method of learning a job is a good method of learning anything, so, good method in any kind of school is likely to be good method in any other kind of school. Of course, good method grows out of good subject matter. If the subject matter is worthless, then even good method cannot redeem it. But generally speaking, our thesis holds true.[6]

THE PROBLEM METHOD. The *problem* is basic to vocational education. So important is it that it becomes a springboard for the discussion of thinking and intelligence in the next chapter.

THE PROJECT METHOD. The project method has had a somewhat stormy history. However, it seems clear that it originated in the field of vocational education and was then taken over into the academic school, where it was tossed around with a view to extracting from it the best features of its vocational application without itself becoming vocational. Its origin and its main characteristics were described (1920) by Snedden:

"A few years ago some of us began using the word 'project' to describe a unit of educative work in which the most prominent feature was some form of positive and concrete achievement. The baking of a loaf of bread, the making of a shirtwaist, the raising of a bushel of corn, the making of a table, the installation of an electric bell outfit — all these, when so undertaken by learners and handled by teachers as to result in a large acquisition of knowledge and experience, were called projects. Projects of this kind might be individual or joint (cooperative). They might be executed in an ordinary lesson. Or they might claim the efforts of the learner for one or more hours per day for several weeks.

"The following were the primary characteristics of projects as thus conceived: (a) The undertaking always possessed a certain unity; (b) The learner clearly conceived the practical end or outcome to

[5] DEWEY, *op. cit.*, p. 209.
[6] F. THEODORE STRUCK, *Creative Teaching, Industrial Arts and Vocational Education* (New York: John Wiley & Sons, Inc., 1938).
NELSON L. BOSSING, *Progressive Methods of Teaching in Secondary Schools* (Boston: Houghton Mifflin Company, 1935).

be attained, and it was always expected that this outcome was full of interest to him, luring him on, as to a definite goal to be won; (c) The standards of achievement were fairly objective — so much so that the learner and his fellows could, in large part, render valuable decisions as to the work — in an amateur or in a commercial sense — or the product; and (d) The undertaking was of such a nature that the learner, in achieving his desired ends, would necessarily have to apply much of his previous knowledge and experience — perhaps heretofore not consciously held as usable in this way (e.g., art, science, mathematics, special to his skill) — and probably would have to acquire also some new knowledge and skills.

"In a sense any concrete job undertaken in a vocational school where the realization of valuable results and products constitutes an important end, might be called a 'project'; that to be an 'educational project' such a job, e.g., turning a spindle, wiring a room, growing a half acre of potatoes, taking commercial charge of three cows for a year, cooking the family breakfast for a month, making ten salable shirtwaists, cooperatively building and selling a cottage, etc., must be of such a nature as to offer large opportunity, not only for the acquisition of new skill and experience in practical manipulation, but also for application of old, and learning of new, 'related knowledge' — art, science, mathematics, administration, hygiene, social science, etc." [7]

The project is obviously something closely akin to what is called in literature "a slice of life." If education is life, if the natural way of learning is through experience, if learning takes place where there is strong motivation, if we learn what we *do,* then the project would seem to provide that perfect integration of subject matter and method that we have been seeking. The problem of curriculum building has always been that of rearranging the facts of life to make them learnable and of grouping them into units both large enough and small enough for comfortable handling. In vocational education the project lends itself admirably to this sort of treatment and, in a sense, every good lesson in a shop is a project. The commercial photographer making his super portrait may easily be employed at it for a whole week of twenty hours in the shop. Not that it takes that long to do a single job commercially, but in school, where he experiments and discusses the problem with his teacher and performs every operation himself, from arrangement of lights and pos-

[7] SNEDDEN, *op. cit.* p. 131.

ing of subject to final retouching and enlargement, this time is well spent.

In the professional field the project, with some modifications, is common enough. Medical student, dental student, law student, cannot be trusted with full charge of patients or clients before actual completion of training, but he can work along with doctor or lawyer and share some of the responsibilities and decisions. In agriculture the project has probably been worked out more effectively than anywhere else. The student, especially if his father is a farmer, can always take charge of some phase of farming, on a small scale, and make himself responsible for the product, whether it be hay, corn, chickens, or milk.

There now seems to be agreement on the essential features of a project, even in the academic field: "First, all agree that it must be problematical in nature. Second, the problem must involve an extended significant unit of activity. A third characteristic is the student's responsibility for the planning and execution of the problematic activity. This was one of the outstanding features of the early agricultural 'home projects.' And finally, the project must be a problem-solving activity of a practical nature." [8]

INDIVIDUALIZED INSTRUCTION. Again, individualized instruction has been almost a *sine qua non* of vocational education, and, incidentally, distinguishes it sharply from any kind of manual training or industrial art that calls for the completion of a series of exercises, each exercise to be finished within a prescribed time. Individual differences mean inevitably different periods of time for the completion of tasks (often projects). Different reactions to tools and processes mean that group instruction is impossible. All the criteria for effective production and competent learning call for individualized instruction. Thus, not only are the externals of adequate shop management and economic use of material provided for, but the different inner needs of students are served.

TRADE AND JOB ANALYSIS. Trade analysis is simply an adaptation of the usual curriculum procedure of breaking down subject matter into suitable teaching units. Instead of breaking down a broad field such as history or literature, the vocational teacher breaks down a trade. Whatever it may be, he determines, out of his experience, what

[8] BOSSING, *op. cit.*, p. 502,

the pupils must know — facts, skills, related technical knowledge. He then determines the order in which these shall be taught, having due regard to the sequence of difficulties as well as to the logic of arrangement demanded by the trade itself. Since the trade must be taught during periods of finite length, the analysis provides instructional material for each period. Since each individual must be reached for instruction at the same time, the teacher's analysis spreads out over many cards, each one of which can be used with different students.

The astute teacher recognizes the fact that *every* lesson need not be on a card, that even trade analysis can be carried to an unhealthy extreme, that one of the mistakes in the early days of vocational education was to carry certain techniques to the extreme, one of these being the job instruction sheet.

No discussion of method in vocational education is complete without reference to the well-known Richards formula:

$$E \propto S + T + I + M$$

This is another way of saying that efficiency on the job varies as the possession of manipulative skill, of technical knowledge, of intelligence, and of morale. The formula has been an effective reminder of the fact that mere training of the muscles is not vocational education. However, in the early days, it was followed to the point where every instruction sheet had to have on it, in addition to instructions for performing an operation, several parallel columns testing related information in science, mathematics, drawing, English, and even industrial history. These sheets were an exceedingly valuable device. When used wisely, they constituted excellent method. But, when handed to boys who could not read or who had difficulty in following directions, they were worse than useless. One of the fundamental rules for good teaching is to vary the procedure. Variety in subject matter and method is more than the spice of school life. It is its essence.[9]

METHODS AND DEVICES. Good methods are eclectic. Note a good lesson in either shop or classroom. It includes a little of each of the following: discussion, lecture, question and answer, visual instruction, individual instruction, demonstration, and drill. Teacher and group move easily from one type to another as the search for facts and the training for skills go on. The efficacy of any particular method

[9] ELROY W. BOLLINGER and G. G. WEAVER, *Occupational Instruction* (New York: Pitman, 1945).

depends upon all the circumstances that have been already enumer-
ated. Even the "lecture" that is usually deadly dull, becomes, on
occasion, a fascinating experience. There must be, of course, the
right ingredients — a facile, dramatic speaker, full of his subject; an
audience with a background rich enough immediately to comprehend the talk; experiments, demonstrations, blackboard illustrations, or other supplementary visual aids; a subject that contributes
to the solution of a problem that concerns the entire audience; and
so on. Of course, the lecture must not be too long. Similarly, a strong
case could be made for whole periods of discussion, of socialized recitation, of question and answer, of visual instruction, even of intensive drill. All of these types of instruction, and many others, have
been described and criticized in great detail elsewhere.[10]

WORK EXPERIENCE: SUPERVISED AND UNSUPERVISED. In the long history
of education we have noted how skills and knowledges that were
originally learned in and around the home have moved into the
schoolhouse. Parents and employers and fellow workers, under modern industrial conditions, have found it more efficient, more economical, and less troublesome, to hand these tasks over to people
called teachers. Yet, in the search for good education we have tried
more and more, to recapture the natural learning situation. So, the
most effective teaching in agriculture is done on supervised programs
where a boy stakes out a project on his father's farm and takes full
responsibility for it under supervision of an agricultural teacher.
This takes education right back to where it started, with, of course,
the very important added factor — the well-trained teacher.

Cooperative programs in industry or business are of essentially the
same nature. The student learns on the job with more or less supervision by foreman or office manager, while the experienced coordi-
nator-teacher establishes a sound relationship between skills learned
at work and theory learned at school. This is also the idea of the
"new apprenticeship," where the school period is only four to eight

[10] STRUCK, op. cit.
BOSSING, op. cit.
ROBERT W. SELVIDGE and VERNE C. FRYKLUND, Principles of Trade and Industrial Teaching (Peoria, Illinois: Manual Arts Press, 1930).
THEODORE H. EATON, Education and Vocations: Principles and Problems of Vocational Education (New York: John Wiley & Sons, 1926).
MILDRED E. LINCOLN, Teaching About Vocational Life (Scranton, Pennsylvania: International Textbook Co., 1937).
WILLIAM H. KILPATRICK, Foundations of Method (New York: The Macmillan Company, 1925).

hours a week as against the half-time arrangement in cooperative education. On the college level, the cooperative plans of Antioch and Bennington have already been described. Here there is undoubtedly less supervision or coordination, but the students are older, maturer. In the professional schools, especially in medicine, internships for clinical service are considered essential for complete training.

Wherever programs of work experience are not feasible, a pale substitute is the class or individual visit to industry for observation of men and women at work. Insofar as such a visit is anticipated by classroom instruction and followed up by reports and discussions, the experience has great value. But, especially for students of high school age, it should always be remembered that we learn what we do and not what we see and hear.[11]

IV. INDIVIDUALITY IN METHOD

Of paramount importance is individuality in both learner and teacher. "Best practice" and commercial standards are norms for every learner, but once he has these norms in mind and muscle, he should be encouraged to experiment, to discover better ways, to exercise his own genius in becoming a better worker, a worthy exponent of his craft or profession. Naturally, the degree to which freedom is permissible or fruitful varies from none at all to considerable, depending upon the temperament and intelligence of the learner. In the professional field such individuality distinguishes the brilliant engineer, actor, lawyer, minister, from the routine worker.

The extent to which uniformity of method should be required of all teachers is always a major problem in supervision. The circumstances are much the same as those with the learner. The brilliant teacher, burning with zeal to communicate his subject to others, may best be let alone. Whether he be machinist, artist, physician, photographer, engineer, or barber, he will convey his message perhaps by sheer inspiration. However, he will probably also scour the field for "best practice" and teach such practice with fervor and with his own elaborations. Were this type of teacher the rule instead of the exception in vocational education or, for the matter of that, in any type

---

[11] Franklin J. Keller and others, "Methods of Teaching (Agriculture, Business, Service, Industry, Homemaking)" in *Vocational Education*, Forty-Second Yearbook, National Society for the Study of Education (Chicago: University of Chicago Press, 1943).

of education, the problem of method would be of no great moment. It is precisely because personalities are what they are, infinite combinations and permutations of interest, temperament, aptitude, and physique, that method is so important. Method is no better than the teacher, but any given teacher is better for good method.

Chapter 10

THINKING AND INTELLIGENCE

I. THINKERS AND DOERS

INTELLECTUAL is a fighting word. It immediately conjures up moral judgment. For, an intellectual may be a "profound thinker" or a "dilettante," a "great statesman" or a "theorizing professor," a "benefactor of mankind" or a "mere visionary," a "thoughtful humanitarian" or a "corrupter of the masses." And all these diverse judgments are probably justified, for "thinking" is a tool, and, like a sharp-edged knife, may, in the hands of surgeon or of desperado, either save life or destroy it.

Common experience supports the notion that much of our early school instruction glances off us harmlessly, but, at odd moments, a livid scar reveals itself, as when Caesar proclaimed, with much authority, "Yon Cassius has a lean and hungry look; he thinks too much: such men are dangerous." He *thinks* too much! And then there was Hamlet.

> "Thus conscience does make cowards of us all,
> And thus the native hue of resolution
> Is sicklied o'er with the pale cast of thought,
> And enterprises of great pitch and moment
> With this regard their currents turned awry
> And lose the name of action."

Thinking makes some men dangerous and others cowardly.

And yet, by and large, thinking, intelligence, "good minds," have been respected, even when feared. The great philosophers, theologians, scientists, the bearers of the torch of learning, have said the words, written the books that embody civilized "thought." They have threshed out and recorded the ideas, have built up the ideologies upon which the lives of the people have been molded. Look at the headings in Parrington's *Main Currents in American Thought:*

"Liberalism and puritanism; germinal ideas; political, social, and economic developments; natural rights, democracy, equalitarianism; universality of moral law; determinism, reprobation; stewards of theocracy." These are all ideas about which the "little man" has been "thinking," but it is the intellectual who formulates, records, and propagandizes.

On the other hand, note the considered judgment of a great anthropologist: [1] "The thought of what we call the educative process is controlled essentially by those ideas which have been transmitted to us by past generations. . . .

"When we bear this in mind we may understand the characteristics of the behavior of the intellectuals. It is a mistake to assume that their mentality is, on the average, appreciably higher than that of the rest of the people. Perhaps a greater number of independent minds find their way into this group and into some other group of individuals who are moderately well-to-do; but their average mentality is surely in no way superior to that of the workingmen, who by the conditions of their youth have been compelled to subsist on the produce of their manual labor. In both groups mediocrity prevails; unusually strong and unusually weak individuals are the exceptions. For this reason the strength of character and intellect that is required for vigorous thought on matters in which intense sentiments are involved is not commonly found — either among the intellectuals or in any other part of the population. This condition, combined with the thoroughness with which the intellectuals have imbibed the traditions of the past, makes the majority of them in all nations conventional. It has the effect that their thoughts are based on traditions, and that the range of their vision is liable to be limited. . . .

"It is therefore not surprising that the masses of the people, whose attachment to the past is surprisingly slight, respond more quickly and more energetically to the urgent demands of the hour than the educated person, and that the ethical ideas of the best among them are human ideas, not those of a segregated past."

In American life who have been the most honored, the "thinkers" or the "doers"? It is hard to say, for again, the record is in the hands of the thinkers, the writers, those who are adept in using symbols, those who say rather than do. Symbols must be interpreted. They lead to diverse, often opposite concepts. In fact, it is a truism that

[1] Reprinted from *Anthropology and Modern Life*, by Franz Boas, pp. 196–99, by permission of W. W. Norton & Company, Inc. Copyright, 1932, by the publishers.

we know a man's thoughts only by his "behavings." We can tell
what he is thinking only by what he *says* he is thinking, or by what
he does. We have no way of seeing directly into his mind. For practical purposes, where there is what we call sincerity, frankness, communion of spirit, sympathetic feeling, we get a pretty good picture
of the other person's mind. But sincerity, frankness, are very rare
qualities. They are too often replaced by selfish desires, ingrained
prejudices, subconscious mind-sets. Then we do not learn what the
other person is thinking. In the first place, he does not say just what
he means. In the second place, it becomes exceedingly difficult to
determine the meaning of what he says. For purposes of interpretation his behavings are very bad.

Then again, it is entirely probable that much of our "thinking"
occurs after the act. We do what we want to do and then, in many
ways, justify our doing it. What we *want* to do is a product of tradition, prejudice, protectiveness. Our explanation is "rationalization," a justification to the rest of the world for our actions.

Repeatedly, teachers are heard to say to hesitant pupils, "Think!"
Or, "Act intelligently!" What does the teacher mean? Is he saying,
"Give me the answer I want" or "Remember what I told you yester-
day" or "Tell me what you saw in the book last night," or does he
really want the pupil to *think*? For all the signs that may be seen
above the blackboard in thousands of classrooms in this country,
admonitions to THINK, the teachers who put them there may
simply want the pupils to RECITE, to give back to the teacher what
they have heard in the classroom or read in a book.

However all this may be, the liberal arts colleges and the academic
high schools have always stressed the importance of learning how
to think, the importance of being intelligent, the importance of dealing effectively with ideas, that one may be an educated person and
a good citizen. On the other hand, vocational schools have always
stressed the importance of doing. No matter how much thinking
may be involved in learning to do, the ability to do is the criterion
of effective living, whether it be that of the auto mechanic, the dressmaker, the seaman, the musician, the artist, the lawyer, or the engineer. Except, perhaps, on the professional level, academic schoolmen and the products of academic schools have attributed very
little thought to the processes of education or accomplishment in
occupations below that level. For them, thinking and doing have existed on different planes.

So, let us face the fact that, over the years, the academicians have placed vocational education in a separate category from academic education. "Our point here is that there is need for a more complete democracy in both these senses not only between student and student but between subject and subject and teacher and teacher. In saying this, we have in mind the powerful, widespread, and very unhappy distinction of atmosphere and general standing between academic and vocational courses. The latter tend to be simply the dumping ground for those who do not succeed in the former." [2] The Harvard professors give a number of reasons: the wish to get ahead, parents' desires that their children shall have what they themselves have lacked, the vague optimistic belief of many young people that they may go to college and hence may need the preparatory subjects, teachers' better preparation in these subjects, and their naturally greater interest in brighter pupils, and simple snobbishness. These are undoubtedly some of the manifest reasons, but they probably grow out of something much more basic, the reverence for "thinking," "thought," "intelligence," "mind." The mysterious quality of the unknown, the lure of the "hard-to-get," the magic of "scholarship," the beauty of symbols, all these shed a purplish light on academic education and make it a measure of intelligence, that precious something with which we all wish to be credited. Just what is this intelligence, and can it, perchance, flourish in vocational schools?

II. WHAT IS INTELLIGENCE?

While intelligence cannot be measured directly, the opportunities of measuring it indirectly through the behavings of its possessor are vast, and during the last fifty years they have been explored extensively, intensively, and often controversially. The resultant definitions of intelligence are legion, yet, when they are boiled down, the differences are, for the most part, in emphasis and not in fundamental concept. An analysis and synthesis by Freeman probably provide the best brief statement:

"Intelligence, then, is the ability to learn acts or to perform new acts that are functionally useful. This definition leads to a distinction between types or forms of intelligence to fit the diversity of kinds of functionally useful acts. Different kinds of acts may be functionally useful to animals and man, to man at different stages of development, or to man in different situations. Some would object to making

2 PAUL H. BUCK and others, *General Education in a Free Society,* report of the Harvard Committee (Cambridge, Massachusetts: Harvard University Press, 1945), p. 27.

the concept as broad as this. They would confine it to what we ordinarily call the intellectual; that is, to abstract thinking. This, however, seems to be an arbitrary restriction of the term. There is a difference in kind between organic adaptation and behavioral adaptation, but there seems to be only a difference in degree between the different types of adaptation that involve learning. We would include, then, such diverse types of learning as are involved in manipulation, performing an act of skill, identifying an object, learning names of objects, forming concepts, and solving puzzles or problems of all sorts. These all are evidently means of functional adaptation.

"It is, of course, possible, and indeed probable, that these forms of learning and of adaptation form a hierarchy. The hierarchy may be of a genetic order and also of a functional order. That is, some may come later in evolution and in the development of the individual, and some may be superior insofar as they enable organisms that possess them to control those that do not. Doubtless there is such a hierarchy. This, however, does not imply that the higher forms can take the place of the lower forms or that a complete measure of intelligence can consist only of those tests that measure the higher forms. The concept of intelligence and tests of intelligence should be broad enough to include the entire range of the hierarchy. Different types of measures of intelligence may be used to measure the ability to make various types of adaptation." [3]

THE HIERARCHY. The mere mention of hierarchy raises the question of moral, social, or even intellectual judgment. Why should abstract thinking be on a higher level than "concrete" thinking? Especially in view of the findings of Boas? Can concrete and abstract intelligences successfully change their places in the world's work? Is it the abstract intelligences who themselves have created prestige for abstract intelligence and placed it at the top of the hierarchy? If concrete intelligences were more facile in the use of words (by definition, they are not at all facile), would they point out that "the ability to learn acts or to perform new acts that are functionally useful" is an especial attribute of concrete intelligences? Practically, we know that the "intelligent" mechanic may consider the "intelligent" professor of philosophy a very dumb creature, and that the professor,

---

[3] FRANK N. FREEMAN, "The Meaning of Intelligence," in *Intelligence: Its Nature and Nurture,* Thirty-Ninth Yearbook, National Society for the Study of Education (Bloomington, Illinois: Public School Publishing Company, 1940), p. 18. Quoted by permission of the Society.

except when he wants his car repaired, may return the compliment. Probably, they are both right. What kind of intelligence would a third person need to decide who is right?

Approaching the problem somewhat differently, Pintner notes four groups of definitions:

"1. Biological: It is general mental adaptability to new problems and conditions of life, or the adaptation of the organism to its environment.

"2. Educational: Intelligence is the ability to learn.

"3. Faculty: An individual is intelligent in proportion as he is able to carry on abstract thinking.

"4. Empirical (behavioristic): Intelligence is merely an evaluation of the efficiency of a reaction or group of reactions under specific circumstances." [4]

As Pintner points out, the differences among psychologists are more apparent than real. For instance, the ability to learn is really the ability of an individual to learn to adjust himself to new problems of life, and the result of this adjustment is a kind of behavior.

WHAT INTELLIGENCE DOES. Getting around to the practical question, What is the use of intelligence? Stoddard brought together what impressed him as the "principal attributes of a functional concept of intelligence," and came to the conclusion that: "Intelligence is the ability to undertake activities that are characterized by (1) difficulty, (2) complexity, (3) abstractness, (4) economy, (5) adaptiveness to a goal, (6) social value, and (7) the emergence of originals, and to maintain such activities under conditions that demand a concentration of energy and a resistance to emotional forces.

"But now must I insert two conditions, without which it is difficult to explain how so many 'intellectual' persons can be so habitually unintelligent. (These persons would do well on mental tests saturated with the demands listed above, with the probable exception of numbers 6 and 7.) The two conditions are concentration of energy and a resistance to intrusive emotional blockings or distortions.

"The first condition postulates a selecting, rejecting, recombining process moving in the direction of larger goals; sheer accumulation of information is the antithesis of intelligent activity. Intelligence, feeding upon an amorphous mass or an endless aggregation of facts, bogs down. It begins to look strangely like the 'standard' school

4 RUDOLPH PINTNER, *Intelligence Testing: Methods and Results* (New York: Henry Holt & Co., 1923), p. 47.

206

curriculum which, by overwhelming the pupil, teaches him to accept a half knowledge about a thousand things as superior to a full and clear understanding of certain basic principles in human knowledge and behavior. It enshrines half-learned, soon-forgotten details while neglecting the few dozen basic principles in the physical, biological, and social sciences that could forever inform and delight the inquiring mind. It is keen on *knowledge about,* and cool toward insight and participation." [5]

It should be noted that Stoddard, in this same article, makes the statement: "In brief, the meaning of intelligence, as it emerges from all child testing, Binet in type, is scholastic aptitude."

WHAT IS GOOD THINKING? Probably the most cherished attribute of the well-educated person is the ability to "think straight." It is also the rarest attribute of any person, well educated or not, if straight thinking is pure thinking, thinking unbiased by feeling, prejudice, tradition, any of those drives that make us *want* to do something regardless of its rationality. Nevertheless, teaching how to think has been a most important goal of the colleges and universities and, of course, under the name of logic, was the backbone of the trivium. The best known, in fact, what might be called the classic discussion of "scientific" thinking, is that of Dewey.[6] This is a detailed formulation of the method that has pervaded the whole field of science and which can be applied in any field where problems must be solved on the basis of available facts. For the purpose of classroom teaching on the secondary level, the essential characteristics of good thinking have been listed [7] as the ability to:

1. Sense the presence of a perplexing problem
2. Recognize clearly the nature of the problem
3. Hold problem in mind as it is studied
4. Venture a bold guess or hypothesis
5. Formulate possible hypothesis or solution
6. Examine critically proposed solutions
7. Cast aside hypothesis found not valid
8. Maintain attitude of suspended judgment
9. Recheck conclusions to test their validity

[5] "Definitions of Intelligence" by GEORGE D. STODDARD, quoted in *Foundations of Education* (New York: Bureau of Publications, Teachers College, Columbia University, 1941).
[6] JOHN DEWEY, *How We Think* (Boston: D. C. Heath and Company, 1910).
[7] NELSON L. BOSSING, *Progressive Methods of Teaching in Secondary Schools* (Boston: Houghton Mifflin Company, 1935), p. 457.

This method of thinking is the method of problem solving. Of course, in the lives of most of us, whether at home, among friends, or on the job, problems are, to a considerable extent, routinized. We speak of going through the daily routine. However, that routine is so broken up with the unexpected, with the new and the unusual, that the average person gets the impression that life is just one problem after another. It is probable that most of these problems are "solved" on the basis of desire, the consequences being what they may. To the extent that they are solved through a process of thinking, they come nearer to making up the life of the "educated man." In any case, teaching young people to solve problems, in other words, teaching them to think, is certainly the task of the school.

INTELLIGENCE AND LANGUAGE. The curriculum of the academic high school and of the liberal arts college is presented to students almost exclusively through language, certainly through symbols. The curriculum of the vocational high school or college is presented in part through concrete objects. Competence in industry and agriculture is measured by ability to make and operate material things. The worker must understand relationships and meanings, but they are relationships and meanings of things and properties that come directly through the senses. If intelligence were to depend largely upon the manipulation and understanding of symbols, many a worker would need, indeed, could have, no intelligence. So it is important to recognize the fact that the standard measure of intelligence, the intelligence quotient, as well as the more or less popular conception of intelligence, is very largely based upon symbolism — language.

"There are important differences among the definitions of intelligence and in the methods and hypotheses with which investigators approach the various problems related to it. But no matter which definition of intelligence one accepts, it is clear that intelligence so defined, even though it may not yet be adequately measured, must play an important part in the attainment of meaning. This is true regardless of whether intelligence be thought of as unified or manifold and regardless of the factors or categories into which its structure is analyzed. In reading the literature pertaining to intelligence, one is impressed by the frequently recurrent use of such terms as generalization, the ability to see relationships, abstract thinking, the ability to make inductions and deductions, verbal ability, inventiveness, and adequate response or adjustment to new problems or sit-

208

uations. All of these factors are involved in the making of mental constructs.

"Special attention should be called to the interrelations of language and intelligence. The predominance of verbal symbols in thinking is generally admitted. Indeed, as previously pointed out, some writers go so far as to identify symbolization and thought; others hold that the higher and more complex mental activities are impossible without language. It is not strange, therefore, that the language part of an intelligence test should strongly influence the total score on the test. In fact, language is deeply involved in most if not all of the factors into which intelligence has been analyzed." [8]

It is this very characteristic of the intelligence quotient, its heavy weighting on the language side, its close correlation with ratings in the academic subjects, that makes it, by inference, a criticism of the practical phases of vocational education.

III. SOME THOUGHTS ABOUT THINKING

The abstraction of abstract thinking from the total thought process is exceedingly difficult, even for the abstract thinker. The effect of emotion, principally subconscious, leading to rationalization, is very great indeed. There is grave doubt that many people, even occasionally, work out their problems by "thinking." "I think I'll do this," usually means, "I am inclined to do this." Then the doer "thinks up" good reasons for doing it. For most of the petty acts of life that is probably as good a way as any. However, a man who is going into business and fails to get all the facts about costs and availability of material and labor, about the number and size of outlets for his product, about the availability of buildings, machines, and transportation, and who goes into a particular business only because he would *like* to be in that kind of business, is naturally headed for disaster. He must first "think" in the truest sense of the term. The enormous number of business failures every year throughout the United States, in times of prosperity as well as depression, is ample evidence of the failure of businessmen, supposedly hard-headed, to think. Even the familiar symbols, signifiying dollars and cents, have been too abstract for them.

[8] ERNEST HORN, "Language and Meaning," in *Psychology of Learning,* Forty-First Yearbook, National Society for the Study of Education (Bloomington, Illinois: Public School Publishing Co., 1942), p. 395. Quoted by permission of the Society.

THINKING ABOUT POLITICS. It is a familiar game of intellectuals to predict just what will be on the editorial page of a particular newspaper after the news of the day is in. It is an easy kind of game for it is heavily loaded in the seer's favor. Whether the newspaper be ranked as capitalist, reactionary and conservative, or communist, revolutionary and radical, it follows a "line." The editorial writer, of course, "thinks" very carefully about the problem, "weighs" it in his mind, and comes out with his "reasoned" judgment. What he actually reasons is that anything that affects the interests of his constituents, that would seriously modify or even destroy the "system" for which his paper stands, is wrong, and starting from that premise, he digs up all the reasons *why* it is wrong.

We all do this, some of the time. The really educated man checks and rechecks, examines his soul, combs his conscience, submits his thinking to his best friend and severest critic. Then he steels himself to the hurts that come when his pet ideas are attacked. Bacon recognized the difficulty when he listed his "idols." In any instance it is virtually impossible to isolate the influences that affect our so-called thinking, but they are suggested in such words and phrases as the closed mind, strong passion, submissiveness to authority, susceptibility to dogma, self-interest, mental laziness, false expectations, inflated ego, inordinate ambition, desire to protect family, and so on. It is a tangled skein, practically impossible to unravel. But it is human nature and it is within those limitations that "thinking" takes place. It is the later psychiatrists — Freud, Jung, and Adler — who have tried to fathom the depths of the subconscious to identify these drives which, if they could ever be brought under one classification, would probably be called attempts at self-realization.

In this connection it should be noted that in all the writings on intelligence there is very little reference to feeling as such. "Straight thinking" is a rarity because feeling is always pulling thinking out of line. The psychologists know this and point out the effects of, say, social position, upon opinion. It is the intense feeling of horror for loss of social position, or the equally intense liking for advancement of social position, that distorts thinking. So with other types of status, professional, political, economic. Incidentally, these classifications do not exclude schoolmen, even those who write books. It takes hard reasoning and clarification of conscience of a high order, to "think straight" — even about vocational education.

Finally, as a sociological note with probable bearing on vocational education, there is this fact: "All the summarized studies tend to show that low cultural environment tends to *depress* I.Q. approximately to the degree agreed to as characteristic of laborers' children, and that a high environment *raises* I.Q. correspondingly." [9]

IV. THINKING IN ACADEMIC OR GENERAL EDUCATION

Good thinking in education should be good thinking in any kind of education. However, with special reference to general education it is particularly pertinent to note an analysis of traits and characteristics of mind so important as to prescribe how general education should be carried out and which abilities should be sought above all others in every part of it.[10] They are to think effectively, to communicate thought, to make relevant judgments, to discriminate among values. Effective thinking includes logical thinking, relational thinking, and imaginative thinking, and each of these corresponds roughly to the three divisions of learning, the natural sciences, the social studies, and the humanities, respectively. Because of their direct application to vocational education, two excerpts from the Report are strikingly relevant:

"The making of relevant judgments involves the ability of the student to bring to bear the whole range of ideas upon the area of experience. It is not now a question of apprehending more relationships within ideas but of applying these to actual facts. The most competent instructor of military science is not necessarily the best officer in the field. An adequate theory of ball playing is conceivable, but an abstract knowledge of it would not make a good ball player any more than a course on poetics, however good, would make a good poet. It is not the power to distinguish or state the universal formula, for separate contemplation, which heightens our skill. It is the power to use the formula in the new concrete situations as they flit past us which education aims to advance. In Plato's myth the philosopher who obtained the vision of the good must return to the cave and use his vision in order to guide himself among the shadows. Initially and inevitably he is confused; only after long habituation is he able to find his way around and properly to apply his concepts to his concrete experience. There is no rule to be learned which could tell the students how to apply rules to cases; the translation

[9] WALTER S. NEFF, "Social Status and Intelligence," in *Foundations of Education, op. cit.,* p. 352.
[10] BUCK and others, *op. cit.,* p. 64.

from theory to practice involves an art all its own and requires the skill which we call sagacity or judgment. . . .

"Education must be so contrived that the young, during the very process of their schooling, will realize the difference between abstractions and facts and will learn to make the transition from thought to action. A young man who has been nourished with ideas exclusively will be tempted by the sin of intellectual pride, thinking himself capable of dealing with any problem, independently of experience. When he later comes into contact with things, he will stumble or perhaps in self-defense withdraw into sterile cleverness. As we have seen, the aptitude of making relevant judgments cannot be developed by theoretical teaching; being an art, it comes from example, practice, and habituation. None the less the teacher can do a great deal; he can relate theoretical content to the student's life at every feasible point, and he can deliberately simulate in the classroom situations from life. Finally, he can bring concrete reports of actual cases for discussion with the students. The essential thing is that the teacher should be constantly aware of the ultimate objectives, never letting means obscure ends, and should be persistent in directing the attention of the student from the symbols to the things they symbolize." [11]

In view of the fact that vocational education combines just such practical education as is demanded in these two quoted paragraphs, with the sciences, the social studies, and the humanities, it appears that it takes full cognizance of the necessity for teaching young people to exercise and develop all the important traits of mind. Vocational education certainly does make the transition from thought to action and makes it in an experienced situation such as can be the only completely effective setting for learning.

V. THINKING IN VOCATIONAL EDUCATION

ACTIVITY AND THINKING. From all the previous discussion it is amply evident that thinking is not a passive process but is rather the necessary accompaniment of activity such as first manifests itself in the baby's groping for control over its muscles, and from there on to the well-coordinated, purposeful activity of the full-grown person. It is this meaningfulness of work that makes it such a potent force for good thinking as well as for good ethics. "For work (as a mental attitude, not as mere external performance) means interest in the

[11] BUCK and others, *op. cit.*, pp. 70–71.

adequate embodiment of a meaning (a suggestion, purpose, aim) in objective form through the use of appropriate materials and appliances. Such an attitude takes advantage of the meanings aroused and built up in free play, but controls their development by seeing to it that they are applied to things and ways consistent with the observable structure of the things themselves." [12] Up to this point we have stressed the learning value of work principally because work is based on interest, thus insuring a learning attitude, and is directed toward a goal, thereby insuring attention and responsibility. Now we see that such a situation inevitably makes an insistent demand upon the mind, and therefore trains the worker in good thinking.

TESTING BELIEFS. Except in science and mathematics, academic subjects do not serve well for the testing of beliefs. In larger and even in smaller social problems the range is so long and the criteria are so subjective that it is exceedingly difficult, usually impossible, to check one's beliefs except in terms of other people's beliefs and of what passes for the community mind. But the checking of beliefs is highly important. "While it is not the business of education to prove every statement made, any more than to teach every possible item of information, it is its business to cultivate deep-seated and effective habits of discriminating tested belief from mere assertions, guesses, and opinions; to develop a lively, sincere, and open-minded preference for conclusions that are properly grounded, and to engrain into the individual's working habits methods of inquiry and reasoning appropriate to the various problems that present themselves." [13] It is precisely in vocational education that these beliefs can be tested, within various ranges of accuracy, depending upon the particular occupation. Where two pieces of metal are threaded so that one will fit into the other, they must fit, or the operation is unsuccessful. The belief, based upon careful planning, that one will fit into the other, is tested, and there is no question as to the outcome. In the training of the physician there can seldom be such precision. So many grains of such and such remedy given to patient X will not produce the same result if given to patient Y, nor even if given to patient X a second time. Nevertheless, by and large, in the vocations there is a minimum of guesswork and a maximum of accurate testing.

[12] JOHN DEWEY, *op. cit.*, p. 163.
[13] JOHN DEWEY, *op. cit.*, p. 27.

MANY TYPES OF THINKING. Vocational education is not merely shop work or laboratory work, but is also science, mathematics, English, history, health, in fact, all the general subjects. Such variety provides for the necessary variations in the thinking process, logical, relational, imaginative, with a view to producing the oft-mentioned, but so seldom realized, well-rounded personality.

STANDARD PROCEDURE IN TEACHING VOCATIONS. The "*I*" in the Richards formula, $E \propto S + T + I + M$, stands for intelligence, the intelligence that demands the best kind of thinking. Take the familiar situation in which an automobile engine just refuses to operate. Along comes the auto repair man. His first task is that of troubleshooter. All that you tell him is that the engine will not go. He may ask you how it "died," or how long you had run it, or a few other seemingly irrelevant questions, but then he goes to work, and systematically tests each feature, either on the engine or leading to it, to find out where the trouble lies. Eliminating one at a time, he finally finds a flaw and concludes that that is the cause of the trouble. He repairs the troublesome element and tries to start the engine. It still doesn't go. He must keep on with his search, testing each unit in the order in which it is most likely to have become defective. He continues this process until finally the engine does start. What has he been doing? He has been *thinking*. He began with an incomplete situation that was full of doubt and perplexity. He had a very definite goal. The engine must be made to run. He conjectured what the trouble might be on the basis of whatever slight evidence the owner could give him or that might lie in the appearance of the engine. Acting on his surmise he tried the carburetor but found it in good condition. Then he made another guess, perhaps that the gas feed line was clogged, but that too was all right. One by one he tried out his conjectures until he discovered just where the trouble lay. He corrected it and then tested out his belief as to whether the engine would run or not. All the time he was thinking and not only finding his way to the correct solution, but also learning about the weaknesses of this particular engine which, at some future time, would probably come back to him for repair. He would have learned something of its nature so that the next repair could probably be made much more quickly.

There is nothing essentially different in the procedure of the doctor who comes to see a patient. He has a little advantage in that a human being can tell how he feels, how the trouble began, whether he ever had had it before. (Even these data are lacking when the patient is a baby.) However, here is a much more complicated and temperamental machine. The doctor must try one thing at a time, starting on a hunch or a conjecture — heart, lungs, pulse, temperature, throat, nose, ears, palpation of abdomen. If he discovers no symptoms at these sources, he may have to go on to urinalysis, blood test, X-ray. He is still trying to find out what is wrong with the machine, and when he gets one or two symptoms he conjectures as to the cause and then tries out his remedies. All the time he has been thinking, putting one and one together to make two and then two and two to make four. He has been recalling patterns of symptoms and similar cases within his experience, always comparing and drawing conclusions. The good auto repair man and the good doctor are both effective thinkers. And they always have in view the "next case," for they are learners.

INTEREST AGAIN. No interest, no learning. No learning, no thinking. The interest factor is certainly strongest in vocational subjects and it naturally follows that the student thinks more effectively in the real situation in which he has a stake.[14] He is also dealing with concrete, clearly defined objects and facts, and he has the benefit of repetitive training in the same thinking problems, both of which are sound aids to effective thinking.

THE LANGUAGE OF VOCATION AND SCIENCE. As has already been pointed out, language can readily be a bar to clear thinking. However, the language of the trades and professions usually refers to very definite, well-defined objects and operations, thus very seldom lending itself to confusion. Thinking with symbols is difficult except when these symbols bear a close and easily discoverable relation to their objects. The worker uses well-defined data.

PERSONALITY AGAIN. A sound program of guidance in vocational education recognizes all types and degrees of intelligence, thereby providing appropriate subject matter and method for all people. Recognition of individual differences makes it possible to cover the whole range instead of confining education to abstract thinkers.

[14] CHARLES A. PROSSER and CHARLES R. ALLEN, *Vocational Education in a Democracy* (New York: The Century Co., 1925), pp. 51–56.

SKILL AND INTELLIGENCE. "There is all the difference in the world whether the acquisition of information is treated as an end in itself, or is made an integral portion of the training of thought. The assumption that information which has been accumulated apart from use in the recognition and solution of the problem may later on be freely employed at will by thought is quite false. The skill at the ready command of intelligence is the skill acquired with the aid of intelligence; the only information which, otherwise and by accident, can be put to logical use is that acquired in the course of thinking. Because the knowledge has been achieved in connection with the needs of specific situations, men of little book-learning are often able to put to effective use every ounce of knowledge they possess; while men of vast erudition are often swamped by the mere bulk of their learning, because memory, rather than thinking, has been operative in obtaining it." [15]

[15] JOHN DEWEY, *op. cit.,* p. 53.

Chapter 11

PHYSICAL AND MENTAL HEALTH

THE most striking contrast between Greek and modern education is found, not in its organization, but in its content, especially in the importance given to gymnastics. In the period of school life from seven to sixteen, fully half — and before the fifth century much more than half — of the boy's time was given to the palaestra. The entire formal education of the ephebic period, including the two years in the gymnasium and the two years garrison duty, likewise consisted of physical training. And yet from all this the Greeks got much more than mere physical development. Moral ends were no less important. *Wholemindedness* or temperance — the control of the passions and the emotions by reason — was thus obtained. Above all, the coordination of thought and action, the fitting of conduct to precept, or word to action, was secured through this same training, and there resulted that harmony between the inner thought life and the outer life of conduct which formed the ideal of the Greeks.

"Games and physical contests were not indulged in haphazardly as with the modern youth, nor participated in by the few for the entertainment of the many. Nor were the standards of excellence the same as modern ones. Success consisted not so much in the winning of the contest as in the evidence given of the proper form of the exercise, the graceful and dignified carriage, the control of temper, and of skill. Running races were usually held in the sand or with lighted torches, so that it can be seen that speed alone was not the test; and the great variety of forms of wrestling indicates that muscular strength was not the chief qualification, nor development of it the aim. Above all other exercises, especially above those forms that called for display of mere force, were prized such games as called for quickness of perception and evidence of carriage or 'pluck.' " [1]

I. THE NEED

The very concept of the primacy of the person carries with it heavy emphasis upon physical and mental health. The nature of individual differences established the importance of these two factors and their close relation to emotional stability. One of the oldest educational slogans has been, "A sound mind in a sound body." Yet, while emphasis has been laid upon play and athletics and much has been preached in the classroom about the importance of health, little attention has been paid to individual differences and still less has been done to see that preachment has been followed by practice.

MODERN VIEWS OF HEALTH. The Greek ideal finds its modern counterpart in psychosomatic medicine, one phase of which has already been mentioned as the conception of temperament as determined by physique — endomorphs, mesomorphs, and ectomorphs. The significance of this conception lies in the realization that the combinations of these three types are almost as many as there are different people. And, by the same reasoning, all people are different, different in everything that goes to make up what we call "personality." To discuss personality and intelligence and ethics without relation to the physiques within which these qualities reside or, perhaps, out of which they evolve, is to ignore a fundamental determinant in education.

However, the Greek ideal cannot be accepted uncritically. Those who abandoned "excess" babies to the elements and left all manual labor to their slaves were no respecters of personality, but rather worshipers of an aristocracy of mind and body. Even Hitler laid great stress on the cultivation of physique, associating it in theory with "race" and in practice with militarism. In and for itself, glowing health is no asset. It leads only to dissipation and domination. A sound physique is *for* something, preferably something socially useful and morally justifiable. Moreover, when the individual has been assisted in reaching his maximum or optimum physical effectiveness, no matter how low that may be on the scale, he is entitled to guidance in adapting himself to as pleasant and remunerative an

[1] From PAUL MONROE, *History of Education*, p. 88. By permission of The Macmillan Company, publishers (1909).

occupation as his body fits him for. The animated mechanism with which he works is an essential part of the personality that commands respect and merits development.

MOTIVATION. Everybody concedes that good health is desirable. Everybody wants to enjoy the advantages of good health. However, adults are notoriously neglectful of health until ill health overtakes them and pain or incapacity or both drive them to the doctor. Again, individual differences mean differences in attitude toward health as well as in health itself. At the other extreme from indifference is the attitude of the hypochondriac, with causeless anxiety about his personal health.

The reasons for neglect are probably many — lack of imagination, low intelligence, inertia, cost of medical service, and dearth of knowledge and practice in using available facilities. Education can do much to stimulate the imagination, to give knowledge, and to overcome inertia. It can also stir up social consciousness so as to provide adequate medical service within the means of the common people. The advances of science, all kinds of tests and treatments — X-ray, vaccines, radium, have worked wonders, but only those in the more favored income brackets can utilize these services and maintain their physical health when twenty-five dollars, say, is an ordinary charge for one visit to a physician, one X-ray picture, two days in the hospital, or a few treatments, and a sum in excess of one or two months' salary of the average worker is considered a fair charge for an operation.

The strongest motivation should lie in the pleasurable emotions that accompany fitness. "This phase of physical fitness refers to the positive side of 'mental hygiene.' It is more than freedom from strain. It is the release of power that comes when one is enthusiastic about the thing he is doing. We have tried to find a better name than pleasurable emotions but so far have been unsuccessful. . . .

" 'One of the most striking things in the development of modern physiology is its gradual recognition of the great value of those pleasurable emotional states which may be classified together under the abused word "joy" and of the harmfulness of the opposite emotional states — anxiety, sorrow, worry, fear, pain, and the like. The condition of happiness, of "joy," is that in which development is unhindered and flourishing; in which the functions are proceeding harmoniously; for worry, fear, unhappiness are the marks of the reverse condition of affairs; something is blocked and is going wrong.

"These pleasurable emotions of the happy individual make it possible to accomplish more with less fatigue. Without this enthusiasm, few men accomplish major achievements. They stop, believing they are tired, long before there is any danger of overdoing. Psychological levels of effort have been reached by men and women suffering from great handicaps — John Milton, Elizabeth Barrett Browning, Kahlil Gibran, and Mohandas Gandhi." [2]

However, probably even stronger motivation lies in the desire for efficiency in one's vocation, or at least for the earning power that accompanies such efficiency. Earning power is desirable for one's own comfort, for pleasurable emotions, but more importantly, for the health and happiness of the wage earner's family. It is this motivation that makes health education an essential phase of vocational education.

Practical experience with people, especially adolescents, indicates that even strong positive motivation is often not enough. As with young children, it must sometimes be as negative as the ultimate withholding of a diploma if the student has not followed all reasonable instructions for the correction of remediable defects. It is probably more to his own interest to "pass" in "health" than in biology or English or any other "subject" in the curriculum. Above and beyond this comparatively low standard, it is hoped that students will acquire knowledges, attitudes, and skills which will help them solve their future health problems. The school can do no less than to keep a watchful eye and a guiding hand on each boy and girl to the end that, at a critical age, he or she may be saved from those acts of commission or omission that result in lifelong physical discomfort or disability.

Each individual is a different problem. There are the fortunate few who have inherited good physiques and good minds, whose habits of living are wholesome, who need give little or no attention to their health. At the other extreme are those with disabilities that require almost constant attention, the severely handicapped and the chronically ill. On the one hand, health education is part of the instructional program for the whole student body. It is part of the teaching curriculum. On the other, it is a phase of guidance, individual and intensive guidance. For several decades health has been one

[2] *Paths to Better Schools,* 1945 Yearbook of the American Association of School Administrators (Washington, D.C.: National Education Association, 1945). The passage in single quotes is from HERBERT S. JENNINGS and others, *Suggestions in Modern Science Concerning Education* (New York: The Macmillan Company, 1917).

of the well-known cardinal principles of education. Due homage has been paid to its importance, yet, positive stipulation as to accomplishment has often been lacking. It is imperative that it be as definitely part of the curriculum as any other "subject."

THE PHYSICAL FITNESS OF WORKERS. Good health results from wholesome health habits. "These habits are ones which the individual should acquire as part of his everyday behavior. It is not enough merely to learn about these things. They are behavior patterns which the individual must acquire through doing. Wholesome health habits should be such as would promote growth and development of the individual and at the same time provide for maximum protection for himself and his fellow beings." [3]

These habits are skills that must be learned. The human body is the kit of tools used for attaining skills and is also the well-adjusted machine that actually exercises skills. Good posture is skill in holding the various parts of the body in place, good carriage is skill in walking, good physical appearance is skill in taking care of the human machine, good tennis playing is skill in making the body hit a ball properly. An efficient body plus a clear directing mind constitute skill on the job, also skill in the home and in other social relationships.

Medical science still has severe limitations. It cannot give normal vision to the color blind. It cannot grow a new arm or leg where one has been lost, although it has done wonders with artificial replacements. When the individual has reached the limit of improvement, he must be adjusted to a vocation for which he is fitted. No matter how great his desire to go to sea, color blindness prevents a boy from ever becoming a deck officer, but he may still gratify his love of ships by shipping out as purser or radio operator. Epileptics may be hazards in the engine room of a freighter, but recent advances in medical science have made it possible for them to become excellent workers, as well as useful citizens, in other capacities.

II. ORGANIZATION

ORGANIZATION. According to size of school and resources of community, the organization may be simple or complex. Considered as a phase of guidance, reference has already been made to it in the chapter on Primacy of the Person. Primarily, the responsibility lies

[3] *Paths to Better Schools*, p. 52.

upon the vocational and educational counselor, whether he is one person serving the whole school or is head of a group of counselors. The small school may have to call upon outside individuals and institutions for all medical and health service. In a large vocational high school, as in New York City, for instance, where the Department of Health cooperates, the following persons take part in the program:

1. Department of Health physician
2. Department of Health nurse
3. Registered nurses assigned to the school as teachers of home nursing and hygiene, who also act as health counselors and maintain liaison between the school staff and the Department of Health
4. Advisors (home room teachers)
5. Health education teachers, including a swimming teacher
6. All subject teachers to the extent that their subjects impinge upon health problems
7. The school and Department of Health call upon all public and private clinics, hospitals, and other agencies for service. They enlist the cooperation of private doctors and dentists where these are preferred by the pupils' parents.
8. The school calls upon or receives offers from Rotary, Kiwanis, and other civic organizations, for funds and services in the promotion of health.

In other words, as a community problem, health must be promoted and conserved by the community.

III. THE PROCEDURE

MEDICAL EXAMINATIONS. The basis of a sound health program is exact knowledge of the physical condition of all students. Thus it becomes necessary to examine each individual *before* entrance to a vocational school, to examine him when he is nearing graduation or approaching the time when he will drop out of school and go to work, to give him a routine examination [4] at annual intervals, and to examine him at any time that he presents evidence of maladjustment, illness, or other difficulty which may have an underlying medical cause.

RECORDS. Careful record is kept of every examination and is, of course, always inspected in conjunction with the health record from

[4] DOROTHY NYSWANDER, *Solving School Health Problems* (New York: Commonwealth Fund, 1942).

previous schools. Every complete health record should be reviewed once a year to select students for special referral to the medical staff for whatever medical examination and follow-up is indicated, to select others for follow-up by the health education teacher or teacher-nurse, to exchange pertinent information concerning the health of each individual with a view to obtaining satisfactory school and work adjustment, and to follow through on previous recommendations. Each case is subject to a joint review by head counselor, health counselor, Board of Education nurse, and student's advisor. Out of such conferences evolves the most effective kind of guidance and health service. At every point the health record, as part of the cumulative record, follows the child throughout his school career.

FOLLOW-UP. Follow-up must be humanly kind, yet relentless. The objective is always development of attitudes and formation of habits such as will carry over into adult life. It constitutes the best motivated kind of *teaching*. However, unless it is firm, unless failure to co-operate results in the withholding of privileges, the whole procedure is meaningless. It culminates in the graduation of a boy or girl who has removed all remediable defects and has attained goals that may be called optimum for that particular individual. Failure to attain these goals means failure to graduate. As drastic as this procedure may seem to some, it has worked marvels in inducing boys and girls, who would otherwise have been satisfied to enter their occupations physically unfit, to make extraordinary efforts, successful efforts, to have their teeth put in good order, to bring their weight up to normal, and to have operations performed for the correction of orthopedic and neurological defects, even for the removal of troublesome appendixes.

PHYSICAL EDUCATION. The valuable contributions of physical education to the health of adolescents in a vocational education program are quite apparent. They are made even more useful through careful adaptation to individual needs as revealed by medical examinations. For those suffering from handicaps, corrective or limited programs are indicated. Unfortunately, uniformity is too often a characteristic in a field where individual differences are most obvious. As in all other phases of vocational education, the needs of the individual, in relation to the demands of society, take precedence over any preconceived notion of physical perfection.

IV. FACULTY PARTICIPATION

As with the entire guidance program, health measures cannot be solely the responsibility of a few specialists. It lies upon the entire faculty, for good health is fundamental to effective exercise of the mind, to development of wholesome emotions, and to acquirement of skills. The advisor is especially concerned, for upon him lies the responsibility of seeing that all services of the school and of the community at large are brought to bear upon the students in his section. It is he who must follow up, and follow up, and follow up. He is *in loco parentis,* and like any good parent, carefully guards the health of his child. From time to time he gives home room lessons on general health problems. As classroom teacher he gives lessons on health as related to his particular trade, especially where occupational hazards are involved.

HEALTH OF FACULTY MEMBERS. "Perhaps the most important mental health factor in the school environment is the personality of the teacher. The teacher or principal who is kind but firm, sympathetic but exacting, and friendly but reserved, exerts a beneficial influence on emotional health. The nagging, scolding, sarcastic, domineering, or emotionally unstable teacher or principal can seriously injure pupils. The same considerations apply to all other school personnel.

"The mental health of pupils requires that teaching methods give ample opportunity for experiencing success without exposing the pupil to excessive fatigue, undue worry or other unfavorable emotional stimulation. Disciplinary measures should consider pupil personality of greater importance than the rigid application of arbitrary rules. Types of examinations and methods of promotion should stimulate each pupil to do the best he can rather than discourage or degrade him. Any system of awards should put emphasis on group cooperation rather than on undue competition among individuals." [5]

SCHOOL HEALTH COUNCIL. To bring home to all faculty members the importance of health and to obtain their cooperation in dealing with health problems, from time to time, the key members of the faculty are brought together as a health council to discuss current problems. Doctors, nurses, counselors, custodian, chairmen of departments,

[5] National Conference for Cooperation in Health Education, *School Health Policies* (New York: Health Education Council, 1946), p. 12.

and principal meet with students, representing the student council, parents representing the parent-teachers' association, and officials, representing the Board of Education. They discuss those many problems that affect the health of boys and girls. Some of these problems are of such nature that they do not ordinarily receive attention under the heading of health, yet they are most important. For instance, cleanliness of building, character of lighting, use of window shades, supply of soap and towels, fatigue factors, and unnecessary stresses and strains imposed upon teachers. These, and many more, are subjects of fruitful discussion when faculty members get together in the interest of their students' health.

V. SOME SPECIAL PROBLEMS

In an age of psychosomatic medicine every advance in "medicine" is, or can be, an advance in personality development, and therefore an advance in occupational adjustment. Indeed, the entire subject of health may be considered in these terms. So, it is patent that a program of vocational education must incorporate every procedure and device that will widen and deepen the individual's occupational availability by intensifying his physical capacity and enriching his personality. Among the newer techniques are those that make eyes, ears, and lungs more useful instruments of effective living.

EYES, EARS, AND LUNGS. The telebinocular is a diagnostic apparatus used in schools and clinics as a screening device for eye defects not revealed by the superficial Snellen Chart. Significant defects are referred to the ophthalmologist for necessary correction. This is also useful in carrying out a remedial reading plan. Group audiometer tests are used to screen out those students who may have a significant loss of hearing. The individual pure tone audiometer is then used for diagnostic purposes so that each student may be given follow-up treatment. This may consist of lip reading, special voice and speech training, and individually fitted hearing aids. Similarly, lungs are subjected to the screening patch test, then to diagnostic X-ray, and appropriate action follows. So with other tests of special physical disabilities.

PHYSIQUE AND THE JOB. Despite the obvious handicaps that poverty offers to maintenance of good health, neither wealth nor high position is a guarantee of physical well-being. Stomach ulcers are a common possession of the rich and the worried. Nervous breakdowns result not from hard work but from insecurity and failure. These maladjustments arise from a vast complex of causes, many of which originate in physical defects. The earlier these defects are detected and undergo treatment or compensation, the more likely is the individual to be adjusted to life in general and his occupation in particular.

Chapter 12

ETHICS AND THE GOOD LIFE

BEYOND everything else, parents want their children to be good. "I want my boy to be a good boy, my girl to be a good girl." In that word "good" lies a wealth of meaning, a differing meaning for each one who uses it, but by and large, there is a sense of positive virtue, doing good as well as being good, being kind to others as well as keeping out of trouble. On a higher level it connotes something spiritual, the bright, shining goodness of a worthy person. Some parents instill that kind of spirit at home and hope the school will foster it, at least, not spoil it. Other parents, not so sure of the beneficent influence of the home, hope the school will somehow make their children better than they are.

There is no clear-cut conception as to how all this is to come about. Vaguely, one would suppose, through the influence of "good" teachers, and the habitual good conduct imposed in the classroom, plus some protection from the inevitable "bad" youngsters. It is questionable as to how much is expected from contact with reading and arithmetic and history and geography. In fact, the stories of people, both real and fictional, pack a great deal of chicanery and plain evil. What parent can trace his offspring's improving conduct to the power of numbers or the story of the Civil War? Yet herein lies, by inference, one of the curious criticisms of "narrow" vocational education. It is too utilitarian, it lacks the cultural and moral values of general education. It has no spiritual content.

However, change the word "utilitarian" to "useful" and there is an immediate brightening of atmosphere. Something really useful has a kind of moral value. If it is "serviceable," a little more so; if it "serves mankind," much more so. Work conceived as activity with a purpose, the product of an artist, of a personality accepting responsibility, in a democracy — all this adds up to a spirituality far removed from utilitarianism. No public school can accept the full burden of a young person's soul life. The home, the community, the church, wield, or should wield, a powerful influence — religious sanctions, mystical insights are theirs to give. The school, especially the vocational school, conceived broadly and deeply as a place where education is life, should provide a wholesome, vivid, and stimulating laboratory in which these finer human traits can flourish.

I. THE MEANING OF ETHICS

THE GOOD LIFE. In the Prologue we asked for the acceptance of certain assumptions. One by one, we have examined these assumptions, elaborated upon them and, we hope, have transformed them into convictions. Probably, in view of its history, the boldest assumption is that of the ethical nature of the vocational school program. In a sense, what we mean by this ethical nature is either stated or implied in all that has preceded. Our conception of work, of personality, of purpose, of democracy — all these are ethical, moral-bearing. They are concerned with values, with conduct, in fact, with everything that constitutes character. We recall the quotation in Chapter 7 to the effect that every statement of educational purposes depends upon the judgment of some person or group as to what is good and what is bad, what is true and what is false, what is ugly and what is beautiful, what is valuable and what is worthless, in the conduct of human affairs. The ethical concept applies to all the other phases of education. Who is the *good* citizen? Who has *good* character? Who uses his leisure time *worthily?* What is a *good* job?

Our assumption was that vocational education is the creative spirit in the mechanic, service rendered by the merchant, justice won by the prosecutor, food raised by the farmer, and life saved by the doctor. It is attitudes, emotions, ethics, conduct, language, and beauty — those attributes that transform jobs into vocations and men and women into their neighbors' keepers and into citizens of the world. A philosophy of education is a philosophy of life, based upon personal experience, community and world experience (present and past), and upon those inner drives and impulses toward a good life, whether they be compounded of the "data and intelligent purpose" of the pragmatist, the "perfection" of the idealist, or the "inner light" or God of the deeply religious. Now, this chapter is about the "ethics" and the "good life" in those assumptions, especially about the life that is good for others as well as for the person who lives it.

One of the most frequently used words in this book is "purpose." Here, as elsewhere, we are speaking of purpose that is *good*. We recall, too, that in the chapter on Primacy of the Person, all schools of philosophy agree that "each person is to be treated always as an end and never merely as a means." Because a philosopher can think of nothing higher or more valuable than personality, the effect on personality is the ultimate test of any social system. In fact, personality is equal to or coterminous with ethics, morals, conduct, spirituality.

The notable significance of this unanimity in philosophical thought is emphasized by a consideration of the dictionary definition of the word "ethics" and of its three divergent theories: "The science of moral duty; more broadly, the science of the ideal human character and the ideal ends of human action. The chief problems with which ethics deals is the *summum bonum,* or highest good, the origin and validity of the sense of duty, and the character and authority of moral obligations. The principal ethical theories are: (1) Such as consider happiness to be the greatest good; these may be *egoistic,* as is usually the case with *hedonistic* and *eudaemonistic;* or *altruistic,* as with *utilitarianism.* (2) Theories of *perfectionism* or *self-realization.* (3) Theories resting upon the relation of man to the universe or to the divine law, as *stoicism, evolutionism, Christian ethics."*

Emphasis upon personality is emphasis upon wholeness, integrity, the complete man in all his relations in life. While, for the sake of clear exposition, it is necessary to discuss the various virtues one at a time, it is essential to keep in mind that, for a person to possess virtue, he must be at one with all of life.

SPIRITUAL VALUES. The test of spiritual value lies in the relation of the individual to all other individuals. Certainly only those values that relate the other person to the self are spiritual. Like the philosophic agreement as to the significance of the personality, "There is a large measure of agreement in American communities on what the spiritual values mean by way of actual personal conduct. Our differences, our lack of community, on them concerns rather the philosophical rationalization and verbalizing of these values. To employ but one example, there is a united community demand that children learn to be just in their dealings with each other. The demand for fair play extends all the way from the sports program to learning to take turns in kindergarten. Indeed, children are more likely to overlook creed and color in their schoolmates than are their elders in their associates. But when it comes to teaching the why and where-fore of just conduct, there is a plethora, almost a confusion, of ad-vice. Some find justification in the natural rights of man, some in the grounds of expediency, some in tested consequences, and some in the ordinance of God." [1]

It is this very personal conduct that is of such exceedingly great importance in school, not for its effect upon school life, not for its contribution to the comfort of the teachers, but for its effect upon the personality that lives with other personalities not only for a few school years but for a full lifetime thereafter.

These spiritual values are what we like to call "standards." Com-menting upon Plato's picture of a man whose personal conduct we would not approve, Livingstone says: "Such a character is not wholly bad. It has moments of energy and intermittent bursts of goodness, but the desire or ambition of the moment masters it — now sex, now money, now something else — and it makes no distinction between good and bad because it has no standards, no principle to rule and discipline it. 'Such a man's life,' as Plato says, 'is subject to no order or restraint, and he has no wish to change an existence which he calls pleasant, free and happy.' But of all lives the life without standards is the most ignoble and barren, sweet in the mouth but bitter in the belly." [2] As a matter of fact, ethics is often defined as the systematic study of the ultimate problems of human conduct, concerning itself with *value*. It is a normative science. It is concerned not so much with the facts of actual human conduct but with its ideal, what it ought to be. It gives rise to Whitehead's well known statement that "moral education is impossible without the habitual vision of great-ness."

II. THE ETHICAL PROBLEMS OF WORK

The entire structure of work relationships is shot through with ethical problems. The sale of a commodity assumes honest represen-tation on the part of the seller and, if it is sold on credit, an honest intention to pay on the part of the buyer. The rendering of a service assumes that the worker will give the full measure of his skill and energy and that the purchaser of the service will pay full value

---

[1] *The Public Schools and Spiritual Values,* Seventh Yearbook, John Dewey Society (New York: Harper & Brothers, 1944), p. 12.
[2] From SIR RICHARD LIVINGSTONE, *On Education,* p. 13. By permission of The Mac-millan Company, publishers (1944).

for it. It is often said that the whole modern financial program, being based on credit, depends for its existence on an evaluation of character, not only of ability to pay but of intention to pay. (Of course, these intentions are measured very coldly in the light of the individual's past performances, but still it is a matter of *good* intention.) When business dealings go wrong, there is frequently the cry of bad faith. It is good faith and good morals that keep any economic or social group in operation. And it is faith or lack of faith that determines a worker's conduct. In one sense, every act he performs is a moral act. So it is even in school. As we have repeated several times, the choice of subject matter is based upon a moral judgment, a judgment as to whether that particular matter truly represents life as it is lived. We have also noted that method, as used in those momentary situations called school, involves moral quality and that the ideas developed through method become moral traits. Every time the teacher makes a decision as to whether a pupil shall be passed or failed, whether he shall be lightly reprimanded or severely punished, whether this or that boy shall be given a heavy responsibility—all these are moral judgments often affecting the lives of the pupils in extraordinary ways.

EXTENT OF WORK RELATIONSHIPS. When reference is made to narrow vocational education it is obvious that work relationships are thought to be confined in factories and offices, places where people go to work, and that outside those factories and offices the workers become consumers, citizens, family members, quite different people from what they are as "workers." Actually nothing of the kind is true. Consider the mother in the home. She works for the entire family, the family is her employer. If she has a servant, she becomes an employer. She also "employs" the husband and the children to work for her in keeping up the home. In these work relationships there arise problems of diligence, skill, hours, working environment, and a hundred other problems involving moral judgment on the part of employer or worker as to the way in which the work is done. As a matter of fact, probably most family troubles arise from conflicting moral judgments as to work in the home.

In the course of "play" the players often hire people to work for them. Golf, tennis, yacht, and other sport clubs employ workers to help the members play. Similarly with social clubs, on a grand scale for the wealthy, on a very moderate scale for others. Those on the lower economic levels have to content themselves with parties in hotels or other public places, where they hire musicians, entertainers, waiters, and so on. These players, in the capacity of consumers, become employers and set up work relationships in order that they may play.

Workers associate themselves in unions and union members are felt to be essentially "workers." However, many of the unions become employers. For instance, the National Maritime Union of 90,000 members employs 500 workers in its headquarters. Some of these, as workers on the union weekly newspaper, *The Pilot,* belong to the Writers' Guild, another union. As an employer, the National Maritime Union must negotiate with its employees, the Writers' Guild. Similarly the New York City Board of Education employs custodians who belong to a union, the members of which, in turn, employ helpers who belong to another union.

Finally, every consumer who buys goods from shopkeepers, gets advice from a physician, has his automobile maintained by an auto mechanic, or lives in a community where there is a policeman, "employs" all these people to work for him, and his relationships with them raise many moral problems.

So, everybody becomes involved in a curiously complex situation that, on one hand, seems to call only for consumer and citizenship morality, but on the other, acquires all the color of an employer-employee relationship. In other words, in our complex and closely interrelated society there is very little of what can be called "pure play." The commercial aspects of play comprehend most of the moralities of work. All that is left for pure play is gaiety and laughter, and adherence to the rules of the game.

INDIVIDUAL AND SOCIAL VIRTUES. These are many. Honesty, truthfulness, love of work, justice, fairness, faithfulness, fulfillment of duty, in fact, all those traits that constitute "character," are requisites of the successful worker, as well as of the worker in all his other life relationships.[3]

These virtues are usually ascribed to, or at least demanded of, the worker, but obviously they must also be possessed by the employer. He too must be honest, truthful, just, fair, and of good character. The occupational virtues certainly work both ways. Otherwise we would not find the Federal Trade Commission outlining sixty-eight methods of unfair competition, among them:

---

[3] FRITZ GIESE, *Philosophie der Arbeit* (Halle: Carl Marhold, 1932). This book includes an extensive and detailed analysis of the ethics of work.

"Misbranding of fabrics and other commodities respecting the materials or ingredients of which they are composed, their quality, origin, or source.

"Unauthorized appropriation of the results of a competitor's ingenuity, labor and expense, thereby avoiding costs otherwise necessarily involved in production.

"Selling rebuilt machines of various descriptions, rebuilt automobile tires, and old motion picture films slightly changed and renamed as and for new products.

"Giving and offering to give premiums of unequal value, the particular premiums received to be determined by lot or chance, thus in effect setting up a lottery.

"Use of pretended exaggerated retail prices in connection with or upon the containers of commodities intended to be sold as bargains at lower figures.

"Imitating or using standard containers customarily associated in the minds of the general purchasing public with standard weights of the product therein contained, to sell to such public such commodity in weights less than the aforementioned standard weights.

"Direct misrepresentation of the composition, nature, or qualities of the product offered and sold.

"Securing business by advertising a 'free trial' offer proposition, when, as a matter of fact, only a 'money back' opportunity is offered the prospective customer.

"Falsely stating that products were made in or came from some locality famous for the quality of such products.

"Stating that products were made by some well and favorably known process, when, as a matter of fact, they were only made in imitation of and by a substitute for such process." [4]

SPECIFIC VOCATIONAL VIRTUES. These specific vocational virtues seem, at first glance, to apply only to work situations. However, again, they are obviously applicable to other so-called play or social situations, or, to put it the other way, the play and social situations really possess, as we have shown, many work elements. Listed among these virtues are will to work, production of adequate quantity and quality, conscientiousness as to time spent, the desire to advance, orderliness, friendliness, self-control, and ability to control others.

[4] "Federal Trade Commission Outline of Sixty-Eight Methods of Unfair Competition," *The Manufacturer*, December, 1929.

COMMUNITY VIRTUES. Patently, classification of virtues as personal and social, specifically vocational, or community virtues, is a more or less artificial device for discussion purposes. Take unemployment, for instance. Perhaps the individual is lazy and does not want to work. Perhaps he is sick and cannot work. Maybe he very much wants to work but cannot find employment. Just where illness or poor physique ends and laziness begins is a fine point for the physician or the social worker. Just how much each individual, as a member of society, is responsible for the unemployment of any other individual, is also a fine point. In any case, continued involuntary unemployment may cause the borderline worker to become voluntarily unemployed.

Is the community responsible for seeing that a worker has a sufficient amount of leisure time to make him a worthwhile worker when he is at work? Is society responsible for the low wages and poverty of the worker, which in turn make him a poor worker and lower his wages still further? Is society or the employer responsible for unhealthy, hazardous work conditions? Who is responsible for the form and pattern of life of the worker, and does it make any difference to anyone but himself and his family?

Finally, whose fault is it if a worker is injured on the job? It certainly becomes difficult to point a finger with any assurance when the primary causes of accident-proneness are listed in descending order as faulty attitude, failure to recognize potential hazards, faulty judgment of speed or distance, impulsiveness, irresponsibility, failing to keep attention constant, nervousness and fear, defective vision, organic diseases, slow reaction, high blood pressure, senility, worry and depression, fatigueability, improper distribution of attention, and inexperience.[5]

III. ETHICS AND DEMOCRACY

If all the virtues we have just been discussing were exercised by all the people, that is to say, if Utopia were suddenly brought into being, they would "strike that delicate balance between my desires and your desires." They would make possible that full and harmonious development of personality, along with a sense of restraint and love that leads to just as full and just as harmonious development of

[5] Reprinted from *The Science of Work* by MORRIS S. VITELES, p. 207, by permission of W. W. Norton & Company, Inc. Copyright, 1934, by the publishers.

all other personalities, known collectively as "society." That would be democracy, and if education accomplished it, education would be democracy.

THE ETHICAL ROOT OF DEMOCRACY. This deep respect for personality, this belief that all human beings have absolute worth, is in accordance with the Judeo-Christian doctrine that every human being has a soul worth saving. While democracy conceives of all men as being equal in a society of men, religion sees them as equal in the eyes of God.

"Jerusalem became a symbol of ideal morality woven on the pattern and the ethics of the family. In the figure are the lines of love, which bind the parents and children; of justice, which is meet among brothers; of charity, which is the sensitive consideration of each for his fellow man. Essential in the spirit and method of democracy is its deep distrust of violence, its hatred of war, its aspiration for peace. Where human personality is highly regarded, there coercion is an absolute evil. The family community is cemented by love in its many aspects, and with love only persuasion is consonant. From the interplay of consideration in mating, from the social impulse in rearing children, from the sense of mutual aid present in the family, the moods and attitudes implied in democracy are derived." [6]

After pointing out that the ethical definition of democracy is not sufficient, but without it we have no definition of democracy at all, Berkson goes on:

"Religion has given full recognition to the fact that men have the power to redirect and to energize their own actions. Much harm has been done in private lives and in social affairs by certain modern schools of psychology which deny the existence of 'will.' It may be freely admitted that the will cannot ever move mountains by direct command, and that sometimes its practical effectiveness cannot be counted on at all. New terms, 'mind set,' 'integrated behavior,' 'purposeful activity,' may be more accurate for scientific study, or more useful for educational purposes. All this has its place, providing it does not make us neglect the more fundamental insight into human character, namely, that man has the power to mobilize his own energies by taking thought in advance, by concentration of emotional attitudes, by setting himself firmly toward a predetermined goal. Religion has grasped the significance of this human potentiality and

[6] I. B. BERKSON, *Preface to an Educational Philosophy* (New York: Columbia University, 1945), p. 26.

has long ago learned that it can be raised by what appear to be immaterial means, by exhortation, encouragement, inspiration, and instilling of faith.

"There is another element of fundamental truth in the religious view: the realization that external changes must be incorporated into the character of each person. The just society cannot be maintained by force of legal enactment alone; right conduct must be supported by the disposition to do right, for no society could enforce its customs and laws only through fear. Besides, the greater part of human relations are beyond the scope of law or even the scrutiny of public opinion. In final analysis, 'Society' is the process of interaction among persons, and 'social ideals' are ways of behaving in intimate personal relations. A social ethics must eventuate in a personality with the attitudes and habits which embody the ideal." [7]

THE SOCIAL ROOTS OF DEMOCRACY. A scanning of the principal theses of the Declaration of Independence immediately brings to light the close parallelism of the political and the religious conceptions of democracy. It states that all men are created equal, that they are endowed by their Creator with certain inalienable rights, that among these are life, liberty and the pursuit of happiness, that to secure these rights governments are instituted among men, that governments derive their just powers from the consent of the governed, and that the people have the right to alter or abolish any form of government which becomes destructive of these human ends. The point is that there are human ends, and that the humans include everybody, without exception. American government, from its inception, has been a moral kind of government. It has been founded on ethical principles. It can be, has been prevented from being wholly moral in actuality by those who have not understood and have not embodied its spiritual purposes. The morality of a nation is the total morality of all its component individuals, those persons whose primacy is the paramount concern of a sound vocational education program, indeed of any social institution designed to maintain and advance the welfare not only of its immediate constituents but of all mankind.

THE DIGNITY OF MAN. Commenting on "General Education in a Free Society," published by Harvard University, and upon "Education for ALL American Youth," President James Bryant Conant,

[7] BERKSON, op. cit., p. 69.

236

who sponsored the Harvard Report and was a member of the Commission that produced the second Report, defined the ends of general education "in terms of an adult behavior essential for the development of a free society in a scientific age, not in terms of societies of the past to which such colorful words as barbarism and civilization have their relevance." [8] That this must be an ethical society is emphasized by the Harvard Report itself:

"This idea is described in many ways, perhaps most commonly in recent times, as that of the dignity of man. To the belief in man's dignity must be added the recognition of his duty to his fellow men. Dignity does not rest on any man as being separate from all other beings, which he in any case cannot be, but springs from his common humanity and exists positively as he makes the common good his own. This concept is essentially that of the Western tradition; the view of man as free and not a slave, an end in himself and not a means. It may have what many believe to be the limitations of humanism, which are those of pride and arise from making man the measure of all things. But it need not have these limitations, since it is equally compatible with the religious view of life. Thus it is similar to the position described at the end of the last chapter as cooperation without uniformity, agreement on the good of man at the level of performance without the necessity of agreement on ultimates, but two points have now been added. First, thus stated, the goal of education is not in conflict with but largely includes the goals of religious education, education in the Western tradition, and education in modern democracy. For these in turn have been seen to involve necessary elements in our common tradition, each to a great extent implied in the others as levels at which it can be understood. Certainly no fruitful way of stating the belief in the dignity and mutual obligation of man can present it as other than, at one and the same time, effective in the present, emerging from the past, and partaking in the nature not of fact but of faith. Second, it has become clear that the common ground between these various views — namely, the impulse to rear students to a received idea of the good — is in fact necessary to education. It is impossible to escape the realization that our society, like any society, rests on common beliefs and that a major task of education is to perpetuate them." [9]

[8] JAMES BRYANT CONANT, *Public Education and the Structure of American Society* (New York: Bureau of Publications, Teachers College, Columbia University, 1945), p. 26.
[9] PAUL H. BUCK and others, *General Education in a Free Society,* report of the Harvard Committee (Cambridge, Massachusetts: Harvard University Press, 1945), p. 46.

IV. TEACHING MORALS

In 1926 the National Education Association Committee on Character Education set up certain conditions for character education that are today as pertinent as ever:

"The least the school may do in its character training efforts is to provide learning conditions which enable the pupil to be honest and sincere with himself. This condition obtains only when the pupil is able to realize that what he is trying to do is valuable to him. He should not be expected to believe this just blindly because someone in authority directs him. He should be able to believe it because his experiences and efforts have led him in close enough relation to the thing he is trying to master to appreciate somewhat his need of it.

"This first right of the pupil to have his personality in its unity and honesty of effort respected by those who seek to guide his learning and to establish right character, is basic to all other considerations in promoting the development of the rich, righteous human life. Indeed, all of the other four qualities are necessary because of this first requisite in any program of character development."

METHODS OF TEACHING. Probably in no phase of methodology could more diverse opinions be elicited than in the field of morals. Some hold that morals cannot be taught at all. They are learned unconsciously in an environment. Others maintain that morals can very definitely be taught through direct classroom instruction. There is still not enough validated evidence to prove that either extreme is right. However, the consensus would seem to be that direct instruction is the least effective method and that therefore, whenever and wherever possible, morals should be learned in the situations in which they are supposed to become effective. If the situation is not likely to arise naturally, it should be "arranged," and preferably dramatized. Charters discusses the following methods: Life situations, individual, indirect, direct, rewards and penalties, suggestion and example, reasoning, personification, dramatization.[10]

As Charters himself points out, "The educators of this country are agreed to a degree quite beyond their custom that all moral education should be indirect." He argues that the great weakness of indirect teaching is its lack of system. On the other hand, if indirect teaching arose out of situations that were true to life, this weakness

10 W. W. CHARTERS, *The Teaching of Ideals* (New York: The Macmillan Company, 1929).

would be overcome. Moreover, if, in these life situations, the individual were to be taught, the results should be outstanding. It is in just this kind of setting that vocational education can be especially effective. The very essence of the teaching of skills and processes, along with related theory and work relationships, is that the situation shall be a replica of life, or at least highly comparable. Whatever virtues inhere in the many other methods (and they are great, especially in suggestion and example, personification, and dramatization) are available to the vocational education program, and they certainly should be used to supplement the individual-life-situation method.

It is exceedingly interesting to note that, while Charters has been discussing the teaching of ideals principally in the elementary school, he falls back finally upon "a technique borrowed from commercial and industrial education and known as *training on the job.*" It is divided into five steps: analysis, demonstration, trial, correction, and follow-up. He illustrates by considering the case of a mother who wishes to apply the ideal of neatness for the first time to her son's closet. She goes through the whole process with him, step by step, individually, of course, showing him his errors and demonstrating right methods, at all times encouraging and holding up to him the ideal of neatness. We recall that neatness is one of our work virtues, and it is easy to see how much more effectively and realistically neatness can be taught to a boy doing a useful job, one that he wants to do, where the goal is a product for which he feels responsibility and pride, and where neatness is merely a by-product, learned more or less unconsciously as part of a life situation. Charters points out that the "training on the job" method merges into the project method which, again, is a product of vocational education.

While the ethics of vocational teachers is not necessarily better than that of academic teachers, it is likely that such ideals as neatness, precision, being assets in the trade, assets which the teacher has presumably realized to have commercial value, are more vividly and effectively taught by teachers with that kind of experience. The situations certainly have a more vibrant air of reality, and, of course, it is patent that the personality of the teacher, his bearing, tone of voice, facial expression, gestures, are all of utmost importance in determining the net result of moral teaching.

V. ETHICS AND VOCATIONAL EDUCATION

Throughout this chapter, by implication, we have emphasized the point that the vocational education program provides, better than any other, opportunities and incentives for teaching morals, the morals of a democratic society. We have pointed out that work relationships are so interwoven with what are called social or family or citizenship relationships, that the virtues acquired in one field permeate those of all others. It is true that we do not have conclusive evidence of the extent of this permeation or of the effectiveness of transfer. As Snedden suggests,[11] the conscientious workman may be a poor father or voter, the hard-working farmer may be stingy and a monopolist. We need more inductive study. However, we are clear that the major worthwhile traits of human nature apply in some degree to all relationships and that the work relationships are varied enough to bring them to bear upon most phases of any one individual's life.

PERSONALITY. Emphasis upon personality, upon an intensive and far-reaching program of guidance, is the major factor in teaching morals. In fact, some maintain that development of personality *is* ethics, that good morals are good personality, and that good personalities are collectively the good society. For, all guidance procedures are concerned with making the individual person "good" — both "good *for something*" and "good per se." It is the process of getting him to choose the "right" action. It is effective only if the situations are real, the stimulus great, and the teacher himself an effective personality.

CONDUCT. Again, conduct, behavior, ethics, morals, may be used interchangeably. The way an individual acts is what the individual *is*. If his aims are those of an adult personality, then the development of that personality eventuates in good conduct.

PURPOSE. The weakness in most academic education is its lack of purpose, of pupil-purpose, of student-purpose. Vocational education is, by definition, directed activity with a purpose, a life purpose, a career, a goal which, when reached, enables the individual not only to support himself but to support others, those he loves. It is not the

[11] DAVID SNEDDEN, *Vocational Education* (New York: The Macmillan Company, 1920), p. 142.

narrow, selfish, utilitarian thing it is so often purported to be. It is a vocation, a calling, something that keeps one moving on, sets one on the road to somewhere. True, there are those who never acquire a purpose or whose purpose is purely hedonistic. There will always be such, but the way to make purpose real is to provide education that taps interests, develops personalities, opens up opportunities, is therefore purposeful. Academic education that eventuates only in "culture," in "good citizenship," in the "educated man," but still leaves him without purpose, is a travesty upon education and a mockery to society.

THE ARTIST. The kind of person we have been describing, the person with a purpose, *is* the artist. Every work of his hands and his brain and his heart is a love song. For him the whole world sings, sings beautifully and truly, and is therefore a moral world.

RESPONSIBILITY. It is this sense of responsibility that ties up into an effective whole the activities of any school. In a vocational school it can be and has been made very real. Responsibility lies with the students and the entire staff. For instance, placement is no mere formal procedure. As a vocational school function, it *must* place the student in the occupation for which he has been trained or, if there has been a change of heart or mind, in one which he wants and likes. This is a responsibility. If the student is required to complete a project, a "masterpiece," for graduation, that project must *be* a masterpiece, and graduation should be impossible without it. If a student is sent out for work experience on the cooperative plan, he must render, on the testimony of his employer, highly satisfactory service. This is a responsibility of the student, and that he carry out his responsibility is a responsibility of the school.

Every vocational school should have an Honor Society open to all students on conditions of service, scholarship, workmanship, character rating, and the like, that are understood by the entire student body and which are attainable by a large percentage of the students, through their own efforts and on their own recognition. The responsibility for attaining high standards should be laid upon all. Similarly, graduation requirements in the realities of life, which become the realities of education, should be set, and it should be the responsibility of the faculty to see that the responsibility of fulfilling those requirements is met by a large percentage of the students.

In all this the head of the school carries the major responsibility of seeing that all these ethical responsibilities are carried out. That is moral education. It is also, in the very best meaning of the word, sound discipline.

INDIVIDUAL TEACHING. The vocational school provides ideal conditions for individual teaching, and therefore, for the development of individual personalities. This occurs in life situations, and the net result is responsible self-direction.

LIFE SITUATIONS. When these life situations are vocational situations, they are readily provided by the vocational school. In the academic schools they do not arise naturally. Yet, Charters makes only one major reference to vocations, that to the Oath of Hippocrates and the codes of approximately 180 American organizations.[12] Right here is the opportunity to use as teaching devices codes that have been drawn up by professional and business men as a result of their own experience. This the vocational school can do very effectively.

MORALE. It is difficult to define morale in industry and business, but it is probably a composite of all we have been discussing. Prosser and Allen believe that vocational education promotes morale in the following ways:

(1) The learner progresses easily
(2) The learner is spared discouragement
(3) The learner develops occupational pride
(4) The learner's training promotes stability
(5) Vocational education turns parasites into workers
(6) Vocational education increases skill and capacity
(7) Vocational education increases the worker's economic lines of efficiency, and thereby enables him to find more than one job in which he can be successful.[13]

DEMOCRACY. In vocational education *everyone* has a chance to succeed. All this is at one with the fundamental tenets of democracy, a moral kind of society.

PERSONAL AND SOCIAL VIRTUES. Since these are related to one's career, and as phases of work relationships pervade personal and social rela-

[12] CHARTERS, *op. cit.,* p. 56.
[13] CHARLES A. PROSSER and CHARLES R. ALLEN, *Vocational Education in a Democracy* (New York: The Century Co., 1925), p. 56 ff.

tionships, the virtues in each sphere reinforce each other. All of them become, to a considerable degree, responsibilities of society.

VOCATION AS A CALLING. The great weakness of academic education is that it puts off consideration of vocation until "education" has been completed. Education is one thing and occupation another. A person learns to live and then to work. It is this kind of divorcement that extracts from vocation all elements of spirituality. It is a real danger. It is only vocational education that accepts and dignifies work, that makes vocation what it should be, an integral part of life, part of the heart and soul and mind of man.

THE LUXURY OF INTEGRITY. "I recall the case of a brilliant young accountant who, shortly after winning his C.P.A., was given an opportunity to make a million dollars, more or less, in a few months time. All he had to do was to approach certain corporations with an offer to split whatever rebates he might earn for them in their filed income tax returns. His share in turn was to be split with the government examiner who supplied the names of such corporations as had legitimate claims for rebates in past tax payments. He told his mother of the glittering opportunity. 'Jim,' she said, 'you know when I come to wake you in the morning I shake you hard and you don't stir?' 'Yes,' he said. 'And then I shake you even harder and you give a little moan?' 'Yes.' 'And finally I shake as hard as I can, and you open one sleepy eye?' 'Yes.' 'I'd hate to come in morning after morning and find you awake.' He turned down the job and has been sleeping soundly ever since." [14]

[14] STUART CHASE, "The Luxury of Integrity," *Harper's Magazine*, August, 1930, p. 342.

Chapter 13

ADMINISTRATION AND
SUPERVISION—LOCAL UNITS

ADMINISTRATION and supervision constitute the arrangements and devices through which the aims of education are carried out in practice. Good administration makes it possible for teachers to do their work effectively, and for boys and girls, young men and women, mature trade and professional workers, to make their lives happier and more efficient. Partly by implication and partly by explicit prescription, administrative and supervisory procedures have been suggested in the discussions of work, scope, personality, subject matter, democracy, intelligence, and ethics. These fundamental concepts applied to effective procedures already current in secondary and higher education, result in sound education from the standpoint of vocation and life. However, they do not automatically determine these procedures, in fact, they create some major, and aggravate some minor problems. It is these special phases that are treated in the present chapter, first, as they affect a local educational unit, and then, as they relate to education on a national scale.

A discussion of administration, indeed a whole book, unless written entirely from secondary sources, must, to be useful, grow naturally out of the writer's experience. Truly, as we have already noted, style is the man. Such writing gives rise to the obvious criticism that this experience, if obtained in a large urban school, does not apply to a small rural school, that procedures effective in one type of community are futile in another. As to details of practice, this is unquestionably true. However, general principles, if sound, should apply in any situation. Long and extensive observation of vocational education in many lands leads us to believe that this is true. So, throughout this book, attempt has been made to set up principles that are generally applicable, and to leave the widest latitude for variations in application. These can be made only by a keen, enthusiastic, intelligent staff that is thoroughly alive to local needs.

I. ORGANIZATION

The intrusion of vocational activities into the all-academic program of the public schools has naturally given rise to as lively a jurisdictional dispute as has ever occurred among trade unions. In one state system there are dual boards of control. In city systems we have frequently had directors of vocational education subordinate to academic administrators possessing no knowledge or understanding of vocations, and no sympathy with education for them. We have had a good deal of "looking down" upon vocational education as something for duller children, and we have had some aggressive independence exhibited by vocational people intent upon compensating for inferiority complex. These have all been natural, perhaps inevitable, phases of the growth of an educational movement. In recent years, as leaders in vocational education have shown their mettle and justified their cause, the controversies have subsided to a considerable extent. Nevertheless, there always remains the question as to who shall decide the when, where, how, what kind, and how much of vocational education in any community. The situation is usually complicated by heavy overweighting of academic teachers whose primary interest is in teaching what they know, and who generally tend to resist the fearsome unknown. Vested interests always play a part.

THE COMMUNITY GETS WHAT IT WANTS. If the community wants vocational education, vocational education it will have. That is what the Board of Education is for, and it will appoint a superintendent to carry out the mandate of the community. The board members and superintendent must all be understanding and sympathetic. They must believe in work, sound concepts of work, as a goal in education. If the superintendent does not have an intimate acquaintance with vocational education, as is too often likely to be the case, then he must find someone who has that intimate knowledge and put him in charge of all vocational activities. Whether, in a large community, he has the title of associate or assistant superintendent, or in a small community, he is a director, supervisor, or teacher-in-charge, makes little difference so long as he has the understanding of both superintendent and Board of Education and the authority to set up a sound program. If such a program is left to an academically trained executive who has, by neither experience nor study, acquired competency in the vocational field, it is doomed before it begins. Any consideration of an "effective" plan of organization, apart from the man who is to administer it, can be only theoretical. It can serve only as a norm, subject to an infinite number of modifications based on local conditions, personal and material.

Assuming the maximum of good will and attention on the part of an administrator, his vocational program can only sputter out into futility if he does not have the liveliest appreciation of the occupational demands of industry, business, agriculture, personal service, the professions, and also of the striking individual differences in the children concerned. Vocational education and vocational educators have often been called "narrow" because they have been contending for something that the academic educators have not understood. Perhaps vocational educators have not fully appreciated the virtues of academic education, but there are two salient facts: one is that the vocational educators have been products of that academic program, and the other is that they have been contending for a place in an academic system already well entrenched. All these psychological and social factors are of paramount importance in determining jurisdiction in a school system.

WHO SHOULD BE THE VOCATIONAL ADMINISTRATOR? To write specifications for an administrator is a dangerous proceeding. In fact, this is true of specifications for any kind of position written by any kind of person. The writer inevitably comes to draw a picture of himself or, by implication, to criticize those he dislikes. It is easy enough to point out that administrators must possess the qualities of "leadership," "intelligence," and "presence." As with any statement of the aims of education, the mere mention of these qualifications constitutes a moral judgment. Certainly the competent administrator must possess them, whatever kinds of behavior they may connote. It is a little easier to prescribe qualifications that can, to a certain extent, be measured. The vocational administrator must know vocations, either through a reasonably long period of actual experience in them, or through a considerable period of intensive study and observation. Preferably, he should have combined both experience and study. He must know academic education. We are past the period when experienced tradesmen, without a thoroughgoing appreciation and understanding of academic education, can administer a vocational program with success. Whatever opinion he may hold as to the futility of much of academic education, he cannot make a place for vocational education unless he can meet the academic people on their own ground. Perhaps it is unfortunate that educational administration must be considered in terms of psychological warfare, but the fact is too patent to be ignored.

Following closely upon the last qualification, the vocational administrator should be well versed in the arts of communication. He must write and speak up for his charge. He must be able to meet and persuade academic schoolmen but, even more important, he must mingle with the public, all of the public. He is, in a very real sense, public relations counselor.

VOCATIONAL EDUCATION FOR EVERYBODY. All this is based upon the notion that vocational education is for everybody. It is based upon the contention that "intelligence" and "thinking" cannot be associated solely with academic education, thus leading to all the evils of educational caste. The best in human values can come out of vocational education, so it must be administered with a view to extracting this "best," and by men and women who not only *know* the best but *are* the best.

The principal thesis of this book is that sound vocational education provides an all-round education for the individual, is, in fact, the best kind of general education. For those who are afraid that vocational education will, under such a program, be swallowed up and debased by academic education, let it be noted that this cannot happen if the administrator of the vocational program meets the foregoing specifications. Knowledge and understanding of, and enthusiasm for, vocational education will prevent such a catastrophe. On the other hand, those who see the danger of segregating vocational education and carrying it on entirely apart from academic education, will note that the administrator who combines good academic education with vocational experience appreciates this danger and is assiduous in avoiding it.

What has been said of the administrator applies, for the most part, to the supervisor. Of both of them it may be said that they are professional persons and, as such, meet the specifications for any other good worker. Each is an artist, keen and enthusiastic about his work of art. He designs the product and feels highly responsible for

247

its successful completion. If he loves children, as he must, his work can be truly a love song.[1]

II. MULTIPLICITY OF OCCUPATIONS

Obviously, even the largest city in the world cannot teach all the trades. Sometimes this fact is cited as conclusive proof of the futility of all vocational education. One might as well argue that since the goal of the encyclopedist is unattainable, all academic education is futile. However, there are other and better approaches.

In the first place, whatever the limitations of a vocational education program may be, it is essential that these limitations be thoroughly appreciated, that within those limitations all known resources be used, and that the public (meaning parents, industrial and business men, and the young people) be made fully aware of those limitations as well as of the opportunities of the program. In a large city there can be specialized schools in each of a dozen or more trades — let us say, printing, auto mechanics, business practice, metal trades, commercial photography, maritime trades, aviation, and so on — whereas, in a very small community, it may be impossible to set up even one shop in one trade. Between these extremes all kinds of combinations and permutations are possible according to the resources of the community and the resourcefulness of the administrator. These variations in schools, both as to trade taught and the place and time of teaching (the very small community may have to resort to the diversified occupations program carried on in commercial shops, stores, or farms) will be detailed in a later chapter. Here it is only necessary to re-emphasize, from an administrative point of view, some of the general principles already developed.

OCCUPATIONAL INFORMATION. Although the teaching of occupational information is a far cry from the teaching of occupational skills, certainly the first approach to vocational education is through a vocational guidance program that brings to young people all possible information *about* occupations. Regardless of limitations of the training program, the school will have stirred up interests, desires, drives, the prerequisites for all education.

These very interests are a goad to the school to provide subject

---

[1] EDWIN A. LEE, "Administration and Supervision of Vocational Education," in *Vocational Education*, Forty-Second Yearbook, National Society for the Study of Education (Chicago: University of Chicago Press, 1943).

matter that will feed these interests. Such subject matter may be presented through one or many of the various types of vocational education. As a matter of fact, much has been written about the importance of letting the curriculum grow out of the interests of the child, but it is a seldom realized ideal. It can be realized.[2]

FAMILIES OF OCCUPATIONS AND MULTI-SKILLED TRADES. From time to time reference is made to families of occupations with the suggestion that schools can teach these "families," thereby making students eligible for entrance into a number of different trades within the family. There is a good deal of value in this conception, but considerable danger in some of the conclusions drawn from it. Take, for instance, the similarity between typing by a secretary in a commercial office and typing by a linotyper in a print shop. While the actual operation is much the same and there are some workers who would be interchangeable, there are so many other conditions surrounding the business office on one hand and the print shop on the other that the same individual is not likely to be attracted equally by both jobs.

During World War II the Army and Navy both found that not only could individual workers transfer readily from a peacetime job to a war job apparently having no relationship, but that entire industrial establishments could be quickly converted. For instance, church organ factories were put to work, with surprisingly little trouble, making airplane parts.

However, it is important to note that young people do not aspire, and probably can never be made to aspire, to efficiency in a "family of occupations." Their interests are directed toward a particular job, with all its surrounding glamor or adventure or precision or machinery or what not. Full use of the young person's interest means that that is the job for which to prepare. If it includes skills and knowledges that are readily applicable to other jobs, well and good. As a matter of fact, this is usually what happens and the "family" is served even though it was not the original objective.

Then, some jobs are multi-skilled. Take, for instance, that of marine engineer. An all-round training for this kind of work includes machine shop practice, electrical maintenance, sheet metal work, pipe fitting, gas engine maintenance, steam turbine and reciprocating engine maintenance. A young man who has gone through

2 FRANKLIN J. KELLER, "Out of Guidance into Curriculum," *Curriculum Journal,* Vol. VIII, No. 8, December, 1937.

this course can take a beginning position in any one of these trades. If, for any reason, it proves more desirable to work ashore than aboard ship, he is well prepared to be a stationary engineer. Earlier we have spoken of the importance of teaching an occupation so that it will radiate into many other phases of knowledge and skill. If this is done, the young person will have become prepared for entrance into many occupations other than those for which he received specific training. So, even in small communities, with severe educational limitations, much can be accomplished.

TRADITIONALISM IN VOCATIONAL EDUCATION. It is a truism that every revolution ends in reaction. Pioneering in vocational education can do the same, in fact, in some instances, *has* done so. Certain old-line standard shops, such as machine, woodworking, electrical, and plumbing, have often been considered the normal, even inevitable, nucleus for any new trade school. There has been some reason, of course. Metal and electrical trades have continued to be a large part of our economy, but certainly woodworking and plumbing have rapidly changed in character and incidence. More than that, newer trades have arrived and even they are rapidly changing. The point is that, unless there are very definite controls, certain elements of vocational education may become as "traditional," nearly as useless as some phases of academic education. These controls must be democratic and, as pointed out in the chapter on Democracy, should originate with large, progressive advisory boards who, in cooperation with the Board of Education, should conduct continuous surveys. We shall return to the topic of advisory boards and continuous surveys, but first we must note another essential control of the dangers arising from the way in which multiplicity of occupations affects the aims of the school.

III. THE FLEXIBLE SCHOOL PROGRAM

In the middle Twenties, just after the Smith-Hughes Law had been passed, and vocational education was really getting on its feet, it was written that, "effective vocational education for any profession, calling, trade, occupation, or job can only be given to the select group of individuals who need it, want it and are able to profit by it. Some schoolmen are not yet convinced that it is futile to train a boy to meet college credit requirements and at the same time try to fit him for a trade. Nor do they recognize, apparently, the misuse of public funds on instruction he will not use and does not expect to use." [3] At the time this was quite true, for the statement refers to the attempt to inject a little vocational education into an essentially academic program. It *was* futile. However, since that time it has been possible to organize vocational education on the basis of the Smith-Hughes mandate of 50 per cent shop work and 50 per cent for all other subjects, in such a way that the major objective of the boy or girl becomes efficiency in the vocation, and college admission provides the opportunity for all the graces, all the perquisites of the "educated man," along with competency to earn a living. The whole emphasis is changed, and the result is far from futility.

This is not to say that *every* pupil in the vocational high school should prepare for college. Far from it. But it does say that if one per cent or three per cent or ten or twenty per cent of the boys and girls who choose to attend vocational schools wish to prepare for college at the same time and have the capacity to do so, they should be given the opportunity. This is of the essence of democracy. Moreover, it is entirely practical. During one half of the day they spend all their time in a shop learning a trade. During the other half of the day, for four years, they take a high school program, comparable to that in an academic high school, including, according to the pupil's election, mathematics from algebra to college geometry, one or two foreign languages, chemistry, biology, physics, American and modern history, economics, and so on. This has been general practice in Metropolitan Vocational High School since 1940, under a charter granted by the Board of Regents of the State of New York, and with the full sanction of the vocational division of the State Department of Education. Somewhere between five and ten per cent of the graduating class actually do enter college or the United States Maritime Academy or New York State Maritime Academy (both of which operate as colleges). Others, who have also acquired college entrance eligibility, do not choose to take advantage of it, but go directly into the trade.

At the other end of the academic scale, as measured by the intelligence quotient, are another ten or fifteen per cent who also spend one half day in shop but whose "academic program" is highly "practical," adapted, "watered down," if you like, to meet their needs. In extreme cases, where pencil and paper produce no results, practically all the time, except for health education, is given to shop work. In

[3] CHARLES A. PROSSER and CHARLES R. ALLEN, *Vocational Education in a Democracy* (New York: The Century Co., 1926), p. 198.

between these extreme groups is a range of pupils who can take related and academic subjects in varying proportions and of varying degrees of difficulty. Their programs meet individual needs. All this is "flexibility of programing," "adapting education to the needs of the child," doing what education should be doing. Individual programing has long been a practice in the best academic high schools, but the choice of subject has often been based on the need for something "easier" rather than for something better adapted to the child's ability. Real flexibility and real individuality can be provided in a vocational program.

Again, there arises the question of the possibility of doing this in a small community. The only answer is that, with desire, inventiveness, personal and professional flexibility, almost as effective results can be obtained in a small as in a large community, as the diversified occupations program indicates. In passing, may it be said that inflexibility arises in the vocational as well as in the academic field. One of the important tasks of the administrator, be he superintendent, director, supervisor, principal, counselor, is always to fight the battle of the child against the immobility of the mossback.

IV. CONTINUOUS SURVEYS

It is exceedingly important to make administrative provision for occupational surveys, especially for those that are intensive and continuous. An original survey determines the vocational school curriculum while its continuation becomes the "curriculum revision" of the academic school. It is one of the correctives for "multiplicity of occupations," for rigidity in shop requirements, and for traditionalism. To bring to the attention of educators and of the public in general the importance of vocational education, the American Vocational Association, then known as the National Society for the Promotion of Industrial Education, sponsored a number of surveys shortly after the passing of the Smith-Hughes Law. They were made in several cities in which the Society planned to hold conventions.[4]

[4] Bureau of Labor Statistics, U. S. Department of Labor, *Vocational Education Survey of Richmond, Virginia,* Bulletin No. 162 (Washington, D.C.: Government Printing Office, 1916).
Bureau of Labor Statistics, U. S. Department of Labor, *Vocational Education Survey of Minneapolis, Minnesota,* Bulletin No. 199, Vocational Education Series No. 1 (Washington, D.C.: Government Printing Office, 1917).
Federal Board for Vocational Education, *Vocational Education Survey: A Discussion of Methods, Procedures, Forms and the Organization of Survey Committees,* Misc. 168.

While considerable value has been derived from over-all, comprehensive surveys of entire communities, and certainly they are desirable when a program of vocational education is being initiated, the best results derive from a systematic, trade-by-trade series of such surveys, each accompanied by experimentation within the school. Some of the survey staff members should also be school staff members who are expected to carry out the program. Advisory board members, specialists from all occupational fields, and teachers in the vocational schools, should all cooperate in discovering what the local and national economy needs in the way of competent workers, and then devise means of providing them. Advisory board members should be alert to check the results of these programs, principally by measuring the competency of those boys and girls who are graduated and enter employment. The program must be kept alive and healthy.[5]

Again, it must be emphasized that the formal survey should be supplemented almost daily by all other means of communication between school and economic life — visits of teachers and students to places of employment, visits of employers' and employees' representatives to school, submission of job analyses and other teaching material to employers and employees for approval, placement of students on cooperative or full-time jobs, regular meetings of advisory boards and school officials for conference on matters of larger policy, and the general, friendly intercourse that anticipates problems, minimizes difficulties, and promotes good will.

V. ADVISORY BOARDS

As vocational education programs develop more and more fully in school systems and, as is expected and hoped, more and more vocational teachers advance to administrative positions, the surer the entire school administration will be as to the validity of its vocational education program. However, at no time will it be free to dispense with the services of advisory boards, if for no other reason than to forestall obsolescence. Of course, the positive and ever-important reason is the democratic one, the need for keeping the schools close and responsive to the people.

Printed in full in WRIGHT and ALLEN, *Supervision of Vocational Education* (New York: John Wiley & Sons, Inc., 1926), p. 351 ff.
[5] From DAVID SNEDDEN, *Vocational Education,* p. 142. By permission of The Macmillan Company, publishers (1920).

If it should appear that excessive emphasis has been placed upon the importance of the advisory board, the reason for such emphasis must be found in the essentiality of democracy. This is based upon the assumption, always to be kept in mind, that the advisory board itself must truly represent employers, employees (unions, if the employees are organized), and the public.

VI. PUBLIC RELATIONS

The public schools belong to the public and the public is entitled to know all about them. Public relations should therefore never be a matter of advertising, of forcing a product upon the public's attention so that it will buy, but rather a natural telling to parents, in their several roles as employers, employees, members of Chambers of Commerce, Rotary Clubs, social clubs, unions, civic organizations, about what is going on in *their* schools. In the small community this is a comparatively easy task. Parents have fairly close contact with teachers, principal, superintendent, and members of the Board of Education. The school and its activities are well known. Certainly children talk about it. However, even in such a community, there is an art to establishing and maintaining good public relations, sometimes necessary to counteract the effect of idle gossip. It should be a simple art, growing out of a sound program, one that meets community needs, and to which the community is therefore highly receptive. Primarily it should be concerned with letting parents and children know what the school has to offer. Beyond that, it should make them aware of what the school would like to offer, and how public support is necessary to make the school what the public wants it really to be. All this is hardly advertising. It is more like an administrative staff report, through a board of directors, to its stockholders.

Once more, the vocational program not only enjoys the advantage of the usual publicity channels of the Board of Education, but it has all the facilities provided by the advisory board on vocational education. Even without thought of publicity effect, everything that the advisory board members do constitutes a channel of information to the public. So, in one sense, a wise and vigorous use of the good offices of the advisory board constitutes an adequate publicity program.

However, there are some additional channels. Visits from employers and employees are certainly not confined to the membership of the advisory board. Every effort is made to get these men and women into the school to observe what is actually going on. They are asked to help, to *do* things for the school. The best friends are those who have contributed services or equipment, but most of all, services. They are asked to speak to appropriate groups. In turn, members of the staff are requested to speak to industrial, commercial, social, and civic groups. Out of meetings of this kind grows newpaper publicity. If the school is alert to opportunities of telling about new and interesting projects, editors will ask for special stories. It is the new thing that is news.

The school has informative, illustrated, good-looking printed material for distribution through all possible channels. This tells the public what it wants to know, what the school can do for young people and mature workers. Radio stations are also interested. Lively discussions, forums, in which prominent persons in the community take part, make a radio program an especially effective means of calling attention to vocational work in the schools.

Vocational schools have the advantage of being able to present more concrete, visual material than academic schools. Products of the shops are incontrovertible evidence of activity in the shops. The shops themselves are much more exciting to older people than the formal classrooms in which they sat as children.

Taking everything into consideration, the public relations job of the vocational school is much simpler and much more effective than that of the academic schools. However, vocational teachers and administrators who, in the past, because of their devotion to the trades, have often been more or less inarticulate, must learn to be expert in the art of communication.[6]

VII. THE VOCATIONAL GUIDANCE PROGRAM

The vocational guidance program is treated in detail in the chapter on Primacy of the Person. At this point it is only necessary to emphasize the extreme importance of administrative support for, understanding of, and sympathy with the purposes of that program. The administrator needs to understand that no vocational education project can be wholly successful without such support and that to operate effectively he must take an active part in it. Many a guidance program, especially in academic schools, has disintegrated be-

[6] BENJAMIN FINE, *Educational Publicity* (New York: Harper & Brothers, 1943).

cause of the ignorance or indifference of the chief administrative officers.

VIII. ETHICS, THE ROAD TO RESPONSIBILITY

Once more, at this point, it is necessary only to point out that the administrator is responsible for giving prestige to projects intended to prove the reliability, integrity, and general responsibility of students. In a very real sense, he sits in judgment, not on the meeting of arbitrary standards — school standards — but on the students' success in meeting standards set up by the community and by the public at large. The standard must be "good" for the young person, as a future man or woman. It must not be a mere passing of subjects, but rather an attainment of adulthood. The students must have accepted the standards for what they are and the administrator must have taken all the necessary steps to win such acceptance. Adult behavior in a democratic society in a scientific age is a goal that spells reality.

IX. MENTAL AND PHYSICAL HEALTH

Everything just said about the vocational guidance program applies in equal measure to the health program. It must be treated as an integral part of vocational education.

X. THE ADMINISTRATOR AS PERSONNEL MANAGER

The peculiarity of the trade teacher's position lies in the fact that he has prepared for and engaged in a trade over a period ranging between five and twenty years and then, often unexpectedly, finds himself engaged in another trade, that of teaching. In one sense, he must begin all over again as learner and not expect to attain full competency for a number of years. Moreover, this new trade presents some rather frightening aspects. It is "white collar," full of college graduates, requires continuous study, is, in short, a profession. The teacher finds himself surrounded all day by lively youngsters. The material with which he works is not as tractable as before. He has to talk more, write more, and make less. Sometimes, as in the maritime trades, he must lead a totally different kind of life. He can spend sixteen hours a day with his family instead of two days a month, or perhaps, a week every six months. The supervision he gets is very different from what he experienced in industry.

The task of the administrator is, literally, to make the teacher feel at home in his new vocation, to encourage him to bring into school the best features of industry, to make the school shop a place of practical learning. The administrator must have an understanding of trade men. He must understand their motives for coming into teaching. He must do everything possible to confirm them in their belief that teaching is a really worthwhile profession, that it is a most challenging kind of work.

In the chapter on Teacher and Counselor much more will be said about the selection and training of teachers. Here, however, it should be noted that such selection, even in a small system, must be as objective as possible. The administrator usually likes to choose his own teachers, often basing his judgment upon the slightest of evidence and relying chiefly upon intuition. He runs the risk of making egregious errors and of laying himself open to charges of favoritism. He would be wise to ask for, or set up himself, objective standards and tests administered by an impartial board of examiners, among whom would be representatives of industry. Certainly the standards used in accepting vocational teachers can be no lower than those for academic teachers. If possible, they should be higher, not as to scholastic attainment, but as to competency in the field for which the teacher is hired. The requisitioning of special help from the industry is the only way of meeting the ignorance of the administrator who, at best, can be proficient in only one or two trades.

XI. BUILDINGS, EQUIPMENT, AND SUPPLIES

In planning for new buildings and equipment, and in ordering supplies, the administrator works through the usual Board of Education channels. However, the very special nature of the physical plant and all that goes into it makes it essential that the architect or the man who writes specifications for equipment or who orders supplies be fully informed of the nature of the material he is handling and be guided by expert advice. Here again the advisory board becomes a very important factor. Shops are planned to meet the highest commercial standards of safety and health; equipment is that of up-to-date industry (with some possible modifications because of the age of the students and the costliness and very special nature of some machines). All this is checked with the advisory board. The administrator sees that these steps are taken.

XII. RESEARCH AND EVALUATION

There has been precious little research in vocational education and many questions, the answers to which would profoundly affect policy, remain unanswered. The administrator cannot maintain any peace of mind until he knows the truth. He cannot sit back and wait for inspiration. In the vocational field he does not find a plethora of "scholars" ready to do research. Therefore he stimulates it. He is always skeptical of traditional standards. For instance, in the chapter on Reality the "time fetish" has been discussed. Nobody knows just how long it takes to learn certain vocations under the best conditions and with any given amount of aptitude. True, no one knows how long it takes to make a good citizen, or indeed, how much the school contributes to total development. But vocational education does better than that. The administrator provides the means of doing it.

Moreover, the effective administrator encourages visitation to other schools and other school systems, to industry, business, farms, wherever the process of job learning goes on, wherever education is functional. Indeed, this curiosity extends to other lands for, as we have been told so often (and we know it to be true), this *is* one world. We must learn what is going on in it.[7]

[7] DAVID SNEDDEN, "The Vocational Education Movement," in *Objectives and Problems of Vocational Education,* Edwin A. Lee, editor (New York: McGraw-Hill Book Co., 1938), p. 372.

Chapter 14

ADMINISTRATION AND SUPERVISION
—LARGER POLICY

I. THE SMITH-HUGHES LAW

THE Smith-Hughes Law was approved on February 23, 1917. It appropriated certain amounts of money for the support of vocational education. At this point it is not our purpose to discuss the law in its entirety, but rather to select one provision that has been subject to drastic criticism by those engaged in academic education and has raised doubts in the minds of some vocational educators. Section 11 reads in part: "That in order to receive the benefits of the appropriations for the salaries of teachers of trade, home economics, and industrial subjects, the state board of any state shall provide in its plan for trade, home economics, and industrial education that such education shall be given in schools or classes under public supervision or control; that *the controlling purpose of such education shall be to fit for useful employment;* that such education shall be of less than college grade and shall be designed to meet the needs of persons over fourteen years of age who are preparing for a trade or industrial pursuit or who have entered upon the work of a trade or industrial pursuit; . . . That such schools or classes giving instruction to persons who have not entered upon employment shall require that *at least half of the time of such instruction be given to practical work on a useful or productive basis, such instruction to extend over not less than nine months per year and not less than thirty hours per week. . . .*"

Again and again this provision, that at least half of the time be given to practical work on a useful or productive basis, has been called a "strait jacket," restricting and hampering efforts to provide a well-rounded education. To somewhat lesser degree but still insistently, it has been urged that thirty hours a week or six hours a day are excessive and should be reduced to the usual five or five and a half hours a day of the academic school.

The arguments for reducing shop time have been various, but they usually simmer down to a desire for more time to teach academic or book work or, as is stated in *Basic Issues in Secondary Education,*[1] "The Committee is firmly convinced that the general pattern of vocational education under the Federal Act providing for 50% vocational training, 25% related work and 25% general or academic work is too inflexible as a plan for the education of youth. The trend in many states is illustrated by California which provides that 'vocational subjects should be scheduled largely in the eleventh and twelfth grades.' With the developments that are taking place in all fields, scientific, technological, cultural and social, as well as vocational, a rephrasing of this formula may be desirable."

The time fetish operates with considerable insistence. The Committee argues with great cogency for flexibility: "The amassing of 'credits' or 'units' required for graduation, regulations relative to 'constants' or 'electives,' requirements as to 'passing marks,' daily and weekly class schedules, courses of study, instructional outlines — these and many other administrative and supervisory devices have a tendency to be mechanical in their effect on the work and activities of the students. The abuse rather than the use of these devices is responsible in part for some of the liabilities in our educational procedures." This is sound doctrine but when, as just noted, such "flexibility" results in the reduction of practical work to a point where it disappears entirely in the ninth and tenth years, then the whole purpose of vocational education is lost.

The Smith-Hughes Law is a "strait jacket" only to those who wish to wear it. The law was passed to encourage a certain type of vocational education that had been sadly neglected. The "half-time practical work" provision was essential to assure the use of federal funds for the purposes for which they had been appropriated:

1. The federal law requires no community in the United States to offer vocational education of any kind; it is purely permissive.

2. After requiring one half time for practical work, the law makes no provision whatsoever for use of the other half. It can be all practical, it can be all academic. The usual practice is to make one half related and one half academic. That is to say, one quarter of the entire time is devoted to related subjects and one quarter to aca-

[1] A report of the Consultative Committee of the New York State Education Department (Albany, New York: University of the State of New York Press, 1945).

demic. Proposals for the profitable use of this time are made to the United States Office of Education by the State Department of Education. For a group of students with high scholastic ability, the law permits 50% practical work and 50% straight academic work, preparing students for both occupation and college entrance.

3. There is nothing in the law that compels a boy to hold a hammer in his hand for three hours each day. "Practical work" means the kind of thing that any worker has to do in pursuit of his occupation. If he moves from a lathe to a desk to read specifications or to write out instructions or to calculate the pitch of a thread, the kind of thing that he will have to do on the job, that is practical work and it is quite conceivable that all practicality can be taken care of in a half day while the other half is devoted to so-called academic subjects *if* that is the kind of program indicated for a particular, individual student and *if*, as has been argued throughout the foregoing pages, the so-called academic subjects are not taught in a vacuum but are an integral part of the preparation of the young person for a life career.

4. Much more important than "time spent" is proficiency attained. Measures of accomplishment in both academic and vocational work are far from satisfactory. No one knows how much one hour of American history for one term contributes to good citizenship. Or why so many boys and girls, after eight years of arithmetic, cannot perform the fundamental operations correctly. The accomplishment of practical jobs in metal or wood or cloth are good measures of attainment in a shop, but nobody knows what would be the minimum, or at least the optimum, time under the most favorable conditions. In other words, research, evaluation, the setting of standards are much more important than the time factor, but the time factor, as embodied in the Smith-Hughes Law, is no bar to the setting of such standards.

5. Since different students can do their shop work at different rates of speed, why not let them do it? There is no reason why one graduate should not know twice as much about the trade as another or, if the trade does not offer enough challenge to keep the best worker busy for four years, why he should not finish the practical work in two, two and a half, three years, and be graduated at the end of that time or, if he needs more time to finish his non-practical work, as is likely, why he should not devote the remaining full time to it. In other words, let flexibility be real flexibility in terms of individual aptitudes and capacities.

A consideration of all these possibilities for flexibility gives the impression that many educators who argue for revision of the law are less interested in making it "more workable" than they are in weakening it in favor of traditional book work. While decrying the Smith-Hughes "strait jacket" they are clamping on a much more rigid and confining strait jacket of their own on the plea that "common learnings," "citizenship," "culture," are of paramount importance. During the nearly three decades of experimentation in individualized vocational education, the present writer has always had the full cooperation of the local Board of Education and the Vocational Division of the State Department of Education in making adjustments to the needs of young people as particular persons. These adjustments have been made under the law. They have been possible, we believe, because of mutual understanding of the aims of sound education and of mutual faith in the integrity of the educators. Of course, this faith had to be based upon a common philosophy of education such as this book presents.

II. FINANCIAL SUPPORT

It is a familiar saying that the people can have any kind of education they are willing to pay for. And it has been a tradition that the local community does the paying. Of course, this tradition was broken during the Civil War by the passing of the Morrill Act establishing the land-grant colleges. In 1917 the Smith-Hughes Law provided federal support for vocational education, and since that time various other types of vocational education have been given federal aid, sometimes on a permanent basis, as in the Department of Agriculture and the Maritime Commission, sometimes on a temporary basis, as was the case with the National Youth Administration and the Civilian Conservation Corps. Whatever form it may take and under whatever jurisdiction it may be given, financial support must grow naturally out of the desire of the people for whatever kind of education they think necessary. Financing is just as truly a function of aims and policies as are curriculum and method.

AN INTEGRATED PROGRAM. The kind of education we have outlined focuses upon the vocational motive and radiates into all phases of life. It considers the individual as a unitary being preparing to take an appropriate place in a unified society. It would seem then that this kind of integrated education is what the people should pay for, and that each local community should pay for it to the extent that it wants it. The community should determine what elements enter into such an education and then supply the wherewithal to provide them. If this procedure were followed throughout the United States, we should have an ideal educational program.

SOME MODIFYING FACTORS. Were it all as simple as this, there would be no problem. However, this seeming simplicity is elusive. If every individual is to have an equal opportunity, no matter where or under what economic conditions he lives, and as a sound democratic doctrine would indicate, obviously a political division larger than town or county must cooperate in financing a program for which the local unit may be too poor to pay. In other words, the first justification for financial aid to education from units larger than town or county is the need for *equalization,* that is, state aid or federal aid, or a combination of both. This is a correlate to the principle that a wealthy community shall contribute more to the state or national treasury than a poor community.

There are special reasons for equalization in vocational education, the principal one being that certain vocations require so few workers in relation to the total population that a few centrally located schools can carry on the complete training program, as is now the case for the maritime occupations, and as would be the case for orange growing or weather forecasting, if such schools were established. State universities serve entire states, tuition free. If they were wholly democratic, they would also pay for board and lodging. All the people of the state must contribute to such a program.

If the people of the entire nation, as represented in Congress, decide that some particular phase of education or of social welfare needs to be stimulated, even though the people as a whole do not wish to pay the full cost of such a program, the states or local communities may be "stimulated" to start such programs, by the offer of partial support. That has been the purpose of the Smith-Hughes Law and of the later George-Reed, George-Ellzey, George-Deen, and George-Barden Laws. These laws have been calculated to stir up communities to carry on activities they had never provided before, and to raise the standards of such vocational education as was already being given. With no higher motive, especially in the initial stages, than that of willingness to do something that somebody else will pay for, much may be accomplished. This has certainly been the effect of these acts, for each year sees a larger proportion of state and local funds spent for vocational education in comparison with the federal funds involved.[2] Whatever may be the shortcomings or the evil effects of federal aid, it is certainly fully justified if it makes vocational education grow where it never grew before, or makes it flourish where it has previously languished.

THE SMITH-HUGHES LAW AND ITS SUCCESSORS. The various federal vocational education laws have served an extremely useful purpose. If the people of the nation decide that vocational education has a place in the entire educational program of the country, they are justified, through the influence of money, in encouraging backward or underprivileged communities to provide better facilities. The use of money for such stimulation is certainly warranted. In recent years great pressure has been brought by national educational bodies to effect national legislation that would enable the poorer communities to provide more and better education, regardless of type. If it turns out to be the will of the nation that this be done, and these larger sums are appropriated, it should be stipulated that a fully adequate amount be devoted to vocational education. It may be argued, and often is, that vocational education has been in the picture long enough to have become an accepted phase of all education, and that further stimulation is both unnecessary and unwholesome. Where this is the case, no harm is done, since the total federal appropriation for all education is not changed. Where it is not the situation, stimulation certainly is still necessary, if the philosophy of this volume is accepted. If it is not the will of the whole people, as represented in the enacting body, and does not have the place that this philosophy mandates, then it is unfortunate for the country at large and for our young people in particular.

OLD TRADITIONS AND NEW PATTERNS. There is no reason why continued federal support should freeze into local educational programs traditions that are unsupported by changes in modern economic life. Using another figure of speech, in the previous section we discussed the alleged "strait jacket" of the 50-25-25 per cent allotment of time. If this were really a strait jacket, and technological advances or economic organization or educational science proved it untenable, the law should be changed. If, however, as we have shown, new emphases, new patterns, new goals, can be developed within the law, then no change is necessary. Nevertheless, it might be highly desirable to write into the law some kind of "stimulus," some kind of reward, for research, evaluation, experimentation, that would keep vocational education in the vanguard of social progress.

Vocational educators have worked against great odds. They have pioneered. In a sense, they have been inventive. But, their "less-than-college-grade" status has been a mental check on the breadth and depth of their thinking. Moreover, the emphasis upon "useful employment" has dulled their sensitivity to some of the more simple factors in useful employment. The necessity of being on the defensive, or of taking the offensive, has tended to make them scornful of, or at least indifferent to, the value of academic education, especially as an indispensable accompaniment of occupational skill. As Mort points out: "The talk of the financing of vocational education without a conceptual design is absurd. The financial program grows out of the conceptual design itself." [3]

Continuous surveys conducted by an Advisory Board on Vocational Education sensitive to the needs of the community should not only discover these needs but should make the entire community conscious of them. Then the community will want vocational education and will get it. It will be willing to pay for it. Moreover, actually the cost of vocational education, once established, exceeds by very little that of traditional academic education. If a community once realizes that the neglect of vocational education is jeopardizing the future of its youth, it will be selfish enough, let us say enlightened enough, to demand real value from its educational program.

THE DANGER OF DILUTION. After all this is said, let it never be forgotten that educational programs are predominantly, almost everywhere, controlled by men and women whose only education, whose only training, whose only occupation have been in the academic field. It is the exceptional school administrator (the number seems fortunately to be growing) who frees himself from the academic, shall we say, "strait jacket," and sees education in its largest aspects. Vested interests, inertia, lack of knowledge, blindness to what is going on in the world, all contribute to the situation. Such ad-

[3] PAUL R. MORT, "Financing Vocational Education," in *Vocational Education,* Forty-Second Yearbook, National Society for the Study of Education (Chicago: University of Chicago Press, 1943), p. 166. Quoted by permission of the Society.

ministrators asseverate, "good academic education is the foundation for all vocational education," or "all school subjects are really vocational," or "we want some vocational education so we are going to put in a shop." Perhaps, when they profess interest in vocational education and then confuse it with industrial arts by installing one shop in one school in a community, they are most dangerous. These are futilities. If there are no safeguards, no mandates, no bulwarks, the weight of the centuries, the curse of traditionalism, the fortuities of academicians, can easily set back our educational program fifty years.

So, we cannot cavalierly dismiss the need for vocational safeguards in federal legislation. It will be some time before enough vocationally minded educators, with vision and exalted purpose, will be in administrative positions where they can provide full, well-rounded education for *all* American youth.

Chapter 15

TYPES OF VOCATIONAL EDUCATION

THE subject matter of education is encyclopedic. The task of the curriculum makers is always to bring a useful portion of it into reasonable compass, and to arrange its many items into some kind of order according to the age, maturity, and comprehension of the learners. The vocational aspect, with its stress on individuality and interest, complicates the problem. Occupations provide a natural and practical classification which, on the less-than-college level, has now become almost a tradition — agricultural, homemaking, industrial, commercial. Beyond lie the professions — engineering, law, medicine, dentistry, theology, and so on. If waste, human and material, is to be avoided, efficiency stepped up, social welfare promoted, society must classify and organize its forces. Therefore, short of personal, tutorial instruction, enough students wanting the same general subject matter and representing some degree of homogeneity in age, outlook, and goal, must be brought together, with like-minded teachers, in an appropriate environment.

However, while subject matter, traditional ways of living, national temperament, technological changes, all call for variations in procedure, the principles of vocational education remain the same, that is to say, fundamental. Their application to particular vocations lies in the hands of administrators and teachers upon whose genius the results of any kind of education ultimately rely. Good methods, for instance, are good methods in any vocation, in fact, in any kind of education, whether it be called vocational, professional, academic, or general. The marked difference between secondary school shop and university lecture hall is only too often evidence of failure of the university to apply sound principles of method, rather than consideration for the various ways in which different people acquire knowledge and skill. There is more than passing interest in the statement of modern surgeons that, after the diagnosis has been made, "any good mechanic can perform the operation." Of course, by "good" they mean *good,* and they mean that the mechanic must have that exquisite coordination of muscles, that intensive knowledge of materials that marks the expert, whether he works on the metal of a man-made machine or on the tissue of a human body. In both cases he must practice and practice and practice, the machinist cutting metal in a shop, the surgeon cutting tissue in an operating theater.

So it goes with all other vocational skills and knowledges. Management of a farm home requires the same kind of understanding of human relationships as does management of store or office or factory.[1]

Therefore, the purpose of this and the succeeding chapter is not to describe the activities of the various types of vocational education and the numerous types of schools in which they are carried on, but to point out how considerations of primacy of the person, of interest and motivation, of reality, democracy, method, intelligence, ethics, and evaluation, find application and usefulness in these traditional fields. Sound education takes many forms. These forms have been described in detail elsewhere.[2]

I. MULTIPLICITY OF OCCUPATIONS

However we may agree upon the general principles of vocational education, we cannot disregard the fact that industrialization has broken down the crafts into thousands of specialties and that advancing technology has created more thousands of new jobs. Even jobs that would seem to be all of one name and class can be very different. Orange growing in Florida and wheat raising in Minnesota are both agriculture, but long experience in one would be of limited value in the other. The 17,452 separate jobs listed in the Dictionary of Occupational Titles *are* separate jobs. However, these differences do not present any insuperable obstacles to adequate training. Natural forces operate to concentrate geographically certain types of jobs and the people interested in them. Even the census brings all of them

1 CHARLES A. PROSSER and CHARLES R. ALLEN, *Vocational Education in a Democracy* (New York: The Century Co., 1925), p. 220.
2 *Vocational Education,* Forty-Second Yearbook, National Society for the Study of Education, prepared by the Society's Committee, Franklin J. Keller, chairman (Chicago: University of Chicago Press, 1943).
F. THEODORE STRUCK, *Vocational Education for a Changing World* (New York: John Wiley & Sons, Inc., 1945).
EDWIN A. LEE, editor, *Objectives and Problems of Vocational Education* (New York: McGraw-Hill Book Co., 1938).

into ten major classifications — agriculture, forestry and fishing, extraction of minerals, manufacturing and mechanical industries, transportation and communications, trade, public service (not elsewhere classified), professional service, domestic and personal service, and clerical occupations. This grouping serves, in a way, to account for the usual fourfold classification of trade school subjects, and, within each of these, for a homogeneity of experience among teachers. The four large groups comprise all kinds of units of administration based not only upon the occupations, but upon age, mentality, and physique of students, upon time of day during which they can attend, upon their previous experience or lack of experience, and upon size of area to be covered. These units are discussed in the next chapter. Here we are concerned with those elements of difference that appear among the four groupings — agricultural, homemaking, industrial, and business education.

II. AGRICULTURE

However much a country may become industrialized, the backbone of its economy lies in agriculture. If agriculture fails to provide enough food, then economic troubles begin. In its early days this country was almost wholly agricultural. Gradually the proportion of workers in agriculture has declined. In 1870 it was 53%, in 1930 it was 21.4%. From 1930 to 1940 the figure declined still further, dropping 13.1% from the 1930 base. The actual number rose from 6,849,772 in 1870 to 8,584,810 in 1880, but the striking fact is that in 1940 it had hardly increased at all over a period of 60 years (8,833,334, rising as high as 11½ million in 1910), while the total number of workers increased from 12,924,951 in 1870, to 52,789,499 in 1940. Agricultural workers constitute approximately 20% of all workers in the country, thus corresponding closely in number to the figure for rural population, which is about 20% of the total population. Despite this decline, the number of workers is still greater than that of any other of the ten census groups except in the manufacturing and mechanical industries. In part, the future number will depend upon advances in chemurgy. Grain may be considered a finished food product, but it may be used to feed cattle to produce milk, which is, in turn, used to manufacture casein, paints, adhesives, textiles, and plastics. When a pound of surplus cheese can be converted into a knitted sweater the problem of estimating a stabilized number of workers in agriculture becomes rather difficult. However, it is clear that a most important group for vocational education will always be those who produce the food that we eat and the many other types of raw material that enter into numerous manufactured products.

METHOD. We have referred to the natural method whereby children in more primitive society learned the occupations of their fathers and mothers, the occupations which they in turn pursued and handed down to *their* children. Where food and clothing and shelter symbolized the everlasting struggle for survival, children learned through imitation, emulation, and immediate stimulus from the parent, to become vocationally proficient. They were taught by the one natural method in which the parents are children's vocational teachers and the community is coincident with work. In the technical sense, there is no such thing as placement, for children are "placed" from the moment they lift their hands to do a chore in home or field. Learning is coterminous with work and the rewards of work are in the product itself.

The method is personal. If the father is intelligent and industrious, his methods are likely to be good, but if he is dull and slipshod, the child not only inherits a low economic status, but is unlikely to rise out of it when he is dependent upon his own work.

Modern agricultural education is only an extension, a clarification, a scientific upgrading of the natural method of learning. The best instruction is based upon projects which young people set up on their parents' farms, or upon whatever plot of ground they can commandeer. The teacher is an experienced farmer who has himself learned the very best methods, and who, by observation, demonstration, personal conference, helps the young farmer to carry through his project according to the best known modern practice. The boy learns to do by doing. He learns to do better by listening and study and application. The time he spends in "school" is probably limited to conferences, library readings, and laboratory experiments plus the usual academic subjects, while his principal learning takes place on the job. Literally, what he learns in school he puts to use outside. All this is the well-known project method.

INTEREST, PERSONALITY, AND EVALUATION. Interest is based on a happy combination of familiarity and novelty. The young farm boy is, perforce, familiar with farm work, and thus is readily excited by it if offered the novelty of better methods, higher production, and, naturally, greater income. He knows his goal and is ready to shoot for it. This is not to say that *every* boy has a burning desire to be a farmer nor that he should have that desire. There is no more reason why farming should be any more hereditary than boatbuilding or medicine or coal mining or the ministry. Actually, probably no more than 60 or 70 per cent, at most, of boys who take agricultural courses, make farming a life work. However, those who do take such courses learn farming under conditions that are highly favorable to the tapping of genuine interest.

The individual project, genuine concern of both teacher and parent, recognition of the community, responsibility for measurable results, — inevitable contacts and communion with other young workers — all these factors are potent in developing a responsible, well-balanced personality. The wholesome independence of the farmer is a traditional trait. Insofar as the boy captures this spirit and puts it to work, not only for himself, but for the community, he is becoming a real person.

Evaluation is automatic and unmistakable. If the boy produces no better crops or cattle or poultry than he would have produced without instruction, then the instruction is futile. Standards for estimating worth of product are clear to himself as well as to teacher and community. He can therefore readily evaluate himself as well as the product. During the entire process the teacher is not only an instructor but, through conferences, follow-ups, and general supervision, the most helpful of personal counselors.

REALITY AND DEMOCRACY. The subject matter grows right out of life, as the boy knows it, and the method is natural. However, as with all work experience on a commercial basis, the subject matter is always arranged for production purposes rather than for learning. Therefore, it becomes the task of the teacher to select and to place in pedagogic order numerous items of farm life so that the young person may profit by them in terms of his previous experience, age, and special ability. The teacher presents related science, provides systematic supervision and evaluation, and stimulates mutual criticism of the group. The sharp eyes of the public, mostly farmers, are on both student and teacher. They are friendly but critical. This public knows that a good curriculum is based upon the needs of individuals and of the community in which these individuals live. It is quite likely that they too go to school for evening lectures and discussions. All this means a school with a real curriculum and a curriculum democratically arrived at.

ETHICS AND INTELLIGENCE. Here is a trade in which the worker can very literally see his product growing before his eyes. Except for those uncontrollable forces of nature — drought, hailstorm, frost, disease — the farmer is the artist, responsible for his work. The pride of the farmer is intense, and he is entitled to it. He assumes great responsibility and carries it out to the end. Not that *all* farmers meet these high standards. There are individual differences among farmers too. There are sharecroppers in the South and migrant workers in the West. But the conditions of farming, and of learning to farm, averaging bad times with good, are highly favorable to drawing out the best there is in a man.

In the sense that we have used the word "intelligence," the ability to learn acts or to perform new acts that are functionally useful, the whole program of agricultural education seems designed to foster it. Every day presents new problems, often emergencies. The "intelligent" farmer is the one who can understand them, meet them head on, and solve them. Not only his livelihood, but often his very existence, depend upon the exercise of that intelligence.

CITIZENSHIP. To detail agricultural education at its best is to describe a project in good citizenship. The balancing of personal and community interests, in fact, their identification, can only mean good civic conduct. However, there are two types of rural organization that seem especially fitted to promote this kind of citizenship. Among boys it is the Future Farmers of America. This is a country-wide organization of secondary school boys determined to "develop competent, aggressive rural and agricultural leadership, create and nurture a love of country life, strengthen the confidence of farm boys and young men in themselves and their work, create more interest in the intelligent choice of farming occupations, encourage members in the development of individual farming programs, encourage members to improve the farm home and its surroundings, participate in worthy undertakings for the improvement of agriculture, develop character, train for useful citizenship, and foster patriotism, participate in cooperative efforts, encourage and practice thrift, encourage improvement in scholarship, and provide and encourage the development of organized rural recreational activities."

While the community cooperative is not primarily an agricultural or even a rural project, it is more likely to succeed and to have its repercussions upon the people themselves in a small, closely knit community. So cooperative canning plants, chicken hatcheries, cotton gins, breeders' associations, fruit marketing, and the like, are not only profitable to those who are members but are assets to the entire community in that they call for very real citizenship.

INDUSTRIALIZATION. The future of the farm, and therefore of agricultural education, cannot be clearly predicted. We know that, because of industrialization, the percentages of both agricultural workers and of total rural population have been rapidly decreasing. Young men and women have been leaving the country to work in the city. The trend has been toward mechanization, bigger farms, and "big business." These changes have robbed the farm and young farmers and young farmers' wives and children of some of the fine qualities we have been reciting, and have been injecting into wholesome surroundings a number of the social evils of industrialization. They have made it necessary for the farmer to become more and more a mechanic and for agricultural education to become more and more industrial. More than that, bigger business means more buying and selling, more accounts, more skills and knowledges of commercial education. Vocational education can do nothing about economic trends. It must go along with them. It is to be hoped that vocational education for rural young people will combine all the best features of agricultural, homemaking, industrial, and commercial education.

III. HOMEMAKING

The status of homemaking education in rural areas is, for girls, almost the same as that of agricultural education for boys. At many points they overlap. The girl learns to milk cows, feed cattle, care for poultry, or even to take full charge of a truck garden. The boy learns to keep the home in repair and to do many domestic chores. They both grow up in their work environment and gradually, under the guidance of father and mother and of older children, learn to become proficient. All the elements of good method, interest, personality, evaluation, reality, democracy, ethics, and intelligence, that make agricultural education a wholesome way of life, could be recited again for homemaking education. The two grow hand in hand. Of course, as the home moves into the village, then into the small town, and finally into the large city, it changes its character markedly and suffers from the same kind of social losses as does agriculture when it becomes industrialized.

SCOPE. The potential scope of homemaking education is, of course, greater than that of any other type because everybody lives in some kind of home even when it is institutionalized, as in large hotels. So, both men and women are possible subjects for homemaking education. Certainly, if the man is not taught all the skills, he should learn some of them, and he should acquire much of the knowledge that is usually reserved entirely for the woman.

CONTRAST WITH INDUSTRIAL EDUCATION. While homemaking education shares many advantages with agricultural education, it is in violent contrast to industrial education. In a normal home, with wise parents, a girl can learn all about homemaking without ever hearing about it in school. She can learn through generous practice and wise guidance. Such a girl needs no school instruction in homemaking. However, such homes are few and they grade all the way from that high level down to very bad. It is in these latter cases that the school, just as in industrial education, steps in to supply those elements that should normally have remained in the home, and makes up for them. The industrialization that, on the one hand, makes the home more livable and comfortable, albeit less educative, has, on the other hand, taken out of the home and put into the factory those processes that were hard, grinding, work.

SOME DIFFERENTIATIONS. For obvious reasons, homemaking is in a very different category from most other vocations.

"Success in the job of homemaking must be judged by such intangible outcomes as the quality of family life, the happiness, health, and sense of security of the family members, or the ability of the family to adjust satisfactorily to emergency demands of unexpected catastrophes. No one hires or fires a homemaker. In the home no rigid qualifications are set by an outsider, no wages are paid, though the wages of the earner may be used or wasted by the homemaker. No marketable standards need be maintained. Each home sets its own standards." [3]

In one sense, homemaking is not vocational at all, that is to say, it does not bring in a money income and it is something that everybody has to do, more or less, just to live. It would therefore seem to

[3] BEULAH I. COON, "Homemaking Education," in *Vocational Education*, Forty-Second Yearbook, National Society for the Study of Education (Chicago: University of Chicago Press, 1943), p. 266. Quoted by permission of the Society.

be a phase of general education. This concept is even more tenable when one recalls that urban life, war necessities, depression, and other economic disturbances have frequently sent the woman out of the home to earn money with which to help maintain the home. In other words, she must have two vocations, or, if you will, one vocation plus an ability to manage and maintain the home. These distinctions are, of course, purely verbal, for the grim fact is that such a woman, for better for worse, unless she can move into a hotel, must at least manage and, more generally, actually maintain the home, whether you call this doubling in occupation or indulging in a hobby.

Placing emphasis upon human relations, especially those between mother and children, homemaking may well deserve classification as a profession, a profession for which adequate training is rarely given and which is certainly never put on a professional basis. If, by the passing of a miracle, all mothers could suddenly become, at one and the same time, adequate teachers, managers, technicians, and laborers there would be very little for the schools to do. In other words, one important task of any school is to make up for the deficiencies of the home. A slight approach to such a miracle has been made in some adult homemaking classes. However, the number of women benefiting from that type of work is pitifully small.

The similarities, even identities, between homemaking and agricultural education indicate that there should be the closest cooperation between the men and women in both fields. Indeed, homemaking education and its results can have a profound effect upon many other types of vocational education "because most wage-earning jobs, except those centering around the farm, are carried on away from the home, the relation between success in homemaking and in other vocations has received very little attention. Undoubtedly the problems existing in the planning and maintenance of city homes have many elements in common with those listed by agriculture and home economics representatives as important parts of both vocational programs. Although, strictly speaking, these are outside the concern of those responsible for training in trade or business, the interrelations of happy home life and success in a job should not be as completely disregarded as they have been in the past. The burden of the homemaking responsibility is usually carried by the woman and is the vocational responsibility in homemaking education. But maintaining a satisfying home life is a cooperative job between men and women, and some aspects of home and family living should be part of the general education of boys as well as of girls, of men as well as of women. Moreover, many men are now carrying responsibility for certain aspects of the homemaking job. Also those phases of education for homemaking which promote the general employability of wage earners should be recognized and incorporated in their educational programs." [4]

A MANY-SIDED EDUCATION. Such a large proportion of all production is devoted to the provision of articles of necessity and comfort for the home and for building the home itself, that homemaking covers a wide field. There are, of course, the well-known manipulative skills, well known because everybody has observed them in the home. Then there is the science that seldom gets into the home except through rule of thumb practice of the housewife. Also, everyone would like, whether or not he or she is conscious of that liking, a "beautiful" home. So Mother must be artistic, or at least, have learned something about art. And finally, psychological, social, even political understanding are essential to successful homemaking. Perhaps in no other trade or profession, call it what you will, is so much expected and so little offered.

INDUSTRIALIZATION. With the preceding statement must be coupled another that seems to point in the opposite direction. Except in hotels, where the home, as we know it, almost disappears, the effect of industrialization on the total labor and worry in any one home, seems not to be very great. Rural electrification helps the farm home, and certainly the vacuum sweeper, electric refrigerator, toaster, percolator, iron, and mixer, all save some manual labor. But the housewife keeps busy just the same. Perhaps the best that can be said is that she does more different things with less backbreaking.

HOME AND COMMUNITY. After all this has been said, the question again arises as to how much effect the school can actually have upon life — upon industry, agriculture, business — upon the home. In the home it sometimes boils down to a struggle between two women, one the actual homemaker, mother of the child, the other the professional homemaker, teacher of the child. The mother sets the standards that the child knows, the teacher sets the standards toward which the child is supposed to aim. If the mother is unreceptive, a second struggle may ensue — child versus mother. The mother may ask whether the homemaking teacher is married, keeps a home, has

[4] COON, op. cit., p. 287.

several children, and what does she know about real homemaking anyway? And why should she invade the sacred precincts of the home? These are pretty heavy odds for the homemaking teacher. However, the whole, once despised trade of nursing has been upgraded into a profession. Nursery schools have become professional ventures. Why not other phases of homemaking? Domestic service, for instance? Perhaps the combination of "electrified" homes and "dignified" maids will be the answer. Of course, there are homes and homes. To speak of the electrified home is to conjure up the picture of a ten-by-ten shack on a Kentucky hillside.

What the homemaking teacher can do for such a home may be great when she is superior in skill, convincing in personality, and socially influential with the mothers and children with whom she works. She may even raise the social and economic tone of the whole community. While education alone cannot *cure* the social and economic ills that produce such a home, it can ameliorate those ills, while other constructive forces are at work. For the people cannot wait. The necessity for good homes is the necessity for good people, and good people are what education is for, and what homemaking education is for.

IV. INDUSTRY

INDUSTRY HAS LEFT HOME. It is industry that has left home and walled itself up in places called plants, factories, where clothing, food, housing, the essentials of life that used to be made in and around the home for those who lived in the home, are now turned out through mass production. The skills acquired in these factories cannot be learned in the natural way that comparable skills are learned on the farm or in the home. At first, children left home along with the jobs, and we had child labor. However, through agitation and legislation, we got the children back again, and now we have them, not in the home but in school. We must educate them, teach them skills and personality and good citizenship. There are seventeen million workers in industry, if we include, along with manufacturing, those occupations classified as transportation, communication, and other public utilities, construction, and mining. That figure is just twice the number of workers in agriculture, forestry, and fisheries, the next nearest classification. We know that the unskilled group is gradually moving up into the semiskilled, while the skilled group is holding its own. It is truly a mechanical age, and at the same

time, a commercial and service age. Education for industry is a
major problem.

HUMAN VALUES. It is in industry that some of the best educational
values, those that are so apparent in agricultural and homemaking
education, can be lost. Personality can be swallowed up in the machine. The final product can be so distant from the individual worker
that he has no interest in it. The plant can be so large that the worker
not only knows practically nothing about what is going on and cares
less, but he certainly has no say in the matter. These values have very
definitely been squeezed out of much of industry, but they can be restored and preserved. In fact, if democracy and individuality are to
retain their places in American life, they must be preserved.

Common observation indicates that many boys have great inherent
interest in things mechanical. This should be fostered, even exploited.
We now have, in most states, compulsory education up to sixteen
years of age, and yet, in many of these same states, the opportunity
to build upon such an interest is often denied.

Whatever the conditions in industry itself, education *for* industry
can be built upon a very real *interest,* the subject matter can be *real,*
and the entire program can be *democratic.* Industrial education lends
itself readily to the best practices in *method* and, recalling once more
our definition of *intelligence,* industrial education certainly offers
wide opportunity for the mind to be at work. The end-product,
project, masterpiece, whatever it be called, offers an accomplishment
that can be readily evaluated by those who are expert in the industry,
and the prospective worker, the graduating mechanic, can be held,
indeed will hold himself, *responsible* for high quality of performance.

PREPARATION FOR ADVANCEMENT. In industry and commerce the
worker may be proprietor, employer, executive, or employee. The
democratic attitude in vocational education means that such education must prepare each individual, if he has the capacity for it, for
advancement to these positions of responsibility. It means that theory,
management, business, and sound general education must accompany training in skills. In other words, nothing less than all-round
development of the individual, within his own limitations, is a mandate upon sound vocational education.

STANDARDS. The mention of general education and theory and business management must not give the impression, at any point in this

discussion, that vocational education should be anything less than education for a vocation. The standards of skill, of knowledge, of intelligence, of morale, must be those of the occupation, the career, in preparation for which the education is being given. There must be no watering down of education in terms of what life actually demands. Evaluation, in terms of real life, must itself be intelligent, sympathetic, and sincere.

THE ROBOT. Lamentations regarding the imminence of complete mechanization of the worker, coupled with advice that all industrial education be abandoned and that academic education take its place, are always highly suspect. It is easy enough to prove that this is a machine age, that machines do much of the work that men used to do, that men, and many, many women, are becoming machine tenders. There are many answers to this kind of reasoning. The census figures do not point to any such calamity. A study of the work that was done by people prior to the industrial age indicates that probably a higher percentage of it was unskilled and backbreaking. The rising percentage of trade and personal service occupations gives even more scope to initiative and personality than heretofore. There are still other answers, but let us accept, for the moment, the gloomiest prediction, the very ultimate in gloom, that *all* occupations will become mechanized. What would be indicated for education? A program of "academic" or "general" education, devoting itself to training for leisure? Preparation for a few hours' button pushing each day, and many hours of play? Blown up to these proportions, the whole thing explodes in absurdity. Allowing for a considerable number of machines that would make machinery to make more machines to enable us to live useless lives, there would still remain one paramount task for the schools and society, that of discovering, creating if necessary, work that required effort, that tapped interest, that was directed toward a worthy goal.

We do not think that any available information makes it probable that we shall have to search out, or actually manufacture opportunities for the highest development of human beings. We think that the task will be to keep up with the opportunities always currently available, to provide appropriate education for capable individuals for the fulfillment of their own destinies and for service to a waiting society. A persistent application of the general principles already discussed should bring about this desideratum.

V. BUSINESS EDUCATION

The rise in numerical importance of clerical, sales, and kindred occupations is a natural accompaniment of technological advance and mass production. In 1870 there were only 81,619 workers in clerical occupations in the whole country. In 1930 there were 4,025,324, the percentage increase being from .6 of 1% to 8.2%. In 1940, when the Bureau of the Census changed its major classifications, it listed 8,307,490 workers in the classification "clerical, sales, and kindred workers." These constituted 16% of the entire labor force. While the number of workers engaged in the production of physical goods dropped from 75.4% to 52.9% from 1870 to 1930, larger and larger numbers engaged in the clerical and sales services necessary for the distribution of those goods.

INDUSTRIALIZATION. This rapid and drastic change in the clerical, distributive, and service fields is a most striking phenomenon. Its parallelism to changes in industry is indicated by the fact that, while men were being taken out of small shops and homes where the handcrafts were pursued, women were being taken out of homes to take care of the corresponding commercial phases. At first commercial work was a matter of penmanship and bookkeeping. Invention of the typewriter started it on to the road of industrialization. Now, all manner of accounting machines, cash registers, dictating machines, and corresponding piece work systems have made commercial work a new "industry." For that reason, business education bears the same close relationship to industrial education as does homemaking education to agricultural education. Checking our criteria, one by one, we find that they can be discussed in practically the same terms, and with only a few variations, as in industrial education. Specialization plays as great a part in business occupations as in industrial. For instance, ability to sell is markedly different from ability to type accurate transcriptions from the dictating machine, ability to operate a bookkeeping machine is quite different from ability to act as private secretary to a corporation executive. This calls for a guidance program for orientation and training of workers in business occupations.

Insofar as occupations become mechanized and repetitive, business occupations, especially clerical, suffer from the same disadvantages as do industrial occupations. However, there is still a preponderance of business occupations that involve close personal relations and demand a maximum of personality, and it is in these that development of personality becomes a most important training feature. It is also notable that business occupations, white-collar jobs, have always been surrounded by an aura of respectability. Especially for girls, work in an office has been deemed much more desirable than work in a factory, and for that reason lower pay has often been acceptable. The desire to work in pleasant surroundings and with "nice people" is a natural and understandable one. It has interfered markedly with any attempt to orient the right persons into either of these fields. Social adaptability has meant more than aptitude, even though it must be conceded that, in many business occupations, personality itself becomes an aptitude.

And this raises another point. The "nice people" that one meets are often marriageable men who create a high turnover in women workers. This in turn means the necessity for training many more replacements. In the early days the demand was met by the establishment of many private business schools which exploited the lack of business training in public schools. The public schools have partly caught up with the situation although there is still a lack of courses based on sound vocational criteria. Increasing recognition of the importance of personality practice has given rise to another type of school — the charm school, again followed to some extent by courses in the public school.

SERVICE OCCUPATIONS. The difficulty of obtaining satisfactory maid service in the home has always been a kind of national joke. The reason is obvious. The worker has no freedom, no security, no limitation as to hours, no social contacts, no training. She is at the beck and call of an often despotic employer and, above all, she is a "servant." Just as the girl would rather work in an office than in a factory, she would rather work in a factory than in a home. For all the mechanization of the home, domestic service is still in demand and there are undoubtedly girls who could provide it if work conditions were changed. Employment conditions are, of course, social and economic in nature, and education can affect them only indirectly. However, it is probable that servants could be assigned to satisfactory positions if they were well trained in the first place, and because of this training, could stipulate the conditions under which they would work. In any case, until the few experiments in this field make their influence more generally felt, domestic service is likely to remain in its present chaotic state. This is a real challenge to vocational education.

The workers in other types of personal service, once held in low esteem, have been able to move into much more favorable positions. The story of the nurse is well known. She is now regarded as a professional woman. The barber used to perform the duties of a surgeon. As a surgeon he has come a long way and is in the top rank in both training and status. As barber, however, he has risen only slightly, although inspection and certification by public health departments and unionization have improved his status. The same applies to beauty operators. However, as long as training is given for the most part in private schools, as is the case with barbering, status is not likely to change very much. The introduction of beauty culture, and in one or two instances barbering, into public vocational schools has given impetus to more favorable consideration of these occupations.

The same can be said of the food trades which, here and there throughout the United States, have been placed on a vocational basis in certain schools. When hotel men and restaurateurs wield their influence in favor of sound training for housekeeping and food service in hotels, restaurants, and boarding-houses, as has been done, for instance, in connection with the Food Trades Vocational High School in New York City, then another group of occupations will have been upgraded.

Another new census classification is "protective service," meaning, for the most part, police and fire protection. The establishment of training courses under public auspices has tended to give dignity and meaning to dangerous occupations the effective performance of which makes possible the safe pursuit of all other occupations. Once again, we see the evolution of the casual "cop" and the volunteer fireman into trained public servants with status.[5]

VI. SOME SPECIAL OCCUPATIONS

The multiplicity of occupations makes it difficult to give appropriate education in all of them. The result has been that vocational schools have concentrated upon the most common occupations and

[5] Irvin S. Noall, "Education for the Service Occupations," in *Vocational Education*, Forty-Second Yearbook, National Society for the Study of Education (Chicago: University of Chicago Press, 1943).

have often standardized them even while changing technologies were demanding revision. This inertia has tended to limit experimentation with other vocations. The continuous survey activities of an advisory board on vocational education should reveal the needs of the community and also the aptitudes and talents of young people for these occupations. For instance, the 1940 census indicates that there are 11,692 actors and actresses and 11,213 dancers, dancing teachers, and chorus girls in the United States. Both of these professions require the most exacting kind of training for successful performance, and yet, until the organization of the High School of Performing Arts in New York City, there was not a vocational high school in the country that offered training in these occupations. Of course, it may be that New York City is the only place where the opportunities for employment justify such a school but, be that as it may, the failure even to consider such occupations indicates a reluctance to cover the legitimate field of occupations. Take a much more populous field, that of musicians and music teachers. The number is 129,256. They are spread all over the country, with a few concentrations such as in New York City and Hollywood. But here again, attempts to teach music on a vocational basis in vocational high schools have been made in only two or three cities. One was started in Metropolitan Vocational High School in New York City in 1938 and has become the nucleus of entertainment occupations in the High School of Performing Arts. While these particular occupations seem to differ markedly in character from industrial or commercial subjects, the fact is that the general principles of good vocational education apply to them just as effectively as to any of the standard trades.

Another neglected field has been that of the maritime trades. A ship is like a floating city. Its operation and maintenance comprehend many arts and skills. The crew must live and eat, so the stewards department must perform all the functions of a good hotel staff. The propulsion of the ship and the maintenance of its mechanical services — light, heat, water, sanitary system, all fall to the lot of the engine department. Here are many trades rolled into one — engineer, machinist, plumber, electrician. The ship must maintain communication with other ships and with land stations. This is the work of the radio operator. He must not only send messages but must maintain his own complicated apparatus. More and more electronic devices are falling to his lot, such as loran and radar. Finally, the captain and his officers must navigate the vessel and be responsible for its cargo. This bald statement covers a myriad of details about a fascinating subject. Yet, training for the sea, promoted in most European countries before World War II, was entirely neglected on the secondary school level in this country until 1937, when, concomitant with the establishment of the United States Maritime Commission, a program was organized in Metropolitan Vocational High School. These occupations are only typical of many others that, in particular places, should become essential parts of the vocational school curriculum. The most casual reference to the census of workers in occupations indicates the failure of vocational education to measure up to its opportunities.

WOMEN'S OCCUPATIONS. Again, except for homemaking, very little special mention need be made of the vocational education of women because the general principles apply in all vocations for all people. It is striking to note how few vocations there are in which women are not engaged in some capacity or other. In the 1940 detailed census classification only the following titles have no figures in the "female" column: railroad conductors, baggagemen, locomotive engineers, locomotive firemen, railroad mechanics and repairmen, railroad freightmen and switchmen, firemen in fire departments, soldiers, sailors, marines, and coast guards. Of course, there immediately springs to mind the fact that the war brought thousands of women into the army, the navy and coast guard, and there were also a good many women railroad conductors. Incidentally, while there were no railroad women mechanics and repair men, there were 1189 women auto mechanics and repair men. And, even in 1940 there were 2053 welders and flame cutters. The war made the "lady welder" a national institution. All this indicates that girls and women should be admitted to any trade in which they show both interest and aptitude, perhaps, within limits, even if no women are engaged in the occupation at the moment. There is no valid reason for the segregation of boys and girls in training for trades for which they may both be employed. Wherever girls have been admitted to the traditional men's trades their influence upon standards and morale has been entirely favorable. For instance, commercial photography is predominantly a man's trade. However, in a commercial photography division of 400 boys in Metropolitan a dozen girls have not only found the environment congenial, with reciprocal feelings on the part of the boys, but they have learned to be good photographers and, upon graduation, have found satisfactory positions. It also works the other way. In cosmetology, which is predominantly a woman's trade, a few boys have been very successful and have headed toward the more highly paid men operators' positions in the trade. Set trade standards and maintain them, keep in mind all the other general principles of vocational education, and let the worker progress. "Male" and "female" will lose even their census significance. It may even be said that girls' trade schools, as such, and, of course, boys' trade schools as such, need never be organized. A school should be organized for the occupation and for the population, male and female, that can benefit from it.

VII. VOCATIONAL–TECHNICAL EDUCATION

There has always been a wide gap between vocational education on the trade level and vocational education as professional education. Obviously, in a technological society where all kinds of services must be rendered, it is more than likely that there will be a gradual increase in technical proficiency from the trade worker up through the top manager, designer, engineer, doctor, lawyer, or other professional person. And this is the fact. So, for many years there have been suggestions and plans and even realizations of a kind of training that would lie somewhere between that of the high school and that of the college. The proposed institution has usually been called a technical institute, sometimes a junior college. The kind of training has, in more recent years, been called "vocational-technical."

INDIVIDUAL APTITUDE AND ORGANIZATIONAL FLEXIBILITY. If high schools and colleges were to build and continually revise their curricula in terms of changing occupational demands and of individual aptitudes, the technical institute, as a separate institution, might not be necessary, for, the essence of such an institute, if it functions at all, is flexibility, even informality, of curriculum, of time spent, and of ultimate objectives. In any case, this is the way in which vocational-technical training may be characterized:

"1. It has as its objective the training of technicians for, or the upgrading of them in, occupations for which professional engineering school graduation is not required.

"2. The jobs for which persons are prepared through vocational-technical training programs include specific technical functions concerned with testing and production, with planning and control, and with supervisory pursuits involved in operation and maintenance.

"3. The pre-employment curricula and supplementary courses are derived from and geared directly to the current needs of industry.

"4. Pre-employment programs are organized as terminal programs rather than those preparatory to more advanced study leading to a college degree.

"5. Vocational-technical programs are most effective when designed for persons who have found their bearings through previous or collateral experience in industry, and desire intensive preparation for their chosen work.

"6. Students in these programs tend to be mature in their attitudes.

"7. Admission and graduation requirements of vocational-technical institutions are usually less formal than those of high schools and colleges, and stress capacity and experience more than academic credits.

"8. Vocational-technical programs take the form of supplementary training for employed workers, with unit courses which are frequently combined with integrated curricula; the former full-time pre-employment or pre-production training; and part-time cooperative training.

"9. A considerable proportion of vocational-technical training, with respect to numbers of students enrolled and student-hours of instruction, is found in supplementary or extension courses for employed workers, as compared with full-time pre-employment training.

"10. Vocational-technical training aims for immediate productivity on completion of the training program; and for the attainment of occupational goals sooner than is usually the case with graduates of engineering colleges.

"11. Methods of teaching are relatively direct with strong emphasis on doing as distinct from book study. Ordinarily, a high proportion of the work is done during the hours of instruction. Individualized instruction material frequently provides opportunity for considerable home study and independent progress.

"12. Teachers for vocational-technical classes are chosen primarily on the basis of practical experience, technical knowledge of industry, knowledge of science pertinent to the field, personal qualities, and ability to teach through programs of orderly experience. For many supplementary programs, teachers are drawn directly from industry on a part-time basis.

"13. Vocational-technical training has great diversity of pattern with respect to the type of institution in which it is offered, the range and character of the course content, the length of the program, and admission requirements.

"14. Supplementary programs vary from a single unit course of a few days or weeks in length to integrated curricula operating over several years on a part-time basis. Pre-employment curricula are commonly one to three years in length.

"15. Vocational-technical training is found at present, on the educational ladder, from grade 10 through grade 14. The more commonly found position is in the upper years of this grade range." [6]

Examination of these criteria indicates that they might very well grow out of the general principles of vocational education that we have already enunciated, or, putting it another way, the attainment of these criteria would require that these general principles be observed. Rigidity of curriculum, inflexible time standards, lack of a guidance program, and failure to maintain a continuous revision of the curriculum through contact with the communities, accounts for the failure of both secondary schools and colleges to provide education for such a group as would be served by technical institutes.

VIII. PROFESSIONAL EDUCATION

In the Middle Ages vocational education comprised the teaching of handicrafts through the apprenticeship system conducted by the guilds, and education for the professions — ministry, law, and medicine, in the universities. One of the most striking phenomena has been the rise of former occupations, some of which could hardly be called crafts, to the status of profession — dentistry, pharmacy, engineering, nursing, and elementary and secondary school teaching. Of course, university teaching was the prerogative of the university graduate. To "know" the liberal arts was to be a teacher of the liberal arts. This rise of the professions has constituted an intellectualization of craft, one that has had certain extremely valuable features but has not been without disadvantages. These become clear when viewed in the light of our criteria.

CRITERIA FOR PROFESSIONAL EDUCATION. Sound individual development is always hampered by the worship of false gods. The very

---

[6] *Vocational-Technical Training for Industrial Occupations,* Report of the Consulting Committee on Vocational-Technical Training appointed by the United States Commissioner of Education, Vocational Division Bulletin No. 228 (Washington, D.C.: Government Printing Office, 1944).

exaltation of professions through setting of difficult entrance requirements, charging of high tuition fees, and emphasis upon theory, has made professional education a most advantageous social asset, one readily sought by men and women whose desire is for happiness through status rather than through devotion to a fitting occupation. The professional schools have set their standards high enough, too high in certain respects, but schools of medicine, for instance, have never made an attempt to recruit the very best prospective physicians, regardless of wealth, race, creed, or color. Until the lower schools and the professional schools themselves manage a personnel program that combs the country for the highest ability, personality always included, and then makes it possible for those best fitted to attend and graduate, the aims of sound vocational education and of the highest social welfare will not have been served. Democracy will have been a mere catchword, for equal opportunity will not have been afforded to all. And interest, motivation, and presumably, aptitude, will have been cheated.

The early methods of professional schools were dubious. With great emphasis upon lecture, textbook, and examination, learning was pretty much a matter of memorization. However, in recent years the practice of having the graduate serve as intern in a hospital and then as visiting physician in a clinic, has injected valid method into a lifeless procedure. Moreover, as in agricultural education, medical education has recaptured some of the advantages of the apprentice system by enabling the young doctor to become proficient in his trade by acting as assistant to an older, experienced practitioner. The case method in law school, field work in engineering, and demonstration or pupil teaching in teachers' colleges have all contributed to the validity and effectiveness of instructional methods. Good teaching methods, with few special modifications, are good teaching methods in all vocations.

As in the vocational high school, methods and subject matter are both likely to be closer to reality, closer to life, more productive of real professional skill, if the school is constantly under criticism of an outside committee of professional men who are aware of the needs of the profession and of the necessity for meeting these needs through sound instruction. Advisory committees on professional education, by whatever name they may be called, are indispensable. They are, of course, always concerned with evaluation of the curriculum and the services of the graduates. An effective curriculum well taught to properly selected students is inevitably a stimulus to development of intelligence. If both faculty and advisory committee maintain the highest ethical standards for the profession and demand them of the students, the students are likely to carry on worthily the highest ideals of the profession.

The more closely one examines problems of vocational education the more he is impressed with the similarity of problems at all educational levels. To take another example, the balancing of training for skill and its attendant acquisition of knowledge, with preparation for citizenship, seems to be no different in trade school from what it is in professional school. Just how one makes a good citizen, what courses should be taught, what activities engaged in, may not yet be altogether clear, but it is clear that young men and women, trained to a high degree of technical proficiency, may not know how to use that proficiency in the interest of their fellow workers, their fellow world citizens. In World War II scientists were accused of preparing the world for destruction, of lacking a moral sense. Certainly they split the atom with ghastly effect. They were antisocial on a grand scale. The problem of making them responsive to the needs of society is the same as that for every other worker. In an age of technology and concentration, where it is difficult to know professional men as individuals, social control and social service are necessary.

Another similarity lies in the attempts of the various professions to close their ranks. This is also a tendency of the trade union. On any level, workers do not themselves have the right to say how many of them there shall be. Neither does society have the right to insist on absolutely free competition such as would result in low standards of public service. There must be, there can be, a happy medium in which each worker attains to happy living while faithfully serving his fellow men. Whatever the procedure turns out to be, the need for such an outcome is inescapable.

Chapter 16

TYPES OF SCHOOLS

A N OCCUPATION can be learned on the job, without any teaching, simply by trial and error. It is learned slowly, badly. Such learning wastes material and human energy. However, when an experienced worker steps in and allows the learner to observe him on the job, then this experienced worker becomes a teacher. If the teacher takes on two or three workers, he probably has a class, and if they all take time off from the job, they can be said to have a school. Wherever a competent worker meets two or more learners and teaches them some phase of an occupation, there is a vocational school. Depending upon time, place, subject matter, method, all that goes to make up sound vocational education, one has a particular type of school. Sometimes the school is right within the plant, sometimes it is entirely separated from the job. At still other times some work is done in each and close cooperation exists between school and plant. If the learner spends approximately the entire day in school, that school is known as a full-time school. If he spends part time in school and part time at work, whether the time be divided 50–50 or one day be spent in school and five on the job, or in any other time combination, the school is called a part-time school. The 50–50 combination is named cooperative, while the half day or full day in school with five days at work, is called continuation school. In apprentice education, the young man usually spends a half day in receiving related instruction and the remainder of the week in shop. The related subjects may be given in a public school or in a plant school. They may be given in the evening, leaving the full week for work, or the employer may allow two hours a week out of working time for related instruction, requiring that apprentices devote two additional hours of their own time to school study.

Evening school work may therefore be of apprentice nature or it may be supplementary teaching that the adult worker desires for his own advancement. If all the instruction is given within the plant and on the job, it is usually known as training within industry. In any case it is obvious that vocational education may take many forms on different time schedules with varied curricula. Whatever the general principles of vocational education may be, they can be carried out only in a student-teacher environment situation. Some of these situations have been found very useful, others less so. It is the purpose of this chapter to describe them.

I. FULL-TIME SCHOOLS

THE THEORY. Full-time schools of all types, whether designated as academic, general, vocational, professional, or otherwise, are predicated upon the assumption that all formal education is best obtained by having the student spend all day, usually five days a week for thirty to forty weeks a year, within a school building in an environment especially prepared for him and with especially trained teachers. Generally speaking, throughout the United States, that is the program for all children up to sixteen years of age. Those who attend college or university are isolated from intimate contact with occupations until they are twenty to twenty-six years of age, a kind of prolonged infancy. Except for those in trade subjects, teachers in general spend their lives in the classroom, before and after they begin to earn a living. Those who have lived in a vocational environment, outside of classroom hours, are, except perhaps in rural areas, the exception. Teaching, which should be the livest and most significant of the professions, is, in effect, a cloistered occupation.

THE LEGAL ASPECT. In the American democratic economy every child is entitled to a basic, appropriate, full-time education up to the age when diminishing returns indicate the desirability of part-time or full-time productive work. The legal sixteen years of age is only a protective minimum which, like the Smith-Hughes Law, serves as a bulwark against the ignorance of a few parents and the selfishness of some employers. Assuming the best-known educational practices, school should not be permitted to "hold" the student any longer than he wishes to be held, that is to say, only as long as he is interested. Society is obligated to provide such "interesting" schools up to the highest age of educability and in the best interests of society. Beyond that age it is bound to provide employment that exercises the skills and knowledges acquired in school. Anything less is a waste of individual personality and a loss to the community at large.

THE TREND. The number of sixteen to seventeen year old youth enrolled in high school has risen between 1890 and 1942 from seven to seventy-two in every one hundred. High school has become practically the standard minimum education, and it is with such a standard in mind that we have discussed the full-time vocational high school. It is our belief that, if due consideration is given to the general principles we have enunciated, especially to primacy of the person, such a school or system of schools will provide satisfactory education for all American youth, whether they are destined for the lowest or highest places on the rungs of the occupational ladder.[1]

FLEXIBILITY. The application of these principles requires utmost flexibility in administration, especially with reference to curriculum. Interpretation of "practical work" and of "nonpractical work" must be made in terms of sound educational criteria. "Practical" means just what it implies: according to practice, best practice. Boys and girls engaged in practices of an occupation should be doing what paid workers do in that occupation, whether it be wielding a hammer, sighting a star, calculating a distance, tracing a delicate line, or passing judgment on the beauty of a tone. Under the auspices of men and women in industry or business or profession there is no great difficulty in determining what these activities should be. Sometimes, limitations of time and facilities make selection more critical, but never impossible. Within range of intelligence, interest, and aptitude, the appropriate kind of practical activity can be found for each student.

The same holds true for the nonpractical, sometimes erroneously called the nonvocational subjects. They may vary from the simplest kind of related number work and specially devised remedial reading to all the requirements and embellishments of a college preparatory high school academic course. This kind of flexibility in subject matter taps the interests of a highly varied group of students and, of course, carries with it the possibility of using the most varied methods. The result is a democratic high school.

THE DEVIATES. The kind of school we have been discussing, if provided with unlimited facilities, both as regards physical plant and personnel, is effective in teaching all students, regardless of deviation from the norm of mentality or physique. Moreover, any true regard

[1] Cf. Educational Policies Commission, *Education for ALL American Youth* (Washington, D.C.: National Education Association, 1944).

for the worth of every individual human being indicates the necessity of allowing him to associate with his so-called normal fellow human beings. However, in actual practice, there are many factors that must be considered in applying the sound general principle of grouping deviates with normals. In some cases the very best interest of the individual deviate, respect for his own personality, may demand some kind of segregation. To take one or two instances: the tubercular require special facilities for the improvement of their health, facilities that would not ordinarily be placed in a building for normal students. Again, healthy individuals should probably not be allowed to associate with the tubercular. Another instance: any considerable number of children of very low mental ability in any one school tends to give that school a reputation for low standards of accomplishment, thus driving out young people of high intelligence with whom those of low intelligence should associate. However "wrong" this attitude of students and parents may be, it is one that very definitely exists and affects school administration. These matters must all be handled on the basis of high educational policy, but such policy must not be so high that it blinds the administrator to facts that in themselves automatically cancel out the benefits of high policy.

Curiously enough, some of the earliest efforts at good vocational education were made in behalf of deviates — especially the poor and the delinquent. We recall the "ragged schools" in England and numerous "reform schools" in this country. We also recall that the first public trade schools came to be regarded as "dumping grounds" for boys and girls who could not get along in any other type of school. So, when vocational schools became operative under the Smith-Hughes Law, the Federal Board for Vocational Education was insistent that they were not for deviates. Vocational schools have always had to struggle against the tendency of teachers and administrators in other types of schools to send their "worst" pupils to them, thus "giving the schools a bad name." They were particularly susceptible to this influence when they stressed shop work to the virtual exclusion of general subjects.

Today there are still two "schools" of thought. For the academicians, segregation is the only sound policy. Wealthier people practice segregation by sending their children to private schools. Those who cannot afford private schools often deplore the fact that their youngsters "must mix with such a poor class of children." They are sure that they don't want their offspring to associate with the mentally subnormal or the delinquent. On the other hand, parents of deviates want their boys and girls to have every advantage of mingling with normal children and the more enlightened educators see the advantage, as well as a certain disadvantage, of such association. Each community handles the problem according to its own lights and facilities and, if respect for worth of the individual is sincere, can probably make either type of program work out successfully. However, the general principle should be to take advantage to the fullest extent of the flexibility of the broadly conceived vocational high school, and begin to segregate only when the best interests of the deviates demand it.

A well-planned program requires that the community take care first, of the physically sound students with varying mental abilities clear down even to institutional cases, and second, of the physically handicapped children with various degrees of mental ability. The initial steps in such a program are the same as those for normal boys and girls. Painstaking vocational guidance enables individuals to work out their vocational programs within the abnormal limitations which they suffer. Modern research, plus a sense of social responsibility, has indicated that only extreme cases of mental or physical deficiency cannot be trained for and placed in some appropriate vocation. Extreme cases are probably institutional anyway and need not be cared for in public schools. Dealing with deviates effectively means the same kind of painstaking activity as for normal students, with the painstaking raised to the nth power of intensity.

Crippled and orthopedic cases, deaf and hard-of-hearing, cardiacs and tubercular, blind and near-blind, and those with speech defects, all require special attention. Health phases of the guidance program are responsible for acquainting both young people and parents with the extent to which specific physical defects determine occupational success or failure. The color-blind boy can never become a deck officer, the tubercular must avoid shops with humid, dust-laden air. Those with foot defects can hardly succeed as traveling salesmen. On the other hand, those without any feet at all can become excellent watch repairers, and the color-blind youth who still wants to go to sea can become a purser or steward. Good will and good guidance help each individual to find an appropriate place.[2]

The same close adherence to sound educational principles, with

[2] CHARLES W. SYLVESTER, "Vocational Education for Handicapped Pupils," in *Vocational Education,* Forty-Second Yearbook, National Society for the Study of Education (Chicago: University of Chicago Press, 1943).

intensive vocational guidance and occupational training, provides effective education for the mentally deficient.[3]

"Many of those who are in correctional institutions would not be there if they had not failed to receive proper education and to acquire marketable vocational skills under normal conditions." [4] While vocational education and all its accompaniments cannot claim to be a sure preventive of delinquency, there can be no question but that some delinquency results from failure to discover a profitable vocation. In any case, a guidance program, especially directed toward abnormal behavior cases, can be effective when the individual is accepted as a human being having worth.

II. PART–TIME COOPERATIVE

THE ORIGIN OF COOPERATIVE EDUCATION. The natural way of learning, learning on the job, is the long way. It is the most effective, but it is slow. It is efficient in what it teaches but, from the learner's point of view, it does not always teach the right thing at the right time. The "job" is established for production purposes, and production, not learning, is its goal. The choice and order of presentation of subject matter is determined by this goal. Under the old apprentice system the learner had plenty of time — four, six, eight, even ten years, to learn his craft, and since he was only one of two or three apprentices, the master worker could give some time to instruction or, at least, to supervision. The old apprenticeship was not adaptable to modern industrial conditions and so gave way to the so-called new apprenticeship in which the employer agrees to give the learner some kind of formal, usually theoretical teaching each week during four or eight hours of working time, or during evening hours. Sometimes this instruction is given by the public school. Such a program, whatever the time arrangement, recognizes the impossibility of complete, effective, and economical learning on the job. It must be supplemented by some kind of "school" work. It sets up a part-time school, and if the school work is extended to half-time — week in and week

---

[3] RICHARD H. HUNGERFORD and WILLIAM H. BRISTOW, "Slower-Learning Pupils — Problems and Issues," *High Points,* March, 1945.
WINIFRED FEMIANI, "The Mentally Retarded Go to High School," *High Points,* November, 1945.
[4] WALTER M. WALLACK, "Vocational Education in Correctional Institutions," in *Vocational Education,* Forty-Second Yearbook, National Society for the Study of Education (Chicago: University of Chicago Press, 1943), p. 335. Quoted by permission of the Society.

out or half day of work and half day of school — the program is known as part-time cooperative education.

No full-time school can be completely successful in reproducing actual work conditions. The shops are never pressed for production. Speed and economy are not essential to meet price conditions. Teachers do not feel the urgent necessity of keeping abreast of modern industrial methods. In academic schools there is, of course, no occupational teaching. As a result of this situation, there has been considerable recognition of the desirability of "work experience" for all young people. If this work experience extends to half the school day and if such subjects as mathematics and science are related to it, the program is called part-time cooperative education. The time may be divided between one week in school and one week on the job, or two weeks in school and two weeks on the job. In any case, the continuity of service desired by the employer is obtained by pairing off two boys so that one is always on the job and one always in school.[5]

VARIOUS TYPES OF COOPERATIVE EDUCATION. Recognition of the importance of coordinating work activity with theoretical instruction has led to many different forms of cooperation. The historic example is that of the United Shoe Machinery Corporation with the public schools of Beverly, Massachusetts, which included all the best features of public-employer cooperation, especially the intimate correlation of practical work in shop and theoretical instruction in school. In recent years, especially since the George-Deen Law became operative in 1937, cooperative education has received greater emphasis in the field of distributive subjects. The Law provides that appropriations to the states for distributive occupational subjects shall be limited to part-time and evening schools. Under this Law large numbers of workers in stores have received the benefit of part-time instruction in school. Of course, all such instruction must be supplemental to daily employment.

THE COOPERATIVE PART-TIME DIVERSIFIED OCCUPATIONS PROGRAM. Organization of an efficient and economical vocational education program has always been an exceedingly difficult problem in the small community, especially one where there are, let us say, only fifteen or twenty boy graduates each year among whom not more than one

[5] CHARLES A. PROSSER and CHARLES R. ALLEN, *Vocational Education in a Democracy* (New York: The Century Co., 1925), p. 225.

or two wish to become farmers. They need vocational education but the community is too small to provide training in more than one or two occupations and certainly too small to absorb all graduates of any one selected occupation. Some means must be found to give training in a number of different occupations that exist in such a community. The answer to this problem has been the cooperative part-time diversified occupations program, developed especially in the South by a group of State Supervisors in Trade and Industrial Education in the Southern Region. "High school students of employable age are enrolled in the program and spend one half of each school day in bona fide employment in their chosen trades or occupations for the purpose of securing organized instruction on the job as student-learners. Two periods of the remaining one-half day of the high school time are devoted to directed and supervised study of technical and related subjects pertinent to the trades or occupations in which the students are engaged. The technical subjects, which are studied on an individual basis, are those subjects which have been approved by a craft or occupational committee as being pertinent. Related subjects are those which are taught on a group basis and include such social subjects as economics, civics, health, safety. Stress is also placed upon the development of good work habits and attitudes. The remaining school time is devoted to the study of regular academic subjects. The pupils included in this type of program are usually high school juniors and seniors, although boys and girls of sixteen years of age and over who can profit from the training are not excluded. Those who wish to do so may graduate from high school with a regular diploma which will permit college entrance. To do this, however, it is necessary for the student upon entering high school to arrange his subjects in such a manner as to gain eight required credits during the first two years. The remaining required two credits plus six electives may be earned during the junior and senior years. Credit is allowed on a vocational basis for time spent in employment and time devoted to the study of technical and related subjects." [6]

This program is obviously an adaptation of the best practices in agricultural education and, to the extent that the employers take a paternal interest in the students and are genuinely concerned in their learning a business or trade, it can be exceedingly effective. It possesses some of the features of old-fashioned apprenticeship with

[6] C. E. RAKESTRAW, "Cooperative Part-Time Diversified Occupations Program," *Occupations: The Vocational Guidance Magazine,* March, 1940.

the later virtues of organized theoretical instruction in school. Moreover, if well planned it does not cut off the student from eligibility for college admission. Even if it has shortcomings as training, it can be effective as guidance. Further, since work is performed in the student's own community, small and closely knit, and boys come together during school time for discussion of their occupations, employers and fellow workers, the program can be most useful as civic education.

The program also has close relationship to the cooperative programs of such colleges as Antioch and Bennington, described in the chapter on Reality. While college programs deviate from the true cooperative type because they do not follow the half-time schedule, and study in college is only indirectly related to work in the field, and the whole combination is more of a guidance than a training program, the students in both high school and college are learning about the occupational world while getting an academic education in school. They are keeping in close touch with the realities of life and, if the academic education is good, are not missing out on any of its graces.

IDEALS AND PRACTICALITY. Well-planned and well-administered cooperative education approaches very closely an ideal type based on sound principles of vocational education. It combines the best methods of work activity and group instruction, it is concerned with the personality and welfare of the individual, it taps a primary interest of the student, it draws its subject matter from reality, and it gives every student an opportunity to learn a business, a trade, or a profession. Recital of the virtues of this type of program raises the question as to why, over the years, cooperative education has been so slow to take hold and has often suffered severe setbacks. The answer is not difficult to find. Employers in business and trade are primarily concerned with production. To live, to exist, an employer must make enough profit to pay himself a salary. If he cannot do this, he goes out of business. This drive for production makes him impatient about taking time, where time is money, to teach somebody to do a job. It takes a far-sighted citizen-employer, or a shrewd, calculating manager to see that sound education of all youth is to his ultimate interest.

Then again, the order of processing for production is different from that for learning. The next job to be done in the shop is likely to require skills that the student-worker has not learned, so he is temporarily unavailable for production. It takes clear-headed planning to adapt production to learning or learning to production, and it takes patience and understanding to close up the gaps when they appear. Moreover, the order in which theory and related technical subjects are learned in school cannot be kept exactly parallel to production in shop. Effort must be made to do so, but there is usually too great acceleration or lag on one side or the other. Tying up shop activity and school work is the task of the coordinator, a combination of first-rate teacher, experienced worker, and superdiplomat. Assuming a reasonably favorable situation in all other respects, the cooperative program stands or falls on his intelligence, enthusiasm, and tact. He must be in and out of the shop or store or other place of employment, back and forth between school and job, and must have frequent talks with employer, student, and teachers. This service is expensive but indispensable. Where it has not been provided, cooperative education has failed.

However, there is a still greater, over-all, difficulty in cooperative education, in fact, in any kind of education which depends upon employers to provide facilities for part of the program. The social-minded employer does all he can to cooperate, and in good times, when business prospers, he is an effective educator, but when business is bad and his books turn red, he "just does not see how he can do it." The employer who is not social-minded may be persuaded to do something in good times, but even then, when he can pay whatever wages are necessary to lure people into his business, he is not enthusiastic about training because he has plenty of marginal money with which to cover the waste of the trial and error method, or to attract workers who have been trained by other employers. So, by and large, employers are likely to say that in good times they do not need to train workers and in bad times they cannot afford to. Cooperative education has had its ups and downs along with the business curve. However, youth does not wait to be born so that training opportunities may coincide with employers' convenience. The public schools must guarantee the best educational opportunities for him, cooperative when possible, full-time in school when not.

This should be the goal of every school — the best possible training facilities on a full-time basis, shops, laboratories, activity everywhere — but the utilization of commercial facilities for the cooperative program, whenever and wherever it is feasible. Such a policy is entirely practical. The Central Needle Trades High School in New York City, a full-time high school, places all its seniors on cooperative jobs, week in and week out, prior to graduation. Metropolitan Vocational High School, also a full-time school, with some excellent facilities for maritime training, including a Liberty Ship, sends its boys out for practical experience on voyages ranging from two weeks to two months, prior to graduation. The pressure of commercial operation as to time, economy, and standards of efficiency, must be experienced to be appreciated and must be appreciated to become a vital part of the student's work habits. Becoming seasick, taking orders from a surly boatswain, sleeping in an uncomfortable bunk, working in a hot boiler room for eight hours a day, are all experiences that cannot be reproduced in school, even on a training ship. Work experiences must be arranged through the industry as represented on advisory boards. This is not too difficult to do when the employers and the unions realize that these young workers are their potential future working force and that the better they are trained, the more production, and profits or wages, will result.

III. PART–TIME CONTINUATION

AN EDUCATIONAL WORKSHOP. The general principles of vocational education were hammered out and tested in what proved to be an extraordinary workshop, the East Side Continuation School, predecessor of Metropolitan Vocational High School. With a one-time peak enrollment of 14,000 boys and girls, attending four hours a week, the resourcefulness of the staff was challenged to the utmost. In a sense, there were ten different schools, with separate records for each group and individual records for each student. The educational contact was brief, the interval between contacts long. The young people were employed in hundreds of different industries and businesses. They represented a tremendous range of intelligence and aptitudes. When the compulsory part-time law first became operative in 1920 the employers objected, the parents vociferated, and many students were recalcitrant. "We left school to go to work and we are now being dragged back." Parents objected principally to loss of wages during time in school and employers bemoaned the absence of workers for one morning or afternoon each week. And in the early stages, it must be confessed, the school had little to offer as compensation for these inconveniences except an intelligent, social-minded, and determined staff of teachers. The goal was a curriculum, equipment, and services that would realize the ideals upon the basis of which the compulsory continuation school law was passed.

In time all this came about with satisfaction, even enthusiasm, on the part of everyone concerned. The very obstacles raised by the situation were a stimulus to educational endeavor. If, under these altogether unusual conditions, skills and knowledges could be acquired, attitudes improved, and social habits formed, then the same can be done in any institution called a school. If the principles we have been emphasizing are thought through in terms of the part-time situation, the continuation school will have been described.

Transition to full-time education was a natural evolution, unplanned and, to a considerable extent, unanticipated. The law required attendance of unemployed boys and girls for twenty hours a week, but enforcement of this provision was exceedingly difficult, almost impossible. However, when the depression of the Thirties set in and thousands of well-paid young workers found themselves at loose ends, they came voluntarily, not only for twenty hours but for thirty and forty hours a week to a school which, by that time, had much to offer them for vocational and general self-improvement. Before long the institution was operating as a two-year full-time vocational high school, and the Board of Education recognized *de jure* what had become a *de facto* situation. Further pressure of numbers and desires made necessary an extension of the course to four years.

Before the full-time development set in, part-time students who were also voluntarily attending evening academic high schools with a view to earning diplomas and entering evening colleges, complained that the imposition of shop work was a "waste of time" for young people who intended to go to college. These complaints led to the introduction of academic subjects paralleling those in day academic high schools and the crediting of continuation school work toward evening high school diplomas. In the depression this academic department became, for students who wished to enter college, the "other 50 per cent" of the Smith-Hughes formula. To it also came adults whose working hours prevented their attendance upon evening high school, but who wished to complete their high school academic education. Until the post-war period when schools throughout the country began to accept veterans, Metropolitan offered the only college-accredited, day time academic courses in the city.

This transition from part-time to full-time, with some variations, was going on all over the country, and in it lay one of the very great services the continuation schools have rendered to youth in this country. Whatever may have been their shortcomings in the early days, and they were many, they more than justified their existence by bringing into being a vast number of full-time vocational high schools that would otherwise probably not have been organized. The attendance at these schools, coupled with lack of employment, convinced most legislatures in states where such schools had been mandated in 1918, 1919, and 1920 (twenty-three states in all), that a higher minimum compulsory age should be established, and caused many of them to fix upon sixteen years. Since, in a number of states, sixteen was the upper continuation school age, continuation schools disappeared in those states, the children being absorbed in full-time schools. The story is told by the figures: whereas in 1924 256,000 boys and girls were enrolled in general continuation schools, by 1946 the number dropped to 81,027. The registration for all types of vocational education, including general continuation school, increased from 1918 to 1942 from 104,186 to 2,624,786, the peak year. During the war the number fell off to about 2,000,000, but in 1947 had risen again to 2,512,105. The number in full-time vocational schools in 1947 was 1,048,248, excluding all those in commercial classes.

The story of the continuation school is a story of social recognition of the worth of youth. In the beginning it was grudging, but it developed gradually into full recognition. Without the initial part-time provisions, the later full-time school would have been established on a much less extensive scale. For the future, the question is whether the full-time minimum compulsory age should remain at sixteen and the continuation age be raised to eighteen, or the full-time age should be raised to eighteen, or the full-time age should be eighteen only for the unemployed with part-time attendance required for the employed. The optimum combination depends pretty largely upon one's conception of the continuation school and its setting within the full-time framework. For instance, while at one time, especially in the early days, it was disastrous to organize a continuation school within a full-time school, the later development of the full-time school, with all its service facilities, made it possible to serve all youth, on either a full-time or part-time basis, in the same building. What are the purposes that must be served?

PURPOSES OF THE CONTINUATION SCHOOL. After a quarter century the purposes of the continuation school, of part-time education for youth, remain the same — the same as for full-time education, but extended as a social service to an even later date than was originally contemplated. "The continuation school provides 'opportunity' tempered by 'guidance.' Stripped of all technical phraseology, the aim of the continuation school is to provide young working boys and girls with those educational advantages of which they have been deprived by economic circumstances and with the social and vocational guidance which is usually omitted from the curriculum of the full-time school. The continuation school commands consideration, however, not as the 'continuation' of activities carried on in any other school, but rather as an institution functioning to prepare the pupil for life itself. Unlike any other type, excepting the cooperative school, the continuation school seeks the immediate betterment of every phase of the worker's life and at the same time directs his attention to varied aspects of the future. The continuation school is not a sop to the unfortunate, nor is it a substitute for a waning apprenticeship system. It occupies a unique and essential position in the present day organization of society. Our institutions, our customs, our community morale are driving forces which find in it an appropriate instrument which they may employ to bring these future men and women into complete harmony with the aspirations of the community. It does this with consideration for the well-being of the individual, with an eye to progress, and hence to the health and advancement of the social body itself.

"The dire needs of those whom it serves should stimulate the development of an exquisite technique lest any precious minute of the allotted four or eight hours a week be made futile and it fail of its mighty attainment. This aim challenges boards of education and school superintendents to provide generous housing and equipment and the most competent teachers for the education of young workers. It becomes a faith, impelling teachers and administrators to inspire individual boys and girls to the loftiest ambitions and thus to accomplish the betterment of the entire community." [7]

The primary, direct, or immediate aims of the continuation school are vocational guidance; placement; coordination; pre-vocational, trade-preparatory and extension training; practical English, arithmetic, civics, history, literature, or any other subjects reasonably desired by the pupils; practical hygiene and physical training. The secondary, indirect, or ultimate aims of the continuation school are the development of each individual to his fullest capacities; the health of the body social and politic.

"As with any lesson plan, it is important that we think of the

[7] FRANKLIN J. KELLER, *Day Schools for Young Workers* (New York: The Century Co., 1924), p. 4.

school in terms of the child's reaction. Were the school organization articulate, it would address the child thus:

" 'Once upon a time your parent would have trained you in the work that you would have to do in the world, or you would have been apprenticed to a master with whom you would have lived and worked. All through the perilous years between fourteen and eighteen you would have been guided and counseled as to your future place in life. But now, with immense factories, stores, and offices, where you are a mere cog in the wheel of industry, where you are hired by chance and fired by circumstance, where you perform one little operation well or ill and only the exceptional child rises above mediocrity, where the blind alley job is much more common than the broad highway to success, we, the state, as represented in the school, shall become your counselor, guide, and friend, to the end that no matter what your riches or your poverty, you will retain contact with the best that is in life.

" 'We intend to help you so that twenty or thirty years hence you will not say, "If I had known when I was a boy what I know now, I would have a different kind of job," or, "If I had only had the right kind of training when I was young, I would be much more advanced in my work than I am now."

" 'And we are going to do that in the most practical and interesting way. We are going to give you a chance to try your hand at as many different kinds of work as possible, knowing that sooner or later you will find your bent. When you have found it, we are going to get you a job in that line of work and then we are going to give you supplementary training along that line so that your advance will be steady and rapid. You will find that when you have availed yourself of all this opportunity you will not only have bettered yourself, but will have become more valuable to the community, a better citizen.' " [8]

As long as the pupil can remain in full-time school with profit to himself and to society, he should be allowed, in fact, invited to do so. If economic circumstances make it appear difficult for him to remain, the state should step in and, through a scholarship or other social device, enable him to continue his school work. If the educational saturation point on the full-time basis has been reached, then the state should continue to guide and supplement until the youth is no longer a youth, but is a man or woman whose feet are set on the road to somewhere. The extent to which part-time continuation

[8] KELLER, *op. cit.*, p. 35.

education is carried on after full-time schooling has been completed is a measure of the social consciousness of society.

IV. APPRENTICESHIP

A FASCINATING STORY. In the whole history of vocational education there is no more interesting subject than that of apprenticeship. In medieval times and even up through the seventeenth century it was the most intensive, pervasive, and effective system of vocational education ever devised. It was full-time education in every sense of the word. The young learner was bound out by his parent to a master craftsman and for periods ranging up to seven years he worked and lived with his employer and, traditionally, married the master's beautiful daughter. Custom molded the apprenticeship system into an instrumentality that, in 1562, was legalized as a national institution "by imposing a compulsory servitude of seven years at least upon all who henceforth wish to enter any industrial calling, and by adopting for the whole country the custom of London, local variations being thus, generally speaking, superseded by one universal practice." [9] The Statute of Artificers was finally repealed in 1814 after economic and political conditions had made such inroads into its provisions that it had become practically inoperative. However, in the 16th century the practice of apprenticing young people constituted a definite and highly organized system of vocational education for young people in trade and manufacture. It was the general rule for them to be working as apprentices. There was no other way of becoming skilled in a craft or trade. So, vocational education was, in a sense, compulsory, and the life of the average working class child in the towns was the life of an apprentice.

The complete life of the apprentice was in the hands of the master, subject to supervision by his guild. Such supervision extended to every phase of living. For instance, "The Merchant Tailors fined a master five shillings for unlawfully beating his apprentice, while another master was fined ten shillings for clothing his boy ill, 'to the great disgrace of the mistery.'" [10] To the extent that the master was skillful at his craft, was interested in teaching it to his apprentice, and was an exemplary character, the resulting training and education were excellent. However, the many rules and regulations of the

[9] From O. JOCELYN DUNLOP, *English Apprenticeship and Child Labor*, p. 60. By permission of The Macmillan Company, publishers (1912).

[10] DUNLOP, *op. cit.*, p. 36.

guilds indicate that these qualities varied considerably among members and that constant vigilance was necessary. As has always been the case with employer and employee associations, their members were, first of all, concerned with their own welfare, so that the practice of apprenticeship was on a high plane only so long as vision and understanding of the members enabled them to identify good training of future craftsmen with their own personal prosperity. However, taken all in all, this kind of training must have been exceedingly effective.

MODERN APPRENTICESHIP. So effective was their training that, despite revolutionary changes in manufacture and commerce, almost general disappearance of the handicrafts and rise of service and distributive trades, persistent attempts have been made to preserve the best features of apprenticeship. Today, while the employer does give trade training and sometimes also related instruction, there are few other similarities between the old and the new apprenticeship. In most states public schools have become compulsory up to sixteen years of age, but subsequent apprenticeship is entirely voluntary on the part of employers, organized employees, and the apprentice. Responsibility for related instruction lies very largely with public vocational schools and supervision is assumed by a joint committee of employers and employees. Apprentices must be sixteen years of age or older. They are often eighteen or nineteen before enrollment. The duration of apprenticeship varies between two and seven years.

Apprenticeship fluctuates with economic and industrial conditions. It was remarked in 1928 by the Director General of Technical Education in France, "There has always been a crisis in apprenticeship." [11] Not only is there a crisis in apprenticeship itself, but the character of training varies markedly with time and circumstance. In the early years of the century there were many so-called "corporation schools" in which all instruction, both practical and related, was provided by the company on company time. In 1912 the total number of apprentices was given as 3946, of whom 2865, or about 73%, were in the machine trades. [12] In recent years the tendency has been to pass over to the public vocational schools the responsibility

[11] International Labor Conference, *Technical and Vocational Education and Apprenticeship* (Geneva: International Labor Office, 1938), p. 165.
[12] Federal Board for Vocational Education, *Apprentice Education*, Bulletin No. 87 (Washington, D.C.: Government Printing Office, 1923), p. 9.

of giving related instruction, thereby establishing a kind of part-time cooperative or continuation education.

THE STANDARDS. In 1937 Congress authorized the Secretary of Labor to set up standards to guide industry in employing and training apprentices, to bring management and labor together to work out plans for training apprentices; to appoint such national committees as were needed; and to promote general acceptances of the standards and procedures agreed upon. In consequence, the Federal Committee on Apprenticeship was organized and has since been offering the Apprentice-Training Service. An apprentice has been defined by the Committee as "a person at least sixteen years of age who is covered by a written agreement registered with a State Apprenticeship Council (where no such council exists registration is with the Federal Committee on Apprenticeship) providing for not less than 4000 hours of reasonably continuous employment for such persons, and for his participation in an approved schedule of work experience through employment, which should be supplemented by 144 hours per year of related classroom instruction." The basic standards provide that this definition be met and that there be "a progressively increasing scale of wages for the apprentice that should average approximately 50 per cent of the journeyman's rate over the period of apprenticeship, that the apprenticeship should be jointly established by the employer and the employee and that adequate supervision and the keeping of records be required for all apprenticeship programs." [13]

APPRENTICESHIP IN MODERN ECONOMY. The conditions under which apprenticeship programs are carried out vary to so great an extent that it is exceedingly difficult to appraise apprenticeship as such. One can say definitely and specifically that when it fully meets the standards of the Federal Committee on Apprenticeship, and is well administered, it serves as an excellent training for those boys who are lucky enough to be enrolled. It has many of the virtues of the well-conducted continuation school program, although it may be lacking in such subjects and activities as are intended to promote civic intelligence. It is a training, not an educational program.

Apprenticeship programs come and go as company and union policies change. Programs are always in process of being instituted

[13] W. F. PATTERSON and M. H. HEDGES, Educating for Industry, Policies and Procedures of a National Apprenticeship System (New York: Prentice-Hall, 1946).

in some places and abandoned in others. They are not stable. For the generality of boys they are not dependable instruments of education. Moreover, they tend to be exclusive. Union members enroll their sons and employers are glad to accept other members of their employees' families. Employers and employees seldom agree as to the optimum number of apprentices. Employers usually want more and unions fewer. Both sides strive to protect their interests, but in the operation some boys of fine aptitude and potentially high skill are kept out of trades where they would be valuable workers.

As a supplementary feature to over-all vocational education, apprenticeship has great value. An outstanding example is the program that the employing printers and printers' unions have carried on for many years in cooperation with the New York School of Printing. However, the school is also conducted as a regular four-year vocational high school to which any boy with desire and aptitude for printing may be admitted. At all times, in a democratic country, the door of opportunity must be kept open to all young people. Moreover, their selection and progress in occupations must be governed by sound guidance in the interest of each individual. Insofar as apprenticeship can meet these conditions, it is an invaluable asset to the total educational program.

V. EVENING SCHOOLS

WHY EVENING SCHOOLS? The term "evening" is obviously only a *time* classification and, in content and quality of instruction, cuts across all other categories. Only in most exceptional cases does it connote objectives very different from those of the types of schools already discussed.

In its inception, the evening school represented an attempt to serve workers who, in their free time, wished to make up for defects in their previous education. They wished to "continue" what had been interrupted. Thus, in England, until the early part of the twentieth century, all "continuation" schools were conducted in the evening or on Sunday and were for "further education." [14] Today, in this country, most evening schools are adjuncts to day schools, offering mature workers the same opportunities provided for young people in the

[14] M. E. SADLER, *Continuation Schools in England and Elsewhere, Their Place in the Educational System of an Industrial and Commercial State* (Manchester: At the University Press, 1907).

daytime, with such modifications and amplifications as are necessary to adapt instruction to older and more experienced students.

The end of the working day is the worst time conceivable for any kind of instruction except that which is purely cultural and pleasurable. Not that related trade instruction may not have a high degree of interest, and therefore pleasure, for the earnest and ambitious worker, but the greatest good to the worker can only result from the maximum application of energy and this must necessarily be low at the end of eight to ten hours of labor. On the other hand, the initiative that drives a worker to an evening school is something not to be discounted, and the sacrifice is undoubtedly evidence of and stimulus to excellent morale. Whatever the time arrangement, a neat balance ought to be struck between incentive to initiative and allowance for fatigue. Weariness of students and teachers is not conducive to the best education.

Realization of this situation brought about, both in England and this country, agitation for further education of adolescents in the day time, with resulting compulsory continuation school laws. In England the law was carried out in only a few sections of the country, but in this country twenty-three states established continuation schools that gave the young worker opportunity for education during what would otherwise have been working hours. There can be no blinking the fact that for young people in a democracy evening schools are only a makeshift for the kind of education they should have received during the regular school day.

SCHOOLS FOR ADULTS. The evening school has therefore become an institution where mature persons, experienced workers, can get extension education through which they may upgrade themselves in their regular occupations. Evening trade schools have usually been organized upon the assumption that the instruction enables the worker to become a better machinist, a better bookkeeper, a better dressmaker, but does not enable him to *change* his occupation. Possibly, in the long run, this is sound policy. However, there are those who, through lack of guidance or opportunity, have been miscast occupationally and should, at least with the benefit of careful guidance, be given a chance to enter a new occupation. Certainly this has been the practice in the professional field, where evening courses may be taken in law and engineering and accounting, although not in medicine. It is difficult to draw the line, but certainly it should not be drawn in such a way as to close the door of opportunity to those

who have initiative and ability to grasp it and who would therefore render worthy service to society.

MECHANICS' INSTITUTES. Notable among evening schools, in England and in this country, have been mechanics' institutes. While all
the features of these institutes have been taken over into public
evening trade schools, the institutes have been pioneers in evening
related technical instruction. They grew out of demands of workers
themselves. At the first meeting of the General Society of Mechanics
and Tradesmen of the City of New York held on January 2, 1786,
the following trades were represented: hatters, potters, carpenters,
tobacconists, butchers, masons, tallow chandlers, sailmakers, coach-
makers, staymakers, coopers, blacksmiths, stonecutters, silversmiths,
ropemakers, tailors, blockmakers, bookbinders, ship joiners, skin-
ners, saddlers, bolters, ship carpenters, hairdressers, bakers. Ever
since that time the Institute has been providing highly efficient evening instruction in related technical subjects.

Mechanics' institutes in England, "though not connected with
either political party, became associated with a point of view that
was distasteful to the more conservative section of English society
because of the opinions of some of their most conspicuous supporters.
The idea of their establishment came from Scotland, but one of the
first mechanics' institutions in England (the Liverpool Mechanics
and Apprentices Library, founded in 1823) is said in the original
circular to have been prompted by the example of New York. The
first object of the mechanics' institutions was the instruction of workingmen in the branches of science which were of practical application to the exercise of their trade." [15]

Vocational education organized on the principles we have been
discussing throughout this volume is so responsive to the demands
of individuals and the requirements of society that it provides education to its constituents wherever, however, and *whenever* it serves
the best interests of all concerned. If it turns out that some adult
workers are served most effectively during the evening hours (these
may be the very early evening hours following immediately upon
the end of the working day), then it offers its services at that time.
A delicate balancing of values in a specific situation is much more
accurate in action than any doctrine as to the appropriateness of such
education in relation to age, fatigue, change of occupation, or stimulus to initiative.

[15] SADLER, *op. cit.*, p. 22.

VI. TRAINING WITHIN INDUSTRY

Just as the term "evening" is a *time* classification, so, "within industry" is a *place* classification. Such training includes apprenticeship and cooperative education. Much of the training by industry has been done in cooperation with public schools. However, supervisory training and job training are definitely industry's business. For this reason it is important to note the tendency to give more attention to the development of individual skill than has heretofore been the case. Welfare of the person seems to have coincided with high plant production.

"Probably the chief difference in job-training programs of present times and those of previous years has been the increased emphasis on progressive or promotional training. This type of training differs from the usual rotational program in that it is possible to assign the new employee to a position of sufficient simplicity for him to proceed intelligently toward more difficult jobs without loss of productivity. Jobs or positions are set up in the ultimate sequential form not for the purpose of facilitating transfer of skill but rather to enable the trainee to apply at each successive position knowledge or skills previously learned on a job during which time he was engaged in actual production. Some organizations have extended this principle over a long period of time and, for example, have been able to teach welding to new workers with the loss of only a few weeks of production during a period of three years. Other organizations are tying in their on-the-job instruction with apprenticeship by bringing the trainees to production performance within a few days on each machine and, by guided experience on other machines or equipment, preparing them for all-around thorough training in a trade. Intensive, on-the-job training methods permit a man to become productively competent within a few days of employment even on tasks which were formerly considered to be so difficult as to require years of experience. For this reason the adjustment of on-the-job training to promotional sequences usually is not planned with the idea of keeping the man on a limited productive effort so much as it is planned with the idea of maintaining the idea and spirit of promotion as a matter of individual development." [16]

Another evidence of employers' interest in workers as individuals,

[16] RUSSELL J. GREENLY, "Vocational Education in Industry," in *Vocational Education,* Forty-Second Yearbook, National Society for the Study of Education (Chicago: University of Chicago Press, 1943), p. 380. Quoted by permission of the Society.

as persons, is the large number of cultural and general information courses offered to employees by corporation schools. Attendance is voluntary and without obligation. With job and company as a focus of interest, occupational activity radiates into many phases of life. Occupational training is accompanied by broad general education.

VII. ADULT EDUCATION

The term "adult education" is an *age* concept. It assumes that mind and soul and hand do not die when they pass out of "school" — the school of youth. It is education for mechanics and for philosophers and for philosopher-mechanics. Its content is whatever men and women are curious enough to learn — to know, to feel, to do. It cuts across time, method, place, and auspices. Evening schools are adult education. Training within industry is adult education. Certainly, in its later stages, apprenticeship is adult education. Correspondence schools, labor forums, private trade schools, organized visits to museums, farmers' conferences with county agents, and lecturers on literature are all adult education. And mothers and veterans, back to high school to earn their diplomas, too, are in adult education.

VOCATIONS AND CULTURE AGAIN. On the adult level it is difficult to say what is vocational and what is general or cultural. Study of vocation may, subconsciously, be motivated by desire to bolster up one's confidence rather than to boost one's salary, and study of literature may be undertaken not for its esthetic value but rather as a possible means of livelihood. Historically, "workers' education" was originally for culture, to make up for the school that never was.

"It is likely to be taken for granted, on first thought, that an engineer's handbook on hydraulics or steel construction is a work of pure utility. Yet the engineering mind finds in the study of the book delight that cannot be sold in the market place. On the other hand, it requires little knowledge of the great books commonly classed as cultural to show that they all bear sharply and directly on the practical issues of life and conduct. We do, no doubt, enjoy the imagery, the stark austerity, and the rhythm of the King James Version. We may take a kindred delight in Hamlet, so many lines of which have become current sayings; in the sonorous prose of Milton; in the mounting spirit of Shelley's Prometheus; in the historic symbolism of Byron and the gorgeous tapestry of Ruskin's climaxes. But who can have intelligence enough to read these works and at the same time separate the form from the thought? As John Morley pointed out long ago, Shakespeare is the poet of feudalism, Milton of militant Protestantism, Shelley of social democracy, and Byron of political democracy. They derived inspiration from forms and ideas of utility and practice. . . .

"Besides, it should be remembered that practical persons *select* the things they propose to consider from among billions of things that may be considered. And when this selecting operation is closely examined, preferences involving values in ethics and esthetics appear on the scene.

"The practical person may also think that his findings and conclusions can be used in only one way. But human beings in actual life will insist on using facts, scientific or otherwise, in various ways. The human being is not a mere economic and political animal. He is a many-sided creature. He is a product of history — of culture. He is a bearer of culture. He does all sorts of things that are not practical at all, such as dying for his country. It is because man is not a purely practical animal that practical leaders are so often defeated in their calculations." [17]

The adult strives, often fumblingly, for an integrated life, and his adult education, when it exists at all, is directed toward fortification of his weaknesses as well as capitalization of his strengths. Vocation pervades "life," *is* a large part of life, and any kind of education inevitably permeates both.

WHY WE NEED ADULT EDUCATION. We need adult education for such diverse purposes as to educate the whole man, to keep our minds open, to base our judgments on facts, to meet the challenge of free choice, to keep abreast of new knowledge, to be wisely destructive, to return to creative endeavor, to prepare for new occupations, to restore unity to life, to insure social stability, to direct social change, to better our social order, to open a new frontier, to liberalize the college curriculum, to improve teachers and teaching, to attain true security, to enlarge our horizons, and to see the view.[18] Therefore, adult education must be free — free to everybody and free in spirit, in mind, and in action. Within the bounds of good manners, no

[17] CHARLES A. BEARD, "Summing Up the Case of Utility vs. Beauty," in *Adult Education in Action*, MARY L. ELY, editor (New York: American Association for Adult Education, 1936).
[18] *Adult Education in Action, op. cit.,* titles of articles in the prologue.

ideas or feelings should be alien. And action should follow. Its methods should be various and ingenious. It should begin with people where they are and then soar to the empyrean. The agency should be catholic and resourceful. There should be individual help and guidance, direction and plan — a way of rescuing adults from the evils of static existence, a way of keeping them zestful, growing — on the road to somewhere.

VIII. TECHNICAL INSTITUTES

Vocational-technical education, as described in the previous chapter, is offered in some trade schools, vocational high schools, technical high schools, junior colleges, engineering colleges, universities, industry, correspondence schools, cooperative courses, *and* in technical institutes. The technical institutes, of course, embody to the fullest extent, these characteristics.

THE MOVEMENT FOR TECHNICAL INSTITUTES. During the last twenty-five years there has been a strong feeling, backed by considerable data, that the technical institute would be the answer to the scarcity of technician personnel in industry. It seemed to be an attempt to crystallize in one type of institution the services that probably could, with flexibility and insight and foresight, be provided by existing institutions. However, the organization of new and separate institutions, with flexibility and informality as guidance policy, would be a wholesome recognition of the individual and societal nature of sound education. Experimentation with such institutes, as is going on in New York State, should prove exceedingly useful to an understanding of vocational education, whatever the other outcomes may be.

Although the Study of the Society for the Promotion of Engineering Education noted that "the needs of the country could scarcely be met by less than 250 institutes, and seemed to call for the creation of a great chain of community institutions having an organic place in city and state educational systems, yet free to achieve their own distinctive character," [19] and this judgment is reaffirmed by the United States Commissioner of Education's Consulting Committee

[19] Society for the Promotion of Engineering Education, *A Study of Technical Institutes,* by W. E. WICKENDEN and R. H. SPAHR (Lancaster, Pennsylvania: The Lancaster Press, 1931).

on Vocational-Technical Training,[20] the number of such institutes is still very small.

"The technician group in industry has not fared so well with respect to opportunity for organized training. Although such schools have been in operation for more than one hundred years, the number of such institutions has been small and the range of offerings has been limited, in the light of industrial needs. Today we find in the United States a great variety of institutions providing some form of vocational-technical training; yet the numbers of students enrolled, the range of courses offered, and the geographical spread of such institutions is entirely incommensurate with the growing demands of widespread industrial enterprise.

"Any study of these programs of vocational-technical training found in the various institutions in the United States is faced with many problems. These institutions vary a great deal from each other in many aspects. The range of programs is great. The organizational patterns differ widely. Nomenclature used by the institutions varies greatly. The philosophy and objectives of one institution may be entirely different from others. Yet these greatly differing institutions are contributing to the training and upgrading of technicians, each in its own way." [21]

SOME FINDINGS AND CONCLUSIONS. The Committee of the Commissioner of Education examined each of the conclusions of the S.P.E.E., bringing them up to date. For the most part, the conclusions proved valid after an interval of thirteen years.[22] Adapted and condensed, they come to the following:

1. Insofar as data are available, it appears that graduates of technical institutes have shown positive adaptability to industry in the following order: supervision in operating departments; plant operation and maintenance; getting on with workmen (human relationships); technical services (drafting, testing, inspection, etc.); team work with associates; cooperation with executives; construction and erection in the field; accepting plant hours and conditions; technical sales work.

[20] *Vocational-Technical Training for Industrial Occupations,* Report of the Consulting Committee on Vocational-Technical Training appointed by the United States Commissioner of Education, Vocational Division Bulletin No. 228 (Washington, D.C.: Government Printing Office, 1944).

[21] *Vocational-Technical Training for Industrial Occupations, op. cit.,* p. 138.

[22] *Vocational-Technical Training for Industrial Occupations, op. cit.,* p. 179 ff.

2. The technical institutes still appear to cater more effectively than engineering colleges to young men who: (a) have had industrial experience; (b) have a career plan definitely mapped; (c) have passed out of a state of book-mindedness; (d) have natural learning processes, which center in actual doing rather than in formal study; (e) for financial or other reasons cannot devote four years or more to study.

3. Technical institutes should have their own distinctive field and character. They have generally failed as departments of engineering colleges.

4. When the S.P.E.E. study was made there was no basis in experience for expecting the junior colleges of a mixed character to do the work of a technical institute successfully. However, since that time, they have entered the field and only time will tell the results of their rather interesting and extensive efforts in this area of education.

5. The day-technical institute with an evening department is the objective to be aimed at wherever possible.

6. The cooperative plan, based on alternate periods of school work and industrial employment, seems particularly well adapted to the aims and levels of age and work of the technical institute.

7. There appears to be a place for the private technical institute with functions similar to those of private schools in other fields.

8. State and private institutions should meet the needs for technical institute education for the smaller cities and rural communities and for the more individual and decentralized occupations.

9. The largest field to be served by the technical institutes appears to be that of training men in the technology of particular industries rather than of generalized engineering courses or broad aims.

10. A lack of solidarity among existing technical institutes has handicapped the development of similar schools over the country at large. They have been unable to create and maintain a recognized status of their own. Some means of closer association seems greatly needed. The beginning of such an organization is under way.

11. The technical institute graduates have received no educational credentials which are nationally recognized. Nothing has actually been done to solve this problem; there has been some discussion. In the minds of many who recognize the psychology of the situation, it appears important that action should be considered which would be sound educationally and professionally.

IX. COLLEGES

"Preparation for a job is one of the major purposes of American colleges of all types today. It is difficult to designate any single group of them as vocational colleges, for the extent to which an institution is devoted to occupational preparation is a matter of degree.

"To attribute the aim of job preparation to higher institutions generally does not violate their historical traditions nor their devotion to liberal and cultural ideals. In the earlier American institutions vocational training did not exclude nor conflict with liberal cultural education. Instead, the two were part and parcel of a unified educational program. In spite of the highly practical nature of many college courses today, the vocational aim is by no means incompatible with more general educational objectives within the same institution. Rather, these two areas of emphasis should contribute significantly to one another's enrichment." [23]

The authors support this statement with data from a number of studies. The conclusions of Haggerty are particularly pertinent:

"Whichever route the investigator takes, he soon comes upon one incontrovertible fact, namely, that higher education in America is saturated with the purpose of preparing men and women to be competent in the work of the world. Higher education in America has from the very beginning been characterized by a vocational purpose, and occupational fitness has always been a desired outcome of higher education. . . . An examination of the fact makes it unmistakable that those who founded our colleges believed, and those who administer them today still believe, that occupational fitness is a legitimate purpose of higher education." [24]

Students themselves proclaim their desire to prepare for a vocation, although the clarity of their conception of what such preparation should be, and the appropriateness of the instructional material, are often open to serious question.

The land-grant colleges are the outstanding examples of vocational education on the post-high school level. The specific purpose of such a college was "to teach certain branches of learning as are related to agriculture and mechanic arts . . . in order to promote the liberal

[23] EURICH and McCAIN, "Programs of Vocational Colleges," in *Vocational Education,* Forty-Second Yearbook, National Society for the Study of Education (Chicago: University of Chicago Press, 1943), p. 435. Quoted by permission of the Society.
[24] MELVIN E. HAGGERTY, "The Educational Program," in *The Evaluation of Higher Institutions,* Vol. III, North Central Association of Colleges and Secondary Schools (Chicago: University of Chicago Press, 1937), pp. 15–56.

and practical education of the industrial classes in the several pursuits and professions of living." As at present constituted, these professions are agriculture, engineering, home economics, arts and sciences, commerce and business, teaching, military education, the armed services, professional veterinary medicine. In other colleges with vocational aims the two professions for which preparation is usually given are engineering and teaching. While Antioch and Bennington do not prepare specifically for professions, through work experience, relation of curriculum material to such experience, and vocational guidance, graduates are equipped for early entrance into a number of varied fields.

COMMON ELEMENTS IN COLLEGE VOCATIONAL PROGRAMS. The characteristics which typical occupation-oriented colleges share [25] are of particular interest in relation to the general principles developed in vocational secondary schools:

1. In recognizing the needs of the locality in which the institutions are located and the adaptation of their programs to serve those needs, these colleges have followed the policy of bringing education close to life, of making it reflect society's needs for services, of bringing education close to reality. They represent a "nation-wide tendency for higher institutions to gear their research and vocational instruction to conditions of their community, state, or region."

2. The tendency to employ more practical techniques to supplement exclusively bookish, academic instruction represents an appreciation of the natural way of learning, especially when the outcome is expected to be a life activity, something which the student will do, a service to society. Preparation for employment in agriculture and industry made this improved methodology imperative.

3. Sound vocational education has always been accompanied by a program of orientation. Training for an unsuitable occupation is almost worse than no training at all. Student personnel programs have been organized to recognize and capitalize upon individual differences. "Through graduate placement bureaus and professional placement offices, higher institutions are assuming a definite responsibility for aiding their graduates to secure jobs."

4. Despite the emphasis upon vocational preparation, these colleges are giving even more attention than ever to general education. Complete development of the student has been the goal.

[25] EURICH and McCAIN, *op. cit.,* p. 447.

X. UNIVERSITIES

From their very inception universities have been vocational institutions. They have prepared for the professions, originally medicine, law, the ministry, and university teaching. To these have been added many others, the most important of which are engineering, commerce, and diplomacy. Those who specialize in scholarship are making a profession of it, in either teaching or writing. In the universities, the keystone of the educational arch, where classical and academic research are carried to its extreme, vocation is the goal.[26]

XI. AREAS OF ADMINISTRATION

So long a list of diverse vocational educational units as we have just completed carries with it both implicit jurisdictional disputes and administrative confusion which, since this country fortunately lacks a strong, dictatorial, central school administration, are bound to occur. As inconvenient as they may be, they are, at least in part, an inevitable product of democracy. Where individual initiative has play, experimentation is inevitable, especially in revolt against tradition. So, whatever the difficulties, they must be accepted along with the benefits of democracy. Arbitrary decisions, off-hand opinions, even emotional appeals, will not suffice. Keeping both democracy and the individual student in focus, and striving for an understanding of origins and motives, will go a long way toward solution of these minor problems.

CONTROVERSIAL ISSUES. 1. Prior to and during part of World War II several social agencies inherited from the depression period (particularly the Civilian Conservation Corps, the National Youth Administration, and the Works Progress Administration) assumed a number of educational administrative functions. NYA schools were rapidly duplicating work that properly belonged to established vocational schools. Moreover, they were under central federal control, whereas the regular schools were operated by the several states and local communities. These emergency agencies were imaginative and did many things that the regular schools should have done and later did do. However, if they had continued their independent way, it is likely that competition and controversy would have injured the whole cause of vocational education.

[26] EURICH and McCAIN, *op. cit.*

2. During the War the United States Maritime Commission established the U. S. Maritime Academy at Kings Point, Long Island. There were already five state maritime academies. The purposes of all of them were exactly the same — the training of future merchant marine deck and engineer officers. During the War there was urgent need for graduates of all the academies. With the coming of peace arose the question as to whether the federal government was in competition with the states. Is the nature of the merchant marine such that training for it should reside in the federal rather than in the state government? Or is the field large enough to absorb the products of a number of state academies? Should the state academies be under control of the U. S. Maritime Commission or of the State Departments of Education? How is uniformity of training to be obtained in a trade where the federal government must necessarily set up the trade standards? Probably there is room for all. State initiative can have an excellent influence upon policy and operation of a federally controlled school.

3. The allocation of Smith-Hughes and other federal funds has given rise to the charge that the federal government has virtually controlled all vocational schools. The original law was written so as to avoid any such eventuality and it has probably succeeded. Each state makes its own plan for vocational education within the framework of the law. The U. S. Office of Education simply sees that the plan conforms with the law. Administration and supervision are entirely in the hands of the state. However, the charge still persists and is always annoying.

4. Within each state there is the problem of control over local schools. Within a city arises the question as to whether vocational and academic schools shall be administered by the same assistant superintendent or director. These problems are not easy to solve. Size and location of school must be reckoned in terms of probable number of students, need of industry, business or profession, transportation, wealth of community, and a dozen other factors. In somewhat modified form, it is the same old issue of little red schoolhouse *vs.* consolidated school. It can be settled only by a balancing of values. For instance, if, as in New York State, there is some evidence, at least a strong feeling, that local colleges are discriminating against applicants of particular race or creed, it may be desirable, as has been proposed, to organize a central state university. If the number of probable students in a county is only large enough to fill one well-organized vocational high school, possibly there should be only

one and that one located so that every child in the county can attend on equal terms, considering facilities for transportation, time consumed in travel, and possible cost of board and lodging. Local pride and jealousy must be subordinated to the highest good of all young people. The same considerations apply to technical institutes which are likely to be more specialized and for older students than the secondary school. Shall there be one institute for all apple growers, ceramics makers, and iron miners in a state, or must classes in these occupations be established all over the state in local multi-trade schools?

5. In Chapter 4 we emphasized the disadvantages of the cosmopolitan high school when directed by a non-cosmopolitan principal. There are very real dangers in such a situation. However, in a community with, say, five hundred high school pupils, it is neither feasible nor desirable to set up a separate trade school which, at best, could offer only two or three trades. The cosmopolitan secondary school is the only solution but, as with any other subject in the curriculum and with any other individual pupil who wants that kind of teaching, the leadership must be understanding, intelligent, sympathetic, and enthusiastic about teaching vocations and must give them the same painstaking administration and supervision as any other phase of school work. An advisory board on vocational education, a feeling of civic responsibility on the part of the community, and guidance from the vocational division of the State Department of Education can be most effective in overcoming those forces that tend to debase, dilute, and generally nullify vocational education surrounded by or buried in a traditional academic environment.

6. As soon as the community grows large enough to build two high schools the question arises as to whether the second shall be a duplicate of the first but in another part of town, or whether each school shall specialize in a different field — perhaps one academic and the other vocational. When the pupil population warrants two *vocational* schools shall they both be general, multi-trade schools, or shall each of them specialize in different vocations? When the community is as large as New York City with its twenty-six officially designated vocational high schools and six other so-called academic high schools that are really vocational, shall each of these schools adopt a specialty, or shall some of them be general and others special? New York City has decided in favor of specialization. Fourteen of the seventy academic and vocational schools have specialized, all of

them located so as to be accessible to every high school student in the city. In each of them one or several vocations are the center of interest, the focus of all activity. These specialties are automotive trades, homemaking, technical subjects, commercial subjects, needle trades, food trades, music, drama, dance, art, science, metal trades, aviation trades, maritime trades, commercial photography, printing, textile trades, electrical trades, and industrial art. The philosophy upon which they have been organized [27] is summarized as follows:

A PHILOSOPHY OF SPECIALIZATION. "1. The harm that can be done by the continuous subjection of a student to situations which demand a competence which cannot reasonably be expected of him is far more serious than a mere waste of time. It is far more serious than the production of students — some of them graduates — who fall far short of a functional knowledge of the subject they have studied, or of a satisfactory mastery of the skills they have been attempting. It may result in producing frustrations, inferiority complexes, and anti-social attitudes of an extremely serious nature. Let him who doubts this read the literature on juvenile delinquency or the various psychological analyses that have been made on the inmates of criminal institutions; or, in milder vein, let him read the various youth studies.

"2. Of all the factors making for success in any line of endeavor, purpose is perhaps the most outstanding. In education, this purpose, to be effective, must be that of the learner — not that of the teacher, the school authorities, or even of society at large. The traditional or academic high school fails to provide a relatively large segment of the adolescent population with such a purpose. However laudable the purpose of the general high school may be in the eyes of those who defend it, there is abundant evidence to show that this purpose has never been taken over or adopted by that segment of youth for whom specialized schools are designed.

"3. The preparation for a vocation does constitute such a purpose. To this segment of the high school population, such preparation seems both intelligible and important. Even in the case of the rather marked positive deviate where the preparation for a vocation is much less immediate, the opportunity to center one's work about a dominant interest, which may or may not one day be used as a back-

[27] *Specialized High Schools in New York City* (New York: Board of Education, 1946).

ground of professional work, can create a situation in which learning is both broader and deeper than that ordinarily found in a general high school.

"4. Except for the positive deviate, there is no real conflict between the specialized high school and the general high school. The needs of most of the students who are now dropping out of school can be met by the curricular offerings of the vocational high schools; hence an expansion in the enrollment of these schools should mean a decrease in the number of dropouts rather than a decrease in the enrollment of the general high schools.

"5. Education in the specialized high schools does not, per se, mean a one-sided or a narrowly specialized education. Vocational and other 'specifics' are not to be substituted for the cultural subjects of the general education; they are rather to be used as a center of motivation. In the vocational school, these 'specifics' are not to be substituted for the cultural subjects; they are to take the place held by the formal subjects now taught in the general high school."

Again, the element of *purpose* is of outstanding importance and is basic in the organization of school units.

Chapter 17

TEACHER AND COUNSELOR

I F WORKERS are artists, the teachers of workers are master artists — virtuosos. A teacher of vocations has chosen the vocation of vocations. His is *the* profession. Time out of mind, teachers — academic teachers — have been told that theirs is a great profession, that for the ills of the world "the remedy is education — more and better education." Here, in vocational education, purporting to prepare young people for all of life, for vocation and its myriad radiations, is a seemingly super-task, one requiring the highest traits of personality, the widest knowledge, and the most exquisite skills. And truly, the teachers should be such as can assume that task.

All that the student should be — artist, personality, knower, doer, an adult behaving ethically in a scientific age — the teacher should be. However he may have learned his trade or profession, however he may have become an exemplary person, he must pass these qualities along to others with all the adeptness of one who has come through the ideal vocational school. Such a school — secondary, college, or university — will have been concerned with all the qualities we have been discussing, and the product — the teacher — is its exemplar.

While trade teachers in vocational schools have come from trades and professions other than that of teaching, the teachers of general subjects have usually known only the academic school. They too should possess all the qualities of the artist, teacher-artist, even if they do not have the skills of the craftsman. Such superiority as they hold in scholarship they must pool with the advantages the trade and professional men and women have in craft skills and knowledges, so that all teachers, regardless of their origin or training, may improve as persons and workers. The unitary character of the individual student can be developed only through the unitary effort of the school.

I. ARTIST

TEACHING IS THE TEACHER'S WORK. For the teacher, his work, teaching, must be activity with a purpose, the purpose being service to potential workers. The purpose must have in it so much that is worthwhile, that is pleasant, that the process of attaining it "must be fun." And the teacher must feel a deep *responsibility* for what he has "made," for the end-product of his efforts, for the lives he has changed, for their ultimate effect on the rest of society. Certainly, if "every work of man should have the nature of a love song," above all, the teacher's work should have that nature.

How many teachers are inspired by the act of teaching? How many find joy in *designing* the act, in *seeing it through,* and *taking the consequences?* All too few, it would seem, but *they* have sung their love song, they have found their work beautiful and good. They are the artists.

Teachers of trades, of crafts, of industry in the narrow sense, find themselves in a peculiar situation. They must have served in a trade long enough, five to ten years, to have become expert in it, to have become artists. Then they enter a new occupation in which they must become artists all over again. To find in one person all the diverse talents that inhere in two vocations is the major problem in the selection of teachers for vocational schools. Fortunately, the good worker takes such pride in his craft that he frequently has a strong desire to convey to others both the sense of pride and the craft, and this impulse finds its outlet in teaching.

THE ESTHETIC NATURE OF TEACHING. Art is most closely associated with teaching as an esthetic activity, the main characteristics of which are spontaneity, self-expression, imagination, imitation, love, and self-relief. "The teacher is like the artist, the pupils are his material through whom he is expressing his ideals. Such an artist-teacher is spontaneous and free in his methods, knowing the rules of the technique of teaching but subordinating them to his own purposes. He is self-expressive in letting his pupils fully into the secrets of his ambition for them as individuals and in showing the ideals regnant in his own life. He is imaginative in handling the familiar material of instruction in new and unfamiliar ways, making contrasts and suggesting comparisons. He is imitative of the great masters of teaching, Socrates, Jesus, Pestalozzi, and Froebel, but in his own independent way. He is animated by the love of teaching, by the love of his pupils, and by the joy he finds in making ideals take root in human lives. And at the end of each day's work, each week's, each year's, there is the sense of having emptied himself, the demand for quiet and rest until the burden of fulness is again present. In this cycle of self-expression and assimilation, of giving forth and taking in, of transferring personality and regaining personality, the teacher finds that he too may be an artist in his work, embodying day by day his ideals of living in the plastic growing material of the nation's youth. Seeing visions constantly himself, he lives to assist others in seeing them, and rejoices daily in his exalted calling. Not all teachers are, nor can hope to become, artists in their work, because their eyes are blind, their ears deaf, their hearts heavy of understanding, their tasks formal, their pupils obnoxious, their work drudgery, and even their ideals ignoble. The difference is rather in the teacher than in the pupil or in the equipment. The artist is an artist in any environment, and so is the unfortunate blockhead. But many teachers have the making of artists in them and do not know it; for these particularly we must work. The artist-teacher works not with brush and canvas, nor with chisel and marble, but with truths and youths, with ideals and nervous systems. He too like the artists of the world is striving to embody the ideal in the real." [1]

THE TEACHER TEACHES WHAT HE IS. The teacher of potential workers, that is, of practically all young people, must himself believe in the importance of work, of the centrality of a career. Such belief becomes part of his personality, he becomes what he believes, and he can get others to be only what he *is*.

II. PERSON

THE TEACHER AS WELL-BALANCED, DEMOCRATIC, WELL-BEHAVED PERSONALITY. The teacher's personality must be big enough to understand *all* personalities. He must have a strong conviction as to the primacy of the person, of his own person as well as of others. Such conviction, implemented by intelligence, can result in his own development, in better balance, in an approximation to the ideal. But the conviction must be strong, and the intelligence keen. For instance, the trade teacher, coming out of an occupational environment where the niceties of speech are ignored, even looked upon with some con-

[1] HERMAN HARRELL HORNE, *The Teacher As Artist* (Boston: Houghton Mifflin Company, 1917), p. 22.

tempt, finds himself at a disadvantage with college-bred academic and technical teachers. The techniques of speech have no intrinsic relationship to the worth of character, but in the mind of the speaker as well as of the hearer, manner of speech has been associated with personality and social status. The trade teacher who is still a learner, who believes in educability, who is convinced that workers can be educated, can apply all these educational principles to himself, thereby gaining poise and confidence for himself and conveying it to his students and fellow workers.

Teachers, too, are individuals with *differences,* which must be recognized. But, while the differences in students cover the entire range, teachers cannot be *too* different. They must always be on the plus side. Whether or not they choose, they are ideals. They are patterns for the young. As we look back over our own school careers, how many such persons can we remember in the teacher's role? Yet, however far short of the ideal most teachers fall, they must ever try to reach it. If the attainment of a well-balanced personality is the end-all of education, and if vocation, both as cause and effect, is bound up with it, then the teacher must be well-balanced. A good physique and mental health are fundamental.

The teacher's personality must be such that there has been distilled out those characteristics that a democratic society (predominantly democratic, at least, the majority) believes to be *good.* Again, it is an ethical problem. Goodness must be democratic goodness.

THE ETHICAL NATURE OF PERSONALITY. In view of the history of vocational education, the boldest assumption is that of its ethical nature. However, it is an assumption fully borne out by the facts. The literature of education, whether written by educators or laymen, is full of expressions such as good citizen, good character, worthy leisure time, and good job. These can result only from good teachers. The concepts of purpose, good purpose, and of responsibility, are ethical and can be realized in educational practice only by ethically minded teachers. For, even when they are least conscious of the process, teachers are setting standards and posting values. Their judgment of worth of individual personality is an ethical judgment. The belief that all human beings have absolute worth is the ethical root of democracy. It is the essence of democracy. It determines not the form, but the spirit of government, of societal control, and it is a very precious thing. It is what takes democracy out of the realm of words and makes of it a reality, a spiritual verity.

THE TEACHER AS AN INTERESTED CRAFTSMAN AND PROFESSIONAL PERSON. If all teachers could be as active and curious as their students, many teacher-training problems would be solved, indeed would disappear. For teachers, like their students, would learn to do by doing, and interest would drive them on. They would be motivated in their careers. They would really teach, for they would like to do what they are doing. The trade teacher must like both his trade and his new profession.

This liking is a complex thing, compounded of egoism and altruism. However, unless the dominant motive is a love of children, of human beings, a desire to see them as well-behaved adults, the teacher can be successful in only a formal way. He often falls short of that. This is not to ignore the natural rewards of teaching — good companionship, sense of power, realization of status, and so on. Nor is it to ignore the "hard work," the "drudgery." But, as with all activity, if it is motivated, the element of drudgery tends to disappear. It is a matter of degree and balance.

Watch the small child walking down the street, wide-eyed with wonderment, discovering the world. Here a colored stone, there a rusty nail, and ahead a dirty stray button. All of these must be picked up and taken home. As he reaches the park he darts toward a brilliant flower, caresses a friendly dog, and makes up to the first child. He would take all of them home too if he were allowed. Intense interest, first-rate attention, and constant activity, and so a rate of learning that surpasses anything at a later stage. If only teachers could be as little children, in this sense, if only they could be curious about all the world, things and people, especially children, they would grow as persons and excel as teachers. The real teacher is an interested person. Loss of interest leads to the deadliness of the assembly line.

It would be difficult to say how many academic teachers developed an early enthusiasm for teaching and held it as a goal throughout the training period. But it is safe to say that it would be a rare person who at sixteen or eighteen years of age became excited about both a trade and teaching as vocation, who planned to spend five or ten years at the trade, and then to teach it. Again, we are speaking of the mechanical trade, the craft, rather than of agriculture or homemaking or business subjects. The fact that the trade teacher was first a trade man or a trade woman indicates that that was the primary drive, and that teaching was an afterthought. Many successful trade teachers have proved that this is a possible combination, that interest in a trade and in teaching may well be combined. However, considerable careful soul-searching is necessary to determine whether attraction to teaching is genuine or has merely to do with the perquisites of the profession. Interest in a trade may very well carry with it the desire to see others engage in it, and therefore the desire to teach. If there is any vocation that should be highly motivated in order to be successfully pursued, it is the profession of teaching, and in the top rank of motivated teaching should be the teaching of vocations. The conditions of vocational education are such that, as with the student, they should be highly conducive to interest and motivation.

Moreover, it is an interest that should never die. When a task is finished, we lose interest in it. But human beings are never finished until they die. Children are insatiable and they live into adulthood. And there are always more of them — more, and all different.

Over half a century ago Barrett Wendell, professor of English at Harvard College, delivered a series of lectures at Lowell Institute in Boston and later embodied them in the best book on English composition to be written during the entire half century. The book is so good because Wendell was not primarily concerned with verbal tricks but rather with English as an expression of life in terms that are warmly, sympathetically human. One of the reasons for weakness of such expression he lays to an "imperfect understanding of the matter in hand." Much of the failure of all types of education, no less of vocational education, can be laid to the failure of teachers to see in each of the youngsters something new, something different, something fresh, something exciting, something challenging.

"Almost everything we see in life, or know, is capable of arousing a good many different emotions. In exaggerated cases we have a fairly clear idea of this; when we see a face distorted with grief, we are aware that on the one hand it is pathetic, and on the other grotesque. When we see a drunkard in the street, we know that he is at once rather funny to look at and a deplorable example of a very insidious vice. But everyday things in life, and everyday works of art — books, pictures, music — generally impress us very indistinctly.

"The simplest example is the best. You take a walk, we will suppose. When you get back, you tell in a general way where you have been. You have walked out, perhaps across a bridge; that is about all you can tell us. Yet when you stop to think, you can see plainly that you can never have taken precisely that walk before, and that you can never take precisely that walk again. At any other moment than the one at which you took it, you yourself must be a little older or a little younger than then. At any other moment you must meet different people and see different objects. What is more, in this world of ours everything about us is constantly, subtly changing, will be changing constantly and subtly so long as life is life. But from that very bridge, where you or I may walk every day, the view is always beautiful to one who loves the great expanse of sky and air; but in no two instances is beauty ever quite the same. As the sun moves, the light is always shifting. As the wind blows, now from one quarter, now from another, the atmosphere is always changing, subtly, slowly, surely. As the clouds shift across the sky, there are changing shadows, and the actual life is changing too. There is hardly a moment when on one side or the other you cannot see a half a dozen craft. There are great dredges near by now, pouring out masses of black smoke and white steam that sometimes blow quickly away and sometimes rise slowly into windless air. Often there are busy little tugboats, pumping noisily about; often, too, lazy coasting schooners at anchor. And on the bridge itself are plenty of human figures: a stolid drawtender or two, with an impudent little spaniel frisking about their heels; young people, apparently engaged in innocent flirtation; laborers trudging along with tin dinner pails; nondescript characters who give color to the report that the place is not always agreeable after dark. Some such things as these everyone must see who walks there. What is more, every single one who sees them must see them with eyes of his own — different eyes from any others that can ever see them. No two of us, as I have reminded you more than once before, can possibly live quite the same life; and so the suggestion that every sight we look on arouses in our minds must differ — slightly and subtly, but surely — as each of us is different from every other. Whoever takes that commonplace walk, then, must have an experience different from any he has had before, or will have again — different, too, more subtly still, from any other man's. Yet all he can commonly tell you, all he commonly tells himself, is that he has walked across the bridge — a thing that anybody can do any day.

"What is true of this very commonplace experience is truer still of experiences that are not commonplace. Each in itself has an individuality peculiarly its own; and each for each one of us an individuality peculiarly our own. Every book that we read, every piece of news that we hear, whatever we know, or see, or feel, is a part of ourselves; and that mysterious thing, our human life in all its inexhaustible subtlety, is made up, for each of us, of these commonplace experiences — and of the few which do not seem commonplace — that we are so apt to neglect. It is the perception of what makes one moment different from another that marks the sympathetic character of the artist; and nothing can do more to make life interesting than a deliberate cultivation of such perception. Nothing is a bore, if one can only bring oneself to look at it with open eyes." [2]

A boy, a girl, a human life in all its exhaustible subtlety; a teacher, an artist! Nothing is a bore, if one can only bring oneself to look at it with open eyes!

III. KNOWER AND DOER

KNOWING AND DOING. Obviously, the teacher must know the facts and possess the skills that he purports to teach — and much more. The teacher of an occupation must know that trade or profession and he must at all times keep up with new knowledge and new techniques, a process that is made regular and comparatively easy through the agency of the advisory board on vocational education. He must be a master of method, which means he must know how people's minds work. Whatever the teacher has to say, whatever he does, and the manner of his doing it, all make an impression upon students and, what is more important, bring about some kind of reaction, favorable or unfavorable, in conduct or emotion. Every teacher has had the experience of hearing a former student say, "I remember so well what you said in class one day, and ever since I have tried to follow your advice. . . ." And then you hear recited words that you had completely forgotten, words that you had uttered casually, and here, after many years, you learn that you had evoked a strong response, that when you least suspected it, you were *teaching*.

The oldest criticism directed toward teachers has been their impracticality. Academic teachers have lived all their lives in schoolrooms, as students and teachers. They have not been doers. Whether teaching trade or theory or academic subjects, the teacher in a vocational school is a doer. The work experience so essential to the education of the student is essential to the teacher. The lack of such experience gives ground for criticism of the training program of agricultural, homemaking, and industrial arts teachers, all of whom are expected to earn bachelor's degrees and at the same time learn enough about their trades to teach them. Work experience becomes incidental rather than basic. Undoubtedly, while living on farms

[2] BARRETT WENDELL, *English Composition* (New York: Charles Scribner's Sons, 1891), p. 262.

and, of course, in homes, considerable experience is "picked up," but the quality of such experience is in no sense standardized, it is rather taken for granted. Teachers of occupations should have known these occupations as serious, bread-winning ventures.

KNOWLEDGE. "Because their knowledge has been achieved in connection with the needs of specific situations, men of little book learning are often able to put to effective use every ounce of knowledge they possess; while men of vast erudition are often swamped by the mere bulk of their learning, because memory, rather than thinking, has been operative in obtaining it." [3] Teachers in vocational schools must have done enough things in specific situations to make their knowledge useful. They cannot lay themselves open to the charge of academicism to which the teachers of academic subjects have always been vulnerable. Vocational teachers must remember that ever since people have worked at all, most of them have learned to work by trial and error. The purpose of vocational education is, among other things, to rationalize and to make economical a wasteful process. Teachers who either talk too much or let students struggle through their work without help are only piling one wasteful institution upon another.

"To some degree every school and college is separated from life by high walls, visible or invisible; it holds reality at arm's length. . . . Abstractions in themselves are meaningless unless connected with experience; and for this reason all education is in some sense premature. . . . Education must be so contrived that the young during the very process of their schooling will realize the difference between abstractions and facts and will learn to make the transition from thought to action. A young man who has been nourished with ideas exclusively will be tempted by the sin of intellectual pride, thinking himself capable of dealing with any problem, independently of experience. When he later comes into contact with things, he will stumble or perhaps in self-defense withdraw into sterile cleverness. As we have seen, the aptitude of making relevant judgments cannot be developed by theoretical teaching; being an art, it comes from example, practice, and habituation. The teacher can do a great deal nonetheless; he can relate theoretical content to the student life at every feasible point, and he can deliberately simulate in the classroom situations from life. Finally, he can bring concrete reports of actual cases for discussion with the students. The essential thing

3 JOHN DEWEY, *How We Think* (Boston: D. C. Heath and Company, 1910), p. 53.

is that the teacher should be constantly aware of the ultimate objectives, never letting means obscure ends, and be persistent in directing the attention of the students from the symbols to the things they symbolize." [4]

Of course, in academic education this is about all the teacher can do, "to direct the attention of the student from the symbols to the things they symbolize." In vocational education, the things are always there. They are being worked with. In them symbols find their origin. Symbols are meaningful because they refer to real things.

METHOD. We recall from the chapter on Methods that "methods remain the personal concern, approach, and attack of an individual, and no catalogue can ever exhaust their diversity of form and tint." And that "every worker might very well sign his product, for, to the practiced eye it will already have borne the earmarks, or better the hallmark, of the maker." Just think what it would mean for every teacher to sign one lesson each day. Sometimes it would be a piece of paper, sometimes a piece of machinery, sometimes the student himself! But the signature would be an indication of responsibility for method; for good method is art. Responsibility would lead him to that kind of inventiveness that he should expect from his students. He would take pride in their "diversity of form and tint." The individuality of the teacher would stimulate the individuality of each student. From the high school shop to the university research laboratory such inventiveness is what leads to all that is most brilliant in modern technology.

INTELLIGENCE. All that we have said about the power of good vocational education to exercise intelligence applies with full force to the teacher. At every moment he is teaching boys and girls to think, to learn acts or to perform new acts that are functionally useful. And that is what the teacher himself may be able to do.

POOLING EXPERIENCE AND SCHOLARSHIP. For reasons that are clear but unfortunate it has been difficult for academic teachers to understand vocational teachers, and vice versa. Even in the same school there are often areas of misunderstanding between scholastically trained teach-

[4] PAUL H. BUCK and others, *General Education in a Free Society,* report of the Harvard Committee (Cambridge, Massachusetts: Harvard University Press, 1945), p. 70.

ers and those who have come up out of industry. On the part of each group there is emphasis upon the value of the subject taught, and entirely too little pedagogical camaraderie, too much stress upon the subject matter, too little upon the human being. This situation is not confined to any one level. It extends from high school to university. "Thus far vocational as well as general education has soft-pedaled a confronting of this whole delicate dynamic area. In short, vocational teachers at all levels have in the future to surround and support the training they offer with a realistic grasp of the total *milieu* in which the work for which they train is to take place. And that realism has to include a democratic bias in all its economic implications. . . .

"Teachers, both general and vocational, have likewise to see their tasks as more nearly identical than is now typically the case. The teacher of liberal arts has to know the contemporary world better. And the teacher of vocational subjects has to be culturally more richly grounded.

"The unified and over-all objective of educating whole persons has to be restored to centrality, both in the training of teachers and the shaping of educational policy by those responsible for curriculum building.

"We will get good workers for our kind of society only as we qualify all our youth to enter that society as persons and citizens no less than as prospective job-holders." [5]

This centrality is something that must be implemented, not merely talked about. Such implementation comes about in various ways, but especially through a vocational guidance or student-personnel program that not only engages highly trained and competent counselors but involves every teacher in the school. It makes teachers, as advisors or sponsors, directly and specifically responsible for pupils and students as human beings. Of course, contributing to the effectiveness of that kind of institution is the careful selection and painstaking training of new teachers.

IV. SELECTION

Despite their important mission in the world, teachers are not drawn from some etherealized upper stratum of humanity. Like their students, they grow up out of the masses. They cannot expect

[5] ORDWAY TEAD, "Learning for Living or Earning?" *The Saturday Review of Literature,* September 15, 1945.

students to be better than are teachers themselves — although, fortunately, many students far outstrip their teachers. To speak of a "distillation of the best" is to say that somebody must do the distilling, some other teachers or men and women who have been teachers. And to each chooser a "good" teacher is one that he likes because the candidate is somewhat like himself or represents the ideal of what the chooser would like to be. For the most part this is the kind of selecting that goes on throughout the country. The superintendent, the high school principal, the supervisor, prefers a teacher because he likes him. Many factors go into this liking, personality ranking highest. Work experience ranks high and, for trade teachers, school record ranks low. Where many teachers are to be selected, as in large cities, certainly objective tests must be used to supplement other data. However they may be revealed, the important thing is to learn whether the prospective teacher has those qualities that are demanded of students in the best vocational programs.[6]

V. TRAINING TEACHERS

EXISTING METHODS. Today there are three existing methods of training teachers for vocational schools. First, agricultural and homemaking teachers get their general education, their teacher-training, and their subject matter (agriculture or homemaking) in a degree-granting college. The same is true of all academic teachers. In other words, whatever they learn about occupational life, except what may have come to them incidentally and casually, they learn in college. Second, men and women are taken from the trade or profession and are given more or less teacher-training before appointment or while in service. They come fully equipped in their occupations, but must learn the new profession of teaching. Third, professional men and women are called to teaching positions in colleges and universities and begin and continue to teach without any training whatsoever. Of course, this is also true of teachers of the liberal arts in colleges and universities.

Here are two extremes: on the one hand, thoroughly adequate experience in the trade or profession but no training for teaching; on the other hand, thoroughgoing preparation for teaching, but inade-

[6] GILBERT G. WEAVER, "Selecting and Training Teachers and Supervisors in Vocational Education," in *Vocational Education*, Forty-Second Yearbook, National Society for the Study of Education (Chicago: University of Chicago Press, 1943).

quate experience in the trade. It is conceded that, although considerable success has been attained by agricultural and homemaking teachers, there is much room for improvement, especially in acquiring a more realistic background of work experience.[7]

The excuse for accepting teachers without any training in the techniques of teaching is that "the well-educated person, full of his subject, needs no techniques." Those who have suffered under thoroughly inept college teaching know that, except in rare instances, this is just not true. And certainly it can be no truer in teaching a profession or trade than it can be in teaching academic subjects. The teacher must "know about life." To know about life, he must know about vocation, and he can know about vocation only by having engaged in it. Generally, it can be said that the best teaching comes from those who are adept in vocation, have as much general education as possible, and have had specific preparation for teaching.

MODERN APPRENTICESHIP, THE IDEAL METHOD. Effective preparation for teaching cannot be of the cold storage variety any more than it can be for any other profession or trade. Work experience accompanied by related instruction (theory) and general education is the answer.[8] Probably the only training that should be given prior to actual teaching is in the mechanical features of classroom method and management. Then the teacher should be placed in a vocational school as an apprentice, under the guidance of a master-teacher, while he takes courses in educational method, theory, and history. These courses can become meaningful only in relation to actual classroom or shop practice. In teaching, as in all other vocations, we learn to do by doing and, on the basis of our doing, we learn to understand, we learn the why and the wherefore by partaking of the wisdom of our predecessors in the profession. This is the essence of the apprenticeship method. Where it has been tried, as in New York City, it has been very successful. However, unless adopted wholeheartedly and financed generously, it is bound to fail. Yet, in the long run, it is the cheapest method, as well as the best, and the oldest.

Of course, the task of helping the teacher to better his teaching

---

[7] WEAVER, op. cit., pp. 155 and 156. Quoted by permission of the Society.
[8] BENJAMIN E. MALLARY, "Vocational Teacher-Training: Its Development and Present Trends," in Objectives and Problems of Vocational Education, Edwin A. Lee, editor (New York: McGraw-Hill Book Company, Inc., 1938), p. 227.

through the use of knowledge acquired in courses is the task of principal and supervisors. Devices for in-service training are essential to the functioning of all training given outside the school building. No matter how high the quality or great the number of teacher-training courses, they can fail utterly in making a good teacher if the school's supervisory program is not planned so as to follow up the results.

COURSES. Courses for industrial teachers have been many and varied. However, they generally group themselves as follows: (1) educational history; (2) trade analysis, job analysis, curriculum making, course of study planning; (3) psychology; (4) education (introductory); (5) methods (general and special); (6) observation and practice; (7) class organization and management; (8) vocational guidance; (9) administration and supervision; (10) special problems; (11) sociology and economics; (12) miscellaneous.[9]

Whatever the names of the courses, whatever ground they may cover, it is most important that the teaching be based upon the same sound general principles of vocational education as these prospective teachers are supposed to use when they teach people younger than themselves. As has been the case with so much professional education, the tendency of professional courses in education is always to revert to the very academic methods that the courses themselves are supposed to eliminate when dealing with students. We learn to teach by teaching, not by talking about it.

VI. TRAINING COUNSELORS

THE COUNSELING PROGRAM. Organization of a vocational school for vocational guidance, for service to each personality in the school, assumes the presence on the staff of highly trained counselors and of teachers who render supplementary but basically important counseling services. What is said here regarding the training of counselors applies to those who have been specially trained for counseling and are highly competent in all its procedures. However, it applies also, only in lesser degree, to all teachers, regardless of special subject taught. The trade teacher leads a triple rather than a double life, he must be a fine craftsman, an excellent teacher, *and* a superior counselor. The interrelationships of a staff organized on this basis are described in the chapter on Primacy of the Person.

[9] WEAVER, *op. cit.*, p. 151.

THE CHARACTER OF COUNSELING.[10] Counseling is certainly a personal service, a very personal service. The actions, the destiny, the very being of the person receiving the service, are changed — if that service is at all effective. We are familiar with all kinds of personal service. If counseling falls into that category, is the counselor a person with a *specific skill* like that of the tailor who makes suits, fitted to our bodies, thereby providing warmth and beauty? Or is the counselor a person who has special knowledge, like that of the lawyer who knows the paths through the tangle of legal underbrush and preying wild life, and protects us from attack by other lawyers? Is he a person with peculiar equipment for affecting our mental and emotional reactions, like a psychiatrist or pastor, who tries to relieve us of our mundane worries, to dissolve our internal conflicts, and thereby to adjust us to a none too hospitable world?

What then do we expect *in* the counselor — skill, knowledge, spirituality? What do we expect *from* the counselor — skill, knowledge, spirituality, power, comfort, what? What personal service do we expect him to render? And do we expect him to be one person or many persons? If we expect all of the foregoing qualities do we expect at the same time that they will be embodied in one person? Or should we depend, for each of them, upon a different person? What are the relationships of the counselor to each of the other personal service people in his field — to the principal, president, registrar, teacher?

Needless to say, any attempt to carry out such a program as we have detailed for vocational education commandeers all the powers of any one counselor, and more likely, those of a number of different counselors. With reference to any single student, counseling involves the impingement upon him of all these services, to the end that he may understand himself, may gain an adequate conception of the world, especially in its occupational phases, and finally, that he may make a satisfactory adjustment to it.

THE SATISFACTORY COUNSELOR. Assuming, for the sake of easy discussion, that one person can perform all the duties of a counselor, what kind of person is he? Obviously he is a person with:

1. Good basic intelligence. He has a mind that can use knowledge,

[10] The material in the remaining paragraphs of this section has been adapted from the Presidential Address of the author at the Convention of the National Vocational Guidance Association held in Atlantic City in May, 1938. The text was published in *Occupations: The Vocational Guidance Magazine*, May, 1938, under the title, "The Revelation and Nurture of Counselors."

whether this has been obtained through experience, through formal teaching, or otherwise.

2. Copious general information. The counselor is a person of culture, in the best sense of the word. He has a wide knowledge of the world and its ways, especially in the field of occupations. While that knowledge need not be encyclopedic, it certainly cannot be meager.

3. Intensive special information. The field of occupations is his special concern. Not only does he know the possibilities for future employment, but the roads of education and training that lead to them. He also knows about people, the motives, the inhibitions, the quirks, the springs that make them the individuals that they are. He knows about men and women and things.

4. Special skills. The counselor is skillful in the employment of certain techniques — the technique of testing, the technique of interviewing, the technique of finding jobs and placing people in them.

5. Special personal qualities. He has both sympathy and objectivity. He has an integrated personality. He certainly must not be one of those who, in the desire to compensate for their own soul-troublings, feel an urge to help everybody else. He is wholesomely energetic and at the same time delicately sensitive to the weaknesses of others. He is, in fact, an extraordinary person.

FINDING THE COUNSELOR. After thus defining the duties of the counselor and writing the specifications for his job, it would seem futile to talk of making a counselor, even of finding the material out of which he might be made. In fact, the chief concern of the administrator is that of *finding* the kind of person who has the potentialities. Probably, counselors are born and not made. In any case, they must be nurtured favorably in their tender years. The administrator must either select them early and train them over a long period; or he must let them select and train themselves, and then weed out the poor ones. The latter method leaves the field wide open and stimulates competition, but is likely to be cruel and wasteful. Wherever the process starts, from all the available talent, self or externally selected, the best combination of talents must be found. How can this be done?

The usual method is to rely upon the same kind of requirements set up for graduation from an academic school. The trouble with this kind of standardization seems to be that there is no way of measuring the degree to which knowledge has been retained, or the extent to which knowledge has translated itself into performance skills. Most important of all, it does not carry with it a guarantee of functioning intelligence.

The question naturally arises: What plan could possibly lead to the valid selection or the adequate training of the kind of person we have described?

The traditional methods of determining the professional worth of vocational counselors in terms of courses taken or points earned is of dubious value. If they are required as a basic qualification, they should be accepted only if the would-be counselor can score high on valid subjective and objective measures of personality and experience in training, regardless of the manner in which these were acquired.

The qualifications of counselors should not go below a certain level of culture, intelligence, scholarship, or achievement. For instance, in scholarship the counselor should be above the average of all the college students in the country.

The profession of counselor is as crucial as that of physician. The selection of counselors should be based upon the welfare of society rather than upon the necessity of providing remunerative occupations for those who desire to be counselors. The mental health of counselors should be outstanding and should be recognized as such by those whose own mental health is similarly outstanding.

Scholarship should be measured by standardized tests in English and two other subjects.

The possession of the bachelor's degree must be set as a minimum standard, but it should in no case be considered in itself a qualification. It could even be waived in cases where tests and other means of measuring scholarship indicate that the candidate is wholly qualified.

The counselor should have specific knowledge of those subjects which are usually included in required courses such as history; philosophy; principles and problems of education; adolescent development; principles of education and vocational guidance; studies in educational and occupational opportunities; counseling methods; psychological tests and guidance; mental hygiene; sociology; economics; labor problems; applied psychology; vocational education; and social case work.

SOME OTHER CRITERIA. There are other criteria, objective enough, but seldom used. For instance, the counselor might be asked, Do you have any children of your own? How old are they? How much time do you spend in counseling them? What has been the result

of your counseling? What is your I.Q.? What magazines do you
read regularly? How much time do you give to them? What books
have you read voluntarily during the last three years? How would
you like to submit such a cumulative record as is now kept of students in good vocational schools? Under what circumstances do you
lose control of your temper? Are you happily married? If you are
not married, why not? During the past three years how many friends
and acquaintances have come to you voluntarily for guidance? How
much of your own time do you give to helping other people? Have
you ever led a boys' or girls' club? And so on and so on.

HOW ARE COUNSELORS MADE? Counselors are not made at all. They
develop out of wise, experienced men and women who have dedicated their personalities and their skills to the education and orientation of young men and women. They may have been trade men or
women, or may have come from the professions. They may have
been academic teachers who persistently and insistently acquainted
themselves at first hand with occupations. Whatever their origin,
they have been eager to learn about life. They who wish to be wise
counselors must first *live* wisely. Then they may help others to live.

VII. PROFESSIONAL ASSOCIATIONS

Vocational education is in the hands of its teachers and administrators. As they grow, it will grow. They and their products, the
boys and girls, the young men and women who have prepared for
vocation and life, are the best public relations counselors. It is they
who convince the people, whose schools they are (in a very special
sense, people's schools), that they are what they purport to be. But
teachers do not grow alone, they grow in association. They learn
from each other. They learn from the best of the academic teachers.
They learn from all who are real educators. Such an association is
the American Vocational Association which, with its predecessors,
for over forty years, has kept vocational education vividly before the
people. The National Society for the Promotion of Industrial Education pressed for the original support of the Smith-Hughes Act and,
through a succession of later acts, the American Vocational Association widened and strengthened this support. It has fought for high
standards of occupational skill in its teachers and for sound teaching methods. In an expanding world economy where vocation and
training for a vocation become more and more important on an

international scale, it is grasping the opportunity of making vocational education education for life in all its phases. The principles of vocational education are fundamental and apply to men and women everywhere. Cooperation with vocational educators and general educators in foreign countries on the basis of these fundamentals should lead to better understanding and should make a contribution to world peace. As members of the American Vocational Association, through its recently organized Committee on International Education, men and women, vocational educators throughout the country can do their part.

COOPERATION WITH GENERAL EDUCATORS. The whole trend of argument in this book has been to break down the sharp division between vocational and general educators and to indicate that the best general education is that which is based upon a sound conception of the centrality of vocation in life. This thesis will hardly be accepted by all so-called "general educators," nor will all the academic high schools and liberal arts colleges become vocational institutions overnight. Nor will all vocational institutions immediately realize their obligation to provide that kind of enriched vocational education that can truly be called general education. In the meanwhile, instead of standing aloof, vocational educators should establish, wherever possible, sound cooperation with those general educators who can conceive of and execute an integrated program. For instance, the sponsorship of *Education for ALL American Youth* by the Educational Policies Commission of the National Education Association indicates that there *is* a large body of educators who are facing the problem of American education with open minds and deep insight. Vocational educators must cooperate with them.

CONVENTION TECHNIQUES. There has been a growing disposition to plan convention meetings on the basis of the panel discussion and to draw into these discussions men and women from other educational fields. This type of programing should be encouraged and intensified. It is essentially an application of good classroom method. While everybody agrees that "speeches" and "speakers" are boring and useless, they still persist. Substitute the panel discussion, followed by general discussion, select wise moderators who will give everyone an opportunity to speak, report the results of the discussions accurately, and members will return to their schools enlightened and stimulated. Vocational educators deal with real problems of education, they talk about life, so their conventions can be of the very greatest benefit to them.

RESEARCH. Research in vocational education has been meager and often inconclusive. No more insistent obligation rests upon vocational educators than that of studying intensively and objectively all their procedures and of evaluating the results. A few well-regimented facts are much more convincing than any amount of opinion. The American Vocational Association has a committee on research that has thus far issued two bulletins, one on the "Occupational Adjustments of Vocational School Graduates," and another, "A Study of Industrial Teacher-Education at the Graduate Level." There should be many more of these bulletins, based on the best-known research techniques and checked for validity by the severest critics. If vocational education is all that we believe it to be, we should be ready and anxious to submit it to the most rigorous evaluation.

VIII. THE TEACHER

Throughout this chapter we have emphasized the necessity of applying to the profession of teaching the same standards that we apply to the occupations taught by those teachers. What is good for the pupil or student is good for the teacher or professor. So, we set up for our own profession the same critical standards that we set up for all other vocations. "An essential factor in the advancement of knowledge is intellectual integrity, the suppression of all wishful thinking and the strictest regard for the claims of evidence. The universal community of educated men is a fellowship of ideals as well as of beliefs. To isolate the activity of thinking from the morals of thinking is to make sophists of the young and to encourage them to argue for the sake of personal victory rather than of the truth. We are not so naive as to suggest that theoretical instruction of the virtues will automatically make a student virtuous. Rather, we assert that the best way to infect the student with a zest for intellectual integrity is to put him near a teacher who is himself selflessly devoted to the truth; so that a spark from the teacher will, so to speak, leap across the desk into the classroom, kindling within the student the flame of intellectual integrity, which will thereafter sustain itself." [11]

The use of the term "workshop" as a device in teacher training

[11] PAUL H. BUCK and others, *op. cit.*, p. 72.

seems to have great significance. "The workshop in a variety of forms convincingly demonstrated its value for the education of teachers in service. A workshop is planned to provide a situation in which teachers may work intensively on problems growing out of their professional situations and so make progress toward the more effective discharge of their professional functions. The focus on problems implies a considerable degree of individualization and a definite pointing toward change of practice. Learning about is related to planning to do. The problem that serves as a starting point may be essentially individual; for example, how to improve a course over which the teacher has a high degree of personal control. Or it may be a large matter, a question, say, of some general curricular adjustment, decision respecting which must be participated in by members of a group." [12] Here is a striking and unusual instance of a definitely vocational, *doing* technique, being adopted in a program for training in an academic profession. And along with the technique come two words redolent of mechanics — "work" and "shop" — a workshop for teachers.

[12] Commission on Teacher Education, *The Improvement of Teacher Education* (Washington, D. C.: American Council on Education, 1946).

Chapter 18

EVALUATION

EVALUATION is the oldest mental and emotional practice in the world. Whenever we say or think "This is good," or "That is bad," we are evaluating. We are measuring accomplishment against some ideal of goodness. Consciously or subconsciously, we are passing judgment upon what we, or somebody else, has done.

A statement of educational purposes is a judgment of some person or group as to what is good and what is bad, what is valuable and what is worthless. It is a statement of preferences, choices, values. This book constitutes such a statement. If it be valid, then vocational education, as actually practiced, should be measured against this ideal, and there should be effective ways of making such measurements. If the statement, or any part of it, is not valid, then the ideal itself should be evaluated in terms of other ideals. There must be a re-evaluation of values. In any case, ideals cannot be pure flashes of intuition or acts of creative imagination, although intuition and imagination are of great importance. They must be based upon experience, the experience of many people, carefully recorded, studied, and generalized. This is research, the basis of a science of education.

I. THE MEANING OF VALUE

VALUES AND STANDARDS. It is obvious, then, that "value" is the opinion of a person, as indicated in the dictionary definition, "the quality or fact of being worth while, excellent, useful, or desirable; worth in a thing whether real or imputed." In the mind of any one person, it is not absolute, because value is also "relative worth or importance; degree of excellence or usefulness; stated in a scale of preferences." In an attempt to approach consensus, we speak of "standards." We recall Livingstone's "But of all lives the life without standards is the most ignoble and barren, sweet in the mouth but bitter in the belly."

For a standard is "that which is set up by authority, custom or general consent, as a model or example; criterion; test; in general, a definite level, degree, material, character, quality, or the like, viewed as that which is proper or adequate for a given purpose." A life without "standards" might be ignoble only in the eyes of the authority who had set up these standards. On the other hand, it might be ignoble because it failed to meet standards arrived at by common consent. So, in any discussion of educational values or standards, we must be especially concerned with *whose* standards they happen to be. To the extent that they are the opinions of people, they are "subjective." To the extent that they are based upon measurements that are commonly accepted, such as the number of words in a particular child's vocabulary, they are objective, or scientific. Of course, the interpretation of the importance of that scientific fact is a matter of opinion, and therefore subjective again. However scientific and objective the standardized intelligence tests may be, they have given rise to no end of controversy as to their "usefulness" for living, in other words, as to the "value" of a high I.Q.

Evaluation in vocational education should deal with the things in this book that we have considered "good" — work, personality, reality, democracy, method, intelligence, physique, and ethics. It should enable us to find out what skills have been attained, what knowledges have been acquired, in terms of the values we have set upon skill and knowledge. It should also enable us to determine the extent to which pupils and students have arrived at "understanding." These are the S and T and I of the Richards formula. That is to say, we should be able to determine whether vocational education, as it exists, measures up to our standards, whether it is "good." However, we should also critically evaluate standards in the light of continuing experience in applying them, that is, re-evaluate the values, thus arriving at higher and better values. And, of course, such higher and better values should suggest better practices.

Periodically we all suffer from educational jitters. They are only a special manifestation of philosophic doubt. Is life worth living? Is war inevitable? Is just and humane government possible? Is the church a beneficent institution? Are we getting too much schooling? Isn't academic education just a racket — hard to take and doesn't prepare you for anything? Is vocational education crassly utilitarian, depriving individuals of culture and confining them to a single and narrowing trade? Aren't we training too many specialists at the expense of versatility? Is this training being given in trades where absorptive capacity is low, but being neglected in trades where absorption is high? And, anyway, don't employers say that they would rather train their own workers, "let the schools just provide good academic education and develop good personalities; we will do the rest"? And so on and so on.

It is fortunate that such questions should be asked — repeatedly, insistently, even belligerently. The public should be ever alert regarding its social institutions. The responsibility of members of boards of education is especially heavy. And the professional staff must know the answers, or, at the very least, must always be searching for them. That is what departments of reference and research are for. Much has been said of "continuous evaluation" and "continuous surveys." Somehow or other, too little actually happens. Be that as it may, the first step in the development of an adequate educational program is always to find out what, at any moment, we have. Then, in some way, to see how good it is in terms of what we want. Next, we must dream a dream about what we ought to have. Finally, in the light of both fact and fancy, we must do something about it.

All this boils down to a few well-known terms — evaluation, survey, compilation, and research.

WHAT IS EVALUATION? As in all other affairs of life, evaluation is as old as education itself. Teachers are always eager to know how much progress their students are making toward certain goals and how that progress can be attained with the greatest economy of time and effort. All the evaluative instruments and techniques in use today may be considered as a modern refinement of a very old practice. Evaluation is the over-all term. Survey, compilation, research, are techniques.

In a narrower sense, however, the concept of evaluation is an outgrowth of the tests and measurements movement which has developed rapidly and has exerted an increasingly powerful influence on education during the past forty years. As a reaction against the earlier subjective and informal character of educational appraisal, testing experts placed great emphasis upon objectivity. As the number of available objective standardized tests increased from a trickle to a flood, thoughtful educators began to realize that pencil-and-paper tests can measure only a part of the outcomes of instruction, and that teachers and guidance workers need information concerning pupil behavior which cannot be obtained by the exclusive use of such instruments. Moreover, most of the earlier standardized tests dealt very largely with factual information.

"To focus tests exclusively on the acquisition and retention of information may recognize objectives of education which are relatively unimportant. Measuring the results of education must be increasingly concerned with such questions as these: Are the children growing in their ability to work together for a common end? Do they show greater skill in collecting and weighing evidence? Are they learning to be fair and tolerant in situations where conflicts arise? Are they sympathetic in the presence of suffering and indignant in the presence of injustice? Do they show greater concern about questions of civic, social and economic importance? Are they using their spending money more wisely? Are they becoming more skillful in doing some useful type of work? . . . These are criteria suitable for estimating the effectiveness of a democratic school system — suitable because directly related to the basic purposes. Until such criteria assume high importance in measuring educational results the stated purposes of education are not likely to penetrate very fully into practice." [1]

In response to such criticism, the test makers began to stress exercises involving development of attitudes, interests, ideals, and habits. The recent Tests of General Educational Development constructed for use of the United States Armed Forces Institute illustrate the new emphasis on behavior in life situations rather than on details, factual, nonfunctioning textbook matter. This general emphasis upon the behavior of a growing individual is what differentiates, in part, evaluation from the earlier concept of tests and measurements. Evaluation is less interested in measuring the body of information which has been or should have been learned, and more interested in discovering in what way the instruction has modified the actual behavior of students. Tests by themselves cannot do this, and so evaluation makes use of questionnaires, case studies, and cumulative records.

Evaluation is more than measurement. All measuring instruments from entirely casual and informal teacher-made classroom tests to the most painstakingly constructed standardized tests cannot by themselves improve teaching or pupil achievement in any subject.

[1] Educational Policies Commission, *The Purposes of Education in an American Democracy* (Washington, D. C.: National Education Association, 1938), p. 153. Republished in *Policies for Education in American Democracy* (Washington, D. C.: National Education Association, 1946).

348

They simply describe a situation in revealing and quantitative terms. A barometer informs the master of a ship that the atmospheric pressure is falling sharply. The master knows what steps must be taken — simply reading the barometer and entering the data in the log are not enough. Similarly, data resulting from the use of standardized tests or other evaluative instruments are of little worth unless the findings are implemented in a definite, practical way. It is this last step that is most essential, but unfortunately most difficult, and therefore least often taken.

A *survey* provides a general or comprehensive view, a scrutinizing view. It is an exceedingly careful and studied inspection. *Compilation* is the act or process of selecting materials for making a book, a statistical table, or the like. The survey and the compilation provide evidence for evaluation, and they are usually preliminary to research. A description of what we have does not tell us whether it is going anywhere, or, if it *is* going somewhere, whether it is worth while going there. Compilation, survey, and research are all necessary for evaluation. Inadequate and inaccurate as they may be, they are the best that the human mind has been able to devise in the long search for knowledge as a basis for action. It is only by their continual use, and by the experience obtained from using them, that they will be made better instruments.

RESEARCH. Research is "studious inquiry or examination; specifically and usually, critical and exhaustive investigation or experimentation, having for its aim the discovery of new facts and their correct interpretation, the revision of accepted conclusions, theories, or laws, in the light of newly discovered facts, or the practical applications of such new and revised conclusions, etc.; also a particular investigation of such character, or a book, article, or the like, presenting the investigator's discoveries; as to give one's full time to research." The term "research" has been too freely applied to inquiries that have not been studious, critical, or exhaustive, and have not been based upon experimentation. Research in education should be as painstaking and as meticulously conducted as any investigation in the physical sciences.

II. NEED FOR EVALUATION

PERSONALITY. The sympathetic and effective guidance of individuals, the development of personality, requires a *comprehensive* body of data. The effectiveness of guidance depends not only upon the intelligence and good wishes of the advisor but upon the most complete knowledge obtainable of the pupil's past and present status. Teachers' marks, I.Q.'s, results of standardized tests, health examinations, records of attendance and punctuality, character traits, work habits — in short, every item called for on a comprehensive cumulative record form — are all valuable. Many facts pertaining to home life do not lend themselves to quantitative description or statistical treatment, but they are among the most significant data obtainable. The cumulative record is more than a guidance tool; it is one of the most effective instruments for evaluating a school's entire program of guidance and instruction.

TEACHERS. To the psychologist, the fact that teachers are so fault-finding with their students suggests that teachers are lacking in their own sense of security. An evaluation program can contribute to their happiness, mental health, and efficiency by furnishing concrete evidence of their accomplishments. Adequate recognition of professional competence can help to build up the teacher's feeling of security and provide the basis for further professional growth. When a school lacks an organized evaluation program, informal appraisals are made on the basis of student data that are not sufficiently comprehensive in scope, such as subject marks, rate of progress through school, performance on uniform examinations, and the like, each of which, though valid in a certain area, does not present a complete picture of the accomplishments of either teachers or their students. If the plan for appraisal is not sufficiently comprehensive, the staff may be in doubt as to whether it is accomplishing the objectives of the curriculum. Teachers may seek security by emphasizing areas of the school's work which produce tangible results — such as coaching for uniform examination — but which may be actually disadvantageous to the work of the school as a whole.

ADMINISTRATION. Thoughtful educators recognize that school policies and procedures are hypotheses which have been deduced from the philosophy of education of the principal. Logic, however, must always give way to experience, and the evaluation program can validate or reject any of the operating hypotheses. Many schools, for example, operate on the hypothesis that education for citizenship may be left entirely to the social studies department, or that student adjustment problems will be solved if a guidance counselor is made available, or that the English department may be held accountable for the widespread use of poor English among the student body. However logical, each of these is only one of a number of possible hypotheses. A teacher of machine shop practice who has only four milling machines available for fifteen boys may believe that in the ensuing educational situation boys learn more about working together for a common end, or about fairness and tolerance in a situation where conflicts are likely to arise, than they do in a formal course in social studies. As a matter of fact, both types of classes contribute to these important goals. Evaluation can determine the contribution of each, and indicate desirable modifications in the school program. Recommendations for change must be recognized as newer hypotheses and again be subjected to experience and continuing appraisal.

COMMUNITY. Evaluation provides excellent opportunity for improved public relations. Destructive criticism of schools is most likely to arise in a community whose citizens are not adequately informed concerning the effectiveness of the educational program for which they are paying. A comprehensive evaluation program provides evidence that should be publicized. Failure of a school or school system to meet pupils' needs is often due to the community's reluctance or inability to provide sufficient funds for education. Evaluation of vocational education through an advisory board on vocational education provides an especially close contact with the community, with resulting sympathy, understanding, and support.

EVALUATING "VALUES" IN VOCATIONAL EDUCATION. Need for evaluation lies in its effect on people — students, teachers, administrators, and men and women of the community. Such effect is brought about by "studious inquiry and critical investigation" of the values attributed to work, democracy, ethics, method, reality, physique, and intelligence. These need to be kept under continual scrutiny.

SELF-EVALUATION. Above all, the program of evaluation should lead the learner, whether a high school, college, or university student, to evaluate himself. Obviously, the teacher, as evaluator of the learner, must, at every point, get the learner to see and understand the bases of evaluation, especially those that will confront him in adult life. Occupationally, his employer will be his most critical evaluator, so it is exceedingly important for the future employee to know what will be expected of him. "The learner should be able to validate his highly personalized (in some cases emotionalized) appraisals against those of the teacher or others who may interpret the evidence from a wider background and with greater objectivity. The learner must not be forced to consider evidence and make decisions which because of immaturity, inexperience, or emotional set, he is incapable of understanding, accepting, or using to advantage. The evaluative process should be consistent with those characteristics of democratic procedure that foster regard for the integrity of the individual and the brotherhood of man." [2]

STUDIES OF EVALUATION. This consciousness of need for evaluation of both secondary and higher education and for self-evaluation at every point has resulted in a number of valuable studies many phases of which are applicable to vocational education.[3]

III. EVALUATION PROCEDURES

FORMULATING THE OBJECTIVES. Objectives of education are an excellent starting place for the development of an evaluation program. The first step requires that a detailed list of more specific objectives be assembled and classified. Since the methods of appraising the acquisition of information are similar in various subject matter fields, this classification can be most economically carried out under the heading, "acquisition of information." Moreover, the methods of instruction appropriate to such a technique as "drawing reasonable inferences from data" are quite similar for subjects in which the content is markedly different.[4]

DEVISING THE TESTING SITUATIONS. Since the purpose of education is to effect desirable changes primarily in *behavior,* it is necessary that

[2] Commission on Teacher Education, American Council on Education, *The Newsletter,* Vol. II, No. 9, June, 1942.
[3] *Evaluating Secondary Education,* Bulletin of the National Association of Secondary School Principals, 26: No. 106, April, 1942.
H. A. GREENE, A. N. JORGENSON, and J. R. GERBERICH, *Measurement and Evaluation in the Secondary School* (New York: Longmans, Green and Co., 1943).
J. P. LEONARD and A. C. EURICH, *An Evaluation of Modern Education* (New York: D. Appleton-Century Co., 1942).
American Educational Research Association Journal, "Methods of Research and Appraisal in Education," Vol. XV, No. 5, December, 1945.
PAUL R. MORT and F. G. CORNELL, *A Guide for Self Appraisal of School Systems* (New York: Bureau of Publications, Teachers College, Columbia University, 1937).
E. R. SMITH, R. W. TYLER, and the Evaluation Staff, "Appraising and Recording Student Progress," Vol. III, *Adventures in American Education* (New York: Harper & Brothers, 1942).
[4] SMITH, TYLER, and the Evaluation Staff, *op. cit.*

352

objectives be measured by behavioral tests whenever possible. It is sometimes useful to know how many books are in a school library, and how many teachers have received their M.A. degrees, but the basic question remains, "What has happened to the pupils?" Regardless of the structure of the school's instructional and guidance programs, if the behavioral test is not met, then the school's work cannot be considered adequate. The best evidence that a new pupil has a functioning knowledge of the school's various guidance services is obtained when the pupil actually avails himself of the needed help. Whether or not the pupils of a given school have an adequate awareness of the need for growth in democratic action can be estimated more reliably by the actual amount of participation in the school's Student Organization than by studying the responses on a written test.

SELECTING EVALUATION METHODS. After the specific objectives of the school program have been defined in terms of behavior, and it has been decided which situations will demonstrate the achievement of those objectives most effectively, there remains the problem of selecting and trying promising evaluation methods. Along with the general growth of the testing movement a considerable number of tests and other evaluative devices have been made available for use in vocational schools. Compared with the number of instruments available for use in academic schools, the number of vocational tests remains very small.[5] The most comprehensive work on evaluative instruments of all types devotes only a small section to "Tests and Reviews: Vocations." [6] The cause of vocational education has been handicapped by the failure of vocational educators to evaluate their own products adequately.

RESULTS. Unless the data obtained from use of evaluative instruments are applied to actual problems within the school, all the time and energy expended in identifying and defining objectives, and devising instruments of appraisal, are largely waste motion. Evaluation should provide evidence concerning the degree to which a school, a teacher, a class, or a pupil is achieving the objectives of the school program.

[5] Louis V. NEWKIRK and H. A. GREENE, *Tests and Measurements in Industrial Education* (New York: John Wiley & Sons, Inc., 1935).
[6] OSCAR K. BUROS, *The Nineteen Forty Mental Measurement Yearbook* (Arlington, Virginia: The Author, 1941).

THE PROCEDURES IN ACADEMIC HIGH SCHOOLS. Generally speaking, evaluation is carried on in academic high schools by means of tests and records. Testing is usually designed to measure achievement, through subject matter examinations composed by the teacher, or through standardized intelligence and reading tests. The cumulative record provides information on both subject achievement and on character. Comparatively few high schools consider centrally functioning guidance committees, grade advisors, or special faculty committees as evaluating agencies. Many regard extracurricular activities, clubs, newspaper and magazine staffs, assemblies, Arista, school dances, athletic events as excellent areas in which to observe success or failure in reaching important objectives.[7]

"The newer evaluation techniques are, for the most part, not being given a chance to demonstrate what they can contribute to the development of a more meaningful evaluation program. Apart from a wide and not always too critical acceptance of the short-answer objective-type examination, the schools show little organized awareness of the possibilities of the newer evaluation techniques for appraisal of interests, attitudes, aptitudes, critical thinking, and personal-social adaptability."[8]

IV. EVALUATION OF VOCATIONAL SUBJECTS

For what purposes may these evaluation techniques be used in the field of vocational education? Obviously, they can be applied to the entire program, but, more particularly, they are applicable to the teaching of a single trade or group of trades, or to the teaching of one kind of subject matter. They can be used to determine the progress of individual students, of special groups of students, or of the entire student body. They are appropriate to the study of types of school organization, especially as compared with industrial and business organizations. They can become a measure of the teaching ability of individual teachers, of groups of teachers in one trade or school subject, or of the entire staff of teachers. They can be extremely effective in determining the efficiency of buildings and equipment.

LIMITATIONS. There is one thing these techniques cannot do, or can do only very imperfectly. In fact, their failure in this respect, unless

[7] HYMEN ALPERN, "Evaluation in the Academic High Schools of New York City," *High Points,* March, 1946.
[8] A. H. LASS and WAYNE WRIGHTSTONE, "Evaluation in the Secondary Schools of New York City," *High Points, op. cit.*

354

properly understood and accounted for, can vitiate any good they may do in the foregoing phases. They cannot measure the spirit, the drive, the philosophy, the essential something that makes real teachers, supervisors, and administrators. The quality of dynamic leadership, of professional integrity, of ingrained humanity, does not lend itself to the techniques of the survey. Schools and school systems have sunk to a state of critical mediocrity or have risen to the heights of public service, just because of one man or one woman. You cannot survey a soul, you cannot survey a school or a school system into existence or even out of existence. Yet Charles A. Prosser (who, incidentally, was vitally concerned with some of the earliest surveys) almost literally created the Federal Board for Vocational Education and developed Dunwoody Institute, and Robert L. Cooley practically made the Milwaukee Vocational School, not because of survey techniques but because these two possessed those imponderables that move the world. However, they used and would have been the first to defend the importance of surveys.

In any study there is one major stumbling block. It is the matter of standards. In fact, the most necessary type of research is that which strives to determine what standards ought to be. The difficulty becomes apparent when we think of ethical standards, moral standards, social standards, all of which are personal standards, and therefore fundamental in setting up educational standards. By the use of precision gauges it is easy to determine whether a gear or bearing is commercially acceptable. It is much more difficult to tell whether the school that has trained a boy to make that gear or bearing has rendered a service to both boy and society or has ruined his life and debauched the community in which he lives. Together, the boy and society are made up of a congeries of muscles, glands, organs, emotions, thoughts, wages, hours, metal, grease, politics, religion, love, greed, all of which affect and are affected by education. Since the Garden of Eden or the primordial ooze (a choice of which also involves standards) we have been trying to set standards of work and play and human intercourse. Any study of education that assumes the standards to have been permanently set does more harm than good. The standards will change as the study progresses. Perhaps it will be necessary to make them up.

Most vocational education surveys have adopted one standard with no hesitation. "The final acid test of any program of vocational education is the ability of the learner to go out from the training course, get a job, and perform the duties of that job at least sufficiently well to meet minimum occupational standards." Suppose the vocational schools in a particular city accepted only ten per cent of the students of secondary school age, that it chose these in the light of their special adaptabilities for three or four of the highly skilled trades, that it trained them intensively for the jobs that would be available, eliminating all along the line those who did not meet the highest trade standards — such a school would meet the "acid test," and yet, as a social institution, would be doing a miserable job. It might even be injuring the few boys whom it trained. But, jump from the early vocational school days to the present, and suppose that all the vocational schools in a city took in all the boys and girls who wished to attend (in other words, avoided exclusiveness), would the program not meet the acid test because *every* learner could not get a job?

There is no intention to labor this argument, but merely to indicate that standards are tricky things and that it would be better not to have them at all than to be fooled by them. The fanatic "redoubles his efforts after he has lost sight of his objectives." In a broad, general way, there is no doubt that employability is the most important test of vocational school efficiency. However, it must be considered as subsidiary to something still broader, that is, adjustment to life as a whole. This means that *all* children must be prepared for vocational competency, that such vocational competency must be a social as well a personal asset, and therefore, that every school, no matter what it calls itself, must think in terms of vocations. This does *not* mean that *any* traditional school can add a shop or two and a counselor, and thereby become a vocational school. It does *not* mean that any vocational school can dilute its vocational work to a tasteless fare of industrial arts, and still remain vocational. There must be standards and there must be a standard for standards.

EXISTING STUDIES. As to vocational education, it is safe to say that few existing studies can be dignified by the name of research. However, in vocational *choice,* individual *diagnosis,* and personnel *selection,* much valuable work has been done. It is only in recent years that this rich product of the industrial psychologists and the personnel men has been acknowledged as useful in vocational education. For a considerable period, anything that smacked of vocational guidance was scorned as a whim of the academic schoolman. It is only on the basis of sound vocational guidance that an equally sound program of vocational education can be built. A comprehensive survey of psychological methods of analyzing job skills and of analyzing individuals appears in *Vocational Guidance Throughout the World.*[9]

A description and evaluation of the most reliable tests make up the valuable volume on *Aptitudes and Aptitude Testing.*[10] Most of these tests have resulted from painstaking research, and Bingham's book constitutes an indispensable handbook for anyone who is assisting young or old people to choose vocations *for which they wish to receive training.* In the field of selection, the first important book, one that is still of great interest as an account of some of the scientific work that came out of the recruitment of the American Army for World War I, is *Trade Tests.*[11]

Falling into the field of evaluation, yet based upon painstaking research, one of the most significant contributions to education in recent years is the "Study of the relations of secondary and higher education in Pennsylvania," [12] promoted by the Carnegie Foundation for the Advancement of Teaching. Concerned with vocational education in only an indirect way, it has vital implications for the field, for, if a similar study, with the title, "The Student and His Skills," or "The Student and His Knowledges and Skills," could be made, it would be of the utmost significance for vocational education.

"The initial purpose of the Pennsylvania inquiry was to reconsider our system of schooling in the light of its obtained results, viewed objectively on their merits irrespective of any particular procedure followed in their production. All are aware that schools and colleges in themselves are at best mere aids or conveniences; they bring together in one place elements which, it is hoped, will stimulate and assist a mind in arriving at an understanding of itself and of its environment. Some individuals become thoroughly well educated without schools or colleges, and the process by which they do so with entirely individual motives and attitudes, illustrates admirably the procedure that must underlie all education. Values that accrue to the

[9] FRANKLIN J. KELLER and MORRIS S. VITELES, *Vocational Guidance Throughout the World* (New York: W. W. Norton & Co., 1937), Ch. VIII and Ch. IX.
[10] WALTER V. BINGHAM, *Aptitudes and Aptitude Testing* (New York: Harper & Brothers, 1937).
[11] J. CROSBY CHAPMAN, *Trade Tests* (New York: Henry Holt and Company, Inc., 1921).
[12] W. S. LEARNED and B. D. WOOD, *The Student and His Knowledge* (New York: The Carnegie Foundation for the Advancement of Teaching, 1938).

individual from his schooling, as from every other source of his mental furniture, accrue solely as his own ability and initiative lead him
to accept and appropriate them. This is what the term 'understanding' means. It is the only secure basis on which even the most elementary educational structure can be reared." [13]

In other words, whether viewed from the standpoint of either
academic preparation for college or vocational preparation for a job,
education is something that must be studied as a whole-life or life-
whole process, in which the school is only an incidental convenience.
For practical considerations this convenience may become a necessity,
but the necessity must be proved by research. A study of the type
reported in *The Student and His Knowledge* is highly desirable in
the field of vocational education.

Another study, not in the field of vocational education, but making
a notable contribution to it, is *Job Satisfaction*.[14] Selecting a fairly
typical community, large enough to include a wide variety of occupations, but small enough to be studied economically, the author
chose New Hope, Pennsylvania, for a survey of job satisfaction.
With the endorsement of a local sponsoring committee, an experienced interviewer called at each residence, asking, but not urging,
each adult to indicate his attitude toward his present or most recent
job by answering thirty-six questions printed on an anonymous report
blank, which was then placed in an envelope and sealed before being
returned to the interviewer. The evidence obtained indicates that the
proportion of workers who are dissatisfied with their jobs is probably less than a third.

The importance of this study lies in the fact that it covers a whole
community rather than a group of workers selected on the basis of
their training or education. It is concerned with *all* workers regardless of their preparation for that work. "Patently, the problem of
adjusting to an occupation is different from that of adjusting to the
multiplication table. Occupations do not stay put, nor do the people
who pursue them. Political, social, economic, mechanical, and psychological influences beat a tattoo on the sensitive soul of the worker.
Therefore vocational guidance is no avocational psychic compensation for the zealous missionary mind of the cloistered school teacher.
Nor is it a playground for the too-pure psychologist. It is a stubborn fact of life with which warmly feeling spirits and coldly

[13] LEARNED and WOOD, *op. cit.*, p. 4.
[14] ROBERT HOPPOCK, *Job Satisfaction* (New York: Harper & Brothers, 1935).

reasoning minds must come to uncompromising grips. Their laboratory is the world of work. Their tools must be the last word in precision.

"It is with something of this sense of cosmic significance and immediate compulsion that the author has pursued his inquiry and marshalled his results. . . . By converging upon the problem from three different points of the human compass, the author has brought the techniques of the personal anecdote, the statistical correlation, and the social survey into a happy triangular union. And, having had practical experience in industry and in the counseling of young people in school, as well as in the general organizational problems coming before the National Occupational Conference, he has been effective, albeit humble, in the application of his findings to the day-to-day problem of occupational adjustment." [15]

Most surveys in the field of vocational education have made attempts at evaluation of going programs. If the evaluation has been objective, the standard has usually been that of employability, without consideration of all the factors that exclude from vocational education a large proportion of those who are entitled to it. Moreover, since the data have resulted from a consideration of employment, relatively short compared with the entire work life of the individual, the results cannot be considered satisfactory. Nevertheless, the employment follow-up study has been a valuable check on the work of any vocational school.

The *survey* has been the most popular form of vocational education study. Since the young people in a community are likely to continue to live and work in it, the natural impulse of the educator has been to find out what employment opportunities that community offers and to base his program upon his findings. So surveys have been concerned with the number of workers in each occupational field and in each type of job, with the opportunities for advancement, with wages and hours, with working conditions, with skills required, and so on.

Back in the early days of World War I, when the National Society for the Promotion of Industrial Education, now the American Vocational Association, was impressing upon the general public the need for vocational education, it was necessary to make community surveys in the grand manner, bringing into cooperation civic, industrial, and political groups. The survey was as much a matter of public relations as it was of educational research. In 1916, 1917, and 1918

[15] HOPPOCK, *op. cit.*, quoted from Foreword by Franklin J. Keller.

studies were made in Minneapolis, Richmond (Virginia), Richmond (Indiana), Indianapolis, New York City, Cleveland, and New Orleans. The Richmond, Virginia, Survey was conducted jointly by the United States Bureau of Education, United States Bureau of Labor Statistics, the Russell Sage Foundation, the National Society for the Promotion of Industrial Education, and the local and state boards of education. Such surveys were necessary at the time, but in the light of certain other considerations to be discussed below, it may be that extensive projects of this character are no longer as important as they once were.[16]

[16] Bureau of Labor Statistics, U. S. Department of Labor, *Vocational Education Survey of Richmond, Virginia,* Bulletin 162 (Washington, D. C.: Government Printing Office, 1916).

Bureau of Labor Statistics, U. S. Department of Labor, *Vocational Education Survey of Minneapolis, Minnesota,* Bulletin 199, Vocational Education Series No. 1 (Washington, D. C.: Government Printing Office, 1917).

Federal Board for Vocational Education, *Vocational Education Survey: A Discussion of Methods, Procedures, Forms, and the Organization of Survey Committees,* Misc. 168. Printed in full in Wright and Allen, *Supervision of Vocational Education* (New York: John Wiley & Sons, Inc., 1926), p. 351 ff.

HOWARD M. BELL, *Matching Youth and Jobs,* American Council on Education, prepared for the American Youth Commission (Washington, D. C.: Government Printing Office, 1940).

ELLSWORTH W. BROOKS, *A Standard Procedure for Administering Commercial Occupational Surveys* (Iowa City, Iowa: State University of Iowa, 1933, master's thesis).

EMILY G. PALMER, *Handbook for the Vocational Education Survey* (Berkeley, California: California State Department of Education, Division of Vocational Education, 1941).

GRAYSON N. KEFAUVER, director, *A Study of Vocational Conditions in the City of Fresno,* General Education Series, No. 2, Division of Vocational Education of the University of California and of the State Board of Education, 1926).

P. G. FRASIER, *A Technique for the Vocational Education Survey of a Local Community* (Des Moines, Iowa: Iowa Board for Vocational Education, 1939).

New York City Board of Education, *General Recommendations on Vocational Education and Guidance* (New York: Vocational Survey Commission, 1932).

FREDERICK J. NICHOLS, "What Are the Steps in the Process Determining the Occupational Opportunities in a Given City?" in *Foundations of Commercial Education,* First Yearbook, Eastern Commercial Teachers' Association (New York: Eastern Commercial Teachers' Association, 1928), pp. 361-70.

Vocational and Practical Arts Education in New York City Schools (New York: Board of Education, 1942).

Vocational Education at the Crossroads (New York: Vocational High School Principals Association, 1943). A critique of the survey, *Vocational and Practical Arts Education in New York City Schools.*

MARGUERITE WYCKOFF ZAPOLEON, *Community Occupational Surveys,* U. S. Office of Education, Vocational Division Bulletin No. 223 (Washington, D. C.: Government Printing Office, 1942).

Joint Legislative Committee on the State Educational System, *Report of the New York City Sub-Committee* (Albany, New York: Williams Press, 1944).

HOWARD A. CAMPION, *Vocational Schools of Essex County, New Jersey* (New York: National Occupational Conference, 1939).

360

The Research Committee of the American Vocational Association has produced two studies, both of which are in the nature of surveys. The purpose of the first [17] is (1) to develop certain procedures and techniques for use in local communities in determining the occupational status of youth, with particular reference to guidance, vocational training, and placement services of the public school, (2) to determine the effectiveness of the occupational training services in a selected area, as a type of study, (3) to present certain critical issues revealed by the study with special reference to the improvement of guidance, vocational education, and placement services in public education. The purpose of the second study [18] is to reveal current practices in industrial teacher-education institutions giving graduate instruction in industrial education, with regard to entrance requirements, residence requirements, kinds of degrees granted, and thesis requirements. As with most other studies of this kind, the series was interrupted by World War II. It is hoped that it will be continued, but with major emphasis upon study of the whole field of workers rather than of selected groups.

Somewhat less pretentious than the survey is the *compilation*. It is sometimes valuable to bring together already existing material in a book or to list sources of information or to compile a bibliography. For instance, the U. S. Office of Education has published a list of 373 studies in agricultural education, with an abstract of each study.[19] The American Youth Commission has listed 2500 books, pamphlets, and articles on American youth, many of them dealing with phases of occupational adjustment.[20] The *Occupational Index,* published monthly, is a continuous bibliography of current publications which contain, or profess to contain, occupational information that will be helpful to an individual choosing a field of work.[21] Obviously, such information should also be useful to all those concerned with the planning of vocational education programs.

[17] Committee on Research, *Occupational Adjustments of Vocational School Graduates* (Washington, D. C.: American Vocational Association, 1940).
[18] Committee on Research, *A Study of Industrial Teacher Education at the Graduate Level* (Washington, D. C.: American Vocational Association, 1941).
[19] U. S. Office of Education, *Summaries of Studies in Agricultural Education* (Washington, D. C.: Government Printing Office, 1935). An annotated bibliography of 373 studies in agricultural education, with a classified subject index and a general evaluation.
[20] LOUIS A. MENEFEE and M. M. CHAMBERS, *American Youth* (Washington, D. C.: American Council on Education, 1938). An annotated bibliography prepared for the American Youth Commission.
[21] *Occupational Index,* published at New York University, Washington Square, New York City.

VOCATIONAL SCHOOL PRACTICE. The first phase of evaluation lies in the selection of students and their distribution to the various courses. In the section, "Selective Factors," in the chapter on Primacy of the Person, this program has been discussed in detail. It includes consideration of interests, achievement in the manual and academic subjects, general behavior, personality, physique and health, special abilities and disabilities. These data must be gathered from the student's record in his previous school, whether elementary, junior high, high, or college, or must be obtained from new and additional tests. In vocational high school, all the devices used in academic high school are applied to the evaluation of academic subjects, character, and all other school relationships whether or not strictly vocational in nature. These have been detailed in the preceding section.

However, to these must be added all those procedures that are useful in evaluating those aptitudes, traits, and abilities belonging more specifically to the job. The ninth year tryout shop cycle has been described under "Selective Factors," also the important device of interview and examination by members of the Advisory Board on Vocational Education representing the particular industry taught in the school. According to the activities in which various schools specialize, special tests are usually developed, such as picture tests in the needle trades, and short-answer tests in aviation. Some schools require candidates for graduation to complete special projects in the senior year — a kind of reversion to the apprentice's masterpiece.

The cumulative record card, constituting the complete picture of the individual, and already drawn in considerable detail in the chapter on Primacy of the Person, is always an ever-ready and extremely valuable tool for evaluation. Not only is it a record of experience and behavior, but it provides a profile resulting from the testing program.[22]

RECOMMENDATIONS FOR FURTHER EVALUATION. A survey of evaluation procedures in New York City vocational high schools [23] makes clear the urgent need for further development and expansion of measuring techniques. Specific recommendations are:

1: Establishment of a central bureau which would give aid and direction to individual schools in measuring techniques

[22] DAVID G. SALTEN, "The Need for a Testing Service in a Vocational High School," High Points, January, 1946.
[23] BENJAMIN FOX, "Evaluation in the Vocational High Schools," High Points, March, 1946.

362

2. Expansion of guidance staffs with necessary assistants to take care of checking, recording, and tabulating test data

3. Research in test construction for measuring the so-called intangibles, such as appreciations, human relationships, personality, etc.

4. In-service courses for teachers in constructing and administering tests

5. Evaluation procedures to measure post-graduate progress and success

6. Greater budgetary provision for tests of all types

V. RESEARCH

While the survey and compilation may very well come within the first part of the definition of research, that is, "studious inquiry or examination," they too often fall short of being "critical and exhaustive investigation or experimentation having for its aim the discovery of new facts and their correct interpretation, the revision of accepted conclusions, theories, or laws in the light of newly discovered facts." Above all, research should mean a reaching out for new knowledge, new principles, upon which better practices can be based. Wherever possible it should be experimental.

COMMON PITFALLS. Use of the term "research" suggests caution. Results may be valuable or useless or harmful according to the care exercised in making the study. Research in vocational education must be subjected to all the usual controls and, perhaps, to a few more. Some of the common pitfalls are discussed in *Summaries of Studies in Agricultural Education.*[24] They are suggested by the following statements:

1. A study has completeness when the data, cases, or instances studied are representative of all parts of the field being studied.

2. Inaccuracy consists of errors of commission. The cause of inaccuracy may be false data, faulty treatment of data, errors in calculation, or unsound assumption.

3. Studies which depend in whole or in part on opinions are subject to bias.

4. The law of single variable is that an effect can be ascribed to a given cause only when the other causes or factors have been kept constant.

[24] U. S. Office of Education, *Summaries of Studies in Agricultural Education, op. cit.*

5. Lack of continuity. The typical situation in research in vocational agriculture is that a research worker selects a problem, studies it for a time, arrives at conclusions, and then discontinues his study.

6. The effect of graduate work. When the student is primarily interested in meeting requirements, he is likely to select a problem which will afford easily available data.

7. The scientific attitude. A scientific viewpoint is prerequisite to a study of real value. The investigator must receive ideas with an open mind. This attitude is conspicuous by its absence when the investigator reaches a conclusion first and then assembles data to prove his conclusion correct.

8. The application of findings. There are studies which have not been carried far enough so that supervisors, teacher trainers, or teachers can see how the findings may be used.

9. Statistical possibilities. The typical study in the field of vocational agriculture uses averages but the use of other measures of central tendency, dispersion, and relationship is infrequent. Calculations of the probable error of differences to determine where the differences are significant is sometimes overlooked. There is evidence that the possibilities of statistical procedure are not generally realized.

KIND OF RESEARCH NEEDED. It is patent that there is a need. There has been some recognition of the need and a tendency to heed it, but, compared with the possibilities, the accomplishment has been very slight indeed. The Federal Vocational Education Acts have made provision for research and service, but the states have done very little in response. This situation naturally gives rise to speculation as to the reason for failure to carry on really authentic research. In light of the outcome is it too expensive in time and money and energy? Are vocational educators incompetent or reluctant to engage in it? Have the academic trends in school systems been too powerful to permit them to do it? Are boards of education too indifferent to the real welfare of the children? One could multiply such conjectures almost indefinitely. It would not be idle to do so, for as long as there is doubt as to the relative value of various types of vocational education, or even as to vocational education itself, some sound basis for resolving that doubt must be found. In the meanwhile, it is pertinent to scan the field for those problems that are making the most urgent bid for solution and would lend themselves to research techniques.

PROBLEMS FOR RESEARCH. 1. There should be intensive case studies of individuals to determine how they came to do the kind of work they do. These should be checked against an evaluation of how well they do that work, and a conjecture as to what kind of work they might have done better. This is the type of study suggested by the Lynds in their survey of community life in Muncie. They add a footnote to an account of The X Family: "The methodological note should be added to this chapter that such a necessarily impressionistic treatment as this is but a prolegomenon to a type of research too little attempted as yet by American social science. There is definite need for the more exact exploration of a socio-economic control system of this sort through the detailed, systematic charting of the individuals affected, in their specific personal and institutional relationships through the controls. A city is made up of individuals, each presenting a pattern of relationships, individual and organizational." [25]

2. Supplementing such a study there should be extensive and intensive studies of what happens to workers in a number of specific industries, that is, the story of their hiring, transfer, advancement, and discharge. Not only would this reveal the work history of each individual but it would indicate the degree to which industry is subject to turnover. Many employers say they would rather train their own workers. Train to what end? For what? How long do workers stay in industry? What industries do they come from and with what training? Koepke did something of the kind in Minnesota. [26]

3. There should be continuous compilation and evaluation of changing technologies in extension of that reported by the National Resources Committee. [27] The results should lead to national policy, to regional policies (state, county, city, or groups of these units), and to local policies (city, town, or sections of these units). There is nothing so deceptive as a trend, but it is the next best thing to the gift of prophecy and we have to use it as best we can.

4. There should be continuous or periodic evaluations of school work, both so-called academic and vocational, by industry, business,

[25] ROBERT S. LYND and HELEN MERRELL LYND, *Middletown in Transition* (New York: Harcourt, Brace and Company, Inc., 1937), p. 100.
[26] C. A. KOEPKE, "A Job Analysis Survey," *Occupations, The Vocational Guidance Magazine*, June, 1934.
[27] National Resources Committee, *Technological Trends and National Policies* (Washington, D. C.: Government Printing Office, 1937).

and professions. This is one of the important functions of advisory boards of vocational education.

5. Supplementing work histories of individuals, as suggested above, there should be studies of the school programs of students of both general and vocational schools, especially in relation to the work in which they ultimately find employment. This would be the old-fashioned follow-up employment study, with modern streamlining. It would be an application of the technique of "The Student and His Knowledges and Skills" to the entire secondary school population, with an extension into the world of work.

6. We recall Hoppock's study of job satisfaction. The reports on many individuals indicated that the workers' satisfaction mounted to something altogether pleasurable, even to the joy of the artist. Studies should be made of these finer aspects of employment, "job joy," "job understanding," and "job personality." Moreover, it is important to know to what extent employers are "satisfied" with their employees, really satisfied, not merely tolerant because they find none better. And what is the relation of this "employer satisfaction" to the vocational education of the employee?

7. There should be a continuing study of the relation of physique and health to job suitability. Especially as a result of the casualties of World War II, many studies have been made in this field and adaptations of mechanisms have been devised to make possible the employment of handicapped men and women. However, little of this has seeped down into vocational education for youths whose handicaps are congenital or the result of civilian accidents. A democratic conception of education that opens up occupational opportunities to all must include everyone who has a physical defect.

8. It has become almost a truism that more people lose their jobs because of personality defects than do those who lack skill and trade knowledge. However, studies of "job temperament" such as would be useful in vocational education guidance programs are sadly lacking. Temperament, what is known in the narrow sense as "personality," offers a wide-open field for research.

9. Similarly, continued and persistent research is necessary on interest, motivation, their relation to learning, and on the nature of happiness as determined by occupation.

10. The exigencies of World War II required that certain kinds of training be given fast and furiously. This was *training,* accompanied by very little indeed that could be called *education.* Moreover, the techniques used were often those with which the schools

were already familiar. However, insofar as they reveal economy in learning, reduce the time factor to the minimum, if not to the optimum, these methods should be studied and adapted to normal civilian vocational education. Several times we have called attention to the "time fetish." The only way to exorcise the spirit that resides in a fetish is to bring it out into the light of day and subject it to that studious examination we call research. Generally speaking, methods of teaching in vocational education have shown considerable advance over those in academic education, but they should be subjected to continuing and vigorous re-examination.

11. Vocational schools have always suffered from the influence of academic teachers and administrators who have automatically directed into them all pupils of low intelligence and directed away from them all those of high intelligence. While we have had some studies of the relation of intelligence to the successful pursuit of vocation, notably that resulting from the study of soldiers in World War I, little has been done on the potentiality of intelligence in the so-called trades. Questions that need to be answered are: What is the relation of academic ratings to shop ratings in vocational schools? Is there any evidence that the I.Q. (or intelligence measured in any other way) is raised by following a vocational education program? There is considerable evidence that the I.Q. is raised by a favorable environment.[28] Does the vocational school provide such environment? What is the correlation between intelligence quotient and ratings in shop work? In other words, what do "gifted" and "dull" mean in a vocational school?

12. Can students who have been successful in shop work in a vocational high school sustain themselves in college? What is the minimum I.Q. of a vocational high school student that warrants his admission to college?

13. What is the minimum I.Q. necessary to succeed in any particular kind of manual work? Or of successful study in a profession? What are the minimum I.Q.'s for various types of occupations for which preparation is given in a vocational high school?

14. What are the characteristics of entering students and how do they differ from those exhibited upon graduation? In other words, what difference has vocational education made in their lives?

[28] FLORENCE L. GOODENOUGH, "New Evidence on Environmental Influence on Intelligence," in *Intelligence: Its Nature and Nurture*, Thirty-Ninth Yearbook, Part I, National Society for the Study of Education (Bloomington, Illinois: Public School Publishing Co., 1940).

15. What degree and kind of intelligence is required on new jobs as compared with the degree and kind of intelligence necessary on old jobs producing the same thing? For instance, old-fashioned hand typesetting as against linotype operation; selling gum and cigarettes as against maintenance of slot machines; making carriages as against making automobile bodies; shoeing horses as against repairing automobile engines; being a family doctor as against being a specialist; being a country lawyer as against being a corporation lawyer?

16. How far can we rely upon vocational education to produce virtues that will apply outside the vocation?

17. The term "curriculum revision" has been common in academic education. It should be equally common in vocational education. While at any one moment the subject matter may be up to date, that moment does not last long. Occupational practices are continually changing. Therefore the curriculum provides a problem for never-ceasing research.

18. Similarly, the testing program requires continuous study and improvement. In line with the theory underlying the Armed Forces Institute Tests of General Educational Development, the tests should, more and more, reveal the ability of individuals to work out problems and to meet new situations.

19. As long as the programs of academic high schools and vocational high schools are strongly differentiated, at least in the minds of lower school teachers and students, if not in fact, it is important to know what motivates some children, and their parents, to choose vocational high schools. This is a problem in articulation that deserves very careful study.

20. Similarly, why do high school graduates choose liberal arts colleges or technical colleges, or professional schools?

21. The American Vocational Association research bulletin on "A Study of Industrial Teacher Education at the Graduate Level" presents questions in the teacher-training field for serious study: Should there be more uniformity than now prevails in minimum undergraduate requirements? What should be the minimum teaching, trade, administrative, or other experience for teacher-trainers? How do the assistantships, fellowships, and other forms of aid to graduate students in industrial education compare with those of other areas such as (1) general education, (2) agriculture, (3) home economics, and (4) business education? What are the most essential qualities or traits for (1) graduate students in industrial arts, (2) graduate

students in vocational-industrial education, (3) teacher-trainers? What are the advantages, disadvantages, and student and faculty viewpoints regarding various forms of final examinations for masters' and doctors' degrees? What graduate credit should be given for courses taught in school shops?

22. To what extent are technological changes destroying our culture, and how far should vocational schools go in combating such destruction? As these changes take place, will more or less vocational education be necessary?

23. To what extent do the humanities contribute to occupational success?

24. How do graduates of liberal arts colleges succeed in occupations compared with graduates of technical or professional schools, where admission to the occupation is open to both? What is the occupational status of graduates of institutions whose curricula are based upon the "great books" theory?

25. There should be an intensive study of institutions, on all levels, elementary, high school, college, and university, that purport to do full justice to both academic and vocational conceptions of education.

26. There should be most careful research, perhaps a synthesis of research, on all the foregoing problems, leading to a re-evaluation of values.

27. In order that all this research may be carried out, there should be, in all public education departments, whether municipal, state, or federal, departments of research, fully equipped and superbly manned.[29]

29 FRANKLIN J. KELLER, "Comparative Vocational Education and Guidance," *History of Education and Comparative Education,* Review of Educational Research, Vol. IX, No. 4 (Washington, D. C.: American Educational Research Association, 1939), pp. 408–11. Includes a bibliography of research in the United States and foreign countries. JOHN M. BREWER, "Contributions of Research to Special Methods: The Practical Arts," in *The Scientific Movement in Education,* Thirty-Seventh Yearbook, Part II, National Society for the Study of Education (Bloomington, Illinois: Public School Publishing Co., 1938), pp. 161–69.
President's Advisory Committee on Education, *Research in the United States Office of Education,* Staff Study No. 19 (Washington, D. C.: Government Printing Office, 1939).
CARTER V. ALEXANDER, *How to Locate Educational Information and Data,* Second Edition, Revised and Expanded (New York: Teachers College, Columbia University Press, 1941).
C. V. GOOD, A. S. BARR, and D. E. SCATES, *The Methodology of Educational Research* (New York: D. Appleton-Century, 1936).
J. C. WRIGHT and CHARLES R. ALLEN, *Administration of Vocational Education* (New

VI. DESIRABLE OUTCOMES

EVALUATION AN INTEGRAL PART OF THE EDUCATIVE PROCESS. Any evaluation program planned and carried out by the school's administrative staff has direct effect upon what takes place in the classroom. Evaluation has beneficial effects on classroom instruction only if it is comprehensive in scope and wisely directed. Otherwise, it may merely give additional support to injudicious or even pernicious instructional procedures. If in a given school, teachers overemphasize the acquisition of details, nonfunctioning, factual knowledge and the instruments of appraisal stress the acquisition of such knowledge, then the evaluation process merely compounds the error. What is perhaps worse, if the teacher recognizes the value of teaching for understanding but is evaluated by the administration on the basis of his students' ability to make simple factual responses out of the textbook, the teacher is liable to impair his teaching in succeeding terms, stressing facts which will enable his students to do well on the tests they have to take. In our traditional schools, memoriter learning, parrot-like reciting, and an excessive emphasis on verbalism are not uncommon. Indeed, this latter is the source of many ills in present-day education.

Several reasons may be given for excessive verbalism in traditional education.[30] Educational psychology of the recent past looked upon teaching as the calling of students' attention to significant facts and skills and then seeing that these facts and skills were mastered. This oversimplified theory of learning also stressed the textbook as the most important source of subject matter. Textbooks and the statements of teachers were considered to be final authorities. As the curriculum expanded, and teachers were required to cover more ground, the learning of facts was stressed because these could be recited back more quickly. Poor teacher personnel emphasized the dependence on facts and books; teachers who had spent their lives in school knew little about the world except what they read. Poor methods of teaching which stressed short individual recitations rather than cooperative group activity increased the hold of verbal-

York: John Wiley & Sons, 1926), chapter on "Establishing and Administering Standards."

[30] DOUGLASS and SPITZER, "The Importance of Teaching for Understanding," in *The Measurement of Understanding*, Forty-Fifth Yearbook, Part I, National Society for the Study of Education (Chicago: University of Chicago Press, 1946), pp. 11–14. Quoted by permission of the Society.

ism. Finally, the separation of school from the student's everyday life activities led to a situation characterized by excessive talk and insufficient meaningful activities.

In the fields of vocational guidance and vocational education, traditional tests and measurements gave the nonverbal aspects of personality their proper emphasis. Elsewhere, however, tests and measurements were enslaved to symbolism. Evaluation must free itself from emphasis upon words if it is to succeed in painting an accurate portrait of student, teacher, or educational situation.

THE OCCUPATION AS A LIFE ACTIVITY. In evaluating vocations and vocational education, the evaluator must keep in mind both the unitary character of the individual's life and the wide variation in individual differences. No enthusiasm for the conception of work as a career, as something that pervades all of one's life, should blind the administrator, teacher, student, or the evaluator, to the fact that there are some people, many of them, who take the attitude of the pretty young girl in the cartoon, talking to her pal on the beach: "There's one nice thing about a job; it fills in the time between breakfast and your date at night."

On the other hand it is significant that the most popular form of modern biographical essay, the "profile," presented in its fullest development in *The New Yorker,* is almost invariably based upon the preoccupation of the subject with his occupation. The element of caricature usually arises from an overemphasis upon the zeal with which the subject carries on his life's work. Whether he be dramatist, manufacturer of meat products, chief petty officer in the Navy, magazine publisher, president of a national union, missionary in China, or aviculturist, his work is his life.

In their quest for "life," the source of desire, the roots of existence, the fundamentals of character, novelist and playwright often find their themes in vocations. The story of a life may very well be the story of an occupation. Again, biography implies a career. In recent years the "doctor books" have had their vogue. World War II provided journalists with an opportunity to sell their own life stories along with comment upon activities in the world at large. The exciting adventures of sailors, soldiers, and explorers are familiar subjects of composition. The less eventful careers of teachers, lawyers, and ministers have had their share of literary treatment. The more humble worker, the baker, the stenographer, the mechanic, the farmer, the fisherman, have all had their day in the pages of books.

Sometimes the more prominent writers have put whole industries into literature, as witness Arnold Bennett's novelization of the management of a luxurious London hotel in his *Imperial Palace*.[31]

An occupational evaluation study might very well be made of these characters in literature in order to gain a true insight into the role of vocations in the lives of workers.

HOW "GOOD" IS VOCATIONAL EDUCATION? When all the evidence is in, when all the surveys have been completed, when all the research has been accomplished, and all the resulting principles have been applied, in other words, when vocational education has been evaluated, vocational education is only as good as someone thinks it is. It has been given "status in a scale of *preferences*," it has been weighed in the scales of human judgment.

"When we have made all pertinent forms of analysis and have traced consequences, how shall we finally determine what motive or what consequence is good or bad? How but in terms of the testimony of persons who experienced the motives and consequences? What other test is there in the last analysis? It is the same in conduct as in esthetics. All the principles laid down by the critics or the philosophers must finally come down to the declaration of some person in the face of some experience that this is good, or this is bad. This is in fact the basis and is in theory the only possible basis." [32]

[31] MARY REBECCA LINGENFELTER, *Vocations in Fiction: An Annotated Bibliography* (Chicago: American Library Association, 1938).
[32] FRANK N. FREEMAN, "The Province of Scientific Inquiry," in *The Scientific Movement in Education, op. cit.*

Chapter 19

PHILOSOPHY OF EDUCATION IN A BEMUSED WORLD

Man is not a separate man, a vain law unto himself, but a member of a great company by whose law he is protected and bound. . . . The acceptance of life means the acceptance of its requirements with its privileges, each a complement of the other. . . . We stand between our forefathers and our sons' sons. Of ourselves we can do nothing. Our life is a means of life, a communication between a faith and a wonder.

CHARLES MORGAN
"Reflections in a Mirror"

I. THE SETTING

WE LIVE and relive our lives in unforgettable dramatic incidents, interspersed with long stretches of quiet routine. So, in the lives of peoples and nations.

There was that night in Bonn. It was during the wickedly cold second winter after victory. We were billeted only for the night and we must see the city, perhaps just feel it in the blackness. So we set forth. Great silvery clouds intermittently obscured the rising moon and left the unlighted streets dark and mysterious. However, whenever a cloud passed, and a flood of moonlight came from above the horizon, throwing the remains of Bonn into sharply silhouetted relief, the curtain rose on a historical drama. Those gaping, ghostly, broken walls were a stage setting for the story of Rome, of Carthage, for all the ruined world that now includes Germany and goodly parts of England, France, Russia — and again, Italy. Beethoven had lived here. Strangely enough, his home was intact. But a great seat of learning, the University of Bonn, lay in ruins.

It takes time to become used to ruins, to live among them. Some say three months, some say never. Inevitably there is some dulling of the senses, but now and again the idiocy of destruction, the poignancy of negation return in great surges of feeling. Months after the Bonn episode, on one cold, foggy morning, the black of night tinged with enough daylight to produce a dull gray, we felt our way through the rubble of the narrow street leading from Hotel Vierjahreszeiten to the Haus der Kunst, in Munich. There they were again, those crumbling, menacing walls, in the workshop of a great liberal educator, Kerschensteiner — and the birthplace of Nazism — seemingly spelling the doom of man.

In 1938 the Bureau International de l'Enseignement Technique, a world-wide organization of vocational educators, held its biennial convention in Berlin, where this chapter is being written. The Kroll Oper was the rostrum from which Hitler was then proclaiming most authentically and vociferously all his weird theories and vile practices, and at this meeting many of his educator mouthpieces were giving good imitations. Fate, or something, gave us the opportunity to stand in the same place and to proclaim the primacy of the person — what this book is about — along with our English and French colleagues, a few lone voices crying in a mental and moral wilderness.

Nine years later, with five other men, we sat around a little table, in an old, makeshift army barracks, surrounded by barbed wire. This was the Augsburg internment camp for top Nazis. Our hosts were a former S.A. general, two S.S. colonels, and a private — all of them prisoners, awaiting trial. We discussed their reasons for being Nazis, their excuses for acting as they did, their feelings regarding their present plight, and their plans for the future — provided they were permitted to make plans. A few days previously we had viewed the wreckage of the Kroll Oper, on the edge of that fantastic waste, once the famed Tiergarten; and not far away, the ironic remains of Hitler's headquarters, the Reich Chancellery. Was this all that a thousand years of learning and culture — and education — had brought about? Was this the empire that was to last a thousand years?

Why, in a volume on the principles of vocational education, is Germany important? At the time of writing it is the seat of infection, the focal point (truly a *Brennpunkt* — a burning point) in a sick world organism. Nowhere else are the symptoms so frightening. It is paradoxical and confusing. "The Germans who with Luther inaugurated the modern Protestant religion and who with Kant and Fichte created the modern moral idealism, and who have been indoctrinated with these Lutheran, Kantian, and Fichtean philosophies for centuries, seem to be the least religious and idealistic in their acts. The British and Americans with their indigenously more empirical, scientific, and pragmatic attitude seem to be the more considerate of others both morally and religiously. Yet many contemporary Anglo-American moral and religious leaders blame science and pragmatism for the ills of our time, and urge that the cure is to be found in a morality and religion independent of science after the manner of Luther, Kant, Fichte, and the Germans." [1]

Walk, mile after mile after mile, through the grim streets of Berlin that provide in mass effect what they lack in instant drama; watch underfed, scantily clothed, beaten-looking Germans emerging from or insinuating themselves into the caves they call homes, and say, "There, but for the grace of God, go I." Germany is a focus of infection and, like its pathological counterpart, must be cleaned out if the entire body politic is to survive. When all the superficialities of mores are discounted, the fundamentals of good education for democracy in Germany can be good education for everybody everywhere. Incidentally, there can be only one more war. It sounds trite to say it, but anyone who lives among these fresh modern ruins — to say nothing of Hiroshima and of Nagasaki and future super-atomic bombs and the, as yet, untried bacteriological weapons — and still thinks there will be anything left to fight about, is insane.

Amid ruins there can be only poverty — dire, essential poverty for all — where everybody has money (pieces of paper called marks, or pounds, or francs) but nobody can buy or sell goods, because goods, products of the good earth, have been destroyed. Factories, offices, homes, and schools are laid waste. Where shall education begin? With warmer, healthier bodies, or with richer spirits and better furnished minds? Is the first task of the educator to provide food and building materials, or is it to animate the soul and stimulate the mind? Obviously, these tasks are complementary, and both are essential. However, in the rebound from war's desolation it is imperative that we recall the primary objectives of education — the thinking and motivation that eventuate in conduct — that it works mainly with ideas and emotions, and only incidentally with the habits that sustain the body.

Feeding a poverty-stricken people makes it possible for them to learn, but it does not determine *what* they learn. It provides them with the decencies of living, but it does not teach them democracy.

[1] From F. S. C. NORTHROP, *The Meeting of East and West*, p. 5. By permission of The Macmillan Company, publishers (1946).

For it is more often the poverty-stricken who respect and help each other, than it is the well-to-do, who usually love their possessions more than they do their fellowmen. It is not the lush-livers, either in Berlin or New York, who believe in, and act upon, a conception of the primacy of the person. So, in times of trouble, whether in post-war devastation or in inter-war prosperity, it is well to remember, with Voltaire, that, greater than the strength of armies is the power of an idea whose time has come. Perhaps primacy of the person is that idea.

DEMOCRACY AND NAZISM. The whole fascist concept was one of the most notorious as well as monstrous adventures in all history — a negation of humanity, indeed, a deliberate physical annihilation of a whole race of human beings. It was opposed not only with guns and bombs, but with an idea. That idea has been so nebulous in the minds of some, and so perverted in the minds of others, that there has been a hesitancy to use it. Its operational meaning has been amply set forth in these pages. However, while this chapter was in process David Lilienthal, under stress of Congressional cross-examination, uttered, straight out of his mind and heart, a creed that made the headlines, and that will undoubtedly long survive the daily papers.

"Traditionally, democracy has been an affirmative doctrine rather than a merely negative one. I believe — and I do so conceive the Constitution of the United States to rest upon, as does religion — the fundamental proposition of the integrity of the individual; and that all government and all private institutions must be designed to promote and to protect and defend the integrity and the dignity of the individual; that that is the essential meaning of the Constitution and the Bill of Rights, as it is essentially the meaning of religion.

"Any form of government therefore, and any other institutions which make means rather than ends, which exalt the state or any other institutions above the importance of men, which place arbitrary power over men, which exalt the state, are contrary to that conception, and therefore I am deeply opposed to them.

"The communistic philosophy, as well as the communistic form of government, fall within this category, for their fundamental tenet is quite to the contrary. The fundamental tenet of communism is that the state is an end in itself, and that therefore the powers which the state exercises over the individual are without any ethical standard to limit them. That I deeply disbelieve.

"It is very easy simply to say one is not a communist. And, of course, if my record requires me to state that very affirmatively, then it is a great disappointment to me. It is very easy to talk about being against communism. It is equally important to believe those things which provide a satisfying and effective alternative. Democracy is that satisfying alternative. Its hope in the world is that it is an affirmative belief, rather than being simply a belief against something else and nothing more.

"One of the tenets of democracy that grow out of this central core of a belief that the individual comes first, that all men are the children of God and their personalities are therefore sacred, carries with it a great belief in civil liberties and their protection, and a repugnance to anyone who would steal from a human being that which is most precious to him — his good name; either by impugning things to him by innuendo or by insinuations. And it is an especially unhappy circumstance that occasionally that is done in the name of democracy. This, I think, can tear our country apart and destroy it if we carry it further.

"I deeply believe in the capacity of democracy to surmount any trials that may lie ahead, provided only we practice it in our daily lives. And among the things we must practice is that, while we seek fervently to ferret out the subversive and antidemocratic forces in the country, we do not at the same time, by hysteria, by resort to innuendo and smears, and other unfortunate tactics, besmirch the very cause that we believe in, and cause a separation among our people, cause one group and one individual to hate another based on mere attacks, unsubstantiated attacks upon loyalty.

"I want to add that part of my conviction is based on my training as an Anglo-American common lawyer. It is the very basis and the great heritage of the English people to this country, which we have maintained, that the strictest rules of creditability of witnesses be maintained and hearsay and gossip shall be excluded in courts of justice. And that, too, is an essential of our democracy.

"And, whether by administrative agencies acting arbitrarily against business organizations, or whether by investigating activities of the legislative branches, whenever those principles of the protection of an individual and his good name against besmirchment by gossip, hearsay and the statements of witnesses who are not subject to cross-examination are not maintained, then, too, we have failed in carrying forward our ideals in respect to democracy. That I deeply believe."

II. UNIVERSALITY WITHIN DIVERSITY

Education is concerned with conduct — conduct based on standards — standards based on emotions and ideas. "The ends of general
education are an adult behavior essential for the development of a
free society in a scientific age." [2] Such meeting of minds, meeting of
spirits, is, historically, the task of philosophy. In one form or another,
each individual restates it to himself — daily. Now and again, it
comes under the spell of great minds and spirits — Confucius,
Buddha, Jesus, Kant. Again, drawing inspiration and reason from
the arts, and in terms of World War II, it appears as an identification of the aesthetic self — the immediately feeling self — with all
nature and humanity, and therefore as respect for both.

"The aesthetic self is a continuum which is as much, and with precisely the same immediacy, in the aesthetic sky, the aesthetic other
person, the aesthetic table, the aesthetic flower, the aesthetic mole-
cule, the aesthetic electron, and the aesthetic ionization, as it is in
the aesthetic self. This explains how it is possible for one to apprehend in his own self-consciousness the blueness of the sky and the
color of the rose and the moving beauty of the sunset with precisely
the same immediacy with which the pain of one's own local tooth-
ache is apprehended. It is only with respect to the differentiations
in this all-embracing aesthetic continuum that the aesthetic self is
different from the aesthetic sky, the aesthetic flower, or any other
human or non-human natural object. Thus, it is quite erroneous to
conceive of a person, after the manner of the Lockean mental substance and traditional modern Anglo-American culture, as a completely local, independent thing having nothing in common with all
other persons and things. There is an all-embracing indeterminate
continuum of feeling common to all creatures in their aesthetic immediacy.

"It must be remembered also that all these aesthetic materials, including the all-embracing aesthetic continuum, are the kind of thing
which can be known only by being immediately experienced. No syn-
tactically formulated, mathematically or logically abstract, indirectly
and experimentally verified theory can ever designate them. They
are, by virtue of this very character, ineffable. They are also emotionally moving. In short, the aesthetic continuum within the essen-

2 JAMES BRYANT CONANT, *Public Education and the Structure of American Society*
(New York: Bureau of Publications, Teachers College, Columbia University, 1946),
p. 26.

tial nature of all things is, to use the language of Shakespeare, such stuff as dreams are made on.' But there are other differentiations in this ineffable, all-embracing aesthetic component than the introspected images which constitute dreams. There are also the equally immediately inspected images which constitute the colors, fragrances, and flavors of the sky, the earth, the flowers, the sea, and other natural objects. The aesthetic component is therefore also the stuff that these are made of." [3]

Vocational education, as conceived in these pages, fits into this framework. It is a kind of education so firmly based upon reality — reality of ideas, emotions, and things — that it cannot afford to be misinterpreted in terms of either the pure verbalism of academicism or the mere utilitarianism of bare training. It is a kind of training so general in its application that it embraces all peoples and all nations, peoples and nations that must live together.

THE IMPORTANCE OF INTERNATIONAL COOPERATION. "Occupational adjustment is interwoven with political and social philosophies, circumstanced by economics, circumscribed by tradition, and circumvented by politicians. Amid this welter of social forces, individual attributes — personality, culture, intellect, physique, all the characteristics that contribute to the making of morally excellent and dynamically effective human beings — must somehow be adapted to the realities of day-to-day existence. If possible, the human beings embodying these attributes must attain not only the good life, but the happy life." [4]

Whatever the contrasting, or even opposing forces among nations — and there are many — among people themselves there is that fundamental desire for the good life, the happy life, and therefore for an occupation, for a career that will enable each individual to attain his desire. Work, among all life's activities, has the character of universality. As well as, perhaps better than, in any other field of human endeavor, international understanding can be reached through an appreciation of people's life occupations. Learning these occupations within a social milieu is vocational education, and as such, taps many common human elements. The most important common element is the child, presumably innocent until corrupted

[3] Northrop, *op. cit.,* p. 461.
[4] Reprinted from *Vocational Guidance Throughout the World,* by FRANKLIN J. KELLER and MORRIS S. VITELES, p. 17, by permission of W. W. Norton & Company, Inc. Copyright 1937 by the publishers.

or indoctrinated by his elders. The other important element is the teacher, the real teacher, the lover of children, who neither corrupts nor indoctrinates, but enables the child to develop in a free atmosphere. Teachers, as a class of workers, as people of good will, should do more to strengthen international bonds than any other group of professional people. During one shattering and another catastrophic war we cooperated in making *things,* in exchanging skills and techniques. It was a great cause and a worthy effort. An equally forceful motive — peace — should enable us to do it again, but this time to lay stress on the making of men and women.

REALITY. All over the world vocational subject matter is more uniform than in any other field of education. Drawing, blueprints, mathematics, are a universal language, understood by technical men everywhere. Science and technology speak in well-known symbols. Vocational intelligence is the same. Methods of teaching are readily comprehended. There is a universality about these phases of education that makes it easy for vocational educators to understand each other even though their mother tongues are different.

National systems of education present many variations. Sometimes they are difficult to comprehend. However, these are just the forms within which the spirit lives. An understanding of their origins is the beginning of an understanding of their persistence. Our own forms of education are often baffling to the foreigner. For instance, it is amazing to many of them that we should have forty-eight different school systems. And yet, as we well know, within this diversity lives the unity — not the uniformity — that we call the American spirit, the spirit that some day — soon — should become the spirit of a united world.

III. NATIONALITY, CULTURE, AND PHILOSOPHIES

CULTURE AND NATIONALITY. In 1916 John Dewey said: "One of the fundamental problems of education in and for a democratic society is set by the conflict of a nationalistic and a wider social aim. The earlier cosmopolitan and 'humanitarian' conception suffered both from vagueness and from lack of definite organs of execution and agencies of administration. In Europe, in the continental states particularly, the new idea of the importance of education for human welfare and progress was captured by national interest and harnessed to do a work whose social aim was definitely narrow and exclusive. The social aim of education and its national aim were identified, and the result was a marked obscuring of the meaning of a social aim.

"This confusion corresponds to the existing situation (1916) of human intercourse. On the other hand, science, commerce, and art transcend national boundaries. They are largely international in quality and method. They involve interdependencies and cooperation among the people inhabiting different countries. At the same time, the idea of national sovereignty has never been accentuated in politics as it is at the present time. Each nation lives in a state of suppressed hostility and incipient war with its neighbor. Each is supposed to be the supreme judge of its own interests, and it is assumed as a matter of course that each has interests which are exclusively its own. To question this is to question the very idea of national sovereignty which is assumed to be basic to political practice and political science. This contradiction (for it is nothing less) between the wider sphere of exclusive and hence potentially hostile pursuits and purposes, exacts of educational theories a clearer conception of the meaning of 'social' as a function and test of education than has yet been attained." [5]

"The comparative approach demands first an appreciation of the intangible, impalpable spiritual and cultural forces which underline educational systems; the factors and forces outside the school matter even more than what goes on inside it. Hence a comparative study of education must be founded on an analysis of the social and political ideals which the school reflects, for the school epitomizes these for transmission and for progress. In order to understand, appreciate, and evaluate the real meaning of the educational system of a nation, it is essential to know something of its history and traditions, of the forces and attitudes governing its social organization, of the political and economic conditions that determine its development. This is all the more true at the present time (1933) when educational systems are organized on a national basis, but, as the history of English education proved, the same principle applies to educational systems which are organized on a voluntary basis with little or no governmental control or supervision. It may, indeed, be claimed that systems which are least controlled by an external government agency, as in England or the United States, better reflect the variety of forces by which the character of a nation is molded than do those systems

[5] From JOHN DEWEY, *Democracy and Education*, p. 113. By permission of The Macmillan Company (1916).

which are subject to rigid centralized control, as France and pre-war
Germany. This fact explains the gap which is so frequently found
between theory and practice in education." [6]

"There is another contribution which the comparative study of
education may hope to make. This is the development of an internationalism based not on emotion or sentiment, but arising from
an appreciative understanding of other nations as well as our own,
from the sense that all nations through their systems of education
are contributing, each in its own way, to the work and progress of
the world, and from a realization of the ambitions and ideals which
each nation is endeavoring to hand on through its schools. A study
of foreign school systems which neglects the search for the hidden
meaning of things found in the schools would merely result in the
acquisition of information about another educational system and
would be of little value as a contribution to the clarification of
thought, to the better development of education as a science, and to
the formulation of a comprehensive, all-embracing philosophy of
education thoroughly rooted in the culture, ideals, and aspirations
which each nation should seek to add to the store of human welfare. . . ." [7]

"In the light of contemporary social philosophies (1937) it might
be concluded that there are, according to one's taste, two kinds of
Utopia. In the first type of ideal state every individual finds himself free to develop, to the fullest extent, his aptitudes and capacities,
along the line of his own peculiar interests. The state provides opportunity for the acquirement of knowledge and skill. It is to be expected that a large number of individuals possessing a wide range of
abilities, will readily find opportunity for their exercise, and that
the totality of individuals known as society or as a nation will reap
the greatest possible benefit. This is individualism and laissez-faire
in the best sense, granting complete freedom of occupational choice,
freedom of opinion, and personal liberty." [8]

IV. A BASIS FOR UNDERSTANDING

Out of all this complex of conflicting social, political, economic
forces emerges the simply motivated, well-intentioned, common

[6] I. L. KANDEL, *Comparative Education* (Boston: Houghton Mifflin Company, 1933),
p. xix.
[7] KANDEL, *op. cit.*, p. xxv.
[8] KELLER and VITELES, *op. cit.*, p. 485.

man, the man in common, about whom education is, throughout the world. Individually and collectively, he is the man of good will. Germany lies in ruins because he became submerged in a morass of hate. Yet it is he who must emerge from the educational process and it is he who must go on to teach his successors, the new generation, to be bearers of good will. How can he, collectively, choose such men and women so that they may be trained to become teachers? This is the problem the world over. In its negative aspects, in Germany, it has been known as denazification. In its positive phases, it means recognition and approval of moral, democratic qualities. It means that teachers must teach children to be better than are the teachers themselves. It is a kind of cosmic pulling up by the bootstraps. The souls of people must rise above the laws of physics. The people of the world must rise above themselves. In so far as school education can perform this task, it must be carried out by superteachers educating more super-teachers until the highest possible level is reached. In other words, sound educational practice is grounded upon integrity of personality, upon respect of each personality for every other personality. This principle is world-wide in its application, assumes the finest in civilization, covers every type of school, and therefore has special significance for vocational education.

COSMIC PATHOLOGY. As in individual medicine and psychology, the abnormal case points up the normal. In world history Germany has been the pathological case, a focus of infection. What seems necessary for her cure, her redemption, is significant for the so-called normal people, the world at large. The prescription seems to be something like this:

1. A search for, a scrutiny of, and an honoring of the finest personalities as the teachers of the young.

2. An exaltation of the best in each people's tradition so that it may not only animate its own members, but may contribute to the culture of all the peoples of the world. It is notable that, however heinously the majority of a people may have sinned (as the Germans certainly have), there are always periods of virtue and minorities of grace that uncover the essential goodness of humanity. In German history these periods and minorities are clear and shining. They can and should become continuities and majorities.

3. As in politics, the history of education is studded with revolt, the sequel to domination and authoritarianism. In general, the edu-

cational "reformers" were those who, like Pestalozzi, would give the child opportunity to develop and express his growing personality, to flower in the warmth of a benevolent environment rather than to wither under the cold repression of his dominating elders. This has been the story in Germany. The latest "revolt" followed World War I, but the period of most intensive authoritarianism was that instituted by the Nazis, which degenerated into all the idiocies and blasphemies of *Rassenkunde* and *Führerprinzip*. It is an oft-repeated psychological truism that no one can teach another (in the didactic sense), but that everyone can learn. Stated differently, no fact, idea, or principle can be forced upon the human organism by another organism. The individual can develop only amid other individuals, willingly, pleasantly, cooperatively, in an atmosphere of freedom and brotherhood. Operationally, this calls for "self-activity," "pupil participation," "student councils," and all those pedagogic and administrative devices that reproduce within the school organization the natural situations among which people learn to live. These are the essence of vocational education, the spirit that makes it and its beneficiaries live. Realistic and cooperative learning are in its very nature.

4. Evolving out of the authoritarian attitude is, in the light of reason and in the warmth of sympathy, one of the most astounding failures in education, the neglect of personality by omission of direct, specific, and recognized means of guidance. For the most part, school teachers and administrators have assumed that the presentation of subject matter carried with it life orientation — a preposterous assumption that persists in every country. The conception of education as a personally conducted tour through the intricate maze of life, or as a process requiring as close supervision as a critical medical case, is old enough, but, as an educational practice, a going concern, it is, strangely and unfortunately, lacking in most schools throughout the world today.

Curiously enough, for a long time Germany has possessed a highly organized program of vocational guidance (*Berufsberatung*). As with so many other sound institutions, the Nazis adapted it to their own ends, "coordinating" every counselor and pupil into servants of the State. Since the end of the war it has again served for orientation of boys and girls into life jobs. However, administered by the Labor Department, service is inadequate in its coverage and in its breadth of vision. As emphasized in the preceding chapters, the child is a developing, educable being from his earliest years, well into maturity, and his life history is the concern of the schools. So, the schools must accept and embrace the responsibility of guidance from the earliest to the latest years. Such guidance must be carried on in cooperation, not only with the Labor Offices, but with the Departments of Health, Social Service, industrial and business concerns, in fact, with the entire complex of economic and social forces. This is a special feature of vocational education.

5. Such a concept postulates a highly sensitive and appreciative attitude toward people — all peoples, and it certainly precludes any underestimate of the intelligence, goodness, or culture of any individual or group of individuals. One day, in Munich, during the difficult reconstruction days, an American officer said to the assembled liaison and security officers, "Never underestimate the intelligence of the Germans. Remember, this was a going concern when somebody set his foot on Plymouth Rock." And so it is with people everywhere, perhaps especially with, historically and internationally, the most troublesome, the East Indians, say, or the Jews, or the Egyptians. Their cultures certainly thrived before Plymouth Rock. To read *Mein Kampf* in the post-war period is both a befouling and cleansing experience. In the light of the deeds of his followers, the obscenities and name-calling of Hitler point up the insane futility of arrogant assumption of superiority and power. It is only when the people are given light — light to see the truth, it is only when the real "iron curtain," the curtain drawn before all history, has been withdrawn, that they can appreciate their fellow humans apart from their groupings by race, creed, or color.

6. At every point in life arises the necessity for taking bearings and plotting one's course. As when traversing the ocean, it is not enough to choose one's goal and then set the rudder. Wind and current, man-made error and mechanical weakness, all contrive to upset one's calculations. So, periodically, there must be new observations and new calculations. In education, this process is evaluation and re-evaluation. We must know where we want to go and whether we are getting there. One of the greatest of educational crimes has its inception in plain, ordinary inertia.

V. THE LINES OF TRANSMISSION

However fervently one may believe that "there is an all-embracing indeterminate continuum of feeling common to all creatures in their esthetic immediacy," such belief does not, in itself, establish or utilize the continuum, and it is that very utilization that is the essence of international cooperation in education, or, what is more important, educational understanding leading to international cooperation. The implementation of such cooperation is of transcendent importance. As has been pointed out, it is in vocational education that the continuum is most easily recognized and most readily put to work. There have been some notable efforts and there are other significant proposals.

INTERNATIONAL LABOR ORGANIZATION. Up to World War II the International Labor Organization was the only body, world-wide in scope, that interested itself in vocational education. Its report on "Technical and Vocational Education and Apprenticeship," issued in 1939, published a "draft recommendation concerning vocational training, and another concerning apprenticeship." These recommendations were general in nature, and included some of the best features of vocational education. At the same time, they made allowance for special conditions existing in the various countries. Whether this body continues as a separate organization or is in some manner integrated with a section of the United Nations, its interests and functions in the fields of vocational education and guidance should be continued and expanded.

BIET. The Bureau International de l'Enseignement Technique (International Bureau of Vocational Education) was a strong organization before the war, with representation from many different countries, but principally from those in Europe. The only Americans attending the Berlin Conference in 1938 were Carter Goodrich, representing the International Labor Organization and later its head; Mrs. Anna L. Burdick, representing the United States Office of Education; and the writer, as an individual member. The organization was supported principally by government subsidies. The headquarters were in Paris with A. Lomont as director. With the war, of course, this organization ceased to exist.

Whatever international action is taken through governmental agencies, it would be a sad day when all individual initiative, as expressed through world-wide voluntary organizations, ceased to exist. In its representation BIET was governmental, but the spirit of its life was in the individual initiative of its members. Whether

386

or not this particular organization is revived, the purpose of a co-operating group of individually concerned workers should be served. BIET was largely European, and it may well be that Europe is too tired to revive the movement. In that case, it obviously falls upon the New World to initiate it, and it is indicated that the American Vocational Association is the body to take up the task. The recent creation of its Committee on International Education indicates the desire and intent to play a major role in bringing about world understanding.

ACADEMIC SCHOOLS. The academic high schools in this country have made considerable effort to promote friendship with the Latin-American countries.[9] This has been done in several ways. Great stress has been laid upon Spanish, which is taught in a great many schools. Much has been said about the teaching of Portuguese but because of lack of competent teachers this has been attempted in a very few places. Many schools study the culture of other countries through all the school subjects, sometimes including vocational subjects. Various types of activity are included: assemblies, Pan-American Day programs, entertainments, illustrated lectures, club activities, correspondence, moving pictures, radio, recordings, newspapers, magazines, exhibits, excursions.

One of the greatest difficulties in getting this kind of work done is to find teachers who are competent and enthusiastic enough to start the activities. Such teachers must be carefully selected. They must be encouraged to travel. They must cooperate with their curriculum revision committees. If the work is to be effective, schools must add new texts and library books, films, records, and other equipment to their current supply. The whole problem bristles with difficulties, but it is challenging, and whatever is done in academic schools is applicable in vocational schools.

UNESCO. Most promising of all educational efforts towards international understanding and peace is the United Nations Educational, Scientific, and Cultural Organization. If well-conceived and administered, it should stimulate and energize the millions of individuals comprehended in the voluntary membership organizations out of which it has arisen — including vocational teachers and administrators throughout the world.

[9] U. S. Office of Education, *Inter-American Friendship Through the Schools,* Bulletin 1941, No. 10 (Washington, D. C.: Government Printing Office, 1941).

WHAT SHALL WE DO? In the framework of whatever organizations exist, or are likely to exist, what can and should we, as vocational educators, do? Certain definite possibilities reveal themselves.

1. Above all, the individual, as man or woman, citizen of the world, must, from day to day, amid the embarrassments of routine and detail, think internationally. Superlatively and transcendently, he must ask himself, "What have I done today that is international?"

2. Vocational educators must join, support, and actively further the objectives of those organizations that have as their aims international understanding, cooperation, and peace.

3. Vocational educators must publish and distribute all kinds of material that will be useful in foreign countries. This is especially pertinent in vocational education where the language of mathematics and drawing is universal. This is always a two-way traffic, for there is no people that does not need help and none that cannot give it.

4. More important than the exchange of material is the exchange of persons and personalities. If integrity of personality is the transcendent factor in education, it is obvious that it is only the impact of personality upon personality throughout the world that can influence new personalities in such a way as to bind them into a new world. Again, this is a two-way line of communication. Not only must visitors become acquainted with foreign educational procedures, but they must learn about manners and customs. They must take back to their homelands not only knowledge of techniques and skills, but also of attitudes and feelings.

Teachers and leaders should be trained for service abroad. They must have wide knowledge and understanding that will make them sympathetic. They must know enough of the foreign language to establish rapport with teachers and children. They must go abroad in a spirit of service and humility. They must be in the truest sense of the word, ambassadors of good will.

5. Teaching in vocational schools should be permeated with facts and viewpoints and attitudes of peoples of foreign countries. Stress should be laid upon the work they do and upon all that is involved in their work life. For instance, whereas academic students exchange letters and books, vocational students might exchange products of their own making. Only to the slightest extent are foreign languages taught in vocational schools. Should they be taught? Certainly not in the old-fashioned, academic, bookish manner. Instruction could well

be built around trades and, above all, there should be the activity and practice that characterize the best modern methods.

6. All these are desirable goals. But we must be realistic. With the best of intentions, vocational educators can do nothing without manpower and money. They have their own jobs, which they must conserve, and their own responsibilities, which they must support. Travel to and life in foreign countries are expensive. Either government or foundations must provide the wherewithal for all activity that requires funds above and beyond what are available for current domestic operations. Perhaps the provision of such funds is one of the major tasks of United Nations and its subsidiary organizations.

VI. THE TEST

The ultimate test of any social system is the facility with which the individual personality can realize itself within the group. The test of an educational program is the positive aid which it gives that individual in attaining, in terms of interest and capacities, his social and occupational goal. The "democracies" have made the path none too easy for the economically handicapped, and often impossible for those with racial or religious disadvantages. In Germany the stratification has been such as to make it virtually impossible for the son of an artisan to break through to the rank of professional. The two-path school system has clinched the matter. Retention in the eight-year *Volkschule* (elementary school) has denied the pupil a training in the prerequisites for university study. Wherever talent struggles for expression and is denied, democracy does not exist.

"If the top jobs are based on hereditary privilege and the bottom ranks are based on hereditary lack of privilege, if all the social pressures emphasize a man's worth solely in terms of his rank and finally prevent other social patterns from developing, then you have something not unlike the Prussian Army. You approximate a caste system for the nation. The converse case is too obvious to require spelling out. Fluidity of social structure (particularly from generation to generation), complexity of social pattern, low visibility of the social structure — all these are desirable if we would have an industrial society composed of individuals who regard themselves as free. In furthering such aims public education is of prime importance." [10]

"It is clear as crystal that in those cases where the type and length

[10] CONANT, *op. cit.*, p. 7.

of education to which a boy or girl is entitled depends on the accident of birth, the subsequent career is likewise largely so determined. In short, to the extent that educational opportunity is determined by family status, education in the modern world makes for social stratification." [11]

A school system must be so organized that the ill effects of stratification are overcome, or stratification itself is eliminated. When *all* graduates of the elementary school may enter a high school devoted to both academic and practical subjects, and *all* students in such a school may qualify upon graduation for either a trade or for college entrance, stratification disappears. Such a program has been the theme of this book.

VII. PERSONALITY AND WORK

In the last analysis, personality is an emotion, an idea, and a mode of conduct. It is love, respect, and good will in action. If all Germans are "incorrigible," all Jews "aggressive," all Frenchmen "dishonest," all Englishmen "superior," all Americans "money-mad," all Russians "barbaric," all Negroes "dumb," and all Japanese "crafty," there can be no continuum, no communication, no respect for personality, no cooperation, no peace. It is a stupid, provincial concept.

"What Toynbee calls 'the parochial sovereign state' is the instrument by which the decline of Western Civilization has been accomplished. In his fourth volume, when he writes of 'the intractability of institutions,' he draws some of his most telling examples from our own history. Both industrialism and democracy, he points out, have been perverted by nationalism. 'Industrialism,' he writes, 'is a cooperative system of work which demands the unification of all the habitable seas on the face of the planet as a common home for the entire living generation of Mankind,' but in a world of parochial states, each striving to improve its economic conditions at the expense of others, industrialism has been a prolific source of wars. As for democracy, Toynbee says that in origin and essence it is 'not parochial but universal, not militant but humanitarian.' 'But,' he continues, 'when this potent spiritual driving-force is diverted into the mechanism of a parochial state, it not only ceases to be beneficent but becomes malignantly subversive.' " [12]

11 CONANT, *op. cit.*, p. 12.
12 GRANVILLE HICKS, "Arnold Toynbee: The Boldest Historian," *Harper's Magazine*, February, 1947, p. 121. The reference is to Toynbee's monumental *Study of History*, published in six volumes by the Oxford University Press at intervals since 1934.

"Love of work" is no wild, fanciful speculation. It is easy enough to cite case after case of workers who just "hold a job" and "make money," hate their bosses and cuss the government. Whatever the percentage of workers with this attitude, these things need not be. The usual criticisms of the higher concept has been a recital of the evils of the assembly line, the supposed ultimate agent in the de-personalizing of human beings. Such criticism has been hard to answer, for the assembly line apparently had come to stay, indeed, to be lengthened and speeded up indefinitely. And yet—

"Mass production rests on three principles: the breaking up of a complex, skilled operation into its component elementary and un-skilled motions; the synchronization of the flow of materials with human operation; and the interchangeability of parts. Of these only the first matters here. In the traditional assembly line each of the ele-mentary motions is performed by a separate worker; the intellectual process of analysis is laid out *in space* with each separate analytical step represented by a separate worker. This would have been the right — in fact, the only right — method if the work were done by single-purpose machine tools, such as a reamer or a trip hammer. But it makes no sense if we use people to do the work.

"The right method, as we found in literally hundreds of instances during the war, is to lay out the assembly in *concept* rather than in space. This means that we still go through the breakdown of the operation into elementary motions. But instead of having each mo-tion performed separately by one worker, a whole sequence of motions is performed one after the other by one worker.

"At Cadillac in Detroit, for instance, completely unskilled and industrially inexperienced Negro women made a high precision aluminum part for aircraft engines, each one turning out a finished product. Every girl worked by a chart which showed in three parallel columns what to do next; what to look for before doing it; speed, temperature, etc.; and what the step accomplished. The worker still did nothing but unskilled motions which were easy to learn; in fact, it took no longer to train these women than it would have taken to train them for orthodox assembly line work. But every girl did a whole operation which brought into play one muscle after the other, thus giving the whole body a chance to rest and a chance to develop a working rhythm. Also each girl could work at her own speed, in itself one of the best means of combating fatigue. And each worker produced an entire product with all the satisfaction that goes with it. As a result, there was not only a highly satisfied and happy laboring force; there was also an extremely efficient one which produced more than could have been produced on the orthodox assembly line." [13]

Apparently, if the will is there, even the assembly line can be conquered, personality preserved, love of work fostered, and vocational education developed as an agency for human development rather than for *training automata.*

VIII. THE HOPE AND THE LIGHT

There was another night in Germany, this time in Stuttgart. The back of winter had been broken. The dreadful cold had abated. The sun was shining again and the leaves on bush and tree were unfolding. The staff of the Education Division had listened to a talk on "cooperative," as opposed to "authoritarian," learning. "Through discussion, criticism, experience, boys and girls will learn the best ways, the right ways." "But, what *is* the right, who sets the standard, what in the criterion of value?" The old, old question. "Would not most psychologists, even while believing thoroughly in the cooperative method of learning, agree that the pursuit of ultimate motive drives one further and further back — the infinite regress — to something inexplicable on scientific grounds, something that seems to yield only to philosophical, some would say, religious, interpretation?" Essentially, must not one look for the hidden spark, the inner light — whatever it is — in the individual, that determines this attitude toward other individuals? Even Toynbee, after tremendous study, has hope in the potentialities of a revival of Christianity. This need not be any particular religion or sect — or even a religion by name. Indeed, as Northrop shows, it is in a synthesis of all religions and philosophies that we must envision unity and hope.

Amid the ruins of Berlin there are published eleven German language newspapers. Among the best of them is *Der Tagesspiegel.* Each morning it prints in the upper left hand corner of the back page a quotation from one of the great liberals, but often from an obscure, sometimes martyred resistant. In the direst of circumstances these voices from the past, both recent and remote, are heartening reminders of those "eternal verities" that we often forget. Hans Scholl was murdered by the Nazis on February 22, 1943. Among his notes appears the following paragraph:

[13] PETER F. DRUCKER, "The Way to Industrial Peace," *Harper's Magazine,* November, 1946, p. 390.

"We always want to cross over to the other shore. We look for a ferry. For it is a deep, entrancing, dark stream, and it is night, without a star in the heavens. There is no path and no bridge. There is only a dim light, protected from the wind on the distant bank, and only one ferry. The name of that ferry is poverty. He who would see the light must first experience poverty, in order to see in the light all the hungry people who, for two thousand years, it has illuminated. Poverty is stronger than riches. Poverty is the power of man to scatter to the winds all excesses without repentance, to evaluate all possessions according to their spiritual worth. Poverty leads man to an absolute choice. The war will bring to Europe the greatest poverty. First of all, hunger and misery will not soften us one whit, because out of ruined cities, ruined countries, ruined and half-exterminated peoples, men will seek the diamonds that, indestructible, lie buried in the rubble."

This is the cleansing that came to Europe — a terrible, scorching sterilization. However necessary, it cannot be risked again, or the light will be extinguished forever. And the next time it will not be Europe alone, but the whole world.

After World War I Germany gave some remarkable evidence of intellectual and social recovery. The Weimar Republic saw many reforms.[14] After World War II they must come again. No nation of people can resign from the human race.

Germany, as a focus of infection, has provided a useful, indeed, an extraordinary "case study." But this book is about vocational education and about all peoples. That is to say, it is about education for all. And it stresses the fact that such education accomplishes its purpose only when it comes through men and women of good will. It needs, beyond everything else, that something that makes people act benevolently toward *all*. What does the thesaurus say? — "bear good will, wish well, take (or feel) an interest in, sympathize with, feel for, treat well, give comfort, do good, benefit, assist, render a service, aid, enter into the feelings of others, practice the golden rule, do as you would be done by."

These trite-sounding words are an expression of the indispensable component of any concept of United Nations, of universal brotherhood, of peace. They connote the ideas that activate the all-embracing indeterminate continuum of feeling common to all creatures without which vocational education, any kind of education, is lifeless and

[14] R. T. ALEXANDER and BERYL PARKER, *The New Education in the German Republic* (New York: John Day, 1929).

meaningless. This indispensable component must penetrate to the individual personality, whoever and wherever he is. He is John Smith, Dmitri Timoshenko, Hans Schmidt, François Pariset, and all the other Joes that this book is about, to whom it wishes to give a chance in life by including *him* in the esthetic continuum and integrating him into life through appropriate education. These things we must deeply believe.

INDEX

398

Home, influence of, on education, 130
Homemaking: 272–276; scope of, 273; contrasted with industrial education, 273; differentiations in, 273; requires varied education, 275; industrialization in, 275; and community, 275
Home-room period, 92
Hook, Sidney, quoted, 147
Hoppock, Robert, quoted, 358
Horizontal mobility, 153
Horn, Ernest, quoted, 208
Horne, Herman Harrell, quoted, 324
Humanities, 153
Hutchins-Adler-Barr, criticisms of, 147–148

I.Q.: 72, 85, 101; fallibility of, 80; and evaluation research, 366
Ideals, in cooperative education, 297
Individual: capacity to learn, 5; development of, 7, 44; potentialities of, 56–57; recognition of, 68; and Catholicism, 69; agreement on importance of, 69; nature of differences in, 72; and method, 89; as separate problem, 219; and social virtues, 231; teaching of, 241
Individuality: complexity of, 70; method in, 198
Individualized instruction, as teaching method, 195
Industrial arts, 82, 150
Industrial education, and homemaking, 273
Industrialization: in agriculture, 272; in homemaking, 275; in business education, 279
Industry: 276–278; morale in, 241; advancement in, 276, 277; human values in, 277; standards, 277; robot, 278; training in, 310
Information, occupational, 247
Integrity, 242
Intellectuals, as thinkers and doers, 200
Intelligence: 72, 215; general, 85; and thinking, 200–215; definition of, 203; hierarchy of, 204; accomplishments of, 205; and language, 207; in agriculture, 271; of teacher, 332
Interest: 72, 86, 109–124, 214; definition of, 111; and effort, 111–112; and feeling, 112; and will, 112; and growth, 113; in vocational education, 121, 148; not an aim in itself, 124; and educa-

tion, 149; as basis of admission to school, 165; in agriculture, 269
International cooperation, importance of, 378
International Labor Organization, 385
Interviews, 87

Jacksonianism, in education, 185
James, William, quoted, 15
Jeffersonianism, in education, 185
Job Satisfaction, 357
Job-teaching, 66
Job-training: 53, 289; and vocational education, 4
Jobs, kinds of, 27
Jung, Carl, quoted, 70

Kandel, I. L., quoted, 380
Keller, Franklin J., quoted, 101, 301–303
Keller and Viteles, quoted, 381
Kindergarten, vocational education in, 113
Knowledge: 152; pieces of, 147; and time fetish, 145; required of teacher, 331

Labor: dignity of, 26; cooperation of education with, 185
Labor-saving devices, 58
Land-grant colleges, 316
Language: and intelligence, 207; of vocation and science, 214
Lass and Wrightstone, quoted, 353
Learned and Wood, quoted, 356
Learning: 109–124; by doing, 35; and motivation, 109; and activity, 151; preparation for, 164; by people, 187
Legal aspect, of full-time education, 290
Leisure, and work, 12
Life: and vocational education, 3; purpose in, 4; and education, 7; purpose of work in, 13; attitude of youth to, 49; adjustment to, 90; preparation for, 159; meaning of good, 227
Life situations, 241
Lilienthal, David, quoted, 375
Liverpool Mechanics and Apprentices' Library, 309
Livingstone, Sir Richard, quoted, 229
Local units, administration and supervision of, 243–257
Luther, Martin, quoted, 38
Lynd, R. S. and H. M., quoted, 364